PUNJAB SOCIETY

About the Editor

Manmohan S. Gill is Reader in the Department of Sociology, Guru Nanak Dev University, Amritsar. He has also served in the capacity of Reader, Academic Staff College and Programme Coordinator, NSS, in the same university. He has worked as Social Scientist with Operation Research Group, a division of Sarabhai Chemicals Ltd., New Delhi in 1982.

Dr. Gill has over 18 years of teaching and research experience. His area of specialization is Rural Sociology and Social Ecology. He has completed three research projects in the subject of untouchability and land relations. He has published numerous papers in the research journals besides making presentations in various academic forums at national and international level. He has authored a book *Spatial Patterns: A Sociological Analysis*.

Dr. Gill is life member of Indian Sociological Society and North-West Indian Sociological Association. He is also the Associate Editor of *Guru Nanak Journal of Sociology*.

PUNJAB SOCIETY

Perspectives and Challenges

Edited by

M.S. GILL

Reader, Department of Sociology
Guru Nanak Dev University, Amritsar, Punjab

CONCEPT PUBLISHING COMPANY, NEW DELHI-110059

ISBN : 81-8069-038-5

First Published 2003

Published and Printed by
Ashok Kumar Mittal
Concept Publishing Company
A/15-16, Commercial Block, Mohan Garden
New Delhi-110059 (INDIA)

Phone : 25351460, 25351794
Fax : 091-11-25357103
Email : publishing@conceptpub.com

FOREWORD

The impulse of development has emerged as a remarkable feature of our times. This is evident from the manner in which it has become a pronounced global concern today. On the basis of the level of development the world stands divided into two blocks : the developed and the underdeveloped, the latter euphemistically called developing. The developing countries are wilfully engaged in the race of development to catch up with the developed ones.

For the developing countries, the impulse of development gained in significance following the end of the era of colonialism which occurred in the middle of the twentieth century. Since then the concept of development itself has grown from economic growth to human development and now further to sustainable development. Its changing connotations notwithstanding, development continues to mean, in the first instance, economic growth. All economic growth takes place in a social milieu and, in turn, has its social fallouts which is what concern sociologists. As for human development, again the prime interest of sociologists lies in the social determinants and consequences of human development. Similarly, in respect of sustainable development the delight of sociologists lies more in the study of socio-cultural sustainability than mere ecological sustainability.

Sociological studies of development began in India with the work of S.C. Dube: 'India's Changing Village'. This was followed by a spate of evaluation studies of development projects including Community Development Project (CDP), Green Revolution (HYVs) and Integrated Rural Development Programme (IRDP). More recently, sociological studies have begun to focus on "economic development and social transformation" and it is emerging as a theme of core sociological concern today.

This book is about the stream of social changes and issues generated by economic development in Punjab, a state known for providing a model of development through agricultural growth in order to discover its socio-cultural facilitators and consequences. It offers a fascinating lab for sociological studies in development. A noted success story of economic development, Punjab's case is also instructive for its seamy side of development. The proof of it lies, among other things, in its having earned the dubious distinction of having the lowest sex-ratio in India.

A collection of twenty-six fascinating papers, the book deals with various social aspects of development in Punjab. In terms of their thrusts, the papers can be broadly classified into five sections: population, agricultural modernization, credit institutions, women, and environment. The papers offer research-based evidence on the trends of socio-cultural change and insightful discussion of emerging issues and problems. Some of the papers present a cogent account of the implications and effects of World Trade Treaty on agricultural development in Punjab. Dr. Manmohan S. Gill has done a skilful job in editing the book. Students of development and policy makers will find the book particularly useful.

S.L. SHARMA
Professor of Sociology (Retd.)
Dean, Arts Faculty
Panjab University, Chandigarh

ACKNOWLEDGEMENTS

I am grateful to all the contributors of the present reader for their keen interest and cooperation to make this venture a success. The present reader represents a tentative framework of the essential reading that we need today to study the contemporary Punjab Society. I shared this judgment with my colleagues in the Department of Sociology, especially Dr. Ranvinder S.Sandhu who motivated me in this endeavour. I owe a deep debt of gratitude to Prof. (retd.) S.L. Sharma, Prof. (retd.) V.S. D'Souza, Prof. Sukhwant Singh Bindra (Political Science), Dr. (Mrs.) Balwinder Arora and Prof. Gurupdesh Singh (English) for their suggestions and moral support. I commend the efforts of the Proprietor and the staff of Concept Publishing Company, New Delhi who helped me to bring to fruition the concept of this reader.

Finally, this work owes much to my mother, my wife, Ravinder and son, Gurwinder for their cooperation and encouragement to complete this work.

M.S. GILL

CONTENTS

SECTION—III

RURAL CREDIT INSTITUTIONS

SECTION—IV

WOMEN EMPOWERMENT

LIST OF CONTRIBUTORS

Kumool Abbi, Lecturer, Department of Sociology, Punjab University, Chandigarh.

B.K. Aggarwal, Professor of Sociology, Department of Economics and Sociology, Punjab Agricultural University, Ludhiana.

R.S. Bawa, Professor (Presently Registrar), Punjab School of Economics, Guru Nanak Dev University, Amritsar.

Vikram Chadha, Professor, Punjab School of Economics, Guru Nanak Dev University, Amritsar.

S.S. Chahal, Economist (Marketing), Department of Economics and Sociology, Punjab Agricultural University, Ludhiana.

G.S. Dhaliwal, Professor of Ecology, Department of Entomology, Punjab Agricultural University, Ludhiana.

M.K. Dhillon, Professor and Head of Family Resource Management, Punjab Agricultural University, Ludhiana.

Anish Dua, Lecturer, Department of Zoology, Guru Nanak Dev University, Amritsar.

Nisha Dua, Research student, Department of Economics and Sociology, Punjab Agricultural University, Ludhiana.

Manmohan S. Gill, Reader, Department of Sociology, Guru Nanak Dev University, Amritsar.

Rajesh Gill, Reader, Department of Sociology, Punjab University, Chandigarh.

Surinder S. Jodhka, Reader in Center for Social System, Jawahar Lal Nehru University, New Delhi.

Sajla Kalra, Research Fellow, Department of Economics and Sociology, Punjab Agricultural University, Ludhiana.

Gian Kaur, Professor, Punjab School of Economics, Guru Nanak Dev University, Amritsar.

Malkit Kaur, Professor, Department of Sociology and Social Anthropology, Punjabi University, Patiala.

Mandeep Kaur, Research Scholar, Department of Economics and Sociology, Punjab Agricultural University, Ludhiana.

Parminder Kaur, Professor of Economics, Department of Economics and Sociology, Punjab Agricultural University, Ludhiana.

Rupinder Kaur, Lecturer in sociology, Mai Bhago College, Ludhiana.

Chander Parkash, Lecturer, Department of Zoology, Guru Nanak Dev University, Amritsar.

P.S. Raikhy, Professor, Punjab School of Economics, Guru Nanak Dev University, Amritsar.

Jasmeet Sandhu, Professor, Department of Sociology, Guru Nanak Dev University, Amritsar.

R.S. Sandhu, Professor, Department of Sociology, Guru Nanak Dev University, Amritsar.

M.K. Sekhon, Assistant Farm Economist, Department of Economics and Sociology, Punjab Agricultural University, Ludhiana.

Shalini Sharma, Assistant Professor of Sociology, Department of Economics and Sociology, Punjab Agricultural University, Ludhiana.

Balwinder Singh, Associate Professor of Ecology, Department of Entomology, Punjab Agricultural University, Ludhiana.

Harnek Singh, Professor of Sociology, Department of Economics and Sociology, Punjab Agricultural University, Ludhiana.

Karam Singh, Director, Agro-Economic Center, Department of Economics and Sociology, Punjab Agricultural University, Ludhiana.

Nirmal Singh, is Senior Statistician, Department of Economics and Sociology, Punjab Agricultural University, Ludhiana.

Rachhpal Singh, Senior Economist, Department of Economics and Sociology, Punjab Agricultural University, Ludhiana.

Sukhdev Singh, Associate Professor of Rural Development, Department of Economics and Sociology, Punjab Agricultural University, Ludhiana.

INTRODUCTION

Punjab has been one of the earliest States, which diffused the ideology of economic development in all sectors of economy. The major challenge has been to evolve a development path that will lead to greater equity, growth and sustainability. Nehru (1954:103) once said that our economy and social structure have outlived their days and it has become a matter of urgent necessity for us to refashion them so that they may promote happiness of all people in things material and spiritual. Following the active intervention of a rational policy of development, Punjab has shown tremendous improvement in production and productivity. The improved economic production gradually and slowly initiated the process of change in the socio-religious ideology based on traditions to modern materialistic class-oriented values. This has transformed the total gamut of social relationships mediated in society.

Further, the development process initiated in Punjab achieved partial modernization of social structure in which innovative, rational, optimistic and entrepreneurial ideology came to replace the conservative and pessimistic one. Nevertheless, certain changes in caste discrimination, marriage, family, women rights have been brought about through a rationality of equality and rational-legal frame of development from the above. But their acceptance at the grassroots seems to be the handiwork of a changed ideology internalized with the pursuit of economic growth. Mass consciousness and potentialities for social mobility were the inherent tendencies of the new social order that came to change all spheres of social life. Supported by rational-legal action of the State through active intervention, the fabrics of social relationships changed. Beside dissolving of the hereditary division of labour, this has transformed the the internal working of social relationships. The social relationships that used to be mediated on the basis of ascribed or ritual roles are giving way to new achievemental roles usually acquired through education, occupation and positions of power and prestige.

The emerging forces of technological, economic and social

developments have eased the rigid system of the society, making sufficient space for inter-group interaction. In the process, struggle among the groups/individuals to secure social and economic dominance is rapidly gaining ground in the social milieu of the society. This has undermined the cooperation—the hallmark of traditional society-based on mutual trust and faith exhibited in strong familial and kin ties to that of mutual compulsiveness (contractual ties) with elements of exploitation, discontentment, frustration, and conflict. Such tendencies are producing alienated individuals, unidimensional men in society for whom valuational and normative systems of the society enforcing social cohesion among groups and communities have no value.

Does such development open avenues for social growth? This poses a major threat to sustain equality with growth and moral values. Punjab provides an interesting contemporary case of social change with complex and contradictory elements such as growth, equity, discontentment, frustration, and so on. This book is a reader with an eye on challenges in front of the Punjab society. Thus, the realm of population growth, urbanization, rural transformation, women empowerment, environmental issues etc. have been given proper place in this reader.

Organization of the Collection

The readings are organized in a manner that highlights different aspects of Punjab society. The book is divided into five sections, representing five mainstreams of the society.

Section-I'Contemporary Punjab' contains six papers: each dealing with important demographic and cultural aspects. Jodhka, through his paper 'Contemporary Punjab: A Brief History', looks into the demographic changes over time. The analysis relates to population, administrative units, density, sex ratio, birth rates, death rates, land holding, working population and other statistical data on Punjab. He concludes that agricultural growth has been responsible for decline of absolute poverty in Punjab. This State has not been able to attract large-scale investment in the industrial sector. Also, Punjab has an average performance in terms of social development. The sex ratio in Punjab is showing a declining trend. Malkit Kaur, in her paper 'Socio-Cultural Correlates of Low Sex Ratio', finds the decline in sex ratio due to the practice of female foeticide in the State. Easy and affordable availability of technology for the determination of the foetus has contributed a lot as far as sex-selective abortions are concerned. The author strongly condemns those religious teachings that advocate not only the killing of girls but also other practices downgrading women in society. Education is one of the factors that may deter gender bias. Exploring this aspect of 'Higher Education in Punjab', Sukhdev Singh finds erosion of ethical values and moral standards among the teachers, the students, and the society at large. Based on the analysis of data collected from fifty-five faculty members of Punjab Agricultural University, Ludhiana, he advocates the decline in moral standards and values to non-recognition of talent, receding professionalism, entry of non-serious students, unionism at different levels and many other variables. At the end, he makes a number of suggestions to improve the standard of higher education.

Another important section of the population is the Scheduled Castes. Its population in Punjab is much higher than what it is at the all India level. Jodhka has touched the issue of untouchability, role of various reform movements, question of Sikh identity, the Singh Sabha Movement, the Ad-Dharmi movement in his paper 'Scheduled Castes in Punjab'. Chamar and Ad-dharmi communities have turned out more successful entrepreneurs than other small and less mobilized groups among the Scheduled Castes. Jodhka holds that the institution of caste is comparatively weak in Punjab. Contrarily, Gill in his paper 'Reservation and Protective Justice' finds it a social reality, which not only provides ground for social exploitation but also avenues for the mobility of Scheduled Castes. The study, based on microanalysis, affirms the perpetuation of structural inequalities despite reservation policy. The author raised the question of constitutional equality in the context of reservation policy. The study is limited to urban populace only and hence needs elaborate macro-analysis. Of course, the analysis points out that reservation provides an opportunity to the lower sections of society to achieve those qualities and attributes on which modern industrial society lays premium essential for social and economic mobility.

Sandhu and Sandhu in their paper 'Urbanization in Punjab' explore the trends and patterns of urbanization through their analysis of statistical data. The article concludes that urbanization is revolving around socio-economically-developed regions and in bigger cities. Despite this, problems emerging with urbanization have not been looked into by the planners and others.

Section-II on 'Agrarian Development, Social Change and Globalization' comprises of six papers. Gill has taken up the issue of changing village social organization in his paper 'Green Revolution and Changing Village Social Organization'. He finds agrarian development has changed social relationships mediated through caste, *Jajmani*, and political systems in rural areas. Social change has been more among the middle and lower castes who have started asserting their numerical strength forcing communities to redefine their web of social relationships besides competing for status in the village social hierarchy. The paper highlights that without proper ideological base to usurp the advantages of mechanization and agricultural development, the rural society is bound to be driven by contradictions and conflicts with elements of progress and regress. In the next paper, 'Dynamics of Caste-Land Relations', Gill has probed the process of leasing in rural society through an analysis of field data. He finds the pattern of land distribution consistent with landowning Jat cultivators who with their hold over land, continue to occupy superordinate position in rural society. No doubt, land has come into market as a commodity but it has not changed hands. The cultivating Jats dominate the lease market as against middle or lower castes. The analysis extrapolates that land is a repository of wealth, power and prestige and Jats through their control maintain their dominant position in rural society.

Another important issue dealt in this section is that of co-operative societies, considered the backbone of rural development in Punjab. Based on primary data, Singh in his paper 'Agricultural Co-operative Service Societies and Rural Development' highlights the infrastructure, financial position, and the functioning of societies. The study infers that faction politics and government control have hampered the functioning of co-operatives and encouraged struggle among groups to control these as a source of power rather than as a delivery system. On the other hand, Chahal and Aggarwal, Milk Co-operatives and Rural Development, come to conclude that milk co-operatives provide employment avenues, raise per capita availability of milk, besides generating fluid cash and thus encourage intercaste interaction because of shared common interests. The authors have not explored the impact of increased benefits among large and medium farmers towards generation of disparities between them and the poor, also the changes in the pattern of social relationships with improved interaction.

In addition, Punjab agriculture has been thrown open to world competition with the implementation of General Agreement on Trade and Tariff (GATT) replaced by World Trade Organization (WTO). Bawa and Raikhy's paper 'Implications of WTO for Agriculture' attempts to visualize the provisions of GATT — 94/WTO and its implications for Punjab agriculture. The WTO provisions have increased the worries of the Punjab farmers who already are not finding market for their foodgrains in the country. In their view, Punjab has tremendous scope to transform WTO challenges into opportunities in the long run, provided State intervenes to take up a market-friendly role by providing infrastructure, technical expertise, storage, market, and the like in addition to setting up agro-processing units. Sharing the above views, Vikram Chadha observes that the State lacks in vision in supporting research and development in agriculture sector. In his paper 'Challenges of Agricultural Research in WTO Regime', Chadha attempts to specify the research needs of the farmers to make them economically viable and internationally competitive. Adoption of genetically engineered crops through proper monitoring is required to sustain the eco-system with maximum profitability on the farm.

Rural credit institutions have contributed a lot in the process of agricultural development by meeting credit needs of the cultivators. This section has five papers that touch upon this issue. Using statistical data available on credit, Sekhon and Kaur in their paper 'Role of Institutional Finance and Government Investment in Capital Formation of Punjab Agriculture', observe that the early period of mechanization has raised demand for fixed assets. This gradually shifted to running expenses with emphasis on investment for high doses of agro-chemicals. The authors conclude that co-operative credit institutions are the major source of investment in the agriculture sector; othes, like commercial banks, act merely as a second fiddle and this accounts for slow capital formation in the agriculture sector. Investment in agriculture, as against that in industrial sector, continues to be less due to small returns and high transaction costs and overdue. Sajla and Singh have explored the role of Regional Rural Banks in Punjab's economy in their study, 'Financing the Weaker Sections'. They have applied the parameter of recovery performance of Gramin Banks. These banks are encouraging rural development with improvement in all the business indicators.

In addition to institutional credit sources, informal or non-institutional credit agencies especially, commission agents too play a dominant role in rural transformation. Gill, Kaur and Gian Kaur in their respective papers have studied this aspect. Paper 'Commission Agents in Rural Setting' by Gill and Rupinder Kaur take up the issue of social and economic relationships in the context of credit needs of the cultivators and provision of this credit by commission agents. Garning the data collected from villages, the authors find that indebtedness of the cultivating class is increasing with escalation in the cost of inputs and heavy social demands and obligations. The dependency of the cultivating class upon commission agents to sustain productivity on the farm with increasing use of agro-chemicals latently has elements of exploitation and subordination. Despite this, both the cultivators and the commission agents maintain close and personal social ties to reinforce economic dependency. Gian Kaur in her paper 'Tenancy and Demand for Agricultural Credit' touches upon the above issue and holds that pure tenants use only one-third of the credit for productive purposes. The analysis is based on the primary data collected from the border village of Amritsar district. The author wants special policy for government lessee especially through institutional credit agencies. Falling in line, Singh and Kaur opine in their paper 'Socio-Economic Adversities of Farmers' that non-farm expenditures are invariably more than that on farm. To cover the gap, farmers divert institutional as well as non-institutional credit and get trapped in a debt circle. The ideology of caste superiority both economically and socially plays havoc and leads to socio-economic adversities to a great extent. The paper lacks class analysis in this regard.

The reading also includes another important issue of women empowerment; which means redistribution of social power and control of resources in favour of women (International Women Conference, 1985). The issue emerged with growing realization that national development and women development are interrelated. Recent constitutional amendments have laid a strong foundation for women's participation in decision-making bodies. This section 'Women Empowerment' includes five readings, probing women's empowerment through politics (Gill), employment in rural development programmes (Singh *et al.* and Abbi), secondary (Singh and Dhillon) and tertiary sector (Gill).

After 73rd and 74th amendments in the Constitution of India, Punjab has been expected, like other States, to recognize women as effective participants in political decision making. Gill has focused the issue that has surfaced out of the experience of women councillors of Chandigarh and Punjab Municipal Committees in her reading on 'Political Empowering of Women'. Her observation based on empirical evidences confirms a continuation of patriarchal structure at familial level, extending further to the level of political participation. Singh *et al.* find a significant role of women, both among farm and non-farm families, in income generating activities through their participation in watershed development. Their comments originate from the analysis of data collected from the Kandhi area of Punjab. The study infers that the nature and extent of women's involvement in agriculture and other developmental activities may vary with occupation, caste, and family status. The focus of Abbi's paper 'Rural Development and Women' is on interlinkage between techno-economic changes centring on the pattern of production and earning a living. Social transformation in women's lives and lifestyles and social identities has been the core of her analysis. The paper highlights the complexity of life of the women, their day-to-day overbusy schedule and race against time that in general remains invisible.

Certainly the women are pushed to work for a variety of circumstances, but what are the feelings and effect on employment have been explored by Singh and Dhillon in their paper "Women Empowerment through Labour Participation in Industrial Sector'. By taking women workers from urban and rural areas as a sample, they come to conclude that employment helps in getting respect from family members and role in decision-making, especially related to household, children and relatives. The last paper of this section, 'Women and Society: Empowering through Work', relates to the perception of status and linkage between status and employment. Gill finds that majority of the educated employed women contemplate their status secondary to that of men. Their service provides opportunities of self-expression, self-actualization and a better lifestyle. A sense of neglèct prevails in their sphere of activities manifestly and latently because of cultural preferences and expectations governing their role behaviour. The author suggests that changing realities should be incorporated into the institutionalized roles and group relations to mitigate gender bias.

Another issue touched upon in this reader is that of environmental stress resulting from demand on scarce resources with the rising standards of people in Punjab. Economic growth has accelerated the process of ecological degradation and in this scenario, economy and ecology are becoming more interwoven—locally, regionally and globally as cause and effect. Against this backdrop, four papers on 'Development and Environment' have been incorporated in this section. Capitalist development based on the theory of growth-manship has altered man-nature relationship. Taking a lead, Gill in his paper 'Development, Environment and Society' has looked into the issue of development, environmental awareness and the role of technology in sustainability of the environment. Using studies conducted in India and abroad and citing examples, he discerns that natural resources got neglected both in the hands of the rich and the poor without realizing the sustenance of economy and people. Taking a social ecologist's position that solution to all environmental problems can only come from within society by a resolution of social inequalities, the author concludes that rich should understand the existence of another underprivileged and underdeveloped sections whose survival depends upon the ideology of sharing the resources rather appropriating these and limiting them to self-interest. Likewise, science and technology should not outrightly reject the knowledge and skills acquired by man through his symbiotic man-nature relationship. Coming to agrarian growth, Dhaliwal *et al.* have dealt the issue of pesticides and its effect on crops and milch cattle. The authors have highlighted the problems of excessive and indiscriminate use of pesticides in their paper 'Pesticides, Environment, and Society'. They hold that despite excessive use and lack of awareness among farmers about its side effects, pesticides will continue to play an important role in agricultural growth. Efforts are afoot to develop sublethal concentrates of agro-chemicals, especially plant protection by chemical industries.

Dua and Parkash's paper 'Status of Stakeholders in Wild Life Protected Areas', specifically and pointedly refers to those people who depend for their livelihood upon the products of Harika Lake. Turning wetlands into tourist resorts may affect the subsistence of such communities. So any plan relating to wetlands should closely watch the interest of the dependent groups.

Associated with the environmental aspect is the moral degradation with improved economic standards. The issue of cultural and moral sustainability is usually left untouched. In this regard, Aggarwal *et al.* in their paper 'Dimensions of Drug Addicts', have tried to approach the above issue. Based on the data collected from the Malwa belt of Punjab, they have tried to associate drug addiction to age, education, family type, and marital status. Their study points out the causes of drug addiction. The authors have suggested the education of the people about the adverse effects of drug abuse and how the pro-active role of drug de-addiction centres may curb this menace and help in building a sustainable healthy society.

Finally, while efforts have been made to comprehend various aspects of Punjab society, it is inevitable that certain other valuable issues have been left out. Such is the nature of a reader of this sort. It is hoped that the present volume would help stimulate interest of scholars in the vibrant Punjab society.

REFERENCE

Nehru, Jawaharlal (1954) *Speeches*, New Delhi, Publication Division, Government of India.

SECTION–I

CONTEMPORARY PUNJAB

1

CONTEMPORARY PUNJAB
A Brief Introduction

SURINDER S. JODHKA

Over the last century or so, the Punjab has seen many changes in its social and political geography. Before its partition in 1947 into the Punjab (East), that remained in India, and the Punjab (West), that went to Pakistan, it used to be a much bigger province and with quite a different social profile. The Indian Punjab was once again divided in 1966 when, in response to a powerful movement by the Sikh Akalis, it was reorganized on linguistic lines. The Hindi speaking parts of the southern Punjab were taken out of its boundary and made into a separate state of Haryana. The non-Punjabi speaking hilly areas were merged with the state of Himachal Pradesh. The newly built capital of Punjab, the planned city of Chandigarh, was made a Union Territory and continued to be the joint capital of both Punjab and Haryana after the reorganization in 1966.

The present state of Punjab has a total area of 50,362 sq. kms. (much smaller than the colonial Punjab when it had a total area of 3,59,179 sq. kms.). It occupies only 1.6 per cent of the total geographical area of India and is inhabited by little more than 2 per cent of India's population. Most of the present day Punjab (more than 90 per cent) is flat plains. It lies between 180 and 320 metres above the sea level. The height is more near the hill and decreases gradually.

Punjab acquired its name from the number of rivers that flowed through the region (the word Punjab in Persian means the land of five rivers). It is a part of the Indo-Gangetic plains that were formed by the elevation of Himalayas. The state also has a small hilly region, the outer range of the Siwalik Hills running along its eastern border. The hilly belt is in the range of six to ten kilometres in width and is also called the *Kandi* area. Compared to the rest of the state, this area has remained relatively less developed.

Punjab is also a border state. Around 553 kms. of India's border with Pakistan passes through the north-western part of Punjab, touching the districts of Amritsar, Gurdaspur and Firozpur. It has also remained "a hot" border. As is the case with the Kandi belt, the areas close to the international border have also remained comparatively much less developed.

Table 1.1: Area, Population, Settlements and Addministrative units 1901-1996

Year	*Area (in kms.)*	*Population (in millions)*	*Settlements (rural and urban)*	*Administrative units*
1901	389,036	26.88	47256	32 districts 43 native states
1911	353,095	24.19	44574	29 districts 15 Punjab states
1921	354,688	24.95	45409	29 districts 15 Punjab states 28 Simla hill states
1931	354,400	29.13	51224	29 districts 15 Punjab states 28 Simla hill states
1941	359,179	35.23	52644	29 districts 16 Punjab states 27 Simla hill states
1951	96,809	12.64	15277	13 districts
1961	122,005	20.35	22879	19 districts
1971	50,362	13.55	12450	11 districts
1981	50,362	16.79	12450	12 districts
1991	50,362	20.19	12915	12 districts
1996	50,362	22.29	12915	17 districts

Source: Gopal Krishan, 1998:13.

Administratively, the state is organized into 4 divisions (Jalandhar, Patiala, Firozpur and Faridkot), 17 districts, 70 sub-divisions/tehsils, 55 sub-tehsils and 137 development blocks (for details about the districts and district headquarters see Tables 1.1, 1.2). The average size of a district in Punjab is around 3000 sq. kms, much smaller than the average size of a district for the country as a whole, which is around 6000 sq. kms. The total number of inhabited villages in the state has been going up steadily. Their number had gone up from 11,625 in 1951 to 12,188 in 1971 and again to 12,428 in 1991. There were also 367 uninhabited villages in the state. As per the most recent census of 2001, the total number of jurisdictional villages in Punjab was 12,729 (break-up for inhabited and uninhabited villages not yet known). This figure had come down 12,795 in the 1991 census. The number of towns or urban agglomerations has also gone up from 110 in 1951 to 120 in 1991 and further to 157 in 2001.

Table 1.2: Districts-wise population, density, sex-ratio, area and district headquarters of Punjab.

District & district headquarter	*Area (sq. kms.)*	*Total Population*	*Density per sq. km*	*Females per 1000 males*
Gurdaspur	3570	1757808	492	903
Amritsar	5088	2505034	492	873
Kapurthala	1633	646647	396	896
Jalandhar	2643	1649205	624	897
Nawanshehar	1258	531253	422	900
Hoshiarpur	3310	1298185	392	924
Rupnagar	2117	902264	426	870
Ludhiana	3762	2426343	645	844
Firozpur	5328	1460082	274	895
Faridkot	1472	451406	307	882
Muktsar	2608	654434	251	880
Moga	2197	771046	351	884
Bhatinda	3401	985301	290	884
Mansa	2150	574662	267	873
Sangrur	5021	1685449	336	870
Patiala	3627	1521330	419	882
Fatehgarh	1177	461520	392	871
Punjab	50362	20281969	403	882

Source: Statistical Abstract, Punjab, 1991, pp. 60.

Of these 139 were statutory towns and the rest 18 were classified as non-statutory or census towns.

Population and Density

According to the 1991 census, the total population of Punjab was 2,02,81,969. As per the available provisional tables of 2001 census, this figure has gone up to 2,42,89,296 persons. The decadal growth rate of the state population during the decade 1971-81 was 23.9 per cent. It came down during the 1981-91 decade to 20.81 per cent, which was lower than the all India average of 23.85 per cent. The population growth rate has further come down to 19.76 per cent during the last decade. The compound annual growth rate of population for Punjab during 1951-91 works out to around 2 per cent.

While population in Punjab has been growing at a rate slower than the country as a whole, the density of population in the state is much higher than the national average. Against the national average of 273, the Punjab in 1991 had a density of 403 persons per sq. kms. It has further increased to 482 in 2001. Interestingly in 1951 the population density of the united Punjab was only 182 (the corresponding figure for India as a whole in 1951 was 117).

The birth rate for the state in the year 1997 was 23.4 per thousand per annum and the death rate for the same year was 7.4. The infant mortality rate has come down considerably during the last two decades—from 89 per thousand per annum in 1980 to 51 per thousand per annum in 1997 (the corresponding figure for India as a whole in 1997 was 71). As shown in Table 1.3 below, in the urban centres of Punjab the infant mortality had come down to as low as 38.

Table 1.3: Birth rate, death rate and infant mortality rate per thousand per annum

Year	*Birth*			*Death Rate*			*Infant mortality rate*		
	Rural	Urban	Total	Rural	Urban	Total	Rural	Urban	Total
1980	30.3	28.3	29.9	9.2	6.6	8.7	96	58	89
1990	28.4	25.6	27.6	8.5	5.8	7.8	66	45	61
1997	24.9	19.0	23.4	7.8	6.1	7.4	54	38	51

Source: Statistical Abstract, Punjab, 1991, pp. 481.

As is the case with other north and north-western states of India, the people of Punjab too have a strong preference for the male child. Punjabi culture celebrates masculinity and puts a high premium on having a male child. The growing demands for dowry too puts a lot of pressure on parents to prefer a male child over daughters. While in the earlier times it was the practice of female infanticide that kept the sex ratio in favour of the male sex, in contemporary times, it is the practice of selective abortions (the female foeticide).

According to the 1991 census, Punjab had 882 females per thousand males, which was much lower than the national average of 927. The only saving grace for Punjab was that while at the all India level, the number of female per thousand males had gone down from 946 in 1951 to 930 in 1971 and further to 927 in 1991, the sex-ratio had been consistently improving in Punjab. The number of females per thousand males had gone up from 844 in 1951 to 865 in 1971 and further up to 882 in 1991. However, as per the current census (2001), the sex ratio has declined to 874. Even more disturbing is the fact that in the age group of 0-6, it has gone down from 875 in 1991 to 793 in 2001.

Interestingly, there is not much difference in the sex-ratio among the different communities in state. As per the available statistics, it has been slightly better among the Sikhs than among the Hindus and the Scheduled Castes of the state. For the years 1971 and 1981, for example the figure for the Sikhs was 865 and 882 while the corresponding numbers for the Hindus of Punjab was 864 and 873 (as in Chaitley, 1995:58).

Being an agrarian belt with a strong patriarchal culture, the people of Punjab continue to have a preference for the male child. While earlier it was the practice of female infanticide now it is the modern method of sex determination tests of the unborn child and selective abortions of female foetus that is used to fulfil the desire of having male children.

People of Punjab take pride in being healthy and tough and the "good food". In terms of health infrastructure the state has experienced progress during the last two decades. From 1656 in 1980, the total number of public and private hospitals in the state had gone up to 2229 by 1998. Of these 2153 were public hospitals (Statistical Abstract, Punjab, 1999, p. 490).

However, the overall progress of the state in providing health infrastructure has been rather slow in Punjab. As shown in Table 1.4, compared to the national average of 22.1 per cent, only 5.7 per cent villages of Punjab had a health sub-centre located within the village. Their accessibility within five kilometres of the village was also lower than the national average. In terms of immunization of children (in the age group of 12 to 23 months), however, Punjab is ahead of many other states. As against the national average of 48.5 per cent, 62 per cent of the children in the relevant age group had been given all the doses in Punjab and there was virtually no gender disparity practiced in the state (see Table 1.5).

Urbanization

The proportion of urban population in Punjab has also been a little higher in the state than the national average. Against the national average of 26.1 per cent, the proportion of urban population in Punjab, as per the 1991 census, was 29.6 per cent (see Table 1.6). The growth rate of the urban population in the state has continued to be among the highest in India. As per the available provisional figures, the proportion of urban population in Punjab in the 2001 census had gone up to 33.95 per cent of the total population. The all India average for the year 2001 is reported to be 29.55 per cent.

Table 1.4: Availability of rural infrastructure (percentages)

Type of infrastructure	*Punjab*	*All India*
Transportation		
Connected with pucca road	81.4	36.8
Bus stop within 2 kms	68.6	64.5
Railway station within 5 kms	21.4	22.4
Communication		
Post-office within 2 kms	78.6	70.2
Telephone within 2 kms	65.7	50.9
Irrigation		
Upto 50 % of gross area irrigated	75.7	34.7
Major source of drinking water		
Piped water	34.3	16.6
Hand pump	48.6	18.4
Other protected source	00.0	13.0
Other unprotected source	17.1	52.0
Education		
Primary school within village	95.7	88.1
Middle school within village	55.7	40.8
Middle school within 5 kms	31.4	31.4
Health		
Sub-centres	5.7	22.1
Sub-centre/hospital within 5 kms	18.6	41.2
Pharmacy	31.4	28.5
Anganwadi centre	35.7	52.8

Source: NCAER Report, 1999:188-89.

Table 1.5: Percentage of children immunized (aged 12-23 months)

Disease immunized against	*Punjab*	*India*
DPT	73.2	57.5
Polio	70.2	58.1
BCG	74.1	64.3
Measles	67.5	52.9
All 8 doses	62.0 (gender disparity 1.00)	48.5 (gender disparity 0.96)

Source: NCAER Report, 1999:1767.

Table 1.6: Population

Subject		*1951*	*1961*	*1971*	*1981*	*1991*
Area (sq. kms)		50,362	50,362	50,362	50,362	50,362
Number of inhabited villages		11625	11947	12188	12342	12428
Number of towns		110	109	108	134	120
Total population (in millions)		9.2	11.1	13.5	16.8	20.3
Rural population (in millions)		7.2	8.6	10.3	12.1	14.3
Urban population (in millions)		2.0	2.5	3.2	4.7	6.0
Population	Punjab	182	221	269	333	403
Density (per km)	India	117	142	177	216	273
% of urban population.	Punjab	21.7	23.1	23.7	27.7	29.6
	India	17.3	18.1	19.9	23.3	26.1
Sex ratio (female	Punjab	844	854	865	879	882
per 1000 males)	India	946	941	930	934	927
Decadal population growth Rate (per cent)		21.6 (21.5)	21.7 (24.8)	23.9 (24.7)	20.8 (23.5)	—
Birth rate (per thousand)		—	—	34.1 (36.3)	30.3 (33.9)	27.7 (29.5)
Death rate (per thousand)		—	—	11.7 (15.9)	9.4 (12.5)	7.8 (9.8)
% of religious communities						
Sikhs		55.7	—	—	—	63.0
Hindus		42.3	—	—	—	34.5
Muslims		0.8	—	—	—	1.2
Christians		1.2	—	—	—	1.1
Others		0.2	—	—	—	0.2
Linguistic groups						
Punjabi		—	—	—	14.6 (40.0)	
Hindi		—	—	—	84.9 (2.8)	

Note: Figures in brackets are the corresponding numbers for India as a whole.
Source: Krishan, 1998:165-66.

Most of the big towns of the north-west region of India, such as, Ludhiana, Jalandhar, Amritsar and Patiala are all located in Punjab. Despite the prolonged political crisis in the state during the 1980s, these urban centres, particularly the industrial town of Ludhiana, have been constantly growing in size. Ludhiana was the first city to become a million-plus city in the entire north-west India. The Punjab currently has two million plus cities, Ludhiana and Amritsar.

Not only has the number of urban settlements increased (from 110 in 1951 to 157 in 2001), the total urban area experienced a rather phenomenal growth during the last four or five decades. The aggregate area under towns in the state was 692 sq. kms. in 1971. By 1991 it had more than doubled and gone up to 1,441 sq. kms. As elsewhere in India, the cities of Punjab are swallowing the lands of neighbouring villages.

Communities and Castes

Despite the popular image of the Punjab being a Sikh state, it was only in 1966, after its reorganization on linguistic basis, that the Sikhs became a majority in the state. As mentioned above, the colonial Punjab was a much bigger province where, in religious terms, the Muslims outnumbered both the Hindus as well as the Sikhs. According to 1911 census the proportion of Muslim population to the total population of the united Punjab was 50.86 per cent and that of the Hindus 36.35 per cent. Only around 12 per cent had reported their religion to be Sikhism (Christians were around 1 per cent).

The population exchange that accompanied partition in 1947 changed the demographic profile of the Punjab very significantly. Almost the entire Sikh and Hindu population of the western Punjab crossed over to the Indian side and the Muslims living on the Indian side left for Pakistan. Thus, in the post-partition Indian Punjab the Hindus came to constitute the majority. However, the Sikhs too gained in demographic terms. Apart from their proportion going up from around 12 per cent to around 35 per cent, they also came to concentrate in some specific districts of the divided Punjab where they constituted more than half of the population. When linguistic surveys were carried out to reorganize the provincial boundaries, Punjab was declared a bilingual state with the Sikh dominated districts being reported as Punjabi speaking areas and the Hindu dominated districts as Hindi speaking areas. The Sikh leadership saw in the new demographic scenario the possibility of a Sikh majority province. After a long drawn struggle, the Punjab was reorganized along linguistic lines in 1966.

According to the 1991 census the Sikhs constituted 63 per cent of the total population of the state while the Hindus were around 34 per cent. Christians and Muslims too had their presence in some pockets of the state but their total populations were not much (see Tables 1.6 and 1.7).

Another important aspect of the demographic composition of religious communities in the Punjab is their uneven rural-urban distribution. Despite being in a minority at the state level, the Hindus overwhelmingly dominate urban Punjab while the Sikhs are concentrated more in rural areas. As shown in Table 1.7, the proportion of the Hindu population is as high as 76.46 per cent in Jalandhar and 76 per cent in Gurdaspur. On the other extreme, the Sikhs constitute 89 per cent of the rural population in Amritsar and nearly 87 per cent in Bhatinda.

Table 1.7: District-wise rural-urban composition of population of different religious communities, 1981 (in percentage)

District	*Rural*				*Urban*			
	Sikhs	*Hindus*	*Chri-stians*	*Mus-lims*	*Sikhs*	*Hindus*	*Chri-stians*	*Mus-lims*
Gurdaspur	51.42	40.21	7.67	0.66	20.11	76.72	2.65	0.47
Amritsar	91.37	6.54	1.99	0.09	43.64	54.91	0.94	0.13
Firozpur	64.19	34.70	0.97	0.10	20.60	76.92	1.92	0.21
Ludhiana	88.31	10.88	0.08	0.66	36.45	61.74	0.42	0.31
Jalandhar	53.54	45.39	0.64	0.36	23.29	75.11	0.73	0.23
Kapurthala	71.52	27.50	0.34	0.56	33.70	65.24	0.35	0.35
Ropar	41.89	56.75	0.76	0.57	22.96	75.35	0.35	0.20
Hoshiarpur	62.00	36.61	0.09	1.23	36.87	60.80	0.50	0.47
Patiala	64.69	33.34	0.16	1.74	35.14	63.64	0.14	0.62
Sangrur	80.15	15.87	0.04	3.85	34.03	50.00	0.6	14.79
Bhatinda	87.69	11.63	0.02	0.55	37.27	61.75	0.21	0.34
Faridkot	90.38	9.02	0.11	0.43	41.55	57.52	0.34	0.13
Punjab	71.30	26.51	1.25	0.89	33.19	64.16	0.72	1.30

Source: As calculated by Abbi and Singh 1997: Appendix 1.

At the ideological and philosophical levels, Sikhism does not approve of caste system. However, in practice caste divisions do exist among Sikhs, though more as an age old 'prejudice' than as an elaborate system of purity and pollution as in some other parts of India. A rather peculiar feature of the caste hierarchy in Punjab is that historically Brahmins have not been much revered in the local imagination. Even among the Hindus of the region the Brahmins do not enjoy the kind of status that they enjoy in some other parts of India. As the well known author, Prakash Tandon wrote in his celebrated book the *Punjab Century*, "That they (the Brahmins) could be the leaders of society, in a position of privilege, I only discovered when I went to live outside the Punjab. With us the Brahmins were an unprivileged class and exercised little or no influence on the community" (Tandon, 1988:73).

Urban Punjab is mostly dominated by the trading castes, mostly Hindus and some Sikhs. The main urban trading castes in Punjab are those of Banias, Khatris and Aroras. Though in terms of numbers they (all trading castes put together) do not constitute more than 10 to 12 per cent of the total population, they control much of the urban trade and industry in the state and economically are quite well off. The Brahmins and the Scheduled Castes also have their presence in the urban Punjab. Apart from the Sikhs from the trading castes, i.e., Khatris and Aroras, many Sikh Jats and the enterprising Ramgarhias (once counted among the backward castes, the artisans) too have been migrating to the urban centres of Punjab.

An interesting feature of the caste structure of rural Punjab is that unlike many other regions, the state has a single landowning dominant caste, i.e. the Jats. Their proportion in the total population of the state would be around 30 to 35 per cent but in most villages of Punjab they constitute the single biggest caste group. They also have control over most of the agricultural land and dominate politically, both at the village level as well as at the state level. Apart from the Jat, more than 80 per cent of the Scheduled Castes (who constitute nearly 30 per cent of the total population of Punjab) also live in the countryside. The other main caste groups are those of Ramgarhias, Sainis, Kambohs and Rais. They together constitute 20 to 25 per cent of the total population of Punjab.

Among all the states of India, the Punjab has the highest proportion of the Scheduled Caste population. The Scheduled Castes accounted for 28.3 per cent of the total population of the Punjab in 1991, much higher than the all-India average of 16.32 per cent (see Table 1.8 and 1.9). In some districts of the state, they make up to 38 per cent of the pópulation. Scheduled Caste population of Punjab was growing at much faster rate than the non-Scheduled Caste population. During 1961 to 1991, the Scheduled Caste population of Punjab grew at an annual rate of 2.83 per cent (all India 2.59) as against the non-Scheduled Caste population growth rate of 1.75 per cent (all India 2.24). By the year 2000, the percentage of their population in the total population of Punjab is likely to have crossed the mark of 30 per cent (for details see the other chapter on the subject in this volume).

The Economy

Punjab has for long been one of the prosperous states of India. In terms of per capita income, Punjab is among the top three states of India. In the year 1995-96, the per capita income of the state at the current prices was Rs. 16,042, much higher than the all India average of Rs. 9,578. Only Goa and Delhi were ahead of Punjab.

Table 1.8: Percentages of the Scheduled Caste Population and Land Holdings of Scheduled Castes in Different States of India (1991)

State/UT	*% of S.C. population to total population*	*S.C. land holdings (% of total holdings)*	*S.C. land holdings (% of total area)*	*Average size of S.C. holdings (hect)*
Andhra Pradesh	15.93	8.81	8.21	0.91
Assam	7.40	0.90	0.99	1.08
Bihar	14.56	12.11	4.90	0.40
Goa	2.08	0.01	Negligible	—
Gujarat	7.41	1.08	2.53	2.30
Haryana	19.75	0.34	0.58	1.65
Himachal Pradesh	25.34	1.39	1.05	0.74
Jammu and Kashmir	Not available	0.63	0.61	0.94
Karnataka	16.38	4.75	7.55	1.56
Kerala	9.92	3.89	0.38	0.10
Madhya Pradesh	14.55	7.87	13.63	1.70
Maharashtra	11.10	5.66	9.57	1.66
Manipur	2.02	0.02	0.04	1.67
Meghalya	0.51	—	—	—
Nagaland	—	—	—	—
Orissa	16.20	4.03	3.45	0.84
Punjab	28.31	0.40	0.72	1.76
Rajasthan	17.29	5.59	18.70	3.29
Sikkim	5.93	0.01	0.02	1.00
Tamil Nadu	19.18	6.74	4.05	0.59
Tripura	16.36	0.36	0.23	0.63
Uttar Pradesh	21.05	24.50	14.31	0.57
West Bengal	23.62	10.89	8.46	0.76

Source: Statistical Abstract, Punjab 1999, pp. 206-07.

Much of the prosperity of Punjab has been achieved through its dynamic agrarian economy. The introduction of green revolution technology during the late 1960s completely transformed the rural economy of Punjab. An increase in the agricultural income also gave a spurt to other sectors of the economy.

Though agriculture continues to be the main occupation of a large proportion of the working population of the state, over the years industrial/ manufacturing sectors have also grown. In fact the share of agriculture has begun to decline in the total income of the state. As shown below in Table 1.10 the share of agriculture in the state GDP came down from 32.22 per cent in 1980-81 to 24.08 per cent in 1998-99. On the other hand, the share secondary sector went up from 18.47 in 1980-81 to 27.52

per cent. The largest proportion in this sector being that of the manufacturing sector.

Table 1.9: District-wise Distribution of Scheduled Caste Population in Punjab, 1981 and 1991

Name of the district	*% S.C. Population (1981)*	*% S.C. Population (1991)*
Gurdaspur	23.69	24.71
Amritsar	26.20	28.03
Kapurthala	26.98	29.47
Jalandhar	36.27	38.15
Hoshiarpur	30.83	33.85
Rupnagar	24.38	24.35
Ludhiana	25.18	24.54
Ferozpur	20.89	21.81
Faridkot	31.67	35.05
Bhatinda	27.01	29.48
Sangrur	25.47	26.75
Patiala	22.12	22.31
Nawanshehar*	—	38.98
Mukatsar*	—	36.44
Moga*	—	30.92
Mansa*	—	28.91
Fatehgarh Sahib*	—	29.89
Punjab	26.87	28.31

*These districts came into existence after 1981.
Source: Statistical Abstract, Punjab 1995.

Table 1.10: Percentage distribution of net state domestic product at factor cost by sectors at constant (1980-81prices)

Sector	*1980-81*	*1998-99*
Primary sector (total)	49.50	42.01
Agriculture	32.22	24.08
Livestock	16.24	17.25
Secondary sector (total)	18.47	27.52
Manufacturing	11.01	21.10
Tertiary sector (total)	32.02	30.47
Transport, communication and trade	16.64	14.29
Finance and real estate	6.81	8.55
Community and personal services	8.58	7.63

Source: Statistical Abstract, Punjab, 1999, pp. 126-7.

More than anything else, the Punjab is known for its enterprising farming. Before anywhere else, it was in the Punjab that the green revolution technology produced miracles. Along with the neighbouring Haryana, western Uttar Pradesh and some pockets of southern and western India, the success of green revolution technology solved the vexing problem of food scarcity of India.

Despite a decline in the share of agriculture/primary sector in the total income or the GDP of the state it continues to employ more than half of the total working population in the state. In the year 1991, agricultural workers accounted for nearly 55 per cent of the total workers (SA Punjab, 1999: 216). The corresponding figure for the year 1980 was 60 per cent (Chadha, 1986:51).

The success of green revolution technology in the state was, to a significant extent, a direct result of the available agricultural infrastructure. Construction of the Bhakra canal system during the early 1950s was the biggest landmark in the development of canal irrigation in the region. Over the years, farmers have also installed a large number of tube-wells in their fields. During 1960-61 to 1990-91, the average number of tube-wells per thousand acres of sown area went up from 1.6 to 76.9. Nearly all the land that can be cultivated is being put to cultivation in Punjab* and nearly 95 per cent of all the cultivated land has an assured source of irrigation available. During this period, the number of tractors available per thousand acres of sown area went up from 0.5 to 28.0 and the use of chemical fertilizers per acre grew from 0.4 kg per acre to nearly 66 kg per acre (Shergill, 1998:2).

Though Punjab occupies less than 2 per cent of the total land area of the country, it began to produce nearly one-fourth of the total food grains of the country and contributed up to two-third of the entire central pool of food grains. In 1980-81, for example, the share of Punjab in the central pool of wheat was 73 per cent and of rice 45 per cent. With the green revolution technology gradually spreading to the other parts of the country as well, Punjab's share in the total food grains production of the country and its contribution to the central pool has been coming down. However, in absolute terms, Punjab farmers continue to grow more and more food grains, particularly wheat and paddy (Punjab still produces around 11 per cent of all the food grains produced in India. Its share in wheat production is 19 per cent and in rice production around 10 per cent).

* The total area being cultivated in Punjab also has seen manifold increase in absolute terms. It went up from 227 thousand hectares in 1960-61 to 2,015 hectares by 1990-91.

Changing Agrarian Relations

Unlike some other parts of the subcontinent, absentee landlordism has never been very strong in Punjab. The region has been known for its hard working, self-cultivating peasants who celebrate the value of *khudkasht* (cultivation with one's own hands). However, as shown below in Table 1.11, Punjab has much larger land holdings than the all India average. While Punjab had 26 per cent of small size holdings (below 1 hectare), the corresponding figure for the country as a whole was 59.4 per cent. But, as in the rest of the country, large proportions of land holdings in the Punjab too were of medium and small size (nearly 70 per cent of all the holdings in the state are below 4 hectares).

Table 1.11: Structure of operational holdings in Punjab and India, 1990-91

Size class	*Punjab*	*India*
Below 1 hectare	26.5	59.4
1 to 2 hectares	18.3	18.8
2 to 4 hectares	25.9	13.1
4 to 10 hectares	23.4	7.1
10 hectares and above	6.0	1.6

Source: *Statistical Abstracts*, Punjab, 1999, pp. 203-04.

Though initially adopted by the better off farmers, all categories of farmers benefited from the green revolution technology. The wage rates of both male and female agricultural labourers increased much faster in Punjab than in other parts of the country. For example, in the early 1980s a male agricultural labourer in Punjab was getting a daily wage of Rs. 18 and a female labourer Rs. 15. The corresponding rate in Maharashtra were Rs. 9.5 and Rs. 6 and in West Bengal Rs. 10.50 and Rs. 8.50. Even in Kerala where agricultural labourers are well organized the wage rates were lesser than Punjab (Rs. 17 for male and Rs. 12 for female labourers; as calculated by Jose, 1988).

Increase in size of cultivable land made possible by the increasing availability of tractors and growing practice of multiple cropping system also increased the demand for labour by many folds. The local landless fulfilled some of this new demand, who switched over from their traditional occupations to agricultural labour. A large number of labourers from the depressed parts of Uttar Pradesh and Bihar also started coming into the villages of Punjab, particularly during the peak seasons when the wages were even higher.

Introduction of new farm technology also transformed the nature of social relations in rural society. While the new technology significantly enhanced the demand for labour, it simultaneously made some of the older occupations redundant. The farmers in the new commercialised agriculture preferred formalized contractual relations with their labourers to the older structures of patronage and clientele. The percentage of agricultural labourers to the total rural workers in Punjab experienced a sharp increase after the green revolution. As per the available statistics, their numbers went up from 8.95 per cent in 1961 to 24.80 per cent in 1971. It again went up to 28.52 per cent in 1981 and further to 30.75 per cent in 1991 (as in Abbi and Singh, 1997:130).

The Marginal Farmers

Until recently, Punjab farmers were considered to be among the most prosperous cultivators in the country. However, the farmers in the whole of Punjab are not a well off category. As discussed above, Punjab too has pockets of backwardness. Since all the cultivable land is already being cultivated, the holding get smaller and smaller as the population grows and families get divided. Some of the districts have very low level of education, particularly in the rural areas. The policies of liberalization and market reforms are also creating peculiar problems for the Punjab farmers. In the newly emerging economic regime, the state is beginning to withdraw from the sphere of economy. On the other hand this process is strengthening the urban trade.

The small cultivators of Punjab had so far survived with the help of the state government in the form of 'minimum support price'. In the open market regime the small farmer or the agricultural sector in general is being placed in a vulnerable situation. The nature of agricultural production is such that all the output comes together and at the time of harvesting there is bound to be a glut in the market. In absence of a secure marketing system, something that had been evolved by the post-independence state, the farmers are likely to find it difficult to deal directly with the traders. The growing indebtedness of the small/marginal farmers and the recent spurt in suicides in rural Punjab, as also in some other parts of India, is an indication of the growing vulnerability of the agrarian sector. While the bigger landowners will survive or may even benefit from the economic reforms, small and marginal landowners are likely to find it difficult to maintain their current levels of living. Given that a high premium is attached to status in the rural society, the crisis for them is indeed serious.

Industry

Punjab is popularly known for its agriculture. The state has not had much heavy investments in industry either from the central government or from the major industrial houses of the country. Punjab has also not been a popular destination for foreign investors. However, despite all these factors, Punjab cannot be considered an industrially backward state.

The state has some flourishing industrial centres and enjoys a leading role in the manufacture of sports goods, hosiery, surgical instruments and cycle parts. As mentioned above the proportion of urban population in Punjab is more than that of the country as a whole, the share of secondary sector, particularly that of the manufacturing sector has been growing in the state over the last three or four decades. Even during the difficult decade of the 1980s when Punjab witnessed a violent movement for a separate nation-state, the industrial sector continued to grow. The share of secondary sector grew from around 18 per cent in 1980-81 to more that 27 per cent in 1998-99. The share of manufacturing sector alone grew from 11 per cent to 21 per cent during the same period (see Table 1.11).

The number of registered factories in the whole of Punjab was 4501 in 1970 and collectively they employed 1,16,806 workers. By 1998, the number of registered factories in the state had gone up to 13,254 giving employment to 4,49,059 persons (see Table 1.12). Though there is some industrial activity in all districts of the state, most factories are concentrated in the three big cities, *viz.*, Ludhiana, Jalandhar and Amritsar (see Table 1.13). Ludhiana has over the years emerged as one of the biggest industrial centres of the entire north-west region. It is also the first million plus city of the region. Apart from these big cities, some of the smaller towns like Mandi Gobindgarh and Rajpura too have a concentration of industrial units.

Table 1.12: Number of factories and workers employed in Punjab, 1970-1998

Year	*Registered working factories*	*Number of workers employed*	*Workers per lakh of population*
1970	4501	116806	862
1980	7053	201735	1206
1990	11396	367513	1770
1998	13254	449059	1909

Source: Statistical Abstracts, Punjab, 1999, pp. 389.

Much of the industry in Punjab is of native origin and of medium and small scale in nature. The labour is mostly unorganised. A large proportion of the labour employed in these industries is also made of migrants from other states. Some of the industries, particularly the sports goods industry in Jalandhar is known to employ child labourers. The wages they earn are too meagre, their living conditions are quite miserable. Given the nature of the industry, most of the jobs are insecure and temporary.

Table 1.13: District-wise number of factories and workers employed, 1998

District	*Registered working factories*	*Number of workers employed*	*Workers per lakh of population*
Gurdaspur	665	12530	634
Amritsar	1655	39748	1447
Kapurthala	401	15447	2081
Jalandhar	1677	47801	2559
Nawanshehar	49	1451	239
Hoshiarpur	476	18463	1262
Rupnagar	465	32202	2961
Ludhiana	4183	148788	4807
Firozpur	507	13829	733
Faridkot	314	8843	1667
Muktsar	190	6499	860
Moga	184	4302	599
Bhatinda	437	15200	1333
Mansa	238	5925	921
Sangrur	857	33050	1685
Patiala	619	29588	1669
Fatehgarh	337	15393	2947
Punjab	13254	449059	1909

Source: *Statistical Abstracts*, Punjab, 1999, pp. 389.

Education and Literacy

In terms of literacy rates, though Punjab has not done as well as states like Kerala, its performance has not been too bad. In 1991 Punjab had a literacy rate of nearly 58.51 per cent, higher than the national average of 52.21. However, as shown in Table 1.14, the state has very sharp inter-district variations. While in the district of Hoshiarpur, 72.08 per cent of the total eligible population was literate, the figure for the Mansa district was only 37 per cent. Similarly, there were significant differences among different categories of population, rural-urban, male-female, Scheduled Castes and others. The Scheduled Castes, for example, had much lower rate of literacy than the rest of the population. There were significant district-wise variations among them as well (see Table 1.14).

Table 1.14: District-wise literacy rates in Punjab, 1991

District	*Rural*	*Urban*	*Male*	*Female*	*Scheduled Castes*	*Total*
Gurdaspur	58.44	73.69	69.55	53.33	47.60	61.84
Amritsar	49.73	73.94	65.07	50.10	33.71	58.08
Kapurthala	58.90	75.84	70.03	55.83	47.82	63.31
Jalandhar	61.48	76.54	75.11	62.05	56.61	68.93
Nawanshehar	63.18	74.44	73.30	54.55	—	64.42
Hoshiarpur	70.61	79.16	80.22	63.34	63.82	72.08
Rupnagar	63.59	81.15	76.49	58.52	57.38	68.15
Ludhiana	62.28	71.71	72.45	61.25	50.48	67.34
Firozpur	40.94	68.36	57.12	37.88	24.40	48.02
Faridkot	42.33	65.45	57.13	41.88	24.27	49.97
Muktsar	40.24	66.34	54.25	37.15	—	46.18
Moga	47.73	67.39	57.37	44.92	—	51.52
Bhatinda	38.97	66.62	53.98	38.04	20.68	46.48
Mansa	32.67	63.52	44.81	28.50	—	37.21
Sangrur	41.25	60.42	56.21	37.67	27.15	45.99
Patiala	49.50	75.21	64.64	48.94	38.53	57.27
Fatehgarh	60.31	73.85	69.45	56.13	—	63.25
Punjab	52.77	72.08	65.66	50.41	41.09	58.51

Source: Statistical Abstracts, Punjab, 1999, pp. 70-71.

Punjab has also been expanding its educational infrastructure over the years. The number of schools at all levels has multiplied during the last three decades (see Table 1.15). According to the NCAER report, the enrolment rate in Punjab was 86.8 with almost insignificant gender based variation (0.95). The corresponding figure for the country as a whole were 71.4 per cent with a male/female ratio of 0.84 (NCAER report, 1999: 105). The drop-out rate in Punjab has been coming down over the years. As per the state government figures, it had come down from 32 per cent in 1992-93 to 21 per cent in 1999 (Department of Social Welfare, 2000).

Table 1.15: Number of schools

Year	*10+2 schools*	*High schools*	*Middle schools*	*Primary schools*
1970	252	1071	1060	7258
1980	157	1912	1498	12383
1990	520	2239	1421	12400
1998	1151	2174	2527	12633

For higher education also, the state has a comparatively good infrastructure. The state has a total of 4 universities including an agricultural university, 8 medical colleges, 18 engineering/architecture colleges and 193 general colleges.

The prosperity brought about by the green revolution also provided many of the landowning rural families with enough surplus income to send their wards to schools and colleges. Investment in education is seen as a medium of social mobility. Once educated, the younger generation, particularly from families with smaller land holdings do not wish to get back to agriculture. However, the nature of growth in the urban industrial sector is such that it does not absorb the educated youth from rural Punjab. Given their rural background, most of them find it difficult to compete for jobs outside Punjab. The obvious consequence is unemployment of ambitious and aspirant upwardly mobile youth. Many of those who joined the militant movement during the 1980s came from this category of the population.

Though the educational infrastructure has expanded in the state, the quality of education being imparted is rather poor, particularly in the government run schools. The situation is particularly depressing in village schools. The number of teachers employed is normally lesser than the number of teachers required. Even those employed do not take their work very seriously. Rarely do the rural schools have enough infrastructure in terms of rooms, labs and furniture required for proper functioning of the school. More ambitious and well to do parents have started sending their children to urban schools. One can also notice mushrooming of private schools, mostly at the nursery and primary level of teaching in the better off villages of Haryana and Punjab. These schools are generally run by some local trust or in some cases even by the panchyats by employing locally available teachers. They mainly attract children from slightly better off families in the village and their main attraction is that they claim to carry out teaching in "English medium".

The Migrant Workers

Migrant labourers, mostly from Uttar Pradesh and Bihar, who initially came in search of better wages to the Punjab countryside have by now become a part and parcel of the state economy. A large number of them are now also employed in urban/industrial sectors.

Being outsiders, they are obviously dependent on the local landowners to give them place to live. They are usually "kept" in the farmers' homestead. The farmers also provide them with whatever they require for their basic consumption requirements. This makes them completely dependent on their employers. Over the year, some of the labourers have also developed "closer" relations with their employers and have begun to even borrow money from them. Local dalits do not like the migrant labourers coming into the village as it weakens their bargaining position *vis-á-vis* the farmers. Those who migrate into Punjab are usually from non-*dalit* castes and given their own caste prejudice, they too maintain distance from the *dalits*. This too makes them completely dependent on their employer farmers.

Given the nature of industry in Punjab, the situation of migrant labourers in the urban sector is no better. Here too, they work according to the wishes of their employers. Rarely do they form unions. Though their earnings are not meagre, their living conditions are quite miserable. A large majority of them live in shanty settlements with virtually no infrastructure to support a healthy living. Being a relatively less industrialized state and most of the towns being small in size, slum dwellers and migrant labourers have not been able to develop any meaningful lobby in the state politics. Though some of them have become registered voters and at election times their votes are sought and bargained for by ambitious politicians, they still do not matter at the state level politics. They do not even have an organized lobby to represent their interests at the local level. The left-wing trade unions and political formations in the state mostly have their following among the "natives".

NGOs and the Vulnerable Groups

Unlike in some other parts of India and the Third World, the NGO movement has been quite weak in the Punjab. Since the state has been a green revolution region and is popularly viewed as being economically developed, internationally funded NGOs do not see it as a priority region. Another factor responsible for the absence of the NGO movement in the state is the political unrest in the state. During the decade of 1980s, when the NGO movement picked up in India, Punjab was experiencing a militant secessionist movement, which would have obviously discouraged activist groups from working in Punjab. Further, since it is a border state with a history of ethnic movements, the government of India continues to treat it as a politically sensitive region which also makes it difficult for the NGOs to get permission to receive international funding for developmental works in the state.

However, though Punjab does not have a vibrant NGO movement, the state has had a long tradition of popular movements. The left-wing organizations have been quite active in the state. Apart from trade union activities, they also have their 'front organizations', that work among vulnerable sections of the society. The *Punjab Istri Sabha* (a women's organization), for example, has been quite actively working on the gender question for a long time.

During the 1980s and 1990s, a large number of local level organizations also came up to support the victims of terrorists and state violence during the militant struggle. Some of them are still working in different parts of the state. Most of these groups identify themselves with one of the two main religious communities of the state, i.e. the Hindus and the Sikhs.

There has also been a gradual growth of some kind of "caste associations'', particularly among the *dalit* caste groups in urban centres. Most of these organizations are not officially registered and would not qualify to be developmental NGOs as such. However, they do seem to be playing an important role in the urban context where the locally migrant *dalits* have little or no support to sustain themselves in times of crisis.

More recently, a large number of formally registered voluntary organizations (the NGOs) have also come up in the state. The new approach of involving voluntary agencies in the implementation of the state welfare programmes have encouraged this process. However, most of them are run/managed by influential people, and they, as an activist put, function like "shops". Their main source of funding is the state government and they claim to work on the state initiated programmes for the vulnerable categories of the population.

Concluding Remarks

Punjab is obviously one of the economically developed states of India. Not only is its average per capita income much higher than for many other states of the Indian Union, but the number of people living in an absolute state of poverty in the state is also much lesser. As per the Planning Commission estimates only 11.77 per cent of the state population was living in poverty in the year 1993-94. The corresponding figure for the country as a whole was 35.97 per cent (Ahluwalia, 2000: 1640). Much of this is obviously a direct consequence of the agricultural growth experienced with the success of green revolution technology. Though much of this new prosperity was cornered by the substantial landholders, the marginal farmers and landless labourers too benefited.

However, despite such a good performance in the field of economic development, the Punjab today is far from being a problem free state. In economic terms, the green revolution is petering out and with the exception of a few pockets, the state is not experiencing any vibrant industrial growth. The decade-long political crisis during the 1980s has had far reaching implications for the state economy. Punjab is not being seen as an attractive venue for large-scale investments either by big industrial houses or by the global capital. The annual economic growth rate of Punjab during the post-liberalization era has been one of the lowest in the country. As per the available estimates, the annual growth rate of Punjab during the period 1991-92 to 1997-98 was only 2.80 per cent. The corresponding figures for Gujarat (7.57), Maharashtra (6.13) and even West Bengal (5.04) were much higher (*ibid.*: 1638).

In terms of social development also Punjab remains a state with average performance. As discussed above, the sex ratio in the state continues one of the lowest in the country and the literacy rate too is only marginally above the national average. More importantly, the state is marked by stark intra-state disparities, something that is rarely highlighted in the literature on Punjab. The performance of the districts of the Malwa region (particularly the districts of Firozpur, Muktsar, Bhatinda, Faridkot, Sangrur and Mansa) has been much poorer than the districts like Ludhiana and Jalandhar. The same is the case with the border areas and the hilly belt (the Kandi area). Not only have these pockets not experienced the kind of economic development experienced elsewhere in the state, in terms of social development also they remain backward. The Malwa region is still ruled by feudal ethos and the literacy rates among the marginal groups like *dalits* is quite low here. The situation is particularly serious among *dalit* women.

The *dalit* population of the state continues to be one of the vulnerable groups. However, there are very significant variations in their status. While the groups like *Ad-Dharmis* and *Chamars* of the Doaba region have experienced considerable social mobility, the situation of *dalits* in the Malwa and Majha (Amritsar and Gurdaspur) districts is still quite bad. The situation is particularly bad among the 'depressed Scheduled Castes'.

Punjab has also been attracting a lot of migrant labour from the states of Uttar Pradesh and Bihar. Though they come to Punjab voluntarily and their earnings are fairly all right, being in an 'alien' land does make them quite vulnerable. At the time of labour scarcity, farmers treat them like bonded slaves.

The process of urbanization and industrialization too have produced new vulnerable social categories, prominent of them being the migrant slum-dwelling labourers and the child labourers—both visible child labourers who work in factories, *dhabas* and restaurants, and the invisible child labourers who work in middle class houses. The social welfare department of the state has virtually no schemes for their protection.

REFERENCES

Abbi, B.L. and Kesar Singh (1997), *Post-Green Revolution Rural Punjab: A Profile of Economic and Socio-Cultural Change (1965-95)*. Chandigarh: CRRID.

Ahluwalia, M.S. (2000), 'Economic Performance of States in Post-Reforms Period', *Economic and Political Weekly*, May 6.

Census of India (2001), *Provisional Population Totals, Punjab* (Series 4). Chandigarh: Director of Census Operations, Punjab.

Chadha, G.K. (1986), *The State and Rural Economic Transformation: The Case of Punjab, 1950-85* New Delhi: Sage.

Chaitley, Y.P. (1995), *Education, Population and Development: A Regional Perspective of Northwest India*. Chandigarh: CRRID.

Government of Punjab (1999), *Statistical Abstract, Punjab 1999*. Chandigarh: Economic and Statistical Organization.

Government of Punjab (1999), *Statistical Abstract, Punjab 1995*. Chandigarh: Economic and Statistical Organization.

Jose, A.V. (1988), 'Agricultural Wages in India', *Economic and Political Weekly*, June 25.

Krishan, G. (1998), 'Demographic Change' in J.S. Grewal and Indu Banga (eds.) *Punjab in Prosperity and Violence*. Chandigarh: Institute of Punjab Studies.

Krishan, G. (1998), 'Urbanization since Independence' in J.S. Grewal and Indu Banga (eds.) *Punjab in Prosperity and Violence*. Chandigarh: Institute of Punjab Studies.

Krishan, G. and Surya Kant (1998), 'Administrative Space' in J.S. Grewal and Indu Banga (eds.) *Punjab in Prosperity and Violence*. Chandigarh: Institute of Punjab Studies.

Randhawa, M.S. (1974), *Green Revolution: A Case Study of Punjab*, Delhi: Vikas Publishing House.

Shergill, H.S. (1998), *Rural Credit and Indebtedness in Punjab*. Chandigarh: Institute of Communication and Development.

Tandon, P. (1988), 'Punjabi Century' (first published 1961) in *Punjabi Saga* (1857—1987). New Delhi: Viking, Penguin Books.

2

THE SCHEDULED CASTES IN CONTEMPORARY PUNJAB

SURINDER S. JODHKA

The Scheduled Castes accounted for 28.3 per cent of the total population of the Punjab in 1991, much higher than the all-India average of 16.32 per cent. In some districts of the state, they made up to 38 per cent of the population. Given the fact that the Scheduled Castes population in Punjab was growing at a faster rate than the rest, their proportion in the total population of the state could be around 30 per cent by now. They are also less urbanized than their counterpart non-Scheduled Castes population and there would be many villages in the state where they would be a majority of the population.

As elsewhere, the Scheduled Castes in the contemporary Punjab are not a homogeneous category. They are made up of diverse communities with their own individual identities and with different levels of cultural disabilities and social development. Strategies for social mobility and participation in political and social reform movements have also been quite varied among them. Through a broad survey of the available secondary source material, I shall try to explore in this paper the changing status of the Scheduled Castes communities in the contemporary Punjab. Using a historical perspective, I shall try to identify specificities of the region and focus on the diverse strategies adopted by different depressed caste groups to ameliorate their status.

The Framework

The institution of caste and the practice of untouchability are widely believed to be the core defining features of the "traditional" social structure of India. Caste has been viewed as an institution that distinguished the traditional India from the West. We have been made to believe, both by the Western discourses on India as well as by our native social anthropologists, that the caste has been around for ages and nothing much had changed in its functioning until the British colonial rulers introduced modern systems of governance and technology. As per this dominant view, the caste existed everywhere in the subcontinent and everyone practiced it. While in Hinduism, the caste system and untouchability had an ideological sanction, the other communities also practiced it, even when not legitimized by their religious philosophy.

However, despite this widely held "commonsense" about the pan-Indian nature of caste, there exists a considerable amount of variation in the manner in which the social relations among the different groups have been structured in different regions. As is widely known, there are different sets of caste groups in different regions of the subcontinent and "the preoccupation with purity and pollution was not equally marked in every part of the country'' (Beteille, 2000: 172). The specific historical trajectory, the patterns of politico-economic changes experienced during the post-independence period and the composition of different ethnic communities determine the actual caste relations in a given region.

Caste and the Contemporary Sikhism

Perhaps the most obvious aspect of the teachings of the first Sikh Guru, Guru Nanak was his opposition to the brahmanical orthodoxy and the caste system. In contrast to the hierarchical values of brahmanical Hinduism, Guru Nanak advocated equality of human beings in relation to God. For him, the aim of salvation was union with God that transcended the cycle of birth and death. He denounced ritualism, ascetic practices, idol worship and the hermit life in jungle. An important aspect of Guru Nanak's philosophy was his emphasis on the values of everyday life, a "this worldliness". He preached that one should attain God while being part of the social world and earning one's living.

The teachings of the Sikh Gurus differed from the brahminical worldview in yet another way. In contrast to caste exclusivism and the practice of untouchability prevalent among the Hindus, the Sikh Gurus emphasized on the need for sharing and communal living. The *kirtan* (the corporate singing) and *langar* (the community kitchen and eating together) were among the new and important institutions introduced by the Gurus. The second Guru standardized the Gurumukhi script, which eventually became a vehicle for the Punjabi language and identity. Earlier Guru Nanak had consciously rejected Sanskrit in preference of the indigenous spoken language. The fifth Guru, Guru Arjun compiled the first canon of the faith, the Adi Granth, that eventually came to be worshipped as the eternal Guru by the Sikhs after the death of the tenth and the last living Gurus.

The Sikh holy book contains writings of many Saints and Sufis of the Bhakti period. This includes the writings of some of the Saints who came from the Shudra (such as Kabir, a weaver; Dhanna, a Jat peasant; and Namdev, a tailor) and untouchable castes (such as Ravidas, a cobbler; Sadhana, a butcher; and Sain, a barber). The Sikh holy book also contains the writings of some Muslim Sufis, such as Sheikh Farid and Bhikan. Of the "five beloved" who were the first to be baptized as Khalsas on the day of Baisakhi in 1699 by the tenth guru, four belonged to the shudra castes.

At the empirical level also, many have reported on the relatively lesser hold of caste on the social relationships among the Sikhs in particular and the Punjabis in general. This is reflected in the writings of colonial administrators as well as in social scientific reports.

Reporting on the problems of the "low castes" in the province, one of the colonial administrators viewed it more in terms of politico-economic disabilities rather than in terms of their being "untouchable" as was the case with the rest of India. A colonial government report, for example, observed in 1920s:

> It would be misleading to attach too great importance to the existence of caste in the Punjab....Not only is it the case that the Brahman has nos practical pre-eminence among Hindus, but as between "caste" and "non-caste" Hindus the distinction is not so strongly marked as to create the political problem found elsewhere in India....(as in Nayar, 1966:20).

Another British author contrasting Punjab with rest of the sub-continent and comparing the caste in Punjab with the class in Europe wrote, "nowhere else in Hindu India does caste sit so lightly or approach so nearly to the social classes of Europe" (Anderson in Nayar, 1966:20). Some of the Western observers went to the extent of saying that the Punjab was a "notable exception" to the caste system in India (O'Malley in Nayar, 1966:20).

More recently some anthropologists have also made similar claims and have argued that caste inequalities in the region were much lesser than elsewhere in India. Comparing the disability experienced by the low castes in Punjab with the rest of India, Saberwal, who studied in a small town of Punjab during the late 1960s writes:

> ...the lowest castes in Punjab had to carry only a light burden of ritual impurities, much lighter, physically and socially, than the burden elsewhere in India (Saberwal, 1976: 7).

Joyce Pettigrew, another anthropologist, goes to the extent of saying that the rural society of Punjab differs radically from the Hindu India because of the absence of caste among the Sikhs. As she writes:

> The social organization and value system, especially of the rural Punjab, differ from that of Hindu India. The prevailing form of social co-operation and the type of political solidarity bear no reference to 'caste' and to rules of purity and pollution, but rather to the family unit and to the values pertaining to that unit, namely, honour, pride and equality, reputation, shame and insult (1975:4).

However, not everyone who has studied Punjab agrees with such a position. Paul Hershman, another anthropologist who carried out his fieldwork in a village near Jalandhar, for example, completely disagrees with the thesis that the ideas of purity and impurity did not exist in Punjab or that caste in the region functioned more like class (Hershman, 1981).

Most other students of Punjab though tend to disagree with Hershman on his contention that the ideas of 'purity' and 'impurity' are as strong in the region as elsewhere in India, agree on the point that caste divisions do exist among the Sikhs. While the structure of hierarchy could be different from other regions of India, one could easily observe some of the typical features of caste system in the Punjab. Though lesser in extent, pollution and avoidance were also practiced in the region particularly in relation to the Scheduled Castes, both among the Hindus as well as among the Sikhs (Nayar, 1966; Singh, I.P., 1975; Singh, H., 1977; Saberwal, 1976). While accepting that caste divisions existed among the Sikhs, the available literature also indicates that the change experienced in the attitudes towards caste during the last century has been quite significant in the region. Evidence for this is available from studies of individual villages or towns, as well as of the social reform movements for the uplift of the "low castes".

I.P. Singh, (1975; 1977), who did a study of a village near Amritsar during the late 1950s provides a fairly good idea about the nature of caste relations in a Sikh village. The Sikhs living in the village were divided into two groups, the Sardars (the upper castes) and the Mazhabis (the lower caste scavengers). The first group included the Jats, Kambohs, Tarkhans, Kumhars, Sunars and Nais (in the Hindu caste hierarchy, they would all be treated as Shudras and with the exception of Jats, they were perhaps all included in the list of Other Backward Classes). Though the agriculturist Jats considered themselves higher than the other groups in this category, Singh observed no feeling of caste-based avoidance or prejudice among them. They visited each other's houses, interdined and attended marriage functions and celebrated most of the festivals together. In terms of the village settlement also, no demarcation existed in the houses of these groups.

However, the Mazhabis, who constituted nearly half of the village population, were treated differently. They lived on one side of the village. They had a separate well while all the other castes used a common well. In the village feasts, where everyone was invited, the Mazhabis sat separately. Since many of them worked as labourers in the fields of the Jat landowners, the latter visited the houses of the Mazhabis but they did so as a patronizing gesture.

There were also occasions where untouchability was either not practiced or its extent had been declining. Many Jats in the village let the Mazhabis enter their houses and did not consider their touch polluting. One of them had also employed a Mazhabi to clean utensils in his house. Practice of untouchability was minimal among the drinkers in the village. The Mazhabis were the traditional brewers of country liquor in the village.

The practice of untouchability was also less in religious affairs. There was only one gurdwara (the Sikh holy place) in the village where everyone was allowed entry. They also sat together while eating food in the gurdwara. The priest, who himself belonged to a low caste (Cheemba, washerman), served all the castes without any discrimination. He had performed all the marriages in the village irrespective of any caste distinction. This was quite in contrast to the way a Brahmin priest functioned. The Brahmin priest used to perform rituals for the Sikhs in the village as well until they began appointing their own priest for the gurdwara. The Brahmin priest served only the upper castes.

The religious reform movements among the Sikhs during the 1920s launched by the Singh Sabhas and Akalis had a lasting impact on the religious life of the Sikhs in the village. The insistence of Sikh reformers to distance the 'community' from Hindus and the legal recognition to wedding through the Sikh rituals, the Anand Karaj, made the village Brahmin priest redundant. Unlike the Brahmin, the Sikh priest could be from any caste and, as mentioned above, the priest in this particular village was from a lower caste. He had been trained to be a priest at the Sikh Missionary College, Amritsar. Priesthood among the Sikhs had thus become an achieved, rather than an ascribed status.

With the exception of Hershman's work, there would hardly be any study of rural Punjab that reports about the superiority of status enjoyed by Brahmins over the Jats (the landowning peasant caste) and the Khatris (mostly in trade and services). Brahmins themselves tended to concede such a framework of ranking. Commenting on the lack of respect enjoyed by the Brahmins in Punjab, Saberwal quotes Chanana:

> In Punjabi the word *Pandat* (Pandit) denotes a Brahman and may connote some respect for the latter. But the word *Bahman* (Brahmin) almost always carries a little contempt (as in Saberwal, 1976:10).

In his study of a small town of Punjab carried out during the late 1960s, Saberwal found a considerable change in attitude towards the traditional ideology of caste (Saberwal, 1973 : 256).

The Mobilizations Against Untouchability in Punjab

Punjab has been witness to a good number of religious reform movements against untouchability. As mentioned above, the founder guru, Guru Nanak and the later Sikh gurus advocated equality of human beings in relation to God and futility of caste division. The Sikh gurus also introduced certain institutions that actively discouraged caste exclusion. More recently, the region experienced several reform movements during the British colonial period.

Along with the British rulers came the Christian missionaries with the intention of spreading the message of the Church in the region. The first to find the appeal of the Church attractive in the region were the members of untouchable castes. The first conversion is reported to have taken place in 1873 when a man named Ditt was baptized in Sialkot. 'To the surprise of the missionaries, Ditt was followed by hundreds of thousands of others from lower castes, and Punjab Christianity became a *de facto* movement' (Juergênsmeyer, 1988:181). By 1890 there were 10,171 Christians living in 525 villages of Punjab and by 1911 their number had gone up to 1,63,994 and by 1921 to over 3,00,000. Most of them came from a particular untouchable caste, the *Chuhras* (scavengers) and mainly hailed from rural areas. Given the nature of the rural power structure, 'conversion to Christianity for these highly vulnerable people was a very risky act of rebellion' (Webster, 1999:96-7). According to Juergensmeyer, the Christian missionaries had not really intentionally targeted the low castes for conversions. 'It was the untouchables who had originally sought out Christianity' (1988: 184). The untouchables obviously saw a potential of social mobility in conversions.

> Originally, the missionaries of the Punjab had only attempted to convert the upper castes, since they regarded others as beyond the reach of the methods they preferred—intellectual argument and moral suasion. The enthusiasm of the first convert, Ditt, and the subsequent lower caste requests for conversion not only baffled the missionaries but embarrassed them: they saw no sensible or moral reason for keeping the lower castes out, yet feared that allowing them in would sully the church's reputation (Juergensmeyer, 1988: 184).

The fears of the missionaries were not unfounded. When a newspaper article in *The Tribune* of October 19, 1892 reported that the rate of conversions would soon turn the Punjab into a Christian region, 'a tremor of fear ran through the upper caste Hindu and Sikh elite' (Juergensmeyer, 1988: 181). There was a virtual competition among the Christians, the Hindus and the Sikhs to win the untouchables over to their side. It was around this time that the militant Hindu reformist organization, the Arya Samaj, made its entry into the Punjab.

Swami Dayanand in Bombay had launched the Arya Samaj in 1875 and in 1877 the Swami visited Lahore. He stayed on in Punjab for nearly eighteen months during his first visit to the province and set up branches of the Samaj in almost all the big towns of the province. Unlike the other Hindu reform movements, Arya Samaj not only attacked other religions who had been converting Hindus into their fold but also severely criticized many of the existing practices of the Hindus including the practice of untouchability. The Swami advocated going back to the ancient Vedic religion wherein untouchables were presumably a part of the Hindu religion. He attacked brahmanical hegemony in religious affairs and emphasized upon the need for spreading modern education among the Hindus. He advocated the inclusion of the lower castes into the Hindu society through a process of religious purification, the *Shuddhi*. Since untouchability was presumed to emanate from ritual impurity, it could be removed through a religious ritual to render untouchables touchable.

At the concrete level, the *Shuddhi* movement was to involve (i) conversion to Hinduism of those belonging to foreign religions; (ii) re-conversion of those who had been converted to a foreign religion; and (iii) initiating steps to raise the status of the low castes within Hinduism.

The first *Shuddhi* ritual was performed nearly five years after the death of Swami Dayanand in 1888 when 70 untouchables belonging to the caste of Odes were solemnized *Shuddhi*. During the year 1901-1910 about sixty to seventy thousand untouchables underwent *Shuddhi* (Pimpley and Sharma, 1985:96). The movement gained further momentum in the following years and more untouchables were "purified" and brought into the Hindu fold.

Did *Shuddhi* make any difference to the untouchables after they were raised to the status of "dwija"? Were they accepted by the upper caste Hindus as their equal?

In their study carried out during the early 1980s, Pimpley and Sharma (1985) found that the movement did not really make any significant difference to the untouchables though it helped the Punjabi Hindu elite in consolidating their position in the region. 'The Punjabi Hindu elite succeeded, in large measure, to retain the untouchable castes in the Hindu fold thereby increasing their political strength.' As far as the untouchables were concerned, they found that a majority of those who went through the *Shuddhi* ceremony ''still suffered from poverty and the stigma of untouchability. Their educational levels were very low. Occupationally they were engaged in agricultural labour force or were in low prestige occupations. Their geographical segregation suggested minimum level of social interaction with other castes. Probably, even after their *Shuddhi*, they did not gain anything except for a symbolic right of reading the Vedas and putting on the sacred thread'' (Pimpley and Sharma, 1985 : 98).

Further, despite their criticism of the Brahmanical orthodoxy within Hinduism, the strategy of Arya Samaj for elevating the status of the untouchables was worked out within the framework of purity and impurity. Though they condemned the practice of untouchability, they did not reject the concept of *varna*. The very notion of *Shuddhi* involved affirmation to the idea of ritual purity as being the criterion for status enhancement.

Though the Arya Samaj initially attacked the so-called foreign religions, i.e. Islam and Christianity, during the course of time as their influence spread they also began to criticize Sikhism. Ever since the days of Sikh gurus, many of the low castes in the region had been a part of the Sikh religion. The reports of low caste Sikhs being enunciated *Shuddhi* and their re-conversion into Hinduism were viewed with much concern by the Sikh middle class leadership. Since the numbers had begun to matter and the communities in the region had become very sensitive about their size, the Sikh leadership was understandably keen to keep the low castes within their fold.

The militant assertion of Hindutva identity by the Arya Samaj had already sparked off a debate on the question of Sikh identity. Sikhs began to assert that theirs was a separate religion and that they should not be clubbed with the Hindus. The practice of untouchability or discrimination against the low castes among the Sikh was attributed to the continued influence of Hinduism on the community. Thus the struggle against caste and untouchability, that were seen as the core Hindu values, was implicated in the movement for a separate religious identity for the Sikhs.

The Singh Sabha movement for the liberation of Sikh Gurdwaras from the Hindu Mahants launched during the 1920 also became a movement for "de-Hinduization" of the Sikh religion. One of the main demands of the movement was "unquestioned entrance to Sikh places of worship" for all (Juergensmeyer, 1988: 28). Some members of the Sikh Khalsa Diwan tried to create their own "depressed class movements" to encourage Scheduled Castes support. The movement was not confined to the liberation of historic Sikh Gurdwaras. Its impact went very far. I.P. Singh in his study of a village in Amritsar district reported that the decline of the Brahmins in the village began around the time these reform movements were launched, i.e. 1922-26. It was after these movements that a low caste Sikh was appointed a priest in the local Gurdwara and he began to give equal treatment to members of all castes in the village (Singh, I.P., 1977: 81-82).

This process seemed to have continued during the post-independence period as well. More significantly perhaps, the rural Sikh elite attributes the change in the status of untouchables in Punjab to the quality of their religion. Reporting about his village, I.P. Singh writes:

> the modern preachers of equality of castes like the Sarpanch and his young friends point it out that what the new law demands is just what the gurus had preached. It is in keeping with the precepts of Sikh religion. There lies the major difference of caste

> structure between a Sikh village and a Hindu village. While in a Hindu village caste hierarchy and differences have religious sanctions behind them, there are no such sanctions in the Sikh religion. Thus it becomes easier to propagate and instill equality of caste relations in a Sikh village (I.P. Singh : 79).

While the Sikh reformers attacked caste, the Sikh leadership, having become aware of the significance of numbers, did not deny the existence of caste among the Sikhs or that the low castes among the Sikhs did not face any disabilities due to their birth. The Sikh leadership, in fact, had to lobby a great deal with the national leadership that along with the Hindus, certain Sikh castes should also be included in the list of the Scheduled Castes for the provision of special benefits and reservations. They were obviously worried that if the reservation benefits were not extended to Sikhs, the low castes among them may declare their religion as Hinduism. Nayar reports that this 'concession was achieved in return for an agreement by the Sikh leaders that no further political demands would be made in the future on behalf of the Sikh community' (Nayar, 1966:238). However, while all the Hindu untouchable castes were given the special privileges, only four sub-castes of untouchable Sikhs were included in the list.

Apart from the competition among the Christians, the Arya Samaji Hindus and the Sikhs, during the colonial period Punjab also witnessed autonomous mobilizations by the local *dalits*. The most important of these was the Ad Dharm movement.

New opportunities opened up by the growing demand of leather goods such as boots and shoes for the British army had brought some prosperity to some of the enterprising members of the Chamar caste. This mobility was particularly evident in the *doaba* region of Punjab where some of the Chamars had even gone to the United States and England and had been a part of the left-wing organizations there. The introduction of secular education along with the social mobility that some individual untouchables experienced provided the social ground for such autonomous mobilizations.

In the favourable atmosphere created by social reformers, by the early 1920s some of the Chamars began to think of their own organization. Most of the early leadership of the Ad Dharm movement had grown under the influence of Arya Samaj but felt uncomfortable with its overall ideology. A Scheduled Caste member of the Arya Samaj from Hoshiarpur, Sant Ram, had begun a new movement for Scheduled Caste mobility within the Samaj, the *Jat Pat Torak Mandal* (Society for the Abolition of Caste). However, soon he had serious conflict with the leadership and left the Samaj.

The Ad Dharm movement took off with the arrival of Mangoo Ram on the scene. Mangoo Ram was son of a rich Chamar but his family had to bear the stigma of untouchability. He spent much of his early life in the United States where he got involved with the Gadar movement. By 1925, he had come back to Punjab. On his return home, he set up a school for lower caste children with the help of Arya Samaj but very soon he distanced himself from the Samaj and took over the Ad Dharm movement.

The Ad Dharm movement saw itself as a new religious movement. They advocated that 'Untouchables were a *qaum*, a distinct religious community similar to those of Muslims, Hindus, and Sikhs, and that the *qaum* had existed from time immemorial' (Juergensmeyer, 1988: 45). When the 1931 Census approached, the Ad Dharmis insisted they be listed as a separate religious community and not be clubbed with the Hindus.

Despite stiff opposition from the local Hindu leadership, their demand was accepted. A total of 418,789 persons reported themselves as Ad Dharmis in the 1931 Punjab Census, almost equal to the Christian population of the province. They accounted for about 1.5 per cent of the total population and around a tenth of the total low caste population of the Punjab. Nearly 80 per cent of the low castes of Jalandhar and Hoshiarpur districts reported themselves as Ad Dharmis (Juergensmeyer, 1988 : 77). In other parts of the Punjab, however, the locally dominant groups were able to thwart the Ad Dharmi drive rather effectively (Khan in Saberwal, 1972: 144). After the census, the Ad Dharm movement was absorbed in Ambedkar's Scheduled Castes Federation that was later transformed into the Republican Party of India. While Ambedkar enjoyed a great deal of influence in Punjab, particularly among the Ad Dharmis and made several visits to the province, few among them followed his strategy of converting to Buddhism for social mobility (Saberwal, 1972: 145).

After independence, the Ad Dharmis were listed as one of the Scheduled Castes of the Punjab and were clubbed with the Hindus once again. Over a period of time they too came to see themselves so. A recent study found that as many as 98.3 per cent of the Ad Dharmis Punjab identified themselves as a "caste group" and only 1.6 per cent of them reported that they were a separate religious community. When asked about their caste before they began reporting themselves as Ad Dharmis, all of them reported to be Chamars (Kamaljot, 1996). Though attempts have been made to revive the Ad Dharm movement during the post-independence period, there has not been much response.

The Scheduled Castes in Contemporary Punjab

As mentioned above, the Scheduled Castes population in the Punjab is not only considerably higher than the national average, their population has also been growing faster than the general population of Punjab. This is perhaps directly linked to their overall backwardness. They accounted for more than half of the total poor in the state both in 1981 as well as in 1991. Educationally also, they have not faired too well. While the literacy rate for the total population of Punjab in 1991 was 58.12 per cent, it was only 41 per cent among the Scheduled Castes. Inspite of some improvement in the literacy rate over the years, the gap between the general population and the Scheduled Castes has remained, more or less, the same. They are also comparatively less urbanized. Compared to 29.55 per cent of urban population for the entire Punjab, only 20.55 per cent of the Scheduled Castes were living in towns and cities in 1991.

These figures clearly indicate that even when the institution of caste was comparatively weaker in the state and the socio-cultural disabilities suffered by the Scheduled Castes were lesser, in terms of developmental indicators, they seem to have not done as well as their counterparts in some other states.

Perhaps the most important initiative taken by the post-independence Indian State for the benefit of the Scheduled Castes was the policy of job reservations. Though not designed to eradicate poverty or unemployment among depressed communities, reservations were expected to create an influential group of elite among them who could provide a leadership to these depressed communities in their struggle for social and economic mobility. The available figures for Punjab show that the Scheduled Castes in the state did indeed avail the benefits of reservations. However, their representation at different levels was uneven. Among all the states of India, the Punjab has the highest proportion of the Scheduled Caste population. While they were over represented at the lower level (Class IV) their proportions declined as one moved up in the job hierarchy. However, even at the top level, their presence was not insignificant (15.32 per cent, Table 2.1).

As elsewhere in India, the Scheduled Castes of Punjab are not a homogenous category. In Punjab they are divided into 37 different caste communities. Though historically they have all been victims of caste oppression and have experienced the stigma of being untouchable, their current status is not similar. The different caste communities differ not only in terms of self-identities but also in terms of their level of social and economic development. The numerical strength of individual caste groups also varies considerably.

Table 2.1: Employment of Scheduled Castes in the Various Departments of the Punjab State Government

	Class I	*Class II*	*Class III*	*Class IV*
Total sanctioned posts	7233	8674	260385	70402
Filled posts	6290	7438	244194	62163
Scheduled Castes	964	1195	41608	25905
% of Scheduled Castes	15.32	16.06	17.03	41.67
Backlog/excess	–9.68	–8.94	–7.97	+16.67

Source: Yadav and Sharma (undated) p. 9 (figures upto March 1993).

Chamars (including Ramdasias and Ad Dharmis) and Mazhabis (including Chuhras and Balmikis) together constitute nearly three-fourth of the total Scheduled Castes population of the Punjab. Most other groups are much smaller in size. The Ad Dharmis and the Chamars have been socially and educationally the most mobile among them. Initially it was the Ad Dharmis and the Chamars who seemed to have cornered a major part of the reserved seats. Subsequently, the state government decided to reserve fifty per cent of the reservation quota for the Mazhabis.

As elsewhere in India, the reservation benefits tended to get monopolized by some individual families among the Scheduled Castes. Most of those holding jobs under the reservation quota are not the first generation beneficiaries. Majority of them is children of those who had already been the beneficiaries of the scheme.

Some of the Chamars and Ad Dharmis have also been extremely successful entrepreneurs. They nearly control the entire surgical industry in the Jalandhar town. About 70 per cent of the big units and about 80 per cent of the medium and small units producing surgical instruments were owned by the Scheduled Castes. Their presence was also quite significant in the sports goods and leather industries in the town.

However, despite such success cases, the overall position of the Scheduled Castes, particularly of the smaller and less mobilized groups, remains rather bleak. It was with the intention of targeting development schemes for such groups that Punjab government identified 13 caste groups as the 'Depressed Scheduled Castes'. Together they account for only 11 per cent of the total Scheduled Castes population. Among these 13 castes, seven are the "de-notified tribes" or the "*Vimukat Jatis*". Since they followed a nomadic way of life, the colonial administration had branded them as "vagrant and criminal tribes". After independence, they were initially called "ex-criminal tribes" but later they were designated as the "de-notified tribes".

Being small in size, they are unable to act as effective pressure groups within the state politics. They have also not been able to produce any influential leaders of their own. Since some of them have also had nomadic lifestyles, they could not accumulate any property for themselves. Compared to the other Scheduled Castes, poverty among them is considerably higher. A study of the depressed Scheduled Castes reported that the number of those living below the poverty line could be as high as 96 per cent of their population. Literacy rates among them were also quite low. Some of these groups (such as Bangali, Bauria and Bazigars) had only around 10 to 12 per cent literate population (Kumar and Kumar, 1996: 11-14). The lack of education also makes them ineligible for the government jobs under the reservation quota.

Occupational Changes

Despite the continued "backwardness" among some of the Scheduled Caste communities, the overall picture has changed a lot. Perhaps the most significant has been the changes in their occupations.

The process of moving away from traditional caste occupations among the Scheduled Castes of Punjab had begun during the colonial period under the influence of social reform movements and it continued during the post-independence period as well. The introduction of new agricultural technology, i.e. the Green Revolution, and the accompanying changes in the rural social structure further accelerated this process. The new technology significantly enhanced the need for labour while simultaneously making some of the older occupations redundant. The introduction of multiple cropping system and mechanization completely transformed the nature of rural labour markets. The farmers in the new commercialized agriculture preferred formalized contractual relations with their labourers to the older structures of patronage and clientele.

The new demand for agricultural labour was partly met by migrant labour from eastern Uttar Pradesh and Bihar and partly by the local Scheduled Castes who switched over from the calling of their castes to agricultural labour. The agricultural labour also gave the local Scheduled Castes a little better status. Economically also their earnings went up. Despite the coming of migrant labour, of the Indian states, the wage rates for agricultural labour have been among the highest in the Punjab.

Occupational shift has taken place among almost all the caste groups. However, it was much more among those who had been part of the reform movements. The Ad Dharmis (the ex-Chamars) and the Mazhabis (the Chuhras who converted to Sikhism) have nearly completely moved away from their traditional occupations. A recent study reported that while 81 per cent of Ad Dharmis had moved away from leather tanning, as many as 96 per cent of the Mazhabis had left their traditional occupation of scavenging (Yadav and Sharma, p. 14). Another study shows that many of the Scheduled Castes from the *doaba* region were trying to move away even from agriculture. While 49.25 per cent of the sample population was still employed in agriculture, as many as 21.75 per cent of them had moved to non-agricultural occupations, ranked higher than the occupation of their parents (Judge, 1997:58). Similarly, Abbi and Singh (1997) found:

> An almost total occupational change among the Scheduled Castes, clean artisans and other non-agricultural castes, de-linking their livelihood pattern from agriculture and agricultural labour. Further, the increasing taking over of agricultural labour and minor supervisory work by the migrant Bhaya labourers, while the local landless labourers commute for grain loading, construction work, tailoring, technical, mechanical and other skilled work (p.91).

Though the change may not be as radical elsewhere in Punjab as reported by these studies (the change has particularly been lesser in the districts of Malwa region), there is no doubt that the traditional structures of dependency among the dominant and the landless castes have weakened considerably. However, while relational structures have seen significant changes, a large majority of the Scheduled Castes population continues to live in poverty and under vulnerable conditions.

Concluding Remarks

The historical evidence on caste relations and the empirical literature available on status of *dalits* in the region clearly shows that though caste has existed in Punjab, the structure of caste hierarchy in the region has been quite different from other parts of the subcontinent (Jodhka, 2000). It certainly does not conform to the manner in which caste has been popularly theorised, viz. the varna system of hierarchy. The Brahmins have not only not enjoyed the kind of status that the varna theory attributes to them, the Brahmanical ideology too has been quite weak in the region. Further, it was not with the British rule that the system of caste hierarchy began to change in the region, the influences of Islam, Sufism and Sikhism had far reaching impacts on the culture and society of Punjab, much before the British introduced "modern" institutions of governance in the region. Even during the present times, Sikhism remains an important ideological force against the caste system and has been often mobilised by various reform movements during the last century.

The economic development experienced in the region during the post-independence period too has brought about many changes in the manner in which caste works in the Punjab today. The new agrarian technology has disintegrated the traditional structures of patronage and loyalty. The process of development during the last five decades or so has also created avenues of employment in urban, semi-urban and rural areas that are "caste-free" in nature. The occupational diversification of the Scheduled Castes of Punjab has been quite significant, at least in some parts of the state. However, a large majority of them still live in conditions of deprivation.

REFERENCES

Abbi, B.L. and Kesar Singh (1997), '*Post-Green Revolution Rural Punjab: Profile of Economic and Socio-Cultural Change* (1965-95). Chandigarh: Centre for Research in Rural and Industrial Development.

Beteille, A. (2000), *Chronicles of Our Time*. New Delhi: Penguin Books India.

Economic and Statistical Organisation (2000) *Statistical Abstract*: Punjab. Chandigarh: Government of Punjab.

Jodhka, S.S. (2000), 'Prejudice without Pollution?: Scheduled Castes in Contemporary Punjab'*Journal of Indian School of Political Economy* (special issue on Scheduled Castes edited by Andre Beteille). Vol. XII (3&4) pp. 381-402.

Judge, P.S. (1997), 'Emerging Trends in the Caste Structure of Punjab'. *The Administrator*. Vol. XLII, January-March. pp. 55-65.

Hershman, Paul (1981), *Punjabi Kinship and Marriage*. Delhi: Hindustan Publishing Corporation.

Juergensmeyer, M. (1988), *Religious Rebels in the Punjab:The Social Vision of Untouchables*. Delhi: Ajanta Publications.

Kamaljot (1996), Religious Reform and Social Mobility: The Case of Ad Dharmis of Punjab. Unpublished M.Phil dissertation, Department of Sociology, Panjab University, Chandigarh.

Kumar, Vinod and Ashok Kumar (1996), *Upward Mobility of Depressed Scheduled Castes in Punjab* (unpublished report). Chandigarh: Institute for Development and Communication.

Nayar, B.R. (1966), *Minority Politics in the Punjab*. New Jersey: Princeton University Press.

Pimpley, P.N. and S.K. Sharma (1985), 'De-Sanskritization of Untouchables: Arya Samaj Movement in Punjab' in P.N. Pimpley and S.K. Sharma (eds.) *Struggle for Status*. New Delhi: B.R. Publishing Corporation. pp. 86-101.

Saberwal, S. (1973), 'Receding Pollution: Intercaste Relations in Urban Punjab', *Sociological Bulletin*. Vol. 22(2). pp. 234-259.

Saberwal, S. (1976), *Mobile Men: Limits to Social Change in Urban India*. New Delhi: Vikas Publishing House.

Singh, H. (1977), 'Caste Ranking in Two Sikh Villages' in H. Singh (ed.) *Caste Among Non-Hindus in India*. New Delhi: National Publishing House. pp. 84-90.

Singh, I.P. (1975), 'A Sikh Village' in M. Singer (ed.) *Traditional India: Structure and Change*. Jaipur: Rawat (Indian reprint). pp. 273-97.

Singh, I.P. (1977), 'Caste in a Sikh Village' in H. Singh (ed.) *Caste Among Non-Hindus in India*. New Delhi: National Publishing House. pp. 66-83.

Webster, John C.B. (1999), 'Leadership in Rural Dalit Conversion Movement' in Joseph T. O'Comell (ed.) *Organizational and Institutional Aspects of Indian Religious Movements*. Shimla: Indian Institution of Advanced Studies. pp. 96-112.

Yadav, B. and A.M. Sharma (undated) *Economic Uplift of Scheduled Castes* (unpublished report). Chandigarh: Institute for Development and Communication.

3

SOCIO-CULTURAL CORRELATES OF LOW SEX RATIO IN PUNJAB

MALKIT KAUR

Whenever, there is any talk of women in development at the National or International level, a very important statistics which is often quoted to show the fact that economic development does not guarantee improvement in the status of women is the sex-ratio of India's economically highly developed state. OXFAM programme co-ordinator (1998) remarked, "The poor status of women in South Asia is not entirely dependent on economic factors and Punjab is, in fact, a prime example of discrimination at work." The state of Punjab has a sex-ratio of 874 as against 933 at the all India level (Census, 2001) and ranks second from bottom among all Indian states. The adjoining state of Haryana (861) is the only state having a sex-ratio lower than Punjab. This fact while reflecting the condition of women in this economically highly developed state of India, also points towards the role of dominant patriarchal ethos and socio-cultural factors in determining the situation.

Sex ratio (number of females per thousand males in the population) is an important indicator which is taken as a measure of the extent of gender equity prevailing in any society at any given time. This indicator has been highly skewed in favour of males in Punjab. At the beginning of twentieth century, sex-ratio for Punjab was at a low of 832 as compared to 972 for India (Census, 1901) reflecting the most imbalanced sex ratio. Such a low sex-ratio of the state is attributed to the high mortality among the females. Patriarchal values, various socio-cultural practices and attitudes have been responsible for this. An attempt has been made in this paper to look into the various socio-cultural factors contributing to the situation and the strategies to improve the situation.

Punjab, being a predominantly peasant society, preference for sons for doing agriculture especially ploughing was clearly evident in the traditional society. Their love for agricultural land which further required males for inheriting and cultivating it placed a premium on sons. The prevalent social system denies women any significant property rights. The practice of hypergamy, whereby the girls had to be married in family above the status of her parental family was also felt as a strain on the family and contributed towards the view that daughters were a burden. The socio-cultural practices of the male-centred kinship system prevalent in the region contribute towards making the position of women vulnerable in the family of marriage, and this lowers her access to resources both within the household and at the societal level. Their continuous neglect in access to resources, health, nutrition, medical care and general care results in high mortality levels and in turn lead to low sex ratio.

The extreme form of devaluation of women was the practice of female infanticide whereby a daughter was killed as soon as she was born. An overall marked deterioration which occurred in the position of women in India during the medieval age, had its greatest impact in north India including Punjab. Repeated foreign invasions created a sense of insecurity in the region. In order to protect the honour of their women from foreign invaders, practices like female infanticide, child marriage, sati, purdah and ban on female education were adopted and encouraged. When Guru Nanak, first guru of Sikhs came on scene, girl infants were killed and women who gave birth to daughter were looked down upon. Guru Nanak through his teachings tried to convince the masses about the importance of women in society. Guru Amardas ji, third Sikh Guru also raised his voice against infanticide and condemned those responsible for this act. Singh Sabha movement also raised voice against purdah system, female infanticide, child marriage, sati, deplorable condition of widows, practice of dowry and extravagant expenditure on marriage ceremonies. These historical forces were expected to have positive influence on the position of women in Punjab. But in spite of progressive spiritual teachings of Sikh Gurus, the situation continued to be far from satisfactory. Talking about the practice of female infanticide in Punjab, Darling (1925) mentioned, "Twenty years ago, a Deputy Commissioner of Jullundur remarked that the girls are sacrificed in order that loans for their marriage expenses may not encumber the land descending to the sons. The birth of a daughter is regarded as the equivalent of a decree of Rs. 2000 against the father. The father's emotions are well described in the *Quran*—And when a daughter is announced to one of them his face becomes black and he is full of wrath. He hides himself from the people because of the evil of that which is announced to him. Shall he keep it with disgrace or burry it in the dust."

Darling further mentions that "One of my authorities is a Sikh official of standing, and he went so far as to say that one reason why village menials do not have to buy their brides is that they do not kill their infant daughters." This indicates that practice of infanticide was prevalent in high castes only. In spite of the shortage of girls, the consequent difficulties in getting girls for marriage and the practice of bride-price, female infanticide was practised. Ludhiana Administrative report mentions about the resultant practice of bride-price, "In the Punjab, where the shortage of women is so great, there is nothing to be said for it, and that it should still exist is a curious commentary on human logic. Incidentally, it must tend to raise the price of brides, and this is now so high that few can purchase without resort to money lender" (Ludhiana, A.R., 1904). These facts speak about the prevalence of the practice of female infanticide in earlier part of the twentieth century. Today, the practice of female infanticide has become a thing of the past, but the neglect of the female child and limited access of female child and women to health, nutrition and medical care still continue. Miller (1981) termed this as 'extended infanticide'.

Earlier studies by Wyon and Gordon (1971), Narangwal study (Kielmann, *et al.*, 1983) and Das Gupta (1987) have clearly indicated neglect of the female infants and babies, differential allocation of food, health and medical care to girls resulting in higher mortality from all causes among the females. Some recent studies — Basu (1991), Punjab Health Department (l991), and Central Social Welfare Board (1998) also reveal these male/female differentials in food, nutrition and health. In addition to this, a very disgraceful practice of female foeticide has not only become popular, but has received social sanction also. Scientific advancement in the field of health has been used by the patriarchal institutions of the society in accordance with their own requirements. The already low sex-ratio of the state may lead to a very alarming situation with the consequent demographic and sociological problems, if this situation continues.

Sex Ratio in Punjab: A Situational Analysis

A look at the sex ratio of states (Census, 2001) reveals that Punjab has a sex ratio of 874, which is significantly lower than the national average of 933 (Table 3.1). Among the 27 states (excluding J & K), Punjab has got 26th rank and only one state, *i.e.* Haryana has a sex-ratio (861), lower than that of Punjab. Kerala state with a sex-ratio of 1058 and the Union territory of Pondicherry with a sex-ratio of 1001 are the only two in the country having a positive sex-ratio, *i.e.* more females than males. Punjab has slipped down to 26th rank among the 27, as compared to the 23rd position it had in 1991. While the national level statistics have shown an improvement of six points, Punjab has experienced a decline of 8 points. Like Punjab, the neighbouring states/UTs of Himachal Pradesh, Haryana and Chandigarh have shown a decline in sex-ratio in the last decade. States which were falling below Punjab in 1991 were Arunachal Pradesh, Haryana, Uttar Pradesh and Sikkim. Out of these Arunachal Pradesh has improved its position tremendously from 859 to 901 (42 points) and Uttar Pradesh has improved from 876 to 898 (22 points), while Punjab has experienced a fall from 882 to 874, thus going further down in hierarchy.

Table 3.1: States of India ranked by sex-ratio (1991 and 2001)

Rank in 1991	*Sex ratio 1991*	*States*	*Sex ratio 2001*	*Rank in 2001*
1	1036	Kerala	1058	1
2	985	Chhatisgarh	990	2
3	976	Himachal Pradesh	970	8
4	974	Tamil Nadu	986	3
5	972	Andhra Pradesh	978	5
6	971	Orissa	972	7
7	967	Goa	960	11
8	960	Karnatka	964	10
9	958	Manipur	978	4
10	955	Meghalaya	975	6
11	945	Tripura	950	12
12	936	Uttaranchal	964	9
13	934	Maharashtra	922	18
14	934	Gujarat	921	20
15	923	Assam	932	16
16	922	Jharkhand	941	13
17	921	Mizoram	938	14
18	912	Madhra Pradesh	920	21
19	910	Rajasthan	922	17
21	907	Bihar	921	19
22	886	Nagaland	909	22
23	882	Punjab	874	26
24	878	Sikkim	875	25
25	876	Uttar Pradesh	898	24
26	865	Haryana	861	27
27	859	Arunachal Pradesh	901	23

Data related to child sex-ratio in the age group of 0-6 presents still more alarming trend. At the national level child sex-ratio has declined from 945 in 1991 to 927 in 2001, a decline of 18 points. This is in contrast to the sex-ratio of total population which has shown an increase. Child sex-ratio has shown a sharp decline in several states, which is the most shocking aspect.

Renowned demographer Ashish Bose (2001) remarks that the 2001 figure is not freak, it is a secular trend. In 1961, the 0-6 sex-ratio was 976, it declined to 964 in 1971, 962 in 1981 and 945 in 1991. But the sharpest decline has been in the past decade.

The Census Commissioner has observed in the census report, "It is clear that sex-ratio in the age-group 0-6 has decreased at a much faster pace than the overall sex-ratio of the country after 1981. The decreasing sex-ratio in this child population perhaps has a cascading effect on population over a period of time leading to diminishing sex-ratio in the country. One thing is clear—the imbalance that has set in at this early age-group is difficult to be removed and would remain to haunt the population for a long time to come. To say the least, demographically the sex-ratio of 927 of the population in the age group of 0-6 does not appear to augur well for the future of the country" (Census, 2001).

Maximum decline in the child sex-ratio is evident for the Punjab state, from 875 to 793 (a decline of 82 points), followed by Haryana from 879 to 820 (59 points), Himachal Pradesh from 951 to 897 (54 points), Chandigarh from 899 to 845 (54 points), Gujarat from 928 to 878 points (50 points) and Delhi from 915 to 865 (50 points). Ashish Bose has used the term DEMARU for these states where D stands for daughters and 'MARU' for killings. He says, "on the basis of 50 points decline in the child sex-ratio, I would classify Punjab, Haryana, Himachal Pradesh and Gujarat as DEMARU states".

A look at the time-series data of this century reveals that while for India sex-ratio has declined from 972 in 1901 to 927 in 1991, for Punjab this has increased from 832 in 1901 to 882 in 1991. Thus the trend for Punjab was encouraging till 1991, except for the fact that increase in the sex-ratio of Punjab noted during the decade of 1981-91 was very less as compared to earlier four decades. This deceleration in the increase was a matter of concern and probable reason considered for this was the increasing trend of female foeticide in the state. This concern was not baseless. Data of this decade (1991-2001) have confirmed our fears and instead of registering an increase, sex-ratio of the state has registered a decline of 8 points whereas National sex-ratio has increased by 6 points

(Census, 2001). A deceleration in the increase in the previous decade (1981-91) and a decline in this decade (1991-2001) is an indication of alarming situation.

A district-wise analysis of sex-ratio (Table 3.2) revealed that sex ratio is highest in Hoshiarpur (935) followed by Nawanshahar (913). Ludhiana represents the district with lowest sex-ratio (824). During the decade of 1991-2001, districts of Muktsar (+6), Mansa (+2), Amritsar (+1), Hoshiarpur (+11) and Nawanshahar (+13) have shown improvement in their sex-ratio. Thus significant improvement in sex-ratio is evident only in two districts of Hoshiarpur and Nawanshahar. On the other hand a significant decline has occurred in Fatehgarh Sahib (–20), Ludhiana (–20), Bhatinda (–19), Patiala (–18), Gurdaspur (–15), Jalandhar (–15), Firozpur (–12) and Kapurthala (–10). Maximum decline is evident in Ludhiana and Fatehgarh Sahib followed by Bhatinda and Patiala. Districts having lowest and highest sex-ratio during 1991 and 2001 census are same, *i.e.* Ludhiana has the lowest rank and Hoshiarpur, the highest rank. District of Hoshiarpur has topped the districts of the state both in terms of total literacy rate (81.40%) as well as female literacy rate (75.56%).

Table 3.2: Ranking of districts of Punjab state by sex-ratio (1991 and 2001)

Rank in 2001	*Sex ratio (2001)*	*State/District*	*Sex-ratio 1991*	*Rank in 1991*	*Change in points (1991-2001)*
–	874	Punjab	882	–	–8
1	935	Hoshiarpur	924	1	+11
2	913	Nawanshahar	900	3	+13
3	888	Gurdaspur	903	2	–15
4	886	Mukatsar	880	11	+6
5	886	Kapurthala	896	5	–10
6	883	Firozpur	895	6	–12
7	883	Moga	884	7	–1
8	882	Jalandhar	897	4	–15
9	881	Faridkot	883	9	–2
10	875	Mansa	873	13	+2
11	874	Amritsar	873	12	+1
12	870	Rupnagar	870	16	–
13	868	Sangrur	870	15	–2
14	865	Bhatinda	884	8	–19
15	864	Patiala	882	10	–18
16	851	Fatehgarh Sahib	871	14	–20
17	824	Ludhiana	844	17	–20

Source: Census of India, 2001, Punjab, Paper 2 of 2001.

As regards the child sex-ratio (0-6 years) (Table 3.3) Moga and Firozpur have the highest sex-ratio (819 each) and Fatehgarh Sahib is at the bottom with the child sex-ratio of 754. As regards the change in the child sex-ratio, none of the districts of Punjab has experienced increase in the sex-ratio in the decade of 1991-2001. All the districts have experienced a decline with maximum decline in Fatehgarh Sahib (–120), followed by Kapurthala (–104), Gurdaspur (–103) and Patiala (–101). In all the districts except Moga (–48 points) all the districts of the state reveal a decline of more than 50 points. The situation as pointed out by Ashish Bose is alarming.

Table 3.3: Child sex-ratio (0-6 age group) in districts of Punjab (1991 and 2001)

State/District	*Sex-ratio (0-6 age group)*		*Change in points*
	1991	2001	
Punjab	875	793	–82
Gurdaspur	878	775	–103
Amritsar	861	783	–78
Kapurthala	879	775	–104
Jalandhar	886	797	–89
Hoshiarpur	884	810	–74
Nawanshahar	900	810	–90
Rupnagar	884	791	–93
Fatehgarh Sahib	874	754	–120
Ludhiana	877	814	–63
Moga	867	819	–48
Firozpur	887	819	–68
Muktsar	858	807	–51
Faridkot	865	805	–60
Bhatinda	860	779	–81
Mansa	873	779	–94
Sangrur	873	784	–89
Patiala	871	770	–101

Source: Census of India, Punjab paper 2 of 2001.

A rural-urban break up of the 0-6 age group (Table 3.4) sex-ratio revealed that disparity in the urban-rural sex-ratio is not very wide, *i.e.* urban (789) and rural (795). But if we see the sex-ratio of the total population, there is great disparity, *i.e.* rural (887) and Urban (848). A district-wise analysis shows that rural child sex-ratio varies between 824 in Firozpur district to 747 in Fatehgarh Sahib district. Districts having, rural child sex-ratio higher than the state average are Firozpur, Jalandhar, Hoshiarpur, Nawanshahar, Ludhiana, Moga, Muktsar and Faridkot. As far as urban sex-ratio is concerned, Gurdaspur has the lowest (729) and

Ludhiana the highest among the districts of the state. Interstingly Ludhiana which otherwise has the lowest sex-ratio in the state, has shown the highest child sex-ratio (0-6 age) in urban areas.

Table 3.4: Rural/urban sex-ratio of districts in Punjab (1991-2001)

State/Districts	*Sex Ratio in 0-6 age group (2001)*			*Change in points from 1991 to 2001*		
	Total	*Rural*	*Urban*	*Total*	*Rural*	*Urban*
Punjab	793	795	789	–82	–83	–77
Gurdaspur	775	789	729	–103	–92	–139
Amritsar	783	789	772	–78	–75	–84
Kapurthala	775	773	779	–104	–102	–112
Jalandhar	797	806	786	–89	–85	–93
Hoshiarpur	810	813	800	–74	–74	–73
Nawanshahar	810	811	805	–90	–87	108
Rupnagar	791	787	800	–93	–96	86
Fatehgarh Sahib	754	747	774	–120	–125	–107
Ludhiana	814	812	816	–63	–74	–53
Moga	819	820	811	–48	–47	–55
Firozpur	819	824	804	–68	–70	–60
Muktsar	807	810	798	–51	–54	–41
Faridkot	805	805	806	–60	–62	–55
Bhatinda	779	789	756	–81	–77	–88
Mansa	779	780	775	–94	–103	–39
Sangur	784	779	798	–89	–98	–65
Patiala	770	764	786	–101	–106	–86

Source: Census of India, Punjab paper 2 of 2001.

Thus a very alarming feature of the census 2001 data is a drastic decline in the 0-6 age group sex-ratio in all the districts of the state. None of the districts of Punjab has shown a positive change and more than that, in none of the districts this decline has been less than 48. Lowest decline of 48 is in Moga district and highest fall of 120 points in Fatehgarh Sahib district. In rural areas also Fatehgarh Sahib district has topped with a decline of 125 points and again Moga has the least decline of 47 points in the child sex-ratio during the last decade of 1991-2001. In urban areas, maximum decline in child sex-ratio is in Gurdaspur (–139 points) and least decline was in Mansa district (–39 points). This pattern of significant decline in child sex-ratio in all the districts of the state is the cause of concern for all of us.

Socio-Cultural Correlates of Sex-ratio

For explaining the sex-ratio imbalances in the Indian population, Entitlement Framework Approach (Sen, 1981) and the Co-operative Conflict Approach to Intra-household Resource allocation (Sen, 1990) have been used by Agnihotri (2000). The excess female mortality, he says, is a result of the inequalities faced by female children in access to life sustaining resources like food, nutrition and health care. It is necessary, therefore, to link the analysis of sex-ratio variations with the issue of allocative behaviour within the household. Higher female mortality due to unequal access to resources can be seen as a case of 'entitlements failure'. Some studies conducted in Punjab have also similar findings. Basu (1991) in her analysis indicated a wide gap in the male-female survival among children of the state. Some earlier studies in Punjab by Wyon and Gorden (1971), Narangwal study (1983) and Dass Gupta (1987) have attributed high female mortality rates to differential allocation of food, health and medical care. Dyson and Moore (1983) have emphasised that Indo-Aryan system of kinship prevalent in north is more hostile and harsh towards females, while the southern kinship system is more female friendly, resulting in the higher chances of survival and more favourable sex-ratios in the south.

Low female labour participation rates have also been found to be correlated with the low sex-ratios (Bardhan, 1974). Agnihotri (2000), says that high female labour participation (FLP) rate emerges as sufficient condition for better sex-ratio but not a necessary condition. He further says that where kinship system ensures survival, the relevance of FLP is marginal, where it does not, FLP is crucial. High FLP increases the value of the females at the societal level and of the female child in the household. Punjab also has the lowest female workforce participation rate (4.41 per cent) among all the states as against 22.3 per cent for the country (Census, 1991). Thus with a kinship system which is harsher to the females, low female workforce participation rates may lead to low sex-ratio.

Differentials in sex-ratios have also been reported among the 'propertied' and 'unpropertied' classes, with propertied groups in the northern India having low sex-ratios (Agnihotri, 2000). Kishwar (1996) in a study of Punjab village also reported that son preference was more pronounced among the propertied rural landholding middle-peasant castes, as compared to the agricultural families. A study in the villages of Sangrur district of Punjab (Wig, 1996) revealed that sex-ratio in 0-6 age group was 980 in SCs and only 840 in other castes. It went on declining in the higher age groups in case of Scheduled Castes and in case of other castes it went on increasing, indicating that once the girl child survives the earlier age groups, her chances of survival are more in other castes as compared to Scheduled Castes. Study also found that in the older age group (60 and above), a dramatic fall in sex-ratio in both the groups is evident, but it is more so in Scheduled Castes (468) as compared to other castes (699). Thus association of caste and age with sex-ratio has been revealed by these studies.

Related to this pattern of low sex-ratio among the propertied castes is the access of women to property rights and the inheritance system. Aggarwal (1994) traces the cause of lower status of women to property rights and inheritance system. The northern social structure denies women any significant property rights which lower their status and also lessens their chances of survival. The practice of dowry very much related to the property rights has been identified as one of the major culprit by Miller (1984) which creates the perception of the girl child as a liability. Kishwar (1996) in her study of Punjab mentions that in these peasant families, heavy amount of dowry is given to compensate the daughter and the son-in-law for denial of daughter's share in land. But this leads to family viewing the daughter as an economic burden and decreases her worth in the family. She further points out that custom of spending more money on marriages was growing among agricultural labourers also. Sometimes the family has to work for years together to pay back the money. This makes birth of girl child an unwelcome event. Thus as a result of Sanskritization, this practice is spreading among the lower castes also.

All the above discussed socio-cultural and economic factors are considered to be contributing towards the general neglect of the female child and the consequent low sex-ratios.

The practice of infanticide, as practised historically has already been discussed. It is being considered that the recent dramatic decline in the 0-6 sex-ratio of Punjab is mainly due to the practice of female foeticide in the state. According to a recent study by UNFPA (2001) based on data generated by the National Family Health Survey I and II conducted in 1990-92 and 1996-98 and the Sample Research Survey has pointed out that female foeticide account for a significant part of the decline in fertility and the increase in the small family norm achieved in Punjab and Haryana, two of the most prosperous states in India. The study revealed that sex abortions (SSAS) accounted for about one-third decline in total fertility rate in urban areas of Haryana, while it contributed to 50 and 80 per cent decline in rural and urban areas of Punjab. Thus female foeticide can be considered as the main probable cause behind the recent drastic fall in the sex-ratio (0-6) of the state.

Conclusion

Preference to have a male child and easy availability of technology for the sex detection of the foetus has resulted in the sex-selective abortions. Thus the action has to be taken on both these fronts. First is to ensure that these pre natal diagnostic techniques are not used for the detection of sex of the foetus, and second to bring about change in people's attitude towards the girl child. While action has to be taken to stop this trend of female foeticide, the question need to be understood in its totality. This is just a symptom of the disease. The root cause of the disease lies in the lower status of women in our society.

George (2001), an activist researcher, who has been actively involved in implementing female infanticide and foeticide prevention programmes all over the country for the past 16 years, says, "If the present trend of unabated pre-natal sex-determination continued for another decade, the region will witness an alarming decline in sex-ratio so much so that the present sex-ratio of 793 (0-6 years) in Punjab would decline by another one-third."

Sabu along with voluntary organisations CEHAT (Centre for Enquiry into Health and Allied Themes) from Mumbai and Masoom from Pune filed a public interest litigation (PIL) after which the Supreme Court directed implementation of Central Diagnostic Techniques (Regulation and Prevention of Misuse) Act, 1994, by June 30 this year. Now the judiciary has done its job. Head Priest of Akal Takht has issued a directive to the Sikh Sangat not to practice this crime of female foeticide. This is a very important step, as the religious leaders, in whom people have faith and conviction, can play a much more important role in persuading the masses against this practice than any law or directions to the law enforcing agencies to ensure the proper implementation of the law. Leaders of other religious organisations should also come forward and join this struggle for saving the girl child. The religious teachings which condemn the killing of girls and other practices downgrading women in society need to be used in support of the cause of gender equality.

Now after the Supreme Court Directive, State Governments have swung into action. Number of steps are being taken to ensure the stricter implementation of the acts like the Medical Termination of Pregnancy

Act, 1992 and the Pre-natal Diagnostic Techniques (Regulation and Prevention of Misuse) Act, 1994. The loopholes in these laws need to be plugged in the light of new technological advancements. Pre-natal sex determination should be linked to the human rights violation and right to life. The victim of this process, i.e. the women who has to undergo abortion and kill her daughter, should not be considered as a party to the crime. Action of course will have to be taken against the persons engaged in conducting of such tests and the doctors conducting these sex-selective abortions, but how much and to what extent must be carefully considered. An action plan has to be prepared and followed involving government, voluntary organisations, doctors, religious leaders, law enforcing agencies, youth and women themselves. Through the organised efforts of enlightened people from different sectors of the society, a movement condemning this practice of female foeticide need to be initiated. The social sanction which has been given to this practice by the society need to be changed to social condemnation of anybody engaging in or being party to such a heinous crime. People need to be made aware about the dangerous consequences of declining sex-ratio. They need to be convinced that a disturbed sex-ratio will mean more violence against women.

The various socio-cultural and economic factors, as pointed out in the paper need to be understood and changed through planned efforts. Status of women in the society has to be improved so that women giving birth to a daughter do not dread the prospect of their daughter being another sufferer like them and are sure that their own life will not be made downgraded in the family with the birth of a girl child.

REFERENCES

Agarwal, B. (1994), *A Field of one's own; Gender and Land rights in South Asia*, Cambridge: Cambridge University Press.

Agnihotri, S.B. (2000), *Sex Ratio Patterns in the Indian Population*, New Delhi : Sage Publication.

Bardhan, P.K. (1974), "On life and death questions", *Economic and Political Weekly*, special issue number 9: 1293-1304.

Basu, Alka M. (1991), "The Gender more vulnerable", *VHAI Bulletin*.

Bose, Ashish (2001), "Towards daughter less nation", *The Tribune*, June 17.

Central Social Welfare Board (1998), *The Tribune*, May 22.

Darling, M.L. (1925), *The Punjab Peasant in Prosperity and Debt*. Columbia : South Asia Books.

Das Gupta, M. (1987), "Selective discrimination against female children in India", *Population Development Review*, 13(1).

Dyson, T. and Moore, H. (1983). "Kinship structure, female autonomy and demographic behaviour", *Population Development Review*, 9(1).

George, Sabu, M. (2001). in Sharma Vidha, "Fighting against female foeticide": *The Tribune*, July 27.

Horowitz, B. and Kishwar, M. (1996). "Family life of agricultural labourers and small farmers in Punjab", in Kishwar, M. and Ruth, V. *In search of answers*, New Delhi, Manohar Publishers & Distributors

Kielmann, *et al.* (1983), *Child and Maternal Health Services in Rural India: Narangwal study*, Vol. I & II, *A World Bank Research Publication*, Baltimore : John Hopkins University Press.

Miller, B.D. (1981). *The Endangered Sex*. Ithaca, N.Y.: Cornell University Press.

Miller, B.D. (1984), "Daughter neglect, momeies work and marriage", *Medical Anthropology*, 8(2) : 109-25.

OXFAM (1998). *The Tribune*, March 8.

Rajput, Pam, Malkit Kaur and Kivan Sharma, (1993). *Civil Child and Family in Punjab. Project Report* submitted to Deptt. of Women and Child Development, Govt. of India, CWSD, Chandigarh : Punjab University.

Sen, A.K. (1981), cited in Agnihotri, S.B. 2000, *op. cit.*

Sen, A.K. (1990), *Ibid.*

UNFPA, (2001), cited in "Foeticide hits Punjab, Haryana Sex-ratio", *The Tribune*, October 17.

Wig, O.P. (1996). Women, work and census in Punjab. *Project Report* sponsored by UNIFEM.

Wyon, J.B. and Gorden, J.E. (1971). *The Khanna Study: Population Problems in Rural Punjab*, Cambridge: Harvard University Press.

4

HIGHER EDUCATION IN PUNJAB

SUKHDEV SINGH

In this paper a modest effort has been made to assess the status of University education and to pinpoint the factors responsible for decline in its standard. As the higher education in any society is of vital importance in the whole education system (Desai: 1998, Arora: 1998, Mohanty: 1995, Singh: 1985, Kapoor: 1977, Hommadi: 1985, Sinha: 1982, Joshi: 1980, UNESCO: 1965). If good primary education is like the strong stem of any tree of a society, higher education is like the fruits of that tree which are reaped in the form of socio-economic, industrial and technological development ultimately leading any nation towards better quality of life. In India higher education has been an integral part of education system since times immemorial, notwithstanding the different nature of higher education in the past. In the post-independence era central and state governments of India have been trying to strengthen the process of higher education, largely on the lines of western countries with a view to build a new and progressive social order based on social justice. It was further realised that reform of education could no longer be postponed with danger to the entire future development of the country because progress in every sector of national life — in industry, agriculture, commerce, communication and health, and the general standard of living depended largely on the quality and adequacy of higher education provided to the people. In the last five decades, a number of Universities, colleges and other institutions of higher education have been established. According to the report of Human Resource Development (1997) there are 226 Universities and 6569 Arts and Science Colleges and 1354 professional colleges in which around 55,32,998 students are getting education of various types. In Punjab, a tiny state of India, there are 4 universities, 177 Arts and Science Colleges and 33 professional colleges in which 1,57,126 students are getting higher education out of which 77,141 are boys and 82,985 are girls.

In the ladder of higher education university education has its own importance and place in almost all the societies of the world. Pandit Jawaharlal Nehru once said "A university stands for humanism, for tolerance, for reason, for progress, for the adventure of ideas and for the search for truth. It stands for the onward march of the human race towards ever high objectives" (Venkatachaliah: 1999). By now, India has sufficient number of universities engaged in various educational pursuits. In spite of this phenomenal growth in the field of higher education, for quite sometime now a general feeling is growing that the standard of higher education is declining (Deshpande: 1999, Srivastava: 1999, Bhandari: 1999, Mohanty: 1995, Faruqui *et al.*: 1994, Desai *et al.*: 1987, Hommadi: 1985). Venkatachaliah observes that unfortunately Indian Universities, in the quality of their research and teaching programmes, have not realised and achieved their own potential. The quality of intellectual life is not uniformly bright. There is an increasing air of indiscipline and irreverence leading to an increasing sense of disenchantment with the universities and their ability to contribute to the development of science and technology. With a view to probe the facts regarding the declining standard of university education, this study was undertaken with the following specific objectives:

(i) Is the standard of university education declining?
(ii) To bring forth the factors/reasons of declining standard of—university education.
(iii) To render suitable suggestions for improving the standard of university education.

Methodology

The study was conducted in Punjab Agricultural University (PAU), Ludhiana which is one of the premier agricultural universities of India. Data were collected from all the five constituent colleges at the main campus, *i.e.* College of Agriculture (COA), College of Basic Sciences and Humanities (COBS&H), College of Agricultural Engineering (COAE), College of Veterinary Sciences (COVS) and College of Home Sciences (COHS). A semi-structured questionnaire schedule containing the basic questions of the investigation was supplied to 15 teacher-respondents of each of the five colleges giving rise to a total sample of 75 teachers spread over the whole university. Teachers of all ranks, *i.e.* Professors, Associate Professors and Assistant Professors were given equal representation in the study. Adequate time of one month was given to the respondents to complete the questionnaire. Six factors *i.e.* economic, social, ethical, psychological, political and miscellaneous were hypothesised as the basic factors for the declining standard of higher education. The teacher-respondents were asked to rank these six factors in accordance with their importance towards falling standard of higher education. The coefficient of concordance (W) given by Kendall (1939) was applied to arrive at the composite ranks assigned to these factors (Conover, 1971). Kendall's coefficient of concordance (W) is defined as:

$$W = 12\,S/[K^2\,n(n^2-1)]$$

where K = number of teacher-respondents

n = number of important factors causing decline in standard of higher education

and $S = \sum_{j=1}^{n}(R_j - \overrightarrow{R_j})^2$

R_j being the total of ranks assigned to the *jth* factor by each of the K respondents.

The value of W always lies between 0 and 1, and it is never negative. The significance of W is tested under the null and alternative hypotheses, $H0$ and $H1$:

$H0$: K sets of rankings are independent (respondents differ amongst each other)
$H1$: K sets of rankings are dependent (respondents are in agreement) by applying χ^2 - test, where χ^2 with $(n-1)$ d.f. is computed by the formula

$$\chi^2 = K\,(n-1)\,W$$

If the calculated value of χ^2 is less than the table value of χ^2 with $(n-1)$ degrees of freedom at desired level of significance, retain the null hypothesis $H0$ of the disagreement among the teacher-respondents, otherwise reject the null hypothesis $H0$ and accept the alternative hypothesis, $H1$ to be true leading to the decision that the respondents are in agreement. In case W turns out to be significant by χ^2 - test implying thereby that the respondents were in agreement, there is a justification to use the average (or total) of these ranks as the composite rank of the factor being considered. Thus to judge the relative importance of a factor, the criterion used was that the lower the value of total R_j for a factor, the more important was the factor and *vice versa*.

Results and Discussion

Pattern of response of the respondents

The extent of response received from the teacher-respondents is exhibited in Table 4.1. Out of the total 75 questionnaire schedules supplied to teachers of various colleges, 55(73.3%) teachers of different ranks responded to the survey with varied level of interest shown to the researcher. College-wise break up of the response indicates that all the teachers (100%) of Veterinary College responded to the survey and showed enough interest and some of them expressed curiosity to know the findings of the research venture. Teachers from College of Agriculture and College of Basic Sciences also gave an encouraging response as 86.7 per cent and 80.0 per cent of them respectively responded to the research effort. However, teachers of College of Home Science and College of Agri-Engineering showed lesser interest in the study as only 60 and 40 per cent teachers of these colleges respectively returned the filled questionnaires. In spite of the repeated visits by the investigator some of the teachers did not entertain the researchers. While some of such teachers pleaded their inability to fill the questionnaire due to paucity of time available with them, a few others were apprehensive for reasons best known to them.

Is the standard of university education declining?

Was the standard of education really declining? This was the first question posed to the respondents. To this query all (100%) of the respondents said "yes" which is indicative of the fact that the standard of university education is really going down. Some of the senior teachers, in their comments on this very phenomenon, recalled the old days which they termed as 'golden days' when atmosphere of research and teaching prevailed all around the campus. Many of the respondents cited examples of the pioneer teachers, in different disciplines, who by their sheer hard work and dedication to the

Table 4.1: Distribution of number of respondents contacted and response received

Name of the College	*Category-wise number of scheduled supplied and response received*							
	Professor		*Associate Professor*		*Assistant Professor*		*Overall*	
	No. of teachers contacted	*No. of responses received*	*No. of teachers contacted*	*No. of responses received*	*No. of teachers contacted*	*No. of responses received*	*No. of teachers contacted*	*No. of responses received*
College of Agriculture	5	4	5	4	5	5	15	13 (86.7)
College of Veterinary Sciences	5	5	5	5	5	5	15	15 (100.0)
College of Home Science	5	–	5	4	5	5	15	9 (60.0)
College of Basic Sciences & Humanities	5	5	5	2	5	5	15	12 (80.0)
College of Agricultural Engineering	5	–	5	1	5	5	15	6 (40.0)
Total	25	14	25	16	25	25	75	55 (73.3)

Note: Figures within parentheses indicate per cent received.

profession, put the name of PAU amongst the institutions of the world reckoned with. Taking a simplistic view, all the teacher-respondents held that the standard of university education has been declining due to various factors as revealed by in-depth analyses of the data which follows.

Relative importance of factors responsible for declining standard of university education

A perusal of Table 4.2 reveals that about half (47.2%) of the respondent-teachers considered erosion of ethical values among the teachers, students and in the society as prime factor, while about one-third (34.6%) considered the economic constraints of the teachers as foremost causative factor responsible for deterioration of standard of education. About a-fifth of the respondent-teachers viewed political interference as foremost factor while 16.3 per cent and 5.4 per cent of them gave 1st rank to miscellaneous and social factors respectively as main factors for declining standard of university education. However, none of the respondent-teachers gave 1st rank to psychological reasons. Economic factor was awarded the second rank by larger percentages, *i.e.* 25.5 per cent followed by 23.6 per cent and 18.2 per cent awarding second rank to ethical and social factors. Kendall's coefficient of concordance *W* worked out to be 0.23 which indicated the degree of concordance between the 55 teacher-respondents with regard to the six factors identified to be the main causes of decline in the standard of university education. The significance of the coefficient of concordance was tested by applying χ^2 test. The value of χ^2 (with 5 d.f.) worked out to be 63.25 which was significant at 1 per cent level of significance. The significance was indicative of the fact that the respondents were in agreement and hence composite ranks can be assigned to the six causative factors according to the magnitude of R_j. As exhibited in the last column of Table 4.2, it was concluded that the ranking of the six factors were: Ethical (1st), Economic (2nd), Social (3rd), Political (4th), Psychological (5th) and Miscellaneous (6th). On the whole, the results of the study indicate that ethical, economic and social factors are the three main factors responsible for declining standard of education while political and psychological factors were next in importance and miscellaneous considerations were the least important.

Factor-wise analysis of declining standard of education

Economic factor : The thrust of the present study has been to bring forth

Table 4.2: Ranking of factors causing decline in standard of university education by respondents-teachers

Factor No. j (n=6)	*Factors*	*Number of teachers assigning ranks 1st to 6th*						*Total No. of teachers assigning ranks (K=55)*	*Total of ranks Rj*	*Ranking of factors according to value of Rj*
		1st	2nd	3rd	4th	5th	6th			
1.	Economic	19(34.6)	14(25.4)	12(21.8)	5(9.1)	3(5.4)	2(3.6)	55(100.0)	130	II
2.	Social	3(5.4)	10(18.2)	25(45.5)	7(12.7)	8(14.6)	2(3.6)	55(100.0)	178	III
3.	Ethical	26(47.2)	13(23.6)	8(14.6)	4(7.3)	4(7.3)	—	55(100.0)	112	I
4.	Psychological	—	8(14.6)	9(16.3)	24(43.6)	6(10.9)	8(14.6)	55(100.0)	217	V
5.	Political	10(18.2)	7(12.7)	2(3.6)	4(7.3)	25(45.5)	7(12.7)	55(100.0)	213	IV
6.	Miscellaneous	9(16.3)	7(12.7)	4(7.3)	4(7.3)	8(14.6)	23(41.8)	55(100.0)	229	VI

Notes :
1. Figures within parentheses indicate per cent of total repondents assigning the rank.
2. Total of ranks R_1 for first factor, viz. Economic (j=1) is computed as [(19×1) + (14×2) + (12×3) + (5×4) + (3x5) + (2x6)] = 130 and similarly for other factors.
3. Coefficient of Concordance $W = \sum 12 (R_j - \bar{R}_j)^2 / (55)^2 (6) (6-1) = 0.23$
4. χ^2 [with (n–1) = 5 d.f] = K(n–1). W =(55) (5) (.23) = 63.25 which is significant at 1% level of significance.

the factors/reasons responsible for deteriorating standard of the university education and data in this regard are presented in Table 4.3 which show the factorwise analysis. Data indicate that under the economic factor, the top ranking causes are less salary, inflation in consumable commodities, and expensive education of the children in that order. Many of the respondent-teachers supported their ideas with several examples. Regarding less salary they contended that in spite of having highest qualification (Ph.D.) the salary is far less than the people working in private and public sectors with simple graduation and post-graduation. Value of the money, they opined, is going down day by day and the dearness allowance given from time to time was far less to compensate the growing financial hardships. Some of the senior teachers compared the value of their present emoluments with those two decades back. Besides, the education of children particularly school education has grown so costly that a single-hand earner teacher hesitates to send his/her children to the public schools. Exorbitant medical expenses, improper/ meagre living accommodation, that also on very high rents, in the city like Ludhiana were the other reasons brought out by the respondents which affect standard of the teaching and research in the university. Some other reasons which undermine the quality of education were less facilities to teachers, engagement of some teachers in secondary occupations, impact of materialism of life style, costly books and journals beyond the reach of teacher's budget etc. As per Kendall's coefficient of concordance the importance of economic reasons from top to bottom came out in the order of ranks presented in the table. These findings are corroborated by some other scholars like Amrik Singh (1985). While commenting upon the low quality of higher education in his book he observed that the second most important reason for declining standard of education is low economic status of teacher. Emoluments are so low and niggard and social prestige so unattractive that teaching has seldom attracted the more talented men and women.

Social Factor : Part B of Table 4.3 depicts the social factor which recede the standard of university education. Data are indicative of the fact that nepotism (1st), corruption (2nd) and regionalism (3rd), are the top ranking social reasons which plague the university education. While filling the questionnaires, many of the respondents have attributed these three reasons as the root cause of declining standard of education. Due to corrupt and *mala fide* practices undeserving persons, who are concerned only with earnings and having least academic aptitudes are occupying

Table 4.3: Ranking of main reasons for declining standard of education within different factors

Factor	*Rea-sons*	*Reasons*	*No. of teachers assigning ranks to the reason (within a particular factor)*						*Total No. of teachers assigning ranks*	*Total of ranks* R_j *
			1st	*2nd*	*3rd*	*4th*	*5th*	*6th*		
A. Economic	1	Less Salary	25(45.4)	17(30.9)	4(7.3)	5(9.2)	2(3.6)	2(3.6)	55 (100)	113 (I)
	2	Inflation	11(20.0)	12(21.8)	11(20.0)	8(14.5)	6(10.9)	7(12.8)	55 (100)	172 (II)
	3	Expensive Education	2(3.6)	6(10.9)	20(36.4)	12(21.8)	9(16.4)	6(10.9)	55 (100)	203 (IV)
	4	Medical Expenses	3(5.4)	6(10.9)	9(16.4)	13(23.7)	21(38.2)	3(5.4)	55 (100)	217 (V)
	5	Improper Accommodation	9(16.4)	8(14.1)	6(10.9)	10(18.2)	13(23.7)	9(16.4)	55 (100)	202 (III)
	6	Any other	1(1.8)	5(9.1)	1(1.8)	3(5.4)	5(9.1)	40(72.8)	55 (100)	292 (VI)
		Computed Statistics	W = 0.32		χ^2 (5 d.f.) = 88.0**					
B. Social	1	Intensified corruption	14(25.4)	17(30.9)	6(10.9)	10(18.2)	8(14.6)	–	55 (100)	146 (II)
	2	Nepotism	15(27.3)	10(18.2)	17(30.9)	8(14.5)	5(9.11)	–	55 (100)	143 (I)
	3	Regionalism	14(25.4)	12(21.8)	12(21.8)	10(18.2)	7(12.8)	–	55 (100)	149 (III)
	4	Maintenance of status	8(14.5)	12(21.8)	16(29.1)	9(16.4)	10(18.2)	–	55 (100)	166 (IV)
	5	Any other	–	–	2(3.6)	6(10.9)	47(85.5)	–	55 (100)	265 (V)
		Computed Statistics	W=0.34		χ^2 (4 d.f.) = 77.9**					
C. Ethical	1	Low involvement in study	9(16.4)	15(27.3)	11(20.0)	9(16.4)	6(10.9)	5(9.0)	55 (100)	168 (III)
	2	Non-serious students	9(16.4)	13(23.6)	20(36.4)	7(12.8)	4(7.3)	2(3.6)	55 (100)	155 (II)
	3	Non-recognition of talent	24(43.4)	14(25.4)	7(12.8)	6(10.9)	4(7.3)	–	55 (100)	117 (I)
	4	Free will	5(5.4)	5(9.1)	6(10.9)	13(23.6)	21(38.2)	7(12.8)	55 (100)	230 (V)
	5	Lack of punctuality and dedication	12(21.8)	6(10.9)	7(12.8)	13(23.6)	12(21.8)	5(9.1)	55 (100)	187 (IV)

(Contd.)

Factor	Reasons	Reasons	No. of teachers assigning ranks to the reason (within a particular factor)						Total No. of teachers assigning ranks	Total of ranks R_j *
			1st	2nd	3rd	4th	5th	6th		
	6	Any other	–	–	1(1.8)	2(3.6)	5(5.5)	49(89.1)	55 (100)	320 (VI)
		Computed Statistics	W = 0.48		χ^2 (5 d.f.) = 79.2**					
D. Psychological	1	Personal tension	16(29.1)	30(54.5)	9(16.4)	–	–	–	55 (100)	103 (II)
	2	Monotony of work	29(52.7)	16(29.1)	10(18.2)	–	–	–	55 (100)	91 (I)
	3	Any other	3(5.5)	3(5.5)	49(89.0)	–	–	–	55 (100)	156 (III)
		Computed Statistics	W = 0.40			χ^2 (2 d.f.) = 44.0**				
E. Political	1	Intensified political interference	33(60.0)	22(40.0)	–	–	–	–	55 (100)	77 (I)
	2	Any other	7(12.7)	48(87.3)	–	–	–	–	55 (100)	103 (II)
		Computed Statistics	W = 0.22		χ^2 (1 d.f.) = 12.3**					
F. Miscellaneous	1	Lack of accountability	12(21.8)	18(32.7)	9(16.5)	12(21.8)	4(7.2)	–	55 (100)	143 (II)
	2	Internal system of examination	16(29.1)	10(18.2)	17(30.9)	7(12.7)	5(9.1)	–	55 (100)	140 (I)
	3	Inbreeding	13(23.6)	10(18.2)	12(21.8)	12(21.8)	8(14.6)	–	55 (100)	157 (III)
	4	Lack of educational equipments	10(18.2)	14(25.4)	4(7.3)	16(29.1)	11(20.0)	–	55 (100)	169 (IV)
	5	Any other	1(1.8)	–	2(2.6)	–	52(94.5)	–	55 (100)	267 (V)
		Computed Statistics		W = 0.37		χ^2 (4 d.f.) = 80.5**				

Notes : 1. Figures within parentheses indicate per cent of total. 2. *Roman numerals within parentheses indicate rank of reasons within a factor according to the value of R_j. 3. ** Indicate significant at 1% level of significance.

positions in university departments leaving the much more deserving candidates in suffering. In this process the mediocrity is thriving in different disciplines. Maintenance of social status by showing hospitality, following custom, traditions and rituals, missing sense of pride as a teacher, were other important social reasons which affect the standard of university education. Increasing tendency of consumerism and hedonism among the teachers due to societal level effects (materialism) also affect the quality of education. Statistical test placed nepotism (1st), corruption (2nd), regionalism (3rd), maintenance of social status (4th), and others on 5th place amongst the social reasons.

Ethical factor : Interestingly ethical factor turned out to be the foremost in causing decline in the standard of university academics. Amongst all the six factors (see Table 4.2) it ranks on the top. Erosion of ethical values and moral standard among the teacher, students and society as a whole, has severely undermined the standard of university education. Among the sub-factors, non-recognition of talent and entry of non-serious students in the university and lukewarm involvement of teachers in academics were the top ranking ethical reasons. About half of the respondents have given lot of illustrations through their written comments on the questionnaire which indicate that university education has not been taken with reverence. Idealism is a value of the past. Work-culture in research and teaching has been damaged beyond repair. Inability to instil the professional outlook among the teachers was another crucial factor. Teacher-taught relationship has not remained pious. In some cases teachers got threats from students for not awarding them higher scores. Furthermore, professional interaction has been replaced by personal and peripheral interest and critical group discussions are missing. The unionistic approach by students and teachers at the cost of professional upliftment, was another major factor deteriorating the standard of university education. Other unethical practices were: influencing the teacher for fetching high grades through base means, declining reading habits among the students due to heavy dependence on 'class notes', less frequency of teacher to the library etc. Besides, squeezing punctuality, dedication to academics on the part of students and teachers, increasing individualism, and loss of missionary zeal have also been found to be responsible for receding educational standards. Statistical analysis ranked the non-recognition of talent as the 1st sub-social cause, followed by non-serious students, lack of involvement in study, lack of punctuality, free will and others.

Psychological : Among the psychological factors monotony and routine academic works were found to be the major causes of lethargy and boredom which erode the enthusiasm of teachers and lessening their interest in academic works. Personal tensions also turned out be an important cause which deflates the academic interest. Although none of the teachers has given 1st rank to psychological reasons yet a few of them have narrated few examples where conflict within the family, within the staff and with authority gave rise to the evasive attitude towards work and over the time some teachers turned more cynic. Lack of self-evaluation, lack of aptitude towards profession, over dominance by non-teaching staff and their attitude to please the bosses only generated a lot of tension among the junior teachers which ultimately made the teacher more remorse in academics. Under psychological factors Kendall's coefficient of concordance placed the monotony to work on the top followed by personal tensions and others.

Political : Ingress of politics in the academic institutions, particularly during the appointments and promotions to higher posts has severely been undermining the standard of university education beside eroding the autonomy of the university. Many of the respondents bemoaned through their comments that increasing trend of favouritism has been ruining the whole education system. Merit has been consistently ignored during selection. Comments of some of the teachers led to the conclusion that this happened due to indifference of intelligentsia towards politics and lack of consistent educational policy at the centre and state level. Mohanty (1995) in his study concludes that politicisation of higher education has posed a serious threat to the quality of higher education. The Gajendragadker committee was very much critical about the politicisation of the system and curb on autonomy of the higher education. Statistically, political factors got fourth rank importance as presented in Table 4.2.

Miscellaneous : Under the miscellaneous factors, internal examination system, non-accountability of the teachers and inbreeding turned out to be the top ranking factors which cut-sized the standard of university education. Many of the respondents reported several instances where they narrated that internal examination system is quite easy for the teacher but the students suffer in this easy going process. Besides, instead of focusing on main discipline the students are kept busy in allied subjects and assignments which are much less beneficial to the students later on.

Employment of the product (students) in their own institution has also been found responsible for this decline. Some of the teachers opined that even if it is necessary, the candidates must be given some exposure in the other institutions. Lack of laboratory equipment (even the very basic requirement), poor library facility, lack of professionalism, non-availability of latest techniques in different disciplines, general deterioration in the society, socialisation of the children in corrupt environment, less representation to young in administration are some of the other reasons which have been affecting the standard of university education.

Conclusions

The study aimed at highlighting the factors which undermine the quality of university education. The composite analysis of the data gathered from the 55 teachers of various ranks of Punjab Agricultural University, led to the conclusion that the standard of university education is declining. Erosion of ethical values and moral standards among the teachers, students and society as a whole turned out to be the prime causes for declining standard of university education. Non-recognition of talent, receding professionalism, entry of non-serious students in the institutions, unionism at different levels, declining reading habits and following the backdoor ways to get good scores by the students turned out to be the main causative factors for declining the standard of higher education. Second most important factor which undermined the quality of education has been economic factor under which less emoluments, expensive children education, inflation, and improper accommodation were the reasons/ causes which ultimately deflated the teacher's interest in providing quality education. Social factor turned out to be the third major factor responsible for squeezing the standard of university education. Intensified nepotism and corruption, regionalism, and entry of mediocres in teaching turned to be major features of social factor. Psychological, political and other miscellaneous factors were placed 4th, 5th and 6th in the overall ranking of factors. Personal tensions, increasing conflicts in the families and with colleagues, ingress of politics in academics at the time of appointments and promotions, no say of intelligentsia in politics, internal examination system inbreeding, lack of basic research facilities in the institutions, growing indiscipline and decreasing reverence of academic institutions turned out to be the other important reasons undermining the standard of university education.

Suggestions

After going through the whole analysis and reasons given by the respondent-teachers, some suggestions are made which may go a long way in improving the standard of higher education:

(1) Talent and merit must be given due recognition and weightage at the time of appointments in the institutions discarding the 'sons of soil approach'. Political interference should be minimised in the academics.

(2) Teachers doing good work be given some special incentives and encouragement to foster the work culture in the institutions.

(3) Product of an institutions should not be absorbed in the same institution. In case it is absolutely necessary on account of sheer merit, sufficient exposure should be given to the selected candidates in outside institutions.

(4) Economic lot of the teachers should be improved by providing better pay-scale, on campus residences, house building loans at nominal rates of interest, subsidised travel and medical facilities.

(5) Newer dignified modes of judging the teacher's accountability in the system need to be developed. Their longer presence in the department may certainly motivate the younger ones for more hard work.

(6) Methods of teaching should be continuously updated by the teachers to make the lectures effective. Use of audio-visual aids, practical demonstrations, field-trips and other innovative teaching techniques can go a long way in improving the standard of education. Therefore, better physical facilities, *i.e.* latest equipments, computers, books, journals and other helping material should be adequately provided.

(7) External examinations must form an essential component of the student's evaluation.

(8) Policy of higher education must lay stress on quality. Unplanned and mushrooming growth of educational institutions should be stopped.

Note: Since, internal examination system prevails in PAU, the findings may vary to a certain extent as compared with other universities.

Acknowledgement: Help rendered by Satnam Kaur, Deep Kamal and Ramandeep towards data collection is gratefully acknowledged.

REFERENCES

Arora, G.S. (1998), Higher Education As a Demerit Good: A Misconceived Move, *University News*, 36(24) June 15.

Bakshi, Gowardhan Lal (1977), *Towards Better Education*, S. Chand & Co., New Delhi, pp. 9-25.

Bhandari, Arvind (1999), Declining Standard of Higher Education, *The Tribune*, June 17th.

Conover. W.J. (1971), *Practical Non-parametric Statistics*, John Wiley & Sons, New York, p. 270.

Desai, A.S. (1998), Government Subsidies for Higher Education, *University News*, 36(24) June 15.

Desai, B.H. Brahmabhatt, A.L. and Pathak, V.A. (1987), Teacher in Higher Education, *University News*, April 20 pp. 6-25.

Deshpande, A.L. (1991), Improving teaching in Higher Education, *University News*, Dec. 16, pp. 29-30.

Faruqui, M.N. & Quereshi, I.A. (1994), Higher Education in India, *University News*, June 6 pp. 1-9.

Gupta, J.P. & Saini S.S. (1988), *Introduction to Statistical Methods*, Kalyani Publishers, New Delhi.

Hommadi, A.H. (1985), *Higher Education in Third World*, Indian Bibliographics Bureau & Balaji Enterprises, Delhi.

Joshi, Ram (1980), *Three Aspects of University Education*, Association of Indian University, New Delhi.

Kanpur, J.N. (1977), *Current Issues in World Higher Education*, S. Chand & Co., New Delhi, pp. 3-5.

Mohanty, Sunil Behari (1995), *Improving University and College Teaching*, A.P.H Publishing Corp., New Delhi, pp. 1-35.

Report *Human Resource Development*, (1997), Ministry of HRD, Govt. of India.

Singh, Amrik (1985), *Redeeming Higher Education*, Ajanta Pub., Delhi.

Sinha, B.N. (1982), *University Teachers and Their Problems*, Puja Publications, New Delhi.

Srivastava, S.P. (1999), University Education in India: Current Problems and Future Challenges, *University News*, Vol. 37, No.18, May 3.

UNESCO (1965). *Access to Higher Education*, Vol. II, International Association of Universities Belgium, pp. 123, 236.

Venkatachaliah, M.N. (1999), Event of the Century, *University News*, May 3, pp. 37, 18.

5

URBANISATION IN PUNJAB
Pattern and Development

R.S. SANDHU & JASMEET SANDHU

Urbanisation is responsible for the overall development of a nation in general and the economic development in particular. According to the Global Report on Human Settlements (UNCHS, 1996) the countries in the South that urbanized most rapidly in the last two decades are generally also those with most rapid urban economic growth and most of the world's largest cities are in the world's largest economies, which is further evidence of this link between economic wealth and cities.

Later half of the 20th century has been a period of rapid urbanisation in the developing countries. Percentage of urban population in these countries increased from 17 per cent in 1950 to 41.2 per cent in 1995 and it is estimated that there would be 64.6 per cent urban dwellers in 2025 in these countries (UNCHS, 1996). On the other hand, India's urbanisation has not been as rapid as in the other developing countries, but its total urban population has increased four and a half times, *i.e.* from 62.01 millions in 1951 to 285.35 millions in 2001 (Census 2001). Although the percentage increase is small yet the total increase in urban population is significant especially due to its large size and its resultant consequences.

Similarly, Punjab has also passed through the same path as far as urbanisation is concerned. Urbanisation has taken different forms in different parts of the country due to historical, ecological and economic factors and also due to the level of development in each state (Dasgupta, 2000). Certain states such as Tamil Nadu, Maharashtra, Gujarat and Karnataka are more urbanised whereas certain others like Orissa, Bihar and Himachal Pradesh are less urbanised. Therefore, it is pertinent that the processes and patterns of urbanisation in each state must be recognised and analysed. Here, an attempt has been made to understand the level, trend and pattern of urbanisation in Punjab in the last five decades, *i.e.* 1951-2001. The article focuses on the present state of Punjab, which was reorganised in 1966. The data have been gleaned from the secondary sources.

Urbanisation in Punjab

Before initiating any discussion on urbanisation in the state, it is pertinent to note that Punjab has been divided twice in the last 54 years and it lost its two capital cities in these divisions. Firstly, Punjab lost its capital city of Lahore to West Pakistan in 1947 and later on at the time of its reorganisation in 1966, its capital city Chandigarh was declared as a Union Territory. Punjab is one of the smaller but prosperous states in India. Like India, it is also predominantly an agrarian state though its urban sector contributes 58.0 per cent towards its G.D.P. (Statistical Abstracts, Punjab; 1999). According to 2001 Census, Punjab's total population stands at 24,289,296 persons, of which 16,043,730 persons reside in rural areas and 8,245,566 persons in urban areas (Census of India 2001, series 4, Punjab). Accordingly, rural population accounts for 66.05 per cent of the state's population whereas urban population constitutes 33.95 per cent of the total state population.

In 1951 the state's total population was 91.57 lakhs, rural population constituted 72.33 lakhs, *i.e.* 79.0 per cent and urban population was 19.24 lakhs, *i.e.* 21.0 per cent. During the last five decades, *i.e.* from 1951 to 2001, the total population of the state has increased to 242 lakhs, an increase of 165.2 per cent. During the same period rural population increased by 121.8 per cent and urban population by 326.5 per cent. In other words, the increase in rural population in the state during 1951-2001 was about 2.7 times, whereas, the urban population increased more than four time, and the level of urbanisation went up from 21.0 per cent in 1951 to 33.95 per cent in 2001.

Table 5.1 shows that the growth rate of urban population during 1951-1961 was 29.06 per cent, which was higher than the growth rate of India's urban population. In the next three decades growth rate of urban population in Punjab remained lower than the all India growth rate. The urban growth rate of the state during 1961-71, 1971-81 and 1981-91 was 25.27 per cent, 44.51 per cent and 29.11 per cent respectively. The lower growth rate of urban population in Punjab during 1961-91 can be due to two reasons. Firstly, Punjab is an agricultural state and the period between 1961-71 and afterwards was period of green revolution in which the rural areas prospered and many small service towns developed which usually supported agricultural and allied activities. These towns usually have lower growth rate as compared to the industrial towns because they mainly perform central place functions for their hinterland. D'Souza (1976) observed that there was functional change of towns in Punjab during 1961-71 rather than higher growth rate of urban population. Another reason for the lower growth rate of urban population in the state was lack of development of industrial towns because of the Punjab Government's policies favouring rural development. Moreover, agricultural development was also more or less uniformly spread in different regions of the state (Bhalla and Chadha, 1981).

Table 5.1: Urbanization in Punjab and India during 1951-2001

Year	*Total Urban Population (in Lakhs)*	*Percentage of Urban Population*		*Growth Rate of Urban Population*		*No. of Towns*
	Punjab	*Punjab*	*India*	*Punjab*	*India*	
1951	19.24	21.0	17.29	20.02	41.42	98
1961	25.58	22.9	17.97	29.06	26.06	106
1971	32.16	23.7	19.41	25.27	38.23	108
1981	46.47	26.1	23.34	44.51	46.34	134
1991	60.01	29.7	25.72	28.45	39.19	120
2001	82.45	33.95	27.78	37.58	31.13	157

Source: Census of India 2001, Series-4, Punjab, Provisional Population Totals, Paper-2 of 2001, Rural-Urban Distribution of Population. Govt. of India, New Delhi, p.27.

Table 5.1 further reveals that during 1991-2001 the urban population of Punjab grew at the rate of 37.58 per cent and this growth rate was higher than the growth rate for India (31.31 %). During this decade there was tremendous increase in number of towns, *i.e.* from 120 in 1991 to 157 in 2001. 41 new towns, were declared for the first time and few old towns were merged with urban agglomerations. So, there was a net addition of 37 towns in this decade. Another important feature of this decade (1991-2001) was the higher growth rate of urban population in the state than the national average. The new towns added about one-fifth (4.4 lakhs) of additional urban population. In 2001 Amritsar city joined Ludhiana as another metropolitan city of the state. In all, class one cities constituted about three-fifths of the total urban population, class II and

III towns together constituted 29.00 per cent of the total population. There was slight decrease in the population in these towns although their number increased. Similarly, Class IV, V and VI towns also increased in number but their share of urban population decreased.

From the above discussion it can be concluded that in the last 50 years (1951-2001) in Punjab, the level of urbanisation has increased by 13 per cent only, whereas urban population has increased more than four times and the number of towns has also increased by 60 per cent (98 to 157) during the same period.

After knowing the increase in level of urbanisation and increase in total urban population in the state, it is pertinent to know how this increase has been distributed in different geographical regions of the state and in different classes of towns in the state.

Pattern of Urbanisation

Geographical Distribution

The pattern of geographical distribution of the urban population in the state is reflected in Map 1. It depicts the level of urbanisation and concentration of urban population in the districts of Punjab. It shows that there is a marked disparity among the districts of Punjab as far as the level of urbanisation is concerned. According to census 2001, Ludhiana district tops in the level of urbanisation and it has more than one-half of its population (55.80 %) residing in urban areas. Nawanshahar is the least urbanised district of the state and it has just one-seventh of its population (13.80 per cent) living in the urban areas. Besides Ludhiana, three other districts which have higher level of urbanisation than the state average are, Jalandhar (47.45 %), Amritsar (40.00 %) and Patiala (34.98 %). These are the districts through which National Highway No.1 (G.T. Road) passes. These four districts accommodate more than one-half (54.46 %) of the state's total urban population. There are two other districts, namely, Fatehgarh and Kapurthala, which are also located on the National Highway No.1, but their level of urbanisation is less than the state and they accommodate only 5 per cent of the state's total urban population. These six districts also form a contiguous belt that divides the state into three broad regions, namely, North Eastern Punjab, Central Punjab and South-western Punjab accommodating 15 per cent, 60 per cent and about 25 per cent of urban population respectively. The central Punjab is the most urbanised of the three regions and all the major cities of the state, namely, Ludhiana, Jalandhar, Amritsar and Patiala are in this region.

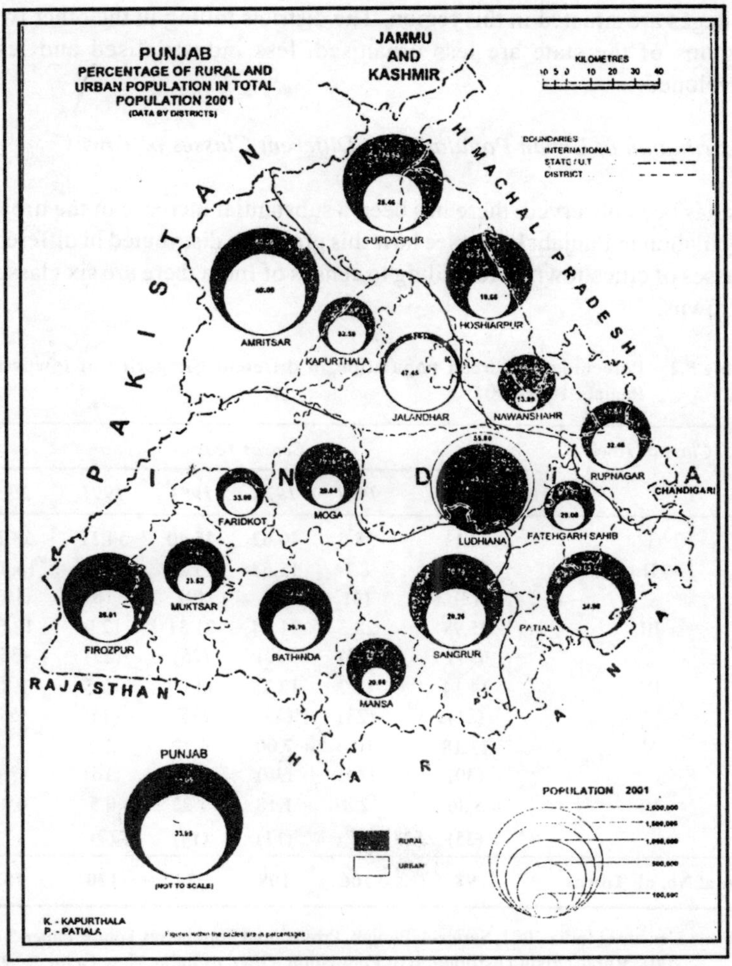

Map I: Punjab: Percentage of Rural and Urban Population

As has been stated earlier, urbanisation and development share a positive relationship. Similarly, the most urbanised region, *i.e.* the central region, is also the most developed region of Punjab. This region is also more industrialised as compared to the other two regions of the state and is the most important region for socio-cultural and economic activities. All the four universities of the state and main medical and engineering colleges are situated in this region. The districts falling in the other two regions of the state are less urbanised, less industrialised and less developed.

Distribution of Urban Population in Different Classes of Towns

As has been observed, there has been a substantial increase in the urban population in Punjab. Let us see how this growth is distributed in different classes of cities/towns. According to census of India there are six classes of towns.

Table 5.2: Percentage of urban population in different categories of towns in Punjab: 1951-2001

Class of Town	*Census Year*					
	1951	*1961*	*1971*	*1981*	*1991*	*2001*
I	33.11	38.5	40.62	45.40	54.31	58.39
II	7.73	8.1	15.68	13.28	19.8	16.46
	(2)	(4)	(8)	(9)	(18)	(19)
III	25.98	28.3	21.74	21.31	12.9	12.50
	(17)	(23)	(22)	(28)	(25)	(35)
IV	14.14	11.2	13.78	11.07	10.5	9.82
	(21)	(23)	(33)	(35)	(44)	(54)
V	13.18	10.0	7.00	6.72	2.0	2.52
	(30)	(34)	(30)	(41)	(16)	(28)
VI	5.36	2.8	1.18	1.22	0.5	0.33
	(25)	(17)	(11)	(14)	(7)	(7)
Total No. of Towns	**98**	**106**	**108**	**134**	**120**	**157**

Source: Census of India 2001, Series-4, Punjab, Provisional Population Totals, Paper-2 of 2001, Rural-Urban Distribution of Population, Govt. of India, New Delhi, p. 27.

Table 5.2 presents number of towns of different classes in Punjab and the percentage distribution of urban population in these towns (class-wise) for the six census years, *i.e.* 1951, 1961, 1971, 1981, 1991 and

2001. It shows that in 1951, there were 98 towns in the state. There were 3 class I cities, namely, Amritsar, Jalandhar and Ludhiana accommodating one-third (33.11 %) of the total urban population, another one- third (33.71 %) of the population was accommodated in 19 class II and III towns, and remaining one-third (32.68 %) of the total urban population of the state was accommodated in 76 class IV, V and VI towns. This pattern of urbanisation showed the even distribution of population in cities of different classes, which is usually found in agricultural surplus states and it tends to promote more equal distribution of urban population than that based on industrialisation.

During the decade 1951-61, the towns of first three classes (class I, II and III) gained in number as well as in the proportion of the urban population accommodated in these towns. On the other hand class IV, V and VI towns of the state mainly lost in terms of proportion of the total urban population in these towns and it decreased from 32.68 per cent in 1951 to 24.8 per cent 1961. The total number of towns also went up from 98 to 106 in this decade but this increase was pocketed by the upper three classes of towns. Situation did not change much in the next decade (1961-71).

The number of towns/urban agglomerations increased from 105 to 134 during 1971-81 due to the creation of 29 new towns in 1981. Subsequently in 1991, 21 of these towns were declassified and 7 new towns were created. As such there was a net loss of 14 towns, *i.e.* the number decreased from 134 in 1981 to 120 in 1991. Table 5.2 also shows that in 1991, class I cities increased in number from 4 to 10 and that these cities also increased their share of urban population from 45.62 per cent in 1981 to 54.31 per cent in 1991. The number of class II towns also increased from 9 to 18 and these towns also gained in terms of their share of urban population. In 1991, 28 class I and II cities and towns of the state together accounted for three-fourths (74.15 %) of the total urban population. On the other hand remaining four classes of towns (class III to VI), which contained 43.70 per cent of the total urban population in 1971, had only 25.85 per cent of the urban population in 1991.

There was tremendous increase in the number of towns in the state during 1991-2001. Their number went up from 120 in 1991 to 157 in 2001. This increase was observed in all the classes of towns except the class VI towns. 41 new towns were declared in the 2001 census for the first time, few old towns were merged with the urban agglomerations and there was a net addition of 37 towns in this decade.

Another feature of this decade (1991-2001) was the higher growth rate of urban population in the state as compared to the national average. The new towns added about one-fifth (4.4 lakhs) of additional urban population. In 2001, Amritsar city also joined Ludhiana city as another metropolitan city of the state. Class I cities had about three-fifth (58.39 %) of the total urban population. Class II and III towns (54 in number) had 29 per cent of the total urban population of the state. There was slight decrease in the proportion of urban population in these towns but their number increased from 43 in 1991 to 54 in 2001. Similarly, number of class IV, V and VI towns also increased but their share of urban population decreased.

Punjab's urban pattern presents a sharp contrast to that of monocentric urbanisation in the states of Maharashtra and West Bengal, where a single metropolis dominates the scene of the state (Dasgupta, 2000). Here, it is spatially dispersed and the biggest city of the state accounts for only one-sixth of the urban population of the state. However, in last few decades the trend is towards the concentration of population in class one cities. At present class one cities accommodate three-fifths of urban population whereas in 1951 they were accommodating only one-third of it. This tendency towards concentration of urban population in big cities could be attributed to increasing inequality in the villages, resulting from the deployment of capital by rich farmers in the cities. The major cities and the developed region of the state are attracting more migrants both from within the state and out of the state which is evident from higher sex ratio in Ludhiana city. It had 189612 total migrants in 1991 out of which about 50 per cent were from within the state and remaining were from other states and other countries (Singh, 2001). Now, industrialisation is also an important factor in the urbanising process.

Urban Development in Punjab

In the preceding analysis it has been observed that in the last 50 years urban population in the state has increased four times whereas population of the state has increased only two and half times (from 91 millions in 1951 to 242 millions in 2001). Cities of the state had inadequate infrastructure and substantial increase in the population could not be accommodated in a planned manner. This has resulted in uncontrolled and haphazard growth, non-conforming land use, excessive strain on urban roads, utilities, services and facilities, substandard and unhygienic buildings, housing shortage, traffic congestion and overall deterioration of the urban environment. In the absence of any urban policy and comprehensive planning legislation in the state, this type of urban development was inevitable. Draft master plans were prepared for 35 towns/cities in the state in the seventies but their non-statutory status made them ineffective. According to a report (1974) of the State Town and Country Planning Department, in Ludhiana, Amritsar and Jalandhar cities, the percentage of planned developed area was only 21.93 per cent, 26.0 per cent and 26.3 per cent respectively. Further, this report revealed that as much as 15 per cent to 20 per cent area under development was without any basic services or amenities whatsoever. Around 30 to 40 per cent of the urban area was with water supply and sewerage system and 40 to 55 per cent was without sewerage system. The situation has not improved much since then, rather it has deteriorated. To present the up-to-date scene of the state of urban development in one of the most populous city of Punjab, *i.e.* Ludhiana, former Urban Development Minister of India (Jagmohan, 1998) made the following comments:

> "Its present population exceeds 1.5 million. It is the biggest money spinner in Punjab and a hosiery capital of the country. Its annual production in this area alone is about 10 billion. And yet it is a city which has 50 per cent of its structures raised without any planning or regulation. About 40 per cent of the population has no access to piped water-supply and 65 per cent has no access to modern sanitary facilities. The level of air pollution is four times more than the toleration limit."

Another interesting feature of urbanisation in Punjab is higher incidence of urban poverty compared to the rural poverty. It is believed that in India there is a higher incidence of poverty in the rural areas and urban poverty is largely a spill over of the rural poverty. Urban poor are actually rural poor who have migrated to urban centres to escape starvation in the countryside. But in Punjab there is higher incidence of poverty in the urban areas as compared to the rural areas and spill over thesis does not hold good in the state. Further, it has been observed that the incidence of rural poverty has always been lower than the urban poverty and that the rural poverty has also been declining at a faster rate than the urban poverty. As a result, the incidence of rural poverty in Punjab has now reached almost a negligible magnitude. In mid-sixties the proportion of urban population below poverty line (48.07%) was less than double the proportion of rural poverty but in early nineties the same was more than three times the proportion of rural poverty (Shergill and Singh, 1998). It will not be wrong to say that there is concentration of poverty in urban areas.

According to census 2001, about one-fifth population of 28 towns lives in slums. But this proportion varies from town to town. *The Tribune* (Chawla, 1997) conducted a survey of slums in the towns of Punjab. It reveals that in Ludhiana city, there were 300 densely populated unauthorised colonies. These were devoid of basic amenities like potable water, sewerage and roads. According to a survey by the Municipal Corporation, there were about 200 small and big slums having more than 50 per cent of the total population. In addition to these slums and unauthorised colonies there were about 20,000 *Jhuggies* which completely lack basic infrastructure. Similarly in Amritsar city there were 200 unauthorised colonies (Bhanwar, 1997). According to the Corporation records, 80 unauthorised colonies have come into existence in the last seven years. There were 52 notified slums, which have 1.5 lakh population. It was true for other cities of the state. Quality of life deteriorates with the size of the city and proportion of slum population is directly related with the size of the city. The unplanned development and the slum population are increasing in a big way because the efforts made by the local and state governments are too meagre to tackle the problem (Sandhu, 1995). Saini (1991) reports that despite huge investments in services through the environmental improvement of Urban Slum Programme, hardly one-third of the slum population in Ludhiana has benefited. It has been noted (Saini 1991 and Sandhu 1995) that objective criteria for the identification and delimitation of the slums are not followed and this consequently leads to the identification of non-slum areas as slums under political pressure and on the other hand real slums are not notified.

Sahota (1996) estimated that housing shortage in the state would be around 6.5 lakh units by the year 2000. Housing provided by the public agencies contributed only 10 per cent to the new housing stock. Sahota's study further reveals that even Punjab Urban Planning and Development Authority (PUDA), the premier public agency that build houses for the urban poor, allocates no more than 6.8 per cent of its resources to shelter the critically urban poor (E.W.S.). Nearly three quarters of its resources go to the housing for the non-poor. He further writes that none of the public corporations and institutions assisting housing in Punjab satisfies any of the efficient criteria in terms of profit, administrative expenses, subsidisation, rates of recovery of loans etc. Sahota recommends that government agencies should get out of the business of constructing houses, townships and urban estates and leave the field for private sector.

An analysis of the level of services in the Punjab towns shows that nearly one-half of the urban households do not have tap water supply within their premises, about one-third are without the toilet facility and about one-seventh of them have to do without electricity (Krishan, 1994).

Punjab has been an agriculturally dominated economy, and the agriculture sector gets the lion's share of funds for development. However, recent data reveal that now urban sector is contributing 58.0 per cent of the total G.D.P. of the state (Statistical Abstract of Punjab, 1999). Information relating to the financing of urban development in the last three five-year plans narrates its own story. During the 6th, 7th and 8th five-year plans, urban development got only Rs.27 crores, Rs. 41 crores and Rs.188 crores respectively, which forms only 2 to 3 per cent of the total outlay of the plans.

Conclusion

From above discussion it can be concluded that there has been urban growth rather than the urban development in the state of Punjab as it has been unplanned and haphazard. As a result quality of urban life has deteriorated. The state seems to be unconcerned about it and is only taking the *ad hoc* measures. State has already enacted Punjab Regional Town Planning Act and it is envisaged that it would help in planning and development but this can happen only if it is handled properly and implemented effectively. Punjabis wake up only when crises overtake them. It is also the case with the urban development. Now state has admitted the unmanageable situations in Ludhiana and other cities of Punjab and state is eager to prepare comprehensive development plan for Ludhiana and wants to take it on top priority (*Tribune*, 1997). But these are only *ad hoc* measures. The state should act in a systematic way. First of all, for the state, where land is scarce and which is now on the threshold of industrialisation, process of urbanisation and urban development needs to be carefully and dispassionately studied.

The state must formulate its urbanisation, urban and regional development strategy that should control all developmental activities on a long-term basis. Cities have an affirmative and constructive role to play in a society. Instead of opting for popular measures which could not be sustained for the healthy development of cities, the state must provide good governance to realise the potential contributions of cities and towns for the economic and social development of the state. If the state government and other stake holders do not intervene immediately and effectively, then, the urban environment is likely to deteriorate further in future and our cites would virtually become unliveable.

REFERENCES

Bhanwar, H.S. (1997), "Civic Agencies Working at Crossroad," *the Sunday Tribune*, 26 January.

Bhalla, G.S. and G.K. Chadha, (1981), *Structural Change in Income Distribution – A Study of the Impact of Green Revolution in the Punjab,* Centre for the Study of Regional Development, J.N.U., New Delhi.

Bhatia, Surjit Singh, (1979), "Azadi pichon Punjab de Sehran da Vikas", *Smajak Vigyan Pattar*, No. 10.

Chawla, K.S., (1997), "Illegal Colonies Sprout in Industrial Hub", *The Tribune*, 23 January.

Census of India 2001 "Series-4, Punjab Provisional Population Total, Paper-2 of 2001, Rural-Urban Distribution of Population, New Delhi.

'Dasgupta, Biplab, (2000), "Contrasting Urban Patterns: West Bengal, Punjab and Kerala", in Amitabh Kundu (ed.) *Inequality, Mobility and Urbanisation: China and India*, Manak, Publication, New Delhi.

D'Souza Victor S. (1976), "Green Revolution and Urbanisation in Punjab during 1961-71", in S. Manzor Alam and V.V. Pokshishevsky (eds.), *Urbanisation in Developing Countries*, Osmania University, Hyderabad.

Govt. of Punjab, (2000), *Statistical Abstract of Punjab (1999)*, Govt. Press, Chandigarh.

Govt. of Punjab, (1974), *Integrated City Development Programmes Ludhiana (1974-79), Amritsar (1976-77 – 1980-81) and Jalandhar (1976-77 – 1980-81)*, Town and Country Planning Department, Chandigarh.

Krishan, Gopal (1994), "Major Urbanisation Issues in Context of Emerging Punjab Situation", Mimeograph, Panjab University, Chandigarh.

Sahota, S.S., (1997), "Public Housing in Punjab", *Indian Express*, March 9.

Saini, L.D., (1991), *Slums in an Industrial City: Case Study of Ludhiana*, Ph.D. Thesis submitted at Punjab University, Chandigarh.

Sandhu, R.S., (1995), "The Infrastructure Development in Slums: an Experience of a Medium Size City in Punjab", *Integrated Urban Infrastructure Development: Seminar Papers*, HSMI, New Delhi.

Sandhu, R.S. and Jasmeet Sandhu, (1999), "Punjab Vich Sehrikaran Ate Sehri Vikas: Vratman Ate Bhivikh", *Smajak Vigyan Pattar*, No. 44-45-46, June-December 1998.

Shergill, H.S. and Gurmail Singh, (1998), "Urban Poverty in Punjab: Trend over 1964-65/1990-91 Period", Presented at a Seminar on Urban Development and Role of Elected Representatives, organised by Institute for Development and Communication, Chandigarh.

Singh, Surjit, (2001), "Regional Migration in India: Some Issues for Urbanisation", in R.S. Sandhu, Sarup Singh and Jasmeet Sandhu (eds.), *Sustainable Human Settlements: The Asian Experience*, Rawat Publication, Jaipur.

The Tribune, (1997), "Plan to Resuscitate Ludhiana", September 3.

UNCHS, (1996), *An Urbanising World: Global Report on Human Settlements*, 1996, Oxford University Press, Oxford.

6

RESERVATION AND PROTECTIVE JUSTICE

MANMOHAN S. GILL

The universal concept of justice in human societies is based on matching of rewards to person's investment and cost or one's investment and contributions. In the traditional Indian socio-cultural context, acquired characteristics like gender, age, caste and so on have been considered as legitimate contributions as compared to the achievements of persons which are becoming a part of the modern secular societies. Homan's (1961) refers this to a theory of distributive justice. The essence of such social justice lies with the way a society allocates its resources to its members. When such ways are perceived as unfair, they lead to negative outcomes. So, acceptance of the norms of distribution of resources is indicative of a harmonious state of affairs and lack of inter-group conflicts. Equality on the other hand, refers to equal distribution irrespective of the amount of contribution. This norm stands out as the highest norm. So as to allocate the resources equitably among the various groups irrespective of superior-subordinate order, the equality norm is related to social justice.

The basis of superior-subordinate can be traced to the steeply hierarchical caste structure in which the lower castes have remained underprivileged and been exploited by those at the top. These oppressed and exploited groups cannot compete with the advanced sections of the society and hence, need protection. Ambedkar has emphasized that certain political rights alone do not constitute the basis of liberty, justice, equality, natural rights, and the rule of law, emphasis has to be laid on social relationships. These objectives can be achieved by providing reservation on the basis of caste. To uplift the poor and the underprivileged in a general process by devising systems for their entry into the realm of equality—the highest norm—has been the first priority of the democratic and secular government. For this, the Constitution of India provides special provisions relating to certain classes of people, namely, the Scheduled Castes, Scheduled Tribes and Anglo-Indians under Articles 16(4) and 335 but no such provision has been made for the vast majority of the Backward classes except under Article 340 where the term socially and educationally backward classes appears. For the welfare of these classes, first commission was set up in 1953 (Kalelkar Commission) and second in 1980 (Mandal Commission). Both the commissions admit that dominating castes are occupying the key points in the society and controlling the destiny of the people. Therefore, reservation is a necessity to uplift these socially and educationally backward classes. This paper attempts to answer the question: Can historical social injustice be removed through the reservation?

Further, backwardness may be expressed in terms of inadequate opportunities of self-development for groups or individuals, especially in economic life and in matters of health, housing, and education. This can be measured from the level of income, extent of literacy, and standard of life. Welfare policy for the Scheduled Castes and backward classes assumes that their backwardness can be removed through it. Reservation is a device to eliminate backwardness arising out of historical conditions of social injustice in which certain groups are located (Sheth, 1987). Reservation helps the struggling groups to regain the lost manhood and human rights (Pawar, 1990). Social reformers like Ambedkar and Sanjivayya Reddy advocated social equality but not at the cost of others or at least at the cost of national interest. Contrarily, Henry (1993) points out that the elite who is by and large from the higher castes fills most of the top positions. Further, the move for privatization on large scale will reduce even the small component of total employment (3 %) in future and will further expose them (Scheduled Castes and backward classes) to the discrimination in the private sector (Thorat, 1998). In this way, the already underprivileged groups will be further marginalised with the process of privatization under new economic policy. An affirmative action through reservation may provide opportunities to discriminated groups to develop capabilities and skills for the emerging society. Through this paper, efforts will be made to understand the attitude of various caste-groups towards the reservation policy.

Objectives

The objectives of the study are as follows:

(i) Reservation policy is a mean to give social justice to the oppressed sections of the society; and
(ii) Reservation on caste lines does not create unequal opportunities for different caste-groups.

Methodology

The study was conducted in the Jalandhar city of Punjab State. In the beginning, efforts were made to gather information on the caste line but due to non-availability of Census data on caste, snowball technique was employed to collect information according to the objectives of the study. In all, 120 respondents belonging to different caste-groups in equal number were interviewed with the help of a pre-tested structured schedule.

Results and Discussion

In addition to reservation policy existing for the Scheduled Castes and Scheduled Tribes, Mandal Commission has recommended reservation to the tune of 27 per cent for the backward classes. Government of India has accepted this recommendation with hesitation after the decision of the Supreme Court in its favour. Khan (1986), Ramaiah (1990), Sheth (1987) and others have supported such reservation for the Scheduled Castes and backward classes. They hold that reservation policy is an affirmative state of action to correct society's negative discrimination against the most disadvantageous groups. Parvathama (1986) argues that continued process of social change through reservation will essentially replace the ascriptive status to achieved one. Contrary to it, Maurya (1999) concludes that in spite of constitutional safeguards and state intervention in favour of the Dalits, their socio-economic condition is deteriorating and the dream of social and economic equality is still a mirage for them. Gill (1989) finds that caste stigma pervades the whole system of our society through reservation. It creates heart burning, jealousy, and frustration among caste Hindus.

In spite of above observation, the respondents in majority hold that through reservation, the political leaders and their kin have been and will be benefited 48.3 % (Table 6.1).

Table 6.1: Attitude towards reservation policy

Attitude	*Caste category*			*Total*
	Scheduled Castes	*Backward Castes*	*Upper Castes*	
Political leaders and their kin will benefit	20 (50.0)	28 (70.0)	10 (25.0)	58 (48.3)
Incompetent, less qualified join service	—	4 (10.0)	18 (45.0)	22 (18.3)
Lead to caste conflicts	4 (10.0)	2 (5.0)	12 (30.0)	18 (15.0)
Improve social and economic status of SC	16 (40.0)	6 (15.0)	—	22 (18.3)
Total	40 (33.3)	40 (33.3)	40 (33.3)	120 (99.9)

The real suffers that is, socially, educationally, and economically backward caste-groups will continue to live a life of misery even with such reservation. Only 18.3 per cent of the respondents hold that policy will improve the socio-economic status of the backward classes. Nearly 18 per cent of the respondents feel that incompetent persons who can manipulate politically will come to occupy positions of importance in society and they will be reaping the fruits of reservation by getting into the service sector. Reservation policy has another negative consequence that it will lead to caste conflicts and caste struggle thereby, jeopardizing the harmonious social system (15.0%). In other words, as competition of contributions is substituted by preferential treatment, it changes patterned functional requisites and thus, tensions and strains are generated in the social system. The outburst at the time of acceptance of recommendations and even afterwards strikes and *dharnas* seem to have their genesis in the changed pattern of functional requisites. Even the prejudicial behaviour adopted by the upper castes against the backward and Scheduled Castes may be attributed to the reservation policy. The movement some attempts is initiated to ameliorate the position of the exploited minority, the majority feels threatened. So as to safeguard its interests, the majority react in the form of manifest actions such as agitation, strikes, etc. (Bains, 1994).

Among the backward castes, 70 per cent respondents hold that politician and their kin will be the beneficiaries of the reservation. The real target group will remain high and dry: 50.0 per cent of the Scheduled Castes and 25.0 per cent of the upper castes shares this opinion. The Scheduled Castes respondents do not accept the idea upheld by 10.0 and 45.0 per cent of the backward and upper castes respectively that reservation is a mean to bring forward the incompetent, incapable, and undeserving persons. On the other hand, 40.0 and 15.0 per cent of the Scheduled Castes and backward castes respectively think that this policy is a mean to improve the social and economic status of the backward castes. Further, most of the upper castes (30.0 %), some of the Scheduled Castes (5.0%) consider that the reservation policy has generated caste struggle and caste conflicts. As a result, social disorganization is taking place as change in the 'part' has its ramification for the 'whole' society. This speaks of the attitude of upper castes towards reservation policy that try to rectify both the numerical and qualitative inadequacy of representation of these sections and a step towards improvement of socio-economic status of the backward classes.

Under the present circumstances, what should be the appropriate course of action? Most of the respondents state that reservation should be given in the field of education and that too, at the time of entry (78.3 per cent, Table 6.2). They should also be helped through stipends, fellowships, and fee concession (93.5 %). In addition, preference may be given for admission to professional and technical courses (70.0%). Reservation at the time of entry to service and in promotion is acceptable to only 36.7 per cent of the respondents. A few states that there should be no reservation (5.0%) and all of them are members of the upper castes.

Table 6.2: Level of reservation

Level	*Caste category*			*Total*
	Scheduled Castes	*Backward Castes*	*Upper Castes*	
Education (at entry)	40 (100.0)	40 (100.0)	14 (35.0)	94 (78.3)
Stipend/Fellowship/Fee concession	40 (100.0)	40 (100.0)	32 (80.0)	112 (93.3)
Admission to professional courses	40 (100.0)	40 (100.0)	4 (10.0)	84 (70.0)
Service (at entry)	40 (100.0)	6 (15.0)	—	46 (36.7)
In promotion	40 (100.0)	6 (15.0)	—	46 (36.7)
No reservation	—	—	6 (15.0)	6 (5.0)

All of the Scheduled Castes and a few of the backward castes (15.0 %) want reservation in services and in promotion but upper castes do not favour this view. Further, all the Scheduled Castes and backward castes want reservation at the time of admission to professional and technical courses; this view is not acceptable to the upper castes (90.0%). Of course, 80.0 per cent of the upper caste respondents say that to uplift these backward sections of the society, stipend, fellowship and fee concession should be granted liberally. Such a view is upheld by all of the Scheduled and backward caste respondents. Likewise, all of them consider reservation should be applicable in the field of education and that too, at the time of entry. Only 35.0 per cent of the upper castes support this point. This again speaks of the difference in the attitude of upper castes *vis-a-vis* Scheduled and backward castes. The former wants to restrict their entry in the field of professional education and services whereas the latter are trying their best to enter into such avenues which help them to gain status and become a part of the industrial structure of the society. Sengupta and Singh (1999) hold that education will atleast suppress the felling of relative deprivation existing among Scheduled Castes. Jain's (1993) argument "education alone would not help in improving the morale of the backward classes; Government services in India carry high prestige and by giving government employment to backward classes, you immediately raise their social status", supports the above view point.

Commission has recommended vocational training for backward classes in technical and professional institutions with financial support to establish them in industrial and business sector. The respondents have supported such move. But the fact is that for village artisans, a big chunk of the other backward classes, there are provisions under IRDP and TRYSEM schemes for setting up industrial/business unit along with training facilities. The evaluation reports highlight the shortcomings as well as financial and administrative snags of such programmes. Maurya and Shrivastava (1999) observe that despite the training under various schemes, the Scheduled Caste entrepreneurs were unable to meet the family requirements through self-employment. Gill (1990) finds that the development with social justice helps economic mobility but not social mobility. Ritual status still defines one's social position in the society. Sachchidanand (1977) holds that the economic elevation helps the depressed classes to come out of their position of subjugation at the hands of economically well-off but it does not bury caste sentiments (Ghanshyam Shah, 1985). So even with economic mobility, structural change leading to social and cultural equality is not possible. On the other hand, opportunities for career advancement will help in breaking the stream of hierarchy based on statuses (Indersen, 1993). Teleologically, these caste groups have to exploit their lower position till society breaks its ascriptive hierarchies and put premium on the capabilities and qualities of the individual by creating healthy opportunities for social and economic mobility.

Theoretically, such mobility is possible in the middle range of the caste hierarchy through the process of sanskritization or acquisition of skills, which help to gain better status. Unless, conducive conditions for equality of opportunities are not provided, structural inequalities and backwardness of lower castes will continue.

In order to guarantee entry of backward classes into the egalitarian structure of the society, the Constitution of India through Articles 15(4) and 16(4) favours preferential treatment for backward classes to achieve equality whereas through Article 16 equality of opportunities in matters of employment or appointment to any office under the State is granted. This article forbids discrimination against any citizen on the ground only of religion, race, caste, sex, descent, place of birth, or residence or any of them. Both the provisions confuse the ideology of the masses. In the study, majority of the respondents (70.7%) states that Constitution provides for equality of opportunities but through the reservation policy unequal opportunity structure is promoted (Table 6.3).

Contrary to it, 29.3 per cent states that reservation for specific castes does not create unequal opportunities. Of those who states that Constitution provides for unequal opportunity structure, 15.6 per cent accepts that reservation policy on the basis of caste increases the extent of already existing inequality. So far as the question of inequality promoted through reservation is concerned, the respondents equally favour and disfavour it.

Scheduled Caste respondents assert that Constitution has provisions of preferential treatment and cannot be said to create inequality or disparity. Therefore, to state that reservation creates unequal opportunity structure will be wrong. Upper castes and backward class respondents emphasize that Constitution accepts equality of opportunities for all but this policy has encouraged inequality and disparity (82.5 and 80.0% respectively). Further, none of the upper caste respondents accepts that Constitution has in its scope a provision for unequal opportunity structure. Nearly 37 per cent of the backward caste respondents state that Constitutional provisions have created unequal opportunity positions for different groups, so as to state that reservation promotes inequality will be wrong (53.3%); but it certainly do so in the view of 46.7 per cent of the backward caste respondents (Table 6.3). From the above analysis, it becomes clear that Constitutional provisions are viewed differently.

The general Indian perception is rooted in the ideology of caste with religious and social sanctions and form part of their social conditions. As such structural change to eliminate or reduce structural inequalities is not possible. All the upper caste respondents and majority of the backward

Table 6.3: Equality and reservation

Constitution grants equality	*Reservation promotes inequality*											
	SC			*BC*			*UC*			*Total*		
	Yes	*No*	*Total*	*Yes*	*No*	*Total*	*Yes*	*No*	*Total*	*Yes*	*No*	*Total*
Yes	—	10 (100)	10 (25.0)	20 (80.0)	5 (20.0)	25 (62.5)	33 (82.5)	7 (17.5)	40 (100.0)	53 (70.7)	22 (29.3)	75 (62.5)
No	—	30 (100.0)	30 (75.0)	7 (46.7)	8 (53.3)	15 (37.5)	—	—	—	7 (15.6)	38 (84.4)	45 (37.5)
Total		40 (100.0)	40 (100.0)	27 (67.5)	13 (32.5)	40 (100.0)	33 (82.5)	7 (17.5)	40 (100.0)	60 (50.0)	60 (50.0)	120 (100.0)

SC = Scheduled Castes
BC = Backward Castes
UC = Upper Castes

castes respondents hold that the basic structural form of Indian society has its roots in caste system. They further state that political parties use such gimmicks to keep themselves in power. So long the political parties overtly or covertly use caste, as a mean to gain power, structural change is not possible. In other words, structural change to reduce inequalities depends upon the ideology supported by the dominant ruling groups. These ruling groups try to propagate that ideology whose basis lies in traditional and religious maintenance and seeks loyalty from the subordinate groups. Subordinate groups since have no ideology of their own, draw their moral and social values from the ideology of the ruling or dominant groups or upper castes. Scheduled Caste respondents and some of the backward caste respondents state that now we are given certain preferences on the basis of our caste, the upper castes should have no reason to grumble. Government through these provisions is trying to ameliorate the conditions of the Scheduled Castes and backward classes and such provisions ought to reduce their exploitation at the hands of superordinate groups. These groups state that reservation policy has increased their consciousness with regard to their caste position. In other words, the subordinate groups are accepting that ideology which justifies their subordinate status in the society. So, only that structural change is possible which serves the political, economic, and social objectives of the upper and ruling castes.

Conclusion

The analysis reveals that reservation policy, of course, is based on caste and caste-based social order but it has provided avenues of social and economic mobility through educational and occupational opportunities to the lower underprivileged castes. The fear of the upper castes that it will leave service sector at the mercy of the incompetent, unqualified, or less qualified and unskilled persons seems to stem from their ideology of caste superiority-inferiority and changing pattern of functional requisites. Evidently, upper castes do not favour reservation in those professional education institutions and service sectors that help the low caste groups to acquire skills necessary for gaining higher status in society.

Further, the politicians and their kin will gain than the deserving ones in their caste category. All caste groups plead that positions in services may be, in due course of time, filled by the less qualified and unskilled kin of the politicians under the garb of reservation policy. This will create unequal opportunity structure for the affluent and less affluent lower castes besides distancing them from other caste groups. Such situation may with the passage of time, lead to polarization of caste groups on increased caste consciousness, thereby, strengthening existing caste conflicts and caste struggles. At least, this will provide leverage to the power brokers to use 'caste' as a mean to gain political power.

The study affirms that structural inequalities created and perpetuated since long cannot be reduced or eliminated through reservation policy. Reservation provides an opportunity to the lower sections of the society to achieve those qualities and attributes on which modern industrial society lays premium. In other words, the lower castes now attain equality and justice denied to them by the upper castes and perpetuated through the socio-religious ideology of 'Karma' and 'Dharma'. So as to bring the lower castes out of their ascriptive syndrome, not making provisions for social justice but education of these groups through reservation, fee concession, stipends, fellowships, etc. has been advocated. This will at least reduce the feeling of relative deprivation besides covering the grounds for real phenomenon of deprivation (as exist in society) through increased level of consciousness and rationality. Such increased level of education inevitably helps one to command means to one's satisfaction despite poverty and adversity. It will also help in self-emancipation and empowerment.

A general opinion that seems to emerge is that Constitution guarantees equal rights to all but reservation provisions create unequal opportunity structure for different groups. Another, reservation on the caste line will bring forth the latent struggle among caste groups to its manifest level. Any special programme with the welfare ideology for the backward or Scheduled Castes will put a question on the concept of equality and social justice as provided in the Constitution. In reality, Constitution through reservation attempts to legitimise the idea of social justice to destabilise inequality created under historical conditions. Reservation and welfare measures for the depressed section has led to the polarization of caste groups (already stated) and is much more evident from the emergence of associations like Scheduled Castes Welfare Association, Non-Scheduled Castes Welfare Association, Anti-Mandal Samiti and others. These associations rather than negating the caste system support it by their very objectives either in favour or against preferential treatment on caste line.

Further, equality is pre-requisite of all human societies whereas equality with social justice is the object to claim rational equality. In this percept, Articles 15(4) and 16(4) in the Constitution legitimizes the idea of equality with social justice in favour of lower strata. In spite of this, any action to legitimize 'equality' put a question on 'social justice' and when 'social justice' is legitimized, the notion of 'equality' comes under cloud. In this context, reservation is a balancing act between the idea of equality and the requirement of social justice.

In short, education of the lower sections of the society is the route to their emancipation and empowerment that will strengthen their ability to compete with others without jeopardizing the orderly development of the society. This will enable them to organize and fight their discrimination and subjugation.

REFERENCES

Bains, R.S. (1994), *Reservation Policy and Anti-Reservationists*, B.R. Publishing Corporation, Delhi.

Gill, M.S. & A.M. Singh (1989), "Reactionary Dissent by Caste Hindu Employee", *Social Change*, Vol. 19, No. 3.

Gill, M.S. (1990), "Weaker Sections and Delivery System", *Prajnan*, Vol, xix.

Henry, Joseph (1993), "Reservation, Caste and Social Justice" in *Strategies for Social Justice*, (IIIT, Delhi), Commonwealth Publications, New Delhi.

Homans, G.C. (1961), *Social Behaviour, its Elementary Forms*, Harcourt, New York.

Indersen, P.V. (1993), *A Strategy for Social Justice: An Alternative to Mandal*, in Strategy for Social Justice, Commonwealth Publications, New Delhi.

Jain, C.S. (1993), "Indian Society in Transition", in *Strategy for Social Justice*, Commonwealth Publications, New Delhi.

Khan, M.A. (1986), *Scheduled Castes and their Status in India*, Uppal Publishing House, New Delhi.

Maurya, R.D. (1999), "The Impact of New Economic Policy on the Socio-Economic Development of the Dalits in India", *Ambedkar Journal of Social Development and Justice*, Vol. 7.

Maurya, R.D. & S.K. Shrivastava (1999), "Entrepreneurship Development among the Scheduled Castes and Scheduled Tribes of Rural India", *Ambedkar Journal of Social Development and Justice*, Vol. 7.

Parvathama, C. (1986), "Caste and Backwardness", *Guru Nanak Journal of Sociology*, Vol. 7, No. 2.

Pawar, I.D. (1990), "Reservation and its Justification", *Kranti Jyoti*.

Ramaiah, A. (1990), "Mandal Commission's Recommendations", *Mainstream*, Vol. 18, August.

Sachchidanand (1977), *The Harijan Elite*, Thomson Press (India) Ltd., Faridabad.

Sengupta, M. & R.G. Singh (1999) "Basic Foundation of Dr. Ambedkar's Philosophy", *Ambedkar Journal of Development and Justice*, Vol. 7.

Shah, Ghanshyam (1985), *Caste, Caste Conflict and Reservation*, Ajanta Publications, New Delhi.

Sheth, D.C. (1987), "Reservation Policy Revisited", *Economic and Political Weekly*, Vol. 46, No. 14.

Thorat, Sukhdeo (1998), "New Economic Policy and its Impact on Employment and Poverty of the Scheduled Castes — Some Observations", *Ambedkar Journal of Development and Justice*, Vol. 6.

SECTION–II

AGRARIAN DEVELOPMENT, SOCIAL CHANGE AND GLOBLAIZATION

7

GREEN REVOLUTION AND CHANGING VILLAGE SOCIAL ORGANIZATION

MANMOHAN S. GILL

Agricultural development in India is characterized by a commitment to achieve maximum increase in agricultural output to support an increasing population and industrialization. In the beginning, areas with assured water from rainfall or irrigation facilities were selected for intensive agricultural development. Gradually, this principle was abandoned and planning process was directed towards adoption of better implements and scientific methods to raise crop yields in all types of areas. This economic rationale paid dividend but the real breakthrough came in 1965 in the form of new varieties of wheat and paddy. This was known as "Green Revolution". The application of modern inputs and controlled irrigation helped in raising the agricultural production in Punjab from 2453 thousand metric tonnes of total cereals in 1960-61 to 25166 thousand metric tonnes in 1999-2000. This had made India reliable to such an extent that it can pursue its independent policies. Three factors, namely, useful improved technology, adequate services and supplies through governmental and cooperative institutions and favourable state's policy have realised the importance of rural society besides giving respect to scientists in attaining agricultural efficiency. In Punjab, the outcome is that the average yield of wheat and rice per hectare at present is 4696 and 3347 kg. respectively. Agrarian revolution had brought forward our pessimist, conservative rural society to the level of innovative, adventurous and of course conflicting one. Such a change has its impact on various elements of village social organization. Also, the transformation of farm sector along with mechanization remoulded the structure of rural economy besides creating several complex problems.

Jajmani System

The village economy prior to green revolution was based on mutual help and recognition expressed in the form of Jajmani system within the village and extended beyond the village in the kinship structure through *vartan-bhanji* system. The technological know-how at that time was based on personal knowledge and experiences of cultivating and supporting castes. Through *Jajmani* system, the cultivating castes were helped by other castes in the process of production and in lieu of their services, the former used to lend the latter all possible help in cash as well as in kind. Though this relationship was based on the principle of superordination and subordination (Bieldman, 1959), yet the reciprocity of relationship maintained a kind of corporation between different castes. The relationship had both cooperative and exploitative nature. Gould (1987), Pocock (1962) and others exphasized the ritual aspect of the relationship (from the notion of purity-pollution), thereby relegating the economic aspect to a secondary position. Rao (1962) says that it is imperative to restrict the *Jajmani* system to the economic and ritual service relationships. Other relationships like caste, kinship and tenurial do overlap.

With mechanization and consequent economic development, the nature of *Jajmani* system has undergone changes and its economic and ritual aspects have visibly weakened (Singh, 1994). The social fabrics of this system too have weakened but not completely uprooted. Still, workers are engaged according to *Jajmani* system (Harnek Singh, 1991 : 80). The traditional *Jajmani* castes have not turned their *kamins* but their offsprings do have especially where land has been redistributed among landless labourers or where right of the tenant over land has been confirmed under tenancy acts. Likewise, the *kamins* have turned their *Jajmans* where the offsprings through education have shifted to non-agricultural occupations. For instance, a Brahmin who holds top position in the traditional hierarchical order, could be a *Jajman* as a landlord and *kamin* as a priest, thereby having two different statuses in the same system. Choudhary (1987) finds the same in the villages of Haryana. In the present changed scenario, status is determined more by the role performed rather than the ritual position of the group or individual.

Further, where *kamins* have changed their traditional occupations by joining urban occupational structure or by taking up caste free occupations made available due to the technological development, traditionally ascribed subordinate position in the *Jajmani* system has been challenged or is not accepted. This is what exactly is happening in the rural society. For all kinds of works especially of a specialized nature such as making gold or silver ornaments, bullock cart, tractor trolley, furniture, shoes etc. payments are made generally in cash. It is the market force that enables the individuals to enter into contractual relationship rather than the social relationship, the crux of *Jajmani* system. This shows the changing nature of *Jajmani* system. Of course, traditional social relationship may be a hurdle to change (Epstein, 1978) but a large section of new generation is settling for cash payments or drifting to new occupations available due to farm mechanization and development. Diwakar (2000) concluded that forced mechanization by the landowning groups has narrowed down the employment opportunities in agriculture sector through isolating poor peasants' strength and in turn, encourages mobility. With such mobility, the attitude towards superordinate class is changing. This makes the distinction between the traditional reality and functional reality.

Above all, the cultivator *Jajmans* prefer to sell their commodities and even produce with the sole motive of marketability and profitability. As a result, cultivators prefer to make payments in cash than in kind at half-yearly intervals. Contrary to it, the labourers and other (*Kamins*) prefer to have these regularly to meet their basic needs. This becomes the cause of conflict but the later has to compromise since, firstly, he is not in a position to dictate terms and secondly, he has this mode of payment since centuries. The cultivator *Jajmans* because of their compulsion of reinvestment for subsequent crop, meeting high prices of inputs and above all their control over land try to impose their way of life which is becoming materialistic day by day and hence prefer to keep transactions in cash rather than in kind. This way, both the cultivator and the labourer share the similarity of situation arising out of their compulsion. A study of farm labour in a Punjab village reveals that the labourers have internalized the technical cultural value of conflict avoidance and have reconciled to the fact of their subordinate role (Singh, 1991). The nature and extent of change in *Jajmani* relationship is a function of the level of development and opportunity structure available in a village and the region (Kumari and Ranga Rao, 1993:45). Thus, the technological development process has changed the attitude of both cultivators (*Jajmans*) and various service castes (*Kamins*). In other words, cooperation based on mutual aspects of social relationships has transformed into another form of cooperation based on mutual compulsiveness. The former leads to solidarity whereas the latter leads to discontentment, frustration and conflict in the long run.

Political System

The process of change is further accentuated with the implementation of Panchayati Raj Institution. Under this, the power and the decision making have shifted to the panchayat at the village level. In the village panchayat, only the elected members can hold the decision making. Earlier there were caste panchayats belonging to a particular caste. These were linked with other nearby villages. The village panchayats on the other hand consisted of village elders and the headship was either hereditary or was elected by consensus. The lower castes had no role in the panchayat affairs which were dominated by the dominant castes comprising of landlords (Buch, 1993). The former either does not exist or does not function. Among Jats of Haryana, caste panchayat is functional (Choudhary, 1987). The traditional village panchayat has been overshadowed by the elected ones. With these elected panchayats, the power of the superordinated or dominant castes does not rest solely on their size of holding but upon the active support of subordinate castes (*Kamins*). Higher ritual status and economic power are not the only decisive factor; numerical strength, whether of the group or caste, ensures one's election to the governing body. A numerically stronger caste may be economically poor and ritually inferior. The power politics at the village level has resulted in alignments between individuals, families, groups and castes—often antagonistic, sometime cooperative and are called factions. Factionalism has become a feature of village life and it influences the decisions of panchayats. In order to hold power, cooperation from varying groups based on caste, family, kin or interest is required. Once the power is attained, it is used to further their own interests and for economic gains of resources. Baviskar (1993) concludes that factions are vital to the economic life of the people as it provides significant power, prestige and patronage to local leader. At the same time, the powerful ones exploit the weaker ones. Hence, the cooperation of mutual social relationships in production process is giving way to cooperation with political goals as one of the binding forces among the groups, families, individuals, castes and kin. In such a cooperation, elements of conflict and mistrust persist. Above this, it is not the caste as a whole that wields and exercises power, but there are multicaste alliances that wield and exercise power.

Mechanization of farm has helped the landowning classes more than the landless peasantry. The upper classes of landowners have cornered the bulk of new prosperity and have consolidated their political power accordingly (Sharma, 1997). This increasing inequality has its impact on the political behaviour of the peasantry. Political incentive rests upon factional leaders who are owners of land and have power and prestige in the village society. They often engage in political competition and even conflict among themselves in pursuit of power and prestige in rural society. Since the middle and lower castes are becoming economically viable, they also engage in factional politics. These mobile groups are relatively independent of landlords but often find themselves in conflict with them. Further, implementation of Mandal Commission might not have provided jobs to the middle castes but has brought significantly positive effect for shaking the roots of feudal power (Diwakar, 2000). The 73rd Amendment of Constitution has led to a democratic plurality. Caste has loosened its grasp in holding fast to feudalism but it has adequately compensated itself in asserting with full force in politics and in concentrating power in its own hands. With every change it emerged stronger than before (Siddiqui, 1993). Above all the electoral compulsions make these factional groups to align with one or the other national parties. On the other hand, landless peasantry continue their dependence on those landlords who respond with paternalistic attitude. With the result, the poor peasantry does not respond actively to such actions which challenge their exploitation in the hands of landowners. Still there is an urge for assertiveness to elevation and equalization of the inferior socio-economic status through the non-traditional path taking its cue from democracy and modernization.

Caste System

Another aspect of village social organization is the caste system that has undergone change due to technical transformation in agriculture. Caste is one of the most important organizing principle in rural society. It governs the organization of kinship. In this system of hierarchical segmentary division, the segments are kept apart by an all pervading concept of ritual pollution. Complex rules of commensality specify the castes from which a particular caste may accept different kinds of food. Caste largely determines occupational choice; certain occupations have been the monopoly of certain specific castes. This defines their way of life, prescribed norms of conduct and expectations besides inter-caste relations. With the advent of new technology and mechanization of agrarian economy, many a new occupations came up which were caste-free. The caste-free occupations have been taken up by the middle and lower castes as these occupations do not demand technical institutional training but training and experience with a skilled professional. This new situation has changed the group cohesiveness which at one time, was based on an unalterable division of labour regulated by irresistible authority of law of nature. This division of labour was stabilized by the doctrine of *karma* and the theory of reincarnation. With the availability of caste-free occupations and change in attitude from a pacific acceptance to a state of assertiveness and confrontation, the culturally prescribed methods of stabilizing caste traditions have lost their validity, thereby floating the rules and norms of conduct of traditional division of labour. Now, within the caste group, members have diverse ways of life, norms of conduct and values as some of them have moved to higher prestige occupations with better economic status than before. With the result, groups and communities are continuously redefining their identity. The changed perception of their position is resisted by those with whom they start competing for status in the caste system. This situation is strengthened by those who move in the occupational category of similar prestige and have gone for sanskritization. With such a process of change, groups and communities delink themselves from their earlier groups and caste status. Along with, these groups and communities start restructuring their past and manipulating their codes and norms to suit their continuously shifted position in the system. With the result, caste loyalty and cooperation among castes inhabiting a village become spontaneous and occasionally these are ordered on castes pattern.

Further, with the economic mobility of middle castes, as well as that of lower castes, the desire to own a piece of land in the village increases. Because of the fact that power has been wielded by landowners, each individual considers land as a symbol of prestige and power. Land owners who are able to secure positions of occupational prestige move to the urban areas. Even the low caste individuals migrate who attain a sufficiently secure urban base. In the process, these groups abandon their subsistence land in favour of interest elsewhere (Sharma, 1993). With such development, land has turned into a commodity freely available for lease, sale and purchase. Also to make the new technology more efficient, the operational size of holding should not be less than 30 hectares. Consequently all the caste groups started purchasing it in small parcels or leasing it in. Since middle castes shifted to caste-free occupations in the early period of agricultural development, the landowners especially the medium farmers began to consolidate their position and even emerged as exploiters of wage labour and other forms of labour extracted from the lower castes, while others have become steadily more impoverished. This process has created a distance between the owner/and share-croppers on the one hand and owner share-croppers and agricultural labourers on the other hand. This process also changed the tenancy system in villages. Land, in the changed scenario is usually leased-out to a cultivator who invariably belongs to upper castes rather than a landless farmer. Secondly, sharecropping is gradually being replaced by fixed land tenancy.

The neo-rich groups comprising of middle and low castes oppose the caste privileges and economic power of the upper castes and finally, challenge the political power of the one time power-holders. Siddiqui (1993) finds that upper strata of society coinciding roughly with upper castes not ready to share political power and control of resources with others on equitable basis, oppose the socio-economic emancipation, uplift and ultimate equalization of deprived castes. This results in the struggle for power at the village level. Interestingly instead of launching a movement for undoing or modifying the system of caste that lay at the root of their social degradation and economic plight, the underprivileged castes took the help of the very same institution to gain political power and economic justice as is being upheld by the upper castes by upholding the religio-cultural belief in the doctrine of *Karma*. Srikanth (1993) has rightly pointed out that with mechanization and green revolution, caste system is losing its rigidity and is increasing become dynamic to meet the new challenges of change in cultural and ideological spheres. In doing so, caste movements, anti-caste movements, and Kisan movements emerge and their leadership is provided by those who are able to arouse the conservative form of organization (based on caste) as well as the radical form challenging the system itself. Consequently, struggles begin to take place for the legal rights on common land, higher wages and ending of '*begar*' (work without payment) among the different caste groups.

In this situation, conflict of interest within the village sharpens and the process continues. Now there are few values which can be said to be common to the whole community and certainly there is no common purpose which inspires all the sections equally.

Conclusion

From the above discussion, it can be discerned that the nature and extent of *Jajmani* relationship has changed from its social and ritual aspect to a more economic one. The co-operation existing in terms of production dependence has transformed into cooperation of mutual compulsiveness with elements of exploitation, discontentment, frustration and conflict. Individuals, families, groups, kins and castes are cooperating in the political pursuit as well but such alignments are to gain power in the village structure to use the resources available for agricultural development. Mechanization of farming has made the middle and lower castes independent of the upper castes. With this, the authority and dominance of the upper dominant landowning castes is challenged. Still feudal values and practices continue to influence the life of rural masses. With new technology and farm mechanization, the underlying stabilizing factors or caste system in the village have transformed their meaning from socio-religious to economic ones. It is this force that enables the groups and communities to move in the caste hierarchy whereby different caste groups are redefining and competing for status in the caste system. The deviation from the traditionally ascribed occupation and the status is higher among the sons and grandsons of lower and middle castes. The economic mobility of these castes has turned them to take a radical posture against their exploitation. Still because of their dependence on landowning castes, these lower castes do not actively respond to such actions. The obvious reason is that the state has not created conditions for the elimination of old ideological system. Without initiating continuous and conscious popular struggle at cultural and ideological level, old values and old practices, would continue to appear as cultural lag. Moreover, green revolution strategy has been implemented with the objective of economic development and not with that of social objective of reducing disparities and modernization. Other features that have started dominating the rural scene are the factional fights, violent behaviour, inter-caste rivalries, inter-caste tensions, disenchantment with progress, and mistrust. Now each village is driven by contradictions and conflicts between individuals, families, groups and castes. Such a situation has not been possible with mechanization under green revolution and it has both elements of development and regression.

REFERENCES

Baviskar, B.S. (1993), "Factional Conflict and the Congress Dilemma in Rural Maharashtra" in Bhat, Kadekar and Ranga Rao (ed.) *Sociology of Development and Change*, Orient Longman, Hyderabad.

Beidelman, T.C. (1959), *A Comparative Analysis of the Jajmani System*, Augustin Incorporated Press, New York.

Buch, M.N. (1993), Review of Rajni Kothari's State Against Democracy in C.F. Siddiqui, *Inter-caste and Inter-Community Relationship,* Commonwealth Publishers, New Delhi.

Chaudhary, R.K. (1987), *Caste and Power Structure in Village India.* Inter-India Publications, New Delhi.

Diwakar, D.M. (2000), *Emerging Agrarian Relation in India,* Manak Publication Pvt. Ltd., New Delhi.

Epstein, (1978), Productive Efficiency and Customary System of Rewards in Rural South India in Potter and Sarre (ed) *Dimensions of Society,* Hazall Waston and Vivey Ltd., Great Britain.

Gould, Harold A. (1978), *The Hindu Caste System : The Scarilization of Social Order,* Chanakya Publication, Delhi.

Kumari, U. Swarna and K. Ranag Rao (1993), "Development and Change: A study in Jajmani Relationship" in Bhatt, Kedekar and Ranga Rao (eds.) *Sociology of Development and Change,* Orient Longman, Hyderabad.

Omvedt, Gail (1982), *Land, Caste and Politics in Indian States (ed),* University of Delhi, Delhi.

Oreinstein, Henry Gaon L. (1965), *Conflict and Cohesion in an Indian Village,* Princeton University Press, New Jersey.

Pocock, David. F. (1962). "Notes on Jajmani Relationships", *Contribution to Indian Sociology,* Vol. VI.

Rao, M.S.A. (1961), "The Jajmani System", *The Economic Weekly,* Vol. XIII.

Sharma, K.L. (1997), *Rural Society in India,* Rawat Publications, Jaipur.

Sharma, Ursula (1993), "Occupational Diversity Revisited: Its implication for the study of class" in Bhatt, Kedekar and Ranga Rao (eds.) *Sociology of Development and Change.* Orient Longman, Hyderabad.

Siddiqui, M.K.A. (1993), *Inter-Caste and Inter-Community Relationship,* Commonwealth Publishers, New Delhi.

Singh, Hernek (1991), "Farm Machination and Rural Labour Relation—A Micro Level Study" in Hansara Shukla (ed) *Social, Economic and Political Implication of Green Revolution,* Classical Publishing Company, New Delhi.

Singh, Sukhdev (1994), *IRDP and District Development: Role and Implementation of D.R.D.A. Scheme,* Deep and Deep Publication, New Delhi.

Srikanth, H. (1993), "Is India still Semi-feudal", *Society and Change,* Vol. IX, No. 1.

8

DYNAMICS OF CASTE-LAND RELATIONS
A Case Study

MANMOHAN S. GILL

Land has been the major source of livelihood in all agrarian societies. In addition to being the source of production, it stratifies rural societies into agrarian classes comprising of owners, tenants and landless labourers. The land-owning class is further divided into big landlords, medium farmers, small farmers and marginal farmers on the basis of land owned by them. The pattern of land distribution is synonymous to social status, power, privileges and social identity. The unequal distribution of land leads to insecure tenancy, exorbitant rents and unequal share-cropping with minimum share of tenants and a privilege to evict the tenant at will. This had been there in the earlier periods of independence of India. As a result, the landowners due to their superordinate status exploited the labourers and tenants to such an extent that the government of that time had to implement a number of tenancy laws. These laws have provisions for keeping the land rents within limits besides securing the position of the tenants. With all such provisions, the landlords/land-owners continued to occupy their economic and political supremacy.

In addition these groups supported that ideology which has been structured within the framework of caste system. Caste system through its commensual relationships maintains a distance between the privileged and underprivileged groups. The privileged groups hold not only economic but also political position in the society. These are the groups who own land in the rural society. In other words, the land hierarchies are based on ascriptive hierarchies of the caste system. During the British rule, these groups ushered the peasantry to such an extent that many a small and marginal farmers turned into virtually a landless labourer class.

In this situation, the landlords started articulating the political and administrative decisions in their favour. This is held to be responsible for agricultural backwardness (Bhaduri, 1973; Diwakar, 2000). Further, the relationship between the landlords and their tenants remained that of a patron and a client.

Of late, the above traditional relationship underwent change under historical, political and social circumstances. Even the ideological and normative basis of the old system gave way to a new set up in which the underprivileged were free to improve their lot and to move in the hierarchy. This had made them not to accept the authority of the landowners meekly but to demand their right. The reformative laws implemented by the government have changed land distribution system and tenancy relations. Abolition of zamindari and jagirdari systems, land ceiling and distribution of surplus land among landless have provided firm standing to the tenants and agricultural labourers; usually belonging to the Scheduled Castes. Judge (1999) finds that allotment of land provides a beneficiary an opportunity to raise in socio-economic status through ownership of and income from land. Since all allottees of the surplus land do not have common interest in land and lack resources, money and contracts, big land owners continue to withhold the land. Despite this, the landowners now find it incongenial to circumvent laws to their favour. In Maharashtra, large scale voluntary transfer of land from absentee landlords had taken place all over the state and most of the tenants had purchased land at rates much lower than the market rates (Paramahamsa, 1975). With the enactment of tenancy laws, the tenants of Tamil Nadu and Kerala have become so powerful that political parties are championing their cause. In Uttar Pradesh, the land management committee of gramsamaj (village adults) decides the legal rights of tillers to the land on the basis of factual evidence. The law provides that for the conferment of ownership right, a cultivator has to prove in the court of law that he has been paying a share of the produce either in cash or in kind to the owners of land and that owner does not cultivate or supervise the cultivation directly. This shows that tenancy laws have supported the tenants.

Studies on tenancy relations reveal that landowners-tenant/ agricultural labourers relations are not smooth. Large land holders are in a position of strength to determine rent and the price of labour because of ownership and their functioning as landlords, money lenders and the major employers. Tillers are still being exploited in various forms by the landowners because many of the tillers are not aware of their legal rights and are exploited *via* extra economic coercion through network of obligation, debt and informal bondage (Diwakar, 2000). Further, at the present historical juncture the size of the operational land-holding is phenomenally small and the proportion of small and marginal land owners in the agricultural population is very high (Census of India, 1991). Under the impact of institutional, technological and demographic factors, the number of large holdings has declined and the proportion of medium and small holdings has increased. Practically in all the states, the proliferation of the holdings at the bottom of land ownership hierarchy is accompanied by a markedly lower increase in the proportion of area owned by them (Sharma, 1995). These small and medium landholders to keep their units viable enter into lease markets. Where cost factor is high, small and marginal land holders lease-out their holdings but their lessees are not to the landless labourers but the medium and large landholders. This is contrary to the traditional view where tenants are presumed to come mainly from the lower category households. Further, the leasing is not done to small and marginal household which means lessor and lessee belong to medium and big households and both are of upper caste. Mandavdhare (1989) in his study of Marathwada region finds that leasing-in is a general practice among big landowners and such transactions are carried over caste lines. Accordingly the exploiter and the exploited belong to the same caste/class and the lower category is excluded. This is not true for all the states. In Andhra Pradesh, Assam, Bihar and some other states, the land is leased-out to household owning less than 5 acres of land and it is done by those owning more than 5 acres (Sharma, 1995). He further states that in Punjab more than half of the acreage is leased-in and leased-out by those who own more than 5 acres of land.

The process of leasing-in and leasing-out has profound effect on agricultural development. Medium and large farmers find it more profitable to lease-in additional land as they have sufficient resources to invest which small and marginal farmers lack. They after leasing-out their land join the class of agricultural labourers thereby giving way to rural prolitarianisation and competition in the lease market. In the present study, attempt has been made to understand the process of leasing-in/leasing-out and its correlated effects. The study addressed to the following pertinent questions:

(a) Which groups are involved in the process of leasing-in and leasing-out?

(b) How do the landowning groups maintain their hold over the land?

(c) What are the consequences of the process of leasing-in and leasing-out?

Methodology

The agricultural production in Punjab has increased manifold during the green revolution and post-green revolution period due to the development of the new technologies and mechanisation and their subsequent adoption on a wider scale. Consolidation of holdings and provisions of electricity and transport facilities have supplemented the process of technological adoption. As a result, the backward, traditional and subsistence agriculture has transformed into advance market and profit-oriented capitalist farming.

Among all the districts of Punjab, Ludhiana is one of the most agriculturally advanced district. From this district, Ludhiana tehsil was selected because of its proximity to Agricultural University and considering that it has experienced greater technological impact as compared to other ones. Two villages from this tehsil were selected arbitrarily.

From these villages, 72 respondents owning land were interviewed with the help of a pre-tested structured interview schedule. The data so collected was statistically analysed.

Results and Discussions

Land being the basic variable in this study, not only determines one's status in the rural society but also provides a basis for interaction among different groups. The analysis of data reveals that 12.5 per cent of the respondents own land up to 1 acre whereas 9.7 per cent have more than 15 acres of land (Table 8.1). Those who own land between 1 to 3 acres constitute 22.2 per cent of the respondents. Majority of the respondents have land between 3 to 7.5 acres (36.1%).

A comparison of owned and operated land explains the operation of land lease market. The size of operated land varies from that owned by many a households. Nearly 10 per cent of the respondents operate up to 1 acre of land, 15.3 per cent between 1 to 3 acres, 25.0 per cent between 3 to 7.5 acres, 22.2 per cent between 7.5 to 15 acres and 27.8 per cent more than 15 acres. Barring the last two categories of land holders, in all the other categories the percentage of farmers has dropped considerably. This is more true in the case of households owning land between 3 to 7.5 acres. Thus medium and large farmers may have gone for leasing-in whereas small and marginal households have leased-out their land. In other words, land lease market is dominated by medium and large farmers as lessee and small and marginal farmers as lessors. Vyas (1970) and Jodha (1981) hold similar view.

Table 8.1: Distribution of resondents according to land owned and land operated

Size of holding (in acres)	*Owned*		*Operated*	
Up to 1 (marginal)	9	(12.5)	7	(9.7)
1 to 3 (marginal)	16	(22.2)	11	(15.3)
3 to 7.5 (small)	26	(36.1)	18	(25.0)
7.5 to 15 (medium)	14	(19.4)	16	(22.2)
More than 15 (large)	7	(9.7)	20	(27.8)
Total	72	(99.9)	72	(100.0)

Note : The mean size of land owned by a house-hold comes out to be about 7 acres.

As in U.P., Bihar and Rajasthan, land is held mostly by Jats. Likewise in Punjab land is predominantly associated with Jats rather than any other caste group.

Data from Table 8.2 discerns that Jats predominate in all land categories and their percentage is the highest (72.2%). Among other caste groups, Chamar households have low representation (8.3%) followed by Arora (6.9%), Ramgarhia (6.9%) and Brahmin (5.6%). They are operating mostly small and marginal holdings. Jats do operate small holdings but their percentage is less as compared to Chamars or Ramgarhias. Medium and largeland holdings are operated by Jats (81.3 and 95.0% respectively). This confirms our contention that land is held by Jats. As they are the owners of the land, they hold better position both economically and socially in the rural society. Further the change in the distribution of ownership and operational landholding has implication towards tenurial relations.

Leasing-in

Landowners generally prefer to lease their land to that household who takes care of the land and develops it. They do not want to lend it to landless tenant especially if he has not means to develop it. In this context, who are the lessees assumes greater importance. Data shows that 66.7

per cent of the total respondents have leased-in land from two to 30 acres (Table 8.3).

Table 8.2: Caste and size of operational landholding

Caste	*Operational landholding (in Acres)*					
	Up to 1	*1 to 3*	*3 to 7.5*	*7.5 to 15*	*Above 15*	*Total*
Arora	–	2 (18.2)	3 (16.7)	–	–	5 (6.9)
Brahmin	–	–	3 (16.7)	–	1 (5.0)	4 (5.6)
Chamar	4 (57.1)	1 (9.1)	–	1 (6.2)	–	6 (8.3)
Jat	2 (28.6)	8 (72.7)	10 (55.5)	13 (81.3)	19 (95.0)	52 (72.2)
Ramgarhia	1 (14.3)	–	2 (11.1)	2 (12.5)	–	5 (6.9)
Total	7 (9.7)	11 (15.3)	18 (25.0)	16 (22.2)	20 (27.8)	72 (100.0)

Table 8.3: Caste and extent of leased-in land

Caste	*Leased-in (in Acres)*					
	Up to 3	*3 to 5*	*5 to 10*	*10 to 20*	*More than 20*	*Total*
Arora	–	1 (9.1)	1 (7.1)	–	–	2 (4.2)
Brahmin	–	–	1 (7.1)	–	–	1 (2.1)
Chamar	–	1 (9.1)	–	–	–	1 (2.1)
Jat	4 (100.0)	9 (81.8)	12 (85.7)	8 (100.0)	11 (100.0)	44 (91.7)
Total	4 (8.3)	11 (22.9)	14 (29.2)	8 (16.7)	11 (22.9)	48 (100.0)

About 23 per cent of the respondents have leased-in more than 20 acres of land whereas 8.3 per cent have leased-in up to 3 acres. Another 22.9 per cent have leased-in 3 to 5 acres; 29.2 per cent from 5 to 10 acres and 16.7 per cent from 10 to 20 acres of land. Data further discerns that those who have leased-in more than 10 acres of land are the members of Jat caste. No doubt Jats preponderate in all land categories thereby giving credential to the fact that land is being leased to those who really cultivate it. Secondly, lease process operates on caste line.

In the opinion of the lessee, the lessor himself or his wards have migrated to other countries (35.4 %; Table 8.4). Nearly 31 per cent lessors have migrated or taken up services/business in the urban areas. Some of the lessors are working as truck drivers, so cannot look after their land. About 15 per cent of the lessees are cultivating the land of their relatives who have gone abroad. The returns from the leased-out land are credited to their accounts in the village. Owing to small size of the holding, 8.3 per cent of lessors have leased-out their land and have taken up dairy. It is found that 10.4 per cent lessors have leased-out to repay bank loan and to avoid litigation. So, the land is leased-out when the lessor migrates to urban area or to other countries or finds his holding uneconomic. In the process of leasing-in the respondents faced no difficulty because the land continues to stand in the name of the owner and not the tenant in revenue records.

Table 8.4: Reasons for leasing-out according to the lessee

Sl No.	*Reason*	*Number*
1.	The lessor or his wards have migrated	17 (35.4)
2.	Service in urban areas	15 (31.3)
3.	Relatives staying abroad	7 (14.6)
4.	Uneconomic holding	4 (8.3)
5.	For the sake of Money	5 (10.4)
	Total	48 (100)

The main purpose of leasing-in is to have the optimum use of the farm machinery and to earn additional income (68.7%, Table 8.5). Such respondents are found to be renting out their tractors and other farm implements to small landholders at the time of sowing and harvesting. Nearly 15 per cent of the lessees report that due to their illiteracy, they cannot get service in urban areas up to their level and to meet family needs land has been leased-in. This keeps them busy as well. In order to avoid forceful occupancy of their relatives land who have settled abroad, 16.7 per cent are cultivating their land on lease basis.

From the above discussion, it may be inferred that Jats enter into large size lease-in transactions which other caste-groups avoid due to lack of money to pay the rent. Also, it is the Jats who lease-out land owing to their services in urban areas or their/their wards, migration to other countries. This process provides them income besides keeping the fertility of land intact. Some lease-out their land to meet family needs and such persons join the rank of agricultural labourers. In the process of leasing, the lessee is benefited as he extensively uses the farm machinery and labour.

Table 8.5: Purpose of leasing-in

Sl No.	*Purpose*	*Number*	
1.	To make proper use of farm machinery	33	(68.7)
2.	To help the relatives by keeping their land under cultivation	8	(16.7)
3.	To meet family needs	7	(14.6)
	Total	48	(100.0)

Leasing-out

Among the respondents, 30.6 per cent are found to lease-out their land. Here again Jats predominate as 72.7 per cent lessors are Jats (Table 8.6).

Table 8.6: Caste and extent of leasing-out

Caste	*Size of leased-out land (in Acres)*				
	Up to 3	*3 to 5*	*5 to 10*	*More than 10*	*Total*
Arora	–	3 (37.5)	–	–	3 (13.7)
Brahmin	–	2 (25.0)	–	–	2 (19.1)
Chamar	1 (33.3)	–	–	–	1 (4.5)
Jat	2 (67.7)	3 (37.5)	5 (100.0)	6 (100.0)	16 (72.7)
Total	3 (13.7)	8 (36.3)	5 (22.7)	5 (27.3)	22 (100.0)

Arora, Brahmin and Chamar constitute negligible percentage. Among all the respondents, 13.7 per cent have leased-out up to 3 acres of land; 36.3 per cent have from 3 to 5; 22.7 per cent have 5 to 10 and 27.3 per cent have more than 10 acres of land. Further, lessees are mainly the Jats in all land categories. This corroborates earlier findings that Jats behold land and there exists a relationship between caste and land-holding. Also the Jats preponderate in lease market.

So far as the purpose of leasing-out is concerned, majority of the lessors state that their family members have migrated and they being old are unable to manage their holdings (36.3%; Table 8.7). The children send remittance for their maintenance while income from leasing-out is credited to the children. In case of 32 per cent of the respondents, husband has gone abroad and the family is staying back with small children to be looked after by the mother. In such cases, too, the land has been leased-out. Those who are working or having business in urban areas are unable to devote time for land cultivation, have leased-out their small uneconomic holding.

Table 8.7: Purpose of leasing-out of land

Sr No.	*Purpose*	*Number*	
1.	Family members staying abroad, myself unable to cultivate	8	(36.3)
2.	Husband staying abroad	7	(31.8)
3.	Business/Service in urban area	4	(18.2)
4.	Small size of holding	3	(13.7)
	Total	22	(100.0)

The caste of the lessee in all the cases is found to be Jat. These Jat cultivators have leased-in land to augment their existing resources (Table 8.8). This is found to be true as 50.0 per cent lessors have cited this as the reason for the lessee to lease-in land. Lessor has faith in the lessee as he is a relative who can be trusted with such right (31.8%). For 18.2 per cent of the lessors, there is no alternative except to lease-out. The land was leased out to the person who has supported his child to go abroad. Secondly, the land is fragmented into small pieces. In one case, the land has been leased under duress otherwise it would have been forcefully occupied by the neighbour landowner.

Table 8.8: Reason for leasing-in according to the lessors

Sr No.	*Reason*	*Number*	
1.	To augment their resources	11	(50.0)
2.	Lessor has faith in lessee	7	(31.8)
3.	No alternative except leasing-out	4	(18.2)
	Total	22	(100.0)

There is no problem in leasing-out the land if it is held by a single person. Where land is held by two or three owners or it turns out to be a disputed land, the problem of sharing the rent arises. In the latter case the land-rent has to be deposited in the court but such cases are very few.

The above analysis thus reveals that land is leased-out to Jat cultivators who look after the interest of the lessor. Land is generally leased out when family members migrate or settle in urban areas or the owner is unable to cultivate land himself. Small landholders also lease-out their land but such cases are found to be few. Further, the lessees augment their existing resources by leasing-in extra land. Of course, lessee must repose the faith of the lessor to avoid coercing of relations at later stage. Lessor tries to avoid litigation with his lessee.

Mortgage

A mortgage is the transfer of an interest in specific immovable property for the purpose of securing the payment of money advanced by way of loan, an existing or future debt or performance of an engagement which may give rise to pecuniary liability. It entails personal obligation/liability to pay. It is a usual phenomenon in rural areas.

As compared to 40.3 per cent respondents who have mortgaged-out their land, none of the respondent is found to have mortgaged-in. Again, Jat cultivators predominate the category of mortgaging their land (82.8% Table 8.9).

Table 8.9: Caste and land mortgaged-out

Caste	*Land Mortgaged-out (in acres)*				
	Up to 3	*3 to 5*	*5 to 10*	*More than 10*	*Total*
Chamar	4 (100.0)	–	–	–	4 (13.8)
Jat	8 (33.3)	14 (58.3)	2 (8.3)	–	24 (82.8)
Ramgharia	1 (100.0)	–	–	–	1 (3.5)
Total	13 (44.8)	14 (48.3)	2 (6.9)	–	29 (100.0)

Among them, 58.3 per cent have mortgaged-out 3 to 5 acres of land and 8.3 per cent from 5 to 10 acres. Approximately 33 per cent have mortgaged land up to 3 acres. Data further discern that of the 13.8 per cent of the Chamar respondent, all have mortgaged-out land up to 3 acres. Similarly all the Ramgarhia respondents fall in the above category. In all, 48.3 per cent of the respondents have mortgaged land between 3 to 5 acres, 44.8 per cent between 5 to 10 acres and the remaining up to 3 acres.

The land has been mortgaged to bank in majority of the cases (82.8 % Table 8.10). Rest have mortgaged it to the rich and influential farmers who lend money to the interested and needy persons. Such respondents have taken loan at the time of the marriage of their daughters (17.2%) and three of them belong to Jat and two to Chamar caste (Table 8.11). One of the respondents has not specified despite persistent enquiry the reason for which he has mortgaged his land and he is a Ramgarhia by caste. About 52 per cent of the respondents have taken loan for tractor from the bank and all belong to Jat caste. Further, 13.8 per cent have secured loan from bank for tubewell. Thus majority of the respondents have secured loan for production purposes.

Table 8.10: Agency to which land is mortgaged

Sr No.	*Agency*	*Number*	
1.	Bank	24	(82.8)
2.	Big farmer-cum-money lender	5	(17.2)
	Total	29	(100.0)

Table 8.11: Reasons for mortgaging-out

Sr No.	*Reason*	*Number*		*Caste*
1.	For Tractor (bank)	15	(51.7)	Jat
2.	For Tubewell (bank)	4	(13.8)	Jat
3.	For dairy (bank)	4	(13.8)	Jat (2); Chamar (2)
4.	Marriage of daughter	5	(17.2)	Jat (2), Chamar (3)
5.	Reasons not specified	1	(3.5)	Ramgharia
	Total	29	(100.0)	

The terms of mortgage vary with the amount of loan taken and the agency from which it has been secured. The rate of interest varies from 24 to 30 per cent if the loan has been taken from private agency. Generally there is no problem in mortgaging the land to bank but mortgaging it to landowner is not without problem. The landowners try to grab it and in such situation the help of village elders/political influential leaders is sought.

Basis of Leasing-in and Leasing-out

The terms of tenancy have shifted from share-cropping to annual rent practically throughout the state. Sharma (1995) has found that share-cropping tenancy has declined significantly in all the states of India. Total cropped area and the intensity of labour/technology use determine the terms of tenancy. In this study, none of the respondents has leased land on share basis: in fact all transactions are made in cash. The annual rent varies from Rs. 5000 to Rs. 6000/acre for irrigated land with facility of tubewell or canal and from Rs. 4000 to Rs. 4500/acre for other types of landholdings. The land rent also varies with the distance from the source of irrigation. Last year the rent was less by about Rs. 1000. In all cases, the electricity/irrigation or repair charges have to be borne by the lessee. So far as the land revenue is concerned, it is paid by the owner but sometime it is shared by the contracted parties depending upon their proximity of relationships. The land lease is made for one year but generally the lessee holds the lease for 4 to 5 years. Lessee is shifted in case of any sort of misunderstanding. Generally the dispute never arises as 'GIRDWARI' is made in the name of the landowner not the tenant. Enquiries with the revenue staff and legal experts on civil suit reveal that Girdwari cannot be transferred and if it has to be, the owner of the land has to be informed. In this way the right of the owner remains in tact. Further, half of the rent is paid in advance and the remaining half at the time of harvesting of first crop. All transactions in kind like grains, rice, dal etc. are deducted at the time of making final payment. Of course, payment for cattle feed is not made.

Land: A Symbol of Prestige

The importance of land in the agrarian society can be gauged from the value a community/group attaches to it. Data reveals that rural people attach too much importance to land and consider it a symbol of prestige (Table 8.12). Nearly 51 per cent hold that it provides identification to our community (Jats) and on its basis affinal ties are extended from family to family. Land also provides emotional satisfaction (38.9%) because one feels attached to one's forefathers who have bestowed upon them the right to landed property. In the view of 52.8 per cent of the respondents land provides security to life. In their opinion, person owning land cannot be hungry in his life, *i.e.* it sustains life. Similar view is shared by 77.8 per cent of the respondents who hold that it provides basic needs. The most striking feature is that it enhances one's matrimonial chances in the community for both the sexes. This fact has pervaded the life of rural society.

Regarding selling of land, most of the respondents disapprove it. But if it has to be sold then it should be sold to the members of the Jat community (Table 8.13). In their opinion, Jats care for the land as mother cares for the child. Majority of the respondents disfavour its selling to the members of the Scheduled Caste community (88.9%) as, firstly, they have no money to pay for it and secondly, they lack necessary infrastructure to cultivate it. Trivedi (1996) in his study finds that 18.1 per cent of the owner Scheduled Castes do not have all the minor facilities at their disposal for cultivation of land and 68.57 per cent of the households are without facilities for doing independent farming. About 24 per cent of the respondents say that when it comes to sale the neighbouring landowner purchases it. They do not allow others to purchase it. Some of the respondents are ready to sell it to anyone who can pay the price and buy the entire holding. This shows that the land remains in the hands of the Jat cultivators.

Table 8.12: Importance of land

Sr No.	*Reason*	*Number*	
1.	Symbol of prestige	72	(100.0)
2.	Provides identification	37	(51.4)
3.	Provides basic needs	56	(77.8)
4.	Provides security to life	38	(52.8)
5.	Provides emotional satisfaction	28	(38.9)

Table 8.13: Sale of land

Sr No.	*To whom and reason thereof*	*Number*	
1.	Jats; they look after it well	58	(80.6)
2.	Not to Scheduled Castes; they have no interest in land	64	(88.9)
3.	To the lessee; do not allow others to buy	32	(44.4)
4.	To anybody who is ready to pay	17	(23.6)

Conclusions

From the analysis of the data, it may be inferred that small and marginal farmers lease-out their land and join the rank of rural proletariat. This at least ensures them work on their farms. The land is leased-in by the medium and big farmers who find it more profitable to lease-in additional land to make optimum use of the farm machinery. This is amply clear from the size of land owned and operated by each household.

The lease market is dominated by the landowning Jat cultivators who are preferred against landless tenants. This feature runs contrary to the theoretical assumption that the tenant is generally a landless person. Sharma (1995) too, has observed a similar phenomenon in the states like Punjab, Haryana, Tamil Nadu, Uttar Pradesh, Bihar and others.

The lessee and the lessor are usually the Jat cultivators who are benefited by the mutual contract of leasing as the lessor or his family is either settled abroad or serving in some urban area or the members of the household who are unable to cultivate it personally. The returns on land are credited to the bank account of the lessor in the former case or used to meet household errands. The lessee on the other hand goes for intensive cultivation. Usually he prefers labour/machine intensive crops. This not only increases agricultural production but also generates employment opportunities for the rural people. This maintains his control over land besides on labour force and provides him social, economic and political status and through it the system of stratification and inequality is perpetuated.

The analysis further shows that many Jat cultivators have taken loan for agricultural or subsidiary purpose from the banks by mortgaging land which is not more than 4 acres in any case. Some have mortgaged land with big and influential landowners who charge exorbitant rate of interest usually ranging from 24 to 30 per cent for meeting their social obligations. The mortgaging of land for machinery or new technology indicates the tendency to exploit the resources of land, irrigation and labour to generate wealth; in short tendency towards capitalisation.

The analysis highlights that the shared tenancy has been replaced by fixed rent tenancy as lessees are paying fixed rent that varies with the distance of leased area from the source of irrigation and the usual rent ranges from Rs. 4000 to 6000 per acre. Even other expenses are borne by the lessee. This indicated that the lessee is reluctant to share the increased output with the lessor/landowner. Such trends have been reported by Bhalla (1983) and Singh (1989), thus supporting the conclusion of the present study. Also the tenancy cannot be inherited as lessor renews the tenancy each year depending upon the prevalent fixed rent for that year. Further, the rules do not permit forceful transfer of land to tenant as change in the revenue records has to be rectified by the original owner of the land.

The study corroborates that land is dear to Jats as it provides prestige, social, economic and emotional security besides identification to the community. The hold of Jats is further justified as the owner, if he has to sell land would prefer Jat landowner cultivating land rather than any other caste group especially the Scheduled Castes. From this it may be concluded that Jats try to maintain their control and hegemony over the subordinate class by controlling the main source of livelihood, i.e. land. Further, inequalities continue to exist more or less in the same way as it existed earlier.

Thus, the study concludes that lessor as well as lessee, both belong to landed class, deny tenancy to the landless tenants (Scheduled Castes) and their relationship is governed by the market force as well as caste status. Bhardwaj and Das (1975) too find the same in some villages of Orissa. This class comprising of Jat cultivators does not want to share the gains of leasing-in with the tenants and through their hold over land control economic resources. As possession of land in agrarian society is a repository of wealth, power, and privileges; the landowners, in this way, not only maintain their superordinate position but also perpetuate inequalities besides keeping a hold of their caste over land.

REFERENCES

Bhaduri, A. (1973), 'A Study in Agricultural Backwardness under Semi Feudalism', *Economic Journal*, Vol. 83.

Bhalla, Sheila, (1983), 'Tenancy Today. New Factors in the Determination of Mode and Level of Rent Payments for Agricultural Land', *Economic and Political Weekly*, Vol. xviii, No. 19, 20, 21.

Bhardwaj, K. and P.K. Das, (1975), "Tenurial Conditions and Mode of Exploitation", *Economic and Political Weekly*, Vol. 10, No. 5-7.

Diwakar, D.M. (2000), *Emerging Agrarian Relations in India*, Manak Publications Pvt. Ltd., New Delhi.

Jodha, N.S. (1981), 'Agricultural Tenancy: Fresh evidence from dry land areas in India', *Economic and Political Weekly*, Vol. xvi.

Judge, P.S. (1999), *Social Change Through Land Reforms*, Rawat Publications, Jaipur.

Mandavdhare, (1989), *Caste and Land Relations in India*, Uppal Publishing House, New Delhi.

Sharma, H.R. (1995), *Agrarian Relations in India*, Har-Anand Publications, New Delhi.

Singh, Iqbal, (1989), 'Agrarian Tenancy in Punjab: Agricultural Impact of Technological Change', *Economic and Political Weekly*, Vol. xxiv, No. 25.

Trivedi, H.R. (1996), *Scheduled Castes Quest for Land and Social Equality*, Concept Publishing Company, New Delhi.

Vyas, V.S. (1970), 'Tenancy in a Dynamic Setting', *Economic and Political Weekly*, Vol. v, No. 26.

9

AGRICULTURAL COOPERATIVE SERVICE SOCIETIES AND RURAL DEVELOPMENT

SUKHDEV SINGH

Farmers of India in general and Punjab in particular have largely been getting support from the Agricultural Cooperative Service Societies which is an important part of the cooperative structure of the country. It is well known that the cooperative credit structure has been one of the most important institutional arrangements for development of agriculture and promoting allied activities in India (Khusro, 1992; Awate, 1994; Baviskar *et al.*, 1994; Sharma, 1995; Singh, 1996; Kuralnathan, 1996; Sholapur, 1997). Though, the cooperative efforts in various fields of life have been a part of Indian Society from time immemorial, but the organised efforts of cooperatives particularly in agriculture got a new turn in 1904 when Cooperative Societies Act was passed. From 1904 to 1947 the development of cooperative sector remained slow due to various reasons, but after independence it has shown a marked increase. Statistics show that agricultural credit including short-term, medium-term and long-term has increased from Rs.2.10 million in 1960-61 to Rs.65,334.2 million during 1992-93. Presently, short-term credit structure consists of 89,000 Primary Agricultural Credit Societies (PACS) at village level, 353 Central Cooperative Banks at district level and 28 state cooperative banks while long term credit structure consists of 717 Primary Land Development Banks and 19 State Development Banks in India. At present, in Punjab, there are 19 Central Cooperative Banks and 4177 Primary Agricultural Cooperative Societies.

The Primary Agricultural Credit, a kingpin of Indian Cooperative Structure, has helped the farmers tremendously in achieving the higher production of various crops besides saving them from the exploitative credit structure of money lenders. It has also helped in bringing the lenders and borrowers closer to each other. The new economic policy (NEP) has thrown the world on a competitive pattern and it is assumed that NEP may give a jolt to cooperative sector for survival. Besides this, there are number of in-built ills which has been hampering the smooth functioning of agricultural cooperative societies. In order to assess the role of these societies and constraints emerging in this era, this study was undertaken with the following specific objectives:

1. To appraise the functioning of Agricultural Cooperative Services Societies.
2. To highlight the major constraints of cooperative societies.
3. To identify the attributes of success/failure of cooperative societies.
4. To render suitable suggestions to improve the functioning of these societies.

Methodology

This study was conducted in four districts, namely, Ludhiana, Patiala, Nawanshahar and Amritsar district of Punjab State in 1997-98. The reasons for choosing these districts was to give adequate representation to the three broad socio-cultural zones of Punjab State, *i.e.* Majha, Doaba and Malwa. District Amritsar represents the Majha, while Nawansahar represents Doaba and Ludhiana and Patiala represent Malwa. Twenty cooperative agricultural service societies were chosen randomly for data collection from the selected districts (five from each district). The data was collected personally with the help of semi-structured schedule. Data were put to tabular analysis.

Profile of the Societies

The basic information about the selected societies such as year of establishment, total membership, number of villages being covered and approximately covered and uncovered areas in which they were functioning, is given in Table 9.1. The Rayya Cooperative Agricultural Service Society in the sample has been found to be the oldest one which was started way back in 1919. On minutely watching the relevant columns of tables, it comes out that 35 per cent societies were started before independence, that too in between 1919 to 1937 while 65 per cent of

Table 9.1: Profile of the sampled cooperative agricultural service societies

District	*Name of Society*	*Year of start*	*Total Members*	*Village covered*	*Total employees*	*Total area (Kanals)*	*Covered area*	*Rooms*	*Stores*
Amritsar	Rayya	1919	380	1	2	1	1/4th	1	1
	Tangran	1965	409	1	3	2	1/4th	1	1
	Pheruman	1936	611	1	4	2	1/5th	1	1
	Khalchian	1959	800	2	5	4	1/4th	3	3
	Nijjar	1987	289	1	2	1	1/4th	2	2
Ludhiana	Bhathal	1978	780	2	5	3	1/4th	2	2
	Hambran	1957	1200	10	4	16	1/3rd	4	5
	Boparai	1929	1460	2	5	1	1/2nd	6	2
	Sudhar	1928	1538	2	4	4	1/2nd	6	2
	Mullanpur	1937	840	1	3	1.5	1/5th	1	1
Nawa-shahar	Saloh	1926	1222	2	4	2	1/3rd	1	1
	Mahilgehlan	1936	1700	2	35	4	1/3rd	15	5
	Chandpur	1982	415	1	1	0.5*	1/3rd*	1*	1*
	Begampur	1978	700	2	2	1	1/4th	2	1
	Dyal	1978	1850	2	3	2	1/4th	2	2
Patiala	Fatehpur-Rajputan	1964	365	3	4	10	1/3rd	2	2
	Suniarheri	1985	240	1	3	3	1/5th	1	1
	Khansian	1988	250	1	2	4	1/5th	1	1
	Behal	1969	832	2	4	3	1/3rd	3	2
	Nainkalan	1970	753	2	3	2	1/3rd	2	1
	Average		841.7	2.05	4.9	3.35		2.85	1.85

* Working on rented building.

sampled societies were established after independence, majority of which came up in the 60s and 70s and latest established society has been Suniarheri which started functioning in 1985 when it was bifurcated from some other village. There is lot of variations in the total membership of societies in the sample. Dyal Cooperative Society has maximum members, *i.e.* 1850 while the lowest number of members was with Suniarheri having 250 members. Most of the members of these societies comprised of farmers of various categories, *i.e.* large, small and marginal. Average number of members of societies under study was 842. Out of the total 20 societies, 40 per cent societies were covering single village in their operation while 50 per cent catered to two villages, one society to three villages, while another one covered as many as ten villages. The average figure for number of villages being covered by these societies came to two. Most of the societies owned 2 to 4 kanals of land while two (Hambran and Fatehpur Rajputan) owned 16 and 10 kanals respectively. The Chandpur society has been carrying out its activities on about half kanal hired (partly built) area. On an average each society owned 3.35 kanals of land. Ninety per cent of the societies had covered 1/3rd to 1/5th of their respective owned area, while 10 per cent societies had covered half of their total area. 80 per cent of the sampled societies have rooms numbering 1 to 3, while 15 per cent 4 to 6 and 5 per cent have 15 rooms for their working. Regarding store facilities 50 per cent societies own single store while 35 per cent have two stores; 5 per cent have 3 stores and 10 per cent have 5 stores. On an average each society own 2.85 (about 3 rooms) and 1.85 (about 2 stores).

Financial Position of the Societies

The functioning of an agricultural cooperative society can be gauged from its financial position. Out of the 20 societies, three had share capital up to Rs. one lac, four between Rs. one to two lacs, six between Rs. two to three lacs and seven had share capital more than Rs. 3 lacs (Table 9.2). The average share capital of the selected societies was Rs.2.92 lacs. As regards the owned fund of the cooperative societies it was found that 11 societies had owned capital below Rs. three lacs, two between Rs. three and six lacs, three between Rs. six and nine lacs, and rest four had owned capital more than nine lacs. The Hambran Cooperative Society has the maximum owned funds of Rs.79.69 lacs. So far as the working capital of the sampled society is concerned, the data reveals that only one cooperative society had working capital less than Rs.10 lacs, while five of them had possessed between Rs.10 to 20 lacs, four had between Rs.20 and 30 lacs, three between Rs.30 and 40 lacs, two between Rs. 40 and 50 lacs and rest five had working capital more than Rs. 50 lacs as on March 31, 1997. The average working capital for the selected societies was Rs. 58.66 lacs. The majority of the societies under this study had deposits less than Rs. one lac, while on the other hand, Mehilgehlan Society, which is a very successful society, had a deposit of nearly Rs. 26 lacs. The Table further indicates that three of the selected societies advanced loans below Rs. 10 lacs, two advanced loans between Rs. 10 and 20 lacs, nine between Rs. 20 and 30 lacs and six more than Rs. 30 lacs.

Information regarding loan outstanding (as on 31-3-1997) shows that five societies had loans outstanding up to Rs. 10 lacs, seven between Rs. 10 to 20 lacs, six between Rs. 20 and 30 lacs and rest two had loans outstanding above Rs. 30 lacs. The average amount of loans outstanding was Rs. 18.16 lacs for the selected 20 cooperative societies. The information rendered by the societies regarding the number of defaulters indicates that nine societies had less than 50 defaulters, six societies had defaulters between 50 to 100 and remaining five societies had more than 100 defaulters. The average number of defaulters for the selected societies was 80.5. Out of the 20 selected cooperative societies two were incurring loss while all other societies were making profits, *i.e.* 90 per cent of the sampled societies were found to be incurring profit while 10 per cent were running in loss.

Table 9.2: Financial position of the societies under study as on 31-3-1997

District	*Name of Society*	*Share Capital*	*Own Fund*	*Working Capital*	*Deposits*	*Loan advanced during year*	*Loan Outstanding at the end of the year*	*No. of defaulters*	*Profit/ Loss*
Amritsar	Rayya	0.95	1.20	23.71	0.56	12.00	0.62	9	+0.62
	Tangran	1.00	0.70	13.00	0.84	7.00	0.70	10	+0.70
	Pheruman	2.09	1.33	23.51	0.27	24.95	5.00	82	+3.40
	Khalchian	2.58	4.24	109.25	0.70	28.86	14.78	161	+0.33
	Nijjar	0.55	2.64	10.70	0.077	5.50	0.28	5	–0.16
Ludhiana	Bhathal	3.80	10.86	35.85	14.72	27.93	20.12	45	+0.30
	Hambran	9.46	79.69	103.02	0.18	90.44	73.53	189	+11.30
	Boparai	4.30	5.23	119.51	49.68	28.08	28.99	120	+5.15
	Sudhar	3.90	19.58	61.98	28.97	25.80	22.88	85	+1.74
	Mullanpur	2.59	8.91	29.68	2.50	25.51	14.62	46	+0.42
Nawa-shahar	Saloh	3.75	6.04	44.97	24.38	33.59	27.82	297	+3.91
	Mahilgehlan	6.82	32.31	409.10	266.63	31.24	22.07	200	+11.70
	Chandpur	1.16	0.03	8.31	0.03	8.59	7.52	54	+0.77
	Begampur	1.75	0.06	19.75	4.73	20.87	12.87	12	+0.14
	Dyal	3.24	0.23	40.90	0.31	41.97	31.71	41	+0.58
Patiala	Fatehpur-Rajputan	2.60	8.40	30.42	1.29	30.07	15.42	52	+8.50
	Suniarheri	2.54	2.65	25.00	0.19	20.81	16.56	71	+3.06
	Khansian	1.35	1.39	15.10	0.26	20.18	12.35	47	+2.15
	Behal	2.68	2.05	35.23	0.07	30.05	24.55	22	+6.25
	Nainkalan	1.25	2.16	14.25	0.85	12.18	10.88	63	–0.90
	Mean	2.92	9.49	58.66	19.85	26.29	18.16	80.55	+6.46

Functions of Societies

Prime function of these societies has been to supply the agricultural inputs which include fertilisers of various types, insecticides, weedicides and mobil oil. Besides supply of agricultural inputs, societies also provide cash money to its members in order to enable them to meet their pressing domestic needs like to come out from the informal debtors so that the agricultural operation goes smoothly. Supply of almost all kinds of consumable domestic goods like sugar, food items, spice, stationery items and clothes to the members as well as non-members of the societies is also an important function of most societies (Table 9.3). Out of total twenty sampled cooperative agricultural service societies, one has been making arrangement for marketing of agricultural produce of its members also. Response towards this activity is highly encouraging and farmers are curious to sell their produce through cooperative instead of selling it to the traditional money lenders who usually cheat to the innocent and ignorant farmers in marketing process in connivance with other people. This society (Mahilgehlan) has turned into a successful model of cooperative societies worth visiting, studying and researching. Other functions of the societies include custom hiring services for agricultural operations, helping the farmers to get loan from the government agencies, etc. Two out of twenty societies have been successfully helping the farmers in custom hiring. Two societies have been running cooperative banks successfully providing all the banking facilities. Establishment of banks have been proving very useful to the farmers and also saving their time and energy.

Table 9.3: Functions of the agricultural service societies

Sr. No.	*Function*	*Yes*	*No*	*Total*
1.	Supply of Agricultural inputs	20(100)	–	20(100)
2.	Supply of cash money for agriculture	18(90)	2(10)	20(100)
3.	Supply of domestic kinds	14(70)	6(30)	20(100)
4.	Arrangement of marketing of end product	1(05)	19(95)	20(100)
5.	Any other	8(40)	12(60)	20(100)

Involvement of Committee Members, Beneficiaries and Women in Functions of Societies

During the course of study it was tried to assess the involvement of committee members and women in the cooperative societies of their respective villages. As told by the respondents (Table 9.4) majority of the committee members (75 %) take part in the functioning of societies. Among the beneficiaries only 40 per cent take active role. The participation of the women in the functioning of the cooperative societies is negligible; only 5 per cent. In all, beneficiaries and women are not involved in the activities of the cooperative societies.

Table 9.4: Involvement of members in the functions of societies

Sr. No.	*Type of Member*	*Yes*	*No*	*Total*
1.	Committee members	15(75)	5(25)	20(100)
2.	Beneficiaries	8(40)	12(60)	20(100)
3.	Women	1(05)	19(95)	20(100)

Constraints/Difficulties of the Societies

The major thrust of the present study has been to highlight the constraints of cooperative agricultural service societies which hamper their smooth functioning. The response towards various queries on constraints of societies has been shown in Table 9.5. One of the major constraints of the societies is imposition of Government agencies like Punjab State Cooperative Supply and Marketing Federation (MARKFED), The Punjab Civil Supply Corporation (PUNSUP), The Punjab State Federation of Consumers Cooperative Wholesale Stores Ltd. (CONSTOFED), etc. for supply of agricultural input as well as domestic commodities. Ninety per cent of the respondents held that imposition of these agencies on cooperative societies by the government has highly undermined the role of cooperative societies. A respondent in an angry mood told in Punjabi tone that these agencies are just like '*Mariya Sap Gal Piya*' (Dead snake in the neck). Another respondent labelled these agencies as hard jaggery in the mouth which neither goes inside the stomach nor comes out. Most of these agencies supply the material of substandard quality to the cooperative societies that too in less quantity, and the societies are forced to accept the material from these agencies. Supply of low quality and quantity of the material to cooperative societies has very strongly been felt by the respondents. They cited numerous examples in this regard. For instance sometimes back CONSTOFED supplied grains (*chanas*) to the cooperative societies which were too poor in quality to feed the animals and it was supplied for human consumption. This practice breeds lot of corruption as societies usually recoup this type of damage from other sides. Respondents further informed that whenever they raise the voice for freedom, government directs that if a society wants to purchase material from open market it will have to sell that material in a stipulated time otherwise penalty would be there. Seventy per cent of the respondents felt that lack of proper infrastructure with the societies is also major constraint because during the rainy season it becomes very difficult to keep goods like fertilizer and other domestic commodities safe. Another notable constraint found during the study has been over control of the government or bureaucracy and interference of petty politicians in the society's work. Sixty per cent respondents told grudgingly that government has throttled the spirit of cooperation in these societies. Instead of making it people's movement, cooperative have been becoming the agencies of government. Poor service conditions of the employees working with cooperative societies have also been becoming constraints in most of the societies. Some of the respondents maintained that employees do not take desired interest in the wòrk largely due to insecurity of their jobs. Easy availability of quality products in the open market also posing competition to the cooperative societies. It is generally known that the multi-national companies have launched many new products in terms of fertilisers, weedicides and pesticides and selling the products at very competitive prices posing threat to the functioning of cooperative structures. It was told by the respondents that some of the farmers even changed their interest to other sources of finance like commercial banks as they offer financial support on very easy terms as crop loans and also commercial banks lend more loan on less security deeds. Further, it was brought out by the respondents that cooperative structure has not been meeting the increased aspirations of the farmers in terms of new technology and cash requirement. Factionalism prevailing in the rural areas is also found to be a hurdle in the smooth functioning of the societies. This phenomenon, according to respondents, becomes evident at the time of election of committee members of these cooperative societies. Interference of the politicians, particularly of the local ones further fuel the fire of factionalism. During the course of study it was noted that winning of maximum elections of cooperative societies becomes the question of prestige for political parties and hence more tension.

Table 9.5: Major constraints of the agricultural cooperative service societies

Sr. No.	*Constraints*	*Yes*	*No*	*Total*
1.	Imposition of Govt. Agencies	18(90)	2(10)	20(100)
2.	Untimely supply of material	16(80)	4(20)	20(100)
3.	Supply of substandard material	15(75)	5(25)	20(100)
4.	Less quantity of supplied material	12(60)	8(40)	20(100)
5.	Lack of proper infrastructure	14(70)	6(30)	20(100)
6.	Govt. control on societies	12(60)	8(40)	20(100)
7.	Poor service conditions of the employee	13(65)	7(35)	20(100)
8.	Any other	12(60)	8(40)	20(100)

Attributes of Success and Failure of Cooperative Societies

During the course of data collection, efforts were made to find out the attributes of success/failure of any cooperative society. From the varied views (Table 9.6) of the respondents five broad attributes have emerged. For a successful cooperative society efficient management is of utmost importance as most of the respondents (90 %) held this factor as a basic requirement. Agricultural cooperative service society can be more successful if it is given freedom to work pertaining to decision making at local level, freedom to purchase the agricultural inputs and consumer goods, freedom to use the profit for expansion of society's work and above all unshackling the clutches of bureaucracy. Commercial orientation of the staff is yet another important factor responsible for making any society a success or failure. Integrity of committee members in particular of chairman and secretary of society is another important attribute for any successful society. The most important aspect of the integrity of the chairman/secretary as told by the respondent, is the honesty, secular outlook and good character. Cooperation of the villagers is yet another crucial factor responsible for achieving the success of any society.

Table 9.6: Attributes of success/failure of cooperative societies

Sr. No.	*Attributes*	*Yes*	*No*	*No response*	*Total*
1.	Efficient management	18(90)	2(10)	–	20
2.	Freedom of work	16(80)	4(20)	–	20
3.	Commercial orientation of the staff	14(70)	6(30)	–	20
4.	Integrity of concerned committee members/secretary	17(85)	1(05)	2(10)	20
5.	Cooperation/interest of the villagers	18(90)	2(10)	–	20

Conclusion

The main aim of the present study has been to assess the performance of Cooperative Agricultural Service Societies in Punjab and to highlight the infirmities under them and render suitable suggestions for improvement. Most of the sampled societies under study came into existence in the 60s and 70s while 1/3rd were established before independence. The oldest society found to be the Rayya Cooperative Society which came into existence in 1919 and the newest was Suniarheri Cooperative Society established in 1985. The average memberships, largely consisting of farmers of various categories, was 842. Majority of the societies have been catering more than one village. Except one (Chandpur), all other societies had 2 to 4 kanals of area having 3 rooms and 2 stores on average. 55 per cent of the societies had their own funds up to 1 lac while all others had more than one lac. The societies possessed 2.92 lacs and 58.6 lacs as their share capitals and working capital on average. Majority of the societies advanced loans in between 10 to 30 lacs during the year of study. Most of the societies were gaining profit notwithstanding some defaulters. Supply of various agricultural inputs and domestic kinds along with some cash money have been the major functions of societies. Most of the committee members were found to be involved in the day to day functioning of the societies. Imposition of government agencies like MARKFED, PUNSUP, CONSTOFED etc. for supply of fertiliser and other commodities to societies, which is usually of substandard and untimely and over interference of government officials in the working of societies highly undermined the smooth functioning of cooperative societies. Availability of quality goods in open market at highly competitive price and easy availability of cash from other commercial banks that also more than cooperative on less security deeds, have been deflating the interest of farmers in cooperative. Well to do farmers have been skipping from cooperatives as cooperatives have not been fulfilling their aspiration in terms of new technology and cash requirements. Populistic policy of government (*Karja Muaafi*), factionalism, increasingly due to politics, and insecurity of staff attached with societies were other factors which have been affecting the smooth functioning of cooperative societies. Efficient management, freedom to work and integrity of attached staff, particularly chairman were found to be major attributes to success of any cooperative venture. From the above, it may be inferred that agricultural service cooperative societies are capable of serving the credit and agricultural input needs of the agrarian class and hence, can have dominant role in rural development. But irregularities, lack of political will and bureaucratic hassles have proved deterrent in development of agricultural production and rural society at large.

Suggestions

On the basis of the study, following suggestions are made which may be helpful in improving the functioning of cooperative societies:

— The agricultural cooperative societies (PACS) should be emancipated from numerous unnecessary restrictions pertaining to purchase of fertilisers and other materials including consumable goods from the government/semi — government agencies. The target should not be imposed by the higher authorities to sell the material (clothes, mobil oil, grains, seeds, etc.) even of low quality. Besides, cooperative societies should be made free to invest their own profit so that they can enhance their activities which will in turn increase the profit of the society.

— As most of the societies expressed their dissatisfaction with the supply of material made by MARKFED/PUNSUP there is a need to reconsider about the linkage of these institutions with the PACS.

— Populist policy followed by the government like loan waiving should not be allowed. Such announcement discourages repayment of loan by the members and hence low recovery of loans hampers the smooth functioning/progress of the societies.

— "*Khudkaashat*" tenants should be allowed to avail the facility of the cooperatives without *Jamabandi* because they are the real needy lot to whom the loans should be advanced.

— Rampant corruption in cooperative sector should be tackled firmly.

— Many a times election of these agricultural service societies led to factionalism in the villages. To overcome this problem consensus leadership should be encouraged. Some honorarium to the president and committee members may maintain their interest in societies' works. Societies' committees should have power to fix the limits of loan to be advanced to its members.

— Political interference should be minimised as it has been noted that the functioning of these societies are highly influenced by the political parties. Societies should have powers to arrest the long-term defaulters (under Section 67 of the Act) to run the societies efficiently.

REFERENCES

Awate M.M. (1994), "Cooperative and Agrarian Transformation: A sociological case study in Maharashtra" in *Problems and Prospects of Development of Cooperative, Voluntarism, Communication, Social Tensions and Weaker Sections in Rural India*, edited by S.N. Pawar, R.B. Patil, Mittal Publications, New Delhi.

Attewood, D.W. and B.S. Baviskar (ed) (1994), *Who Shares Cooperatives and Rural Developmen*? Oxford University Press.

Baviskar, B.S. and D.W. Attewood. (1994), Fertile grounds: Why do cooperative flourish in western India? In *Problems and Prospects of Development of Cooperative, Voluntarism, Communication, Social Tensions and Weaker Sections in Rural India,* edited by S.N. Pawar, R.B. Patil, Mittal Publications, New Delhi.

Kavita Sharma, (1995), "Performance of Primary Agricultural Cooperatives Societies in Himachal Pradesh. *Man & Development,* March.

Khusro, A.M. (1992), 'Neglecting Cooperatives.' *Indian Express,* Dec. 15.

Kuralnathan, Manickan (1996), Agriculture Cooperatives in Asia and the Pacific (India-1) *Asian Productivity Organisation*, Tokyo, Japan.

Memoria, C.B. (1989), *Agricultural Cooperative Structure in India*, Kitab Mahal, Allahabad

Sajjan Singh, (1996), Agriculture Cooperations in Asia and the Pacific, (India-2) *Asian Productivity Organisation,* Tokyo, Japan.

Shollapur, M.R. (1997), Analysis of effectiveness of credit cycle: An experience of the primary cooperative credit societies in Karnataka State, *Indian Economic Review*, July, pp. 30-48.

10

MILK CO-OPERATIVES *VIS-À-VIS* RURAL DEVELOPMENT

S.S. CHAHAL & B.K. AGGARWAL

Operation Flood is a well-known programme initiated with an objective to strengthen the dairy industry, through the network of the milk producers' co-operative societies (MPCS) in the rural areas of the Punjab state. The milk co-operatives as such act as a catalyst in promoting economic progress of the rural-folk by providing assured market for milk and supply of dairy inputs including compounded feeds, veterinary and artificial insemination services in rural areas.

The structure of dairy co-operatives in the State consists of MPCS at the village level, milk supply union at the district level and co-operative dairy federation at the apex level. The Punjab State Co-operative Milk Producers' Federation Limited (MILKFED) has envisaged giving impetus to the milk production in state on a continuous basis. As a result, the milk production in Punjab has shown a quantum jump from 32.21 lakh tonnes in 1980-81 to 77.06 lakh tonnes in 1999-2000. This has enhanced the availability of milk from 541 to 875 gm per capita in the above-mentioned period. Dairy development has, thus, assumed a position of paramount importance in the rural economy of the state. These co-operatives have an immense potential for creating self-employment and supplementing the incomes of the dairy farmers, especially of the small and marginal ones, and landless wage earners.

Nevertheless, the dairy development programme implemented on co-operative principles has helped to raise milk production, which in turn became an instrument in augmenting the incomes of dairy farmers. However, it is noticed that there is hardly any study conducted to assess the role of milk co-operatives in strengthening the dairy industry of the state. Keeping this in view, the present study has been undertaken to examine the role of milk co-operatives in the rural development of Punjab.

Data and Methodology

The data pertaining to the number of co-operative societies, their membership, value of milk and milk products procured, number of milch animals, share of livestock in total income of Punjab for the period 1980-81 to 1999-2000 were collected from Statistical Abstracts of Punjab. The data relating to pattern of income from dairy for members and non-members of milk co-operative societies was taken from the Ph.D. dissertation of Chahal (1991) and same was updated for the years 1992-93 and 1999-2000. The tabular analysis was used to achieve the stipulated objectives of the present study.

Results and Discussion

The results of analyses of these data have been discussed under the following sub-heads:

Growth of Milk Co-operative Societies

Milk traders commonly exploit the dairy farmers on various accounts such as paying lower price for milk, irregular payment, etc. To overcome these problems, the Planning Commission of India felt the need to organize the small dairy farmers so that the milk production enterprise becomes a profitable venture. This would not only ensure adequate supplies of fresh milk and other milk products to the urban consumers but also bring handsome returns to the milk producers.

The pattern of growth of milk co-operative societies and their membership has been depicted in Table 10.1. A perusal of the data shows that there were 2593 MPCS in 1980-81, which increased to 5372 in 1999-2000. This exhibited a growth of 107.17 per cent over 1980-81. The pattern of membership reveals that it increased by 3.11 times in 1999-2000 over 1980-81. Further split up of data reveals that the per cent of villages owning a co-operative society has increased from 21.01 in 1980-81 to 43.53 per cent in 1999-2000. The membership per society also reflected an increasing trend as it increased from 37 to 56 in the above said periods. This clearly shows that the milk co-operative movement in the State is picking up with every passing year. The studies conducted by Sidhu and Sidhu (1986) and Chahal (1991) brought out another interesting aspect that in the case of successful co-operative societies a major chunk of membership of these societies has been constituted by weaker sections of the rural population. This has created a sense of equality among masses in rural areas. As all the members, irrespective of their social and economic status, have to stand in same queue for the disposal of the milk. This has encouraged the weaker sections to take up dairying extensively through self-financing or Integrated Rural Development Programme. This in turn helped them to improve their economic status. These findings are in consonance with the study conducted by Devasia (1986).

Table 10.1: Trend in the growth of milk producers' co-operative societies (MPCS) and their membership in Punjab, 1980-81 to 1999-2000

Year	*Societies (No.)*	*Membership ('000s)*	*Villages having MPCS (Per cent)*	*Membership (Per society)*
1980-81	2593	96.75	21.01	37
1983-84	3356	139.77	27.19	42
1986-87	4640	186.52	37.60	40
1989-90	5143	240.39	41.67	47
1992-93	5034	262.06	40.79	52
1993-94	5033	262.06	40.78	52
1994-95	4861	265.12	39.39	53
1995-96	5061	286.50	41.06	57
1996-97	5264	289.02	42.65	55
1997-98	5253	291.31	42.56	55
1998-99	5329	297.74	43.18	56
1999-2000	5372	300.58	43.53	56

Source: Statistical Abstracts of Punjab, 1981-2000.

Volume of Business and Pattern of Profit

With the growth of the milkco-operative societies, the volume of business has been showing an increasing trend. As more people are taking to dairying, the volume of milk available per society has increased over the period. The volume of business per society has increased from Rs. 19.78 thousand in 1980-81 to Rs. 381.43 thousand during 1999-2000 (Table 10.2).

As such, volume of business has increased by 19.28 times over the period under study. The volume of business per member also depicted a similar pattern. This became possible with increasing number of societies earning profit during the study period. The results further reveal that the percentage of societies earning profit has increased from 45 in 1980-81 to 74 in 1999-2000. The profit per society registered an increase by about 19.93 times during the period of study. Similarly, the profit per member depicted a growth of nearly 1200 per cent in 1999-2000 over the base year. It is pertinent to mention that the profit accruing to the co-operative societies is distributed to members in the form of bonus. This facility is not available with any other milk marketing system. Bonus not only helps to boost rural development but also attracts fellow dairy farmers to adopt co-operatives for the disposal of their milk. The milk co-operatives, therefore, ensure better deal to milk-sellers, which in turn helps them to supplement their income by removing unemployment/underemployment. As such, this helps the members to improve upon their economic status and way of life.

Table 10.2: Performance of milk producers' co-operative societies in Punjab, 1981-81 to 1999-2000

Year	*Volume of business per MPCS (Rs. '000s)*	*Volume of business per Member (Rs.)*	*MPCS earning profit (%)*	*Profit per MPCS (Rs.)*	*Profit per Member (Rs.)*
1980-81	19.78	530	45	439	12
1983-84	46.65	1120	55	866	21
1986-87	77.94	1939	60	1524	38
1989-90	89.06	1905	64	1592	34
1992-93	173.83	3339	61	4036	78
1993-94	173.86	3339	61	4044	78
1994-95	202.09	3705	68	5703	93
1995-96	302.47	5343	71	5061	101
1996-97	300.07	5465	71	5613	102
1997-98	263.09	7186	71	7504	135
1998-99	290.04	5191	67	6683	120
1999-2000	381.43	6817	74	8749	156

Source: Statistical Abstracts of Punjab, 1981-2000.

Milch Animal Scenario

With the launching of Operation Flood Programme the milk co-operatives have been further strengthened. This has resulted into assured market for milk in the rural areas. It helps to provide competitive market for milk, thereby, saving the milk sellers from the exploitation of private milk traders in the state. This has encouraged the rural masses to take up dairying enterprise more extensively. It has also resulted into increase in the number of milch animals. An examination of Table 10.3 exhibits that the number of milch animals has increased from 6145 thousand in 1966 to 8810 thousand in 1997. Similarly the number of milking buffaloes has shown a spectacular growth for the same period. However, the number of cows has shown decreasing trend after 1972. As such, number of cows stands approximately at 2639 thousand in 1997. But this negative trend may not be taken alarmingly as the low yielding *desi cow* breeds are being replaced by the exotic/crossbred cows which are high yielding. Thus, rearing of high yielding crossbred cows helped to remove unnecessary burden on the economy by way of saving costly feed and fodder fed to *desi cows*.

Table 10.3: Trend in growth of milch animals in Punjab, 1966-1997

('000s)

Year	*Number of Cows*	*Number of Buffaloes*	*Total number of milch animals*
1966	3162	2983	6145
1972	3390	3796	7186
1977	3312	4110	7422
1990	2832	5578	8410
1993	2800	5731	8531
1997	2639	6171	8810

The dairy farmers responded positively to animals breeding programme for improvement of their stock. The animals inseminated artificially have increased from 250 in 1980-81 to 105029 in 1989-90 (Chahal and Singh, 1993). This trend is still continuing which helps to have high yielding stocks with the dairy farmers.

The results reveal that with the adoption of animal breeding programme and with better management by the dairy farmers, the milk production has increased from 3221 thousand tonnes in 1980-81 to 7706 thousand tonnes in 1999-2000 in the state (Table 10.4). This increase in milk production not only enhanced the per capita availability of milk but also proved a means for the augmentation of the income of the dairy farmers. The per capita availability of milk has increased from 541 to 875 gm per day during the study period. The marketable surplus for the corresponding period has increased from 2024 to 4854 thousand tonnes in the state. This evidence is enough to prove that the milk co-operatives helped the milk producers to supplement their incomes with adoption of dairy enterprise.

Table 10.4: Performance of dairying in Punjab, 1980-81 through 1999-2000

Year	*Milk production ('000s tonnes)*	*Milk availability per capita (gm/day)*	*Marketable Surplus* (000 tonnes)*
1980-81	3221	541	2024
1983-84	3700	570	2331
1986-87	4302	623	2710
1989-90	4972	675	3132
1992-93	5583	735	3517
1993-94	5970	770	3761
1994-95	6215	788	3915
1995-96	6424	798	4047
1996-97	6755	825	4255
1997-98	7165	845	4513
1998-99	7394	855	4658
1999-2000	7706	875	4854

Source: Statistical Abstracts of Punjab, 1981-2000.

Income Status

The results discussed earlier brought out that the dairy co-operatives have brought perceptible change by way of creating more employment opportunities for dairy farmers in the rural areas. It would be rather useful to examine the status of dairying in generating income at macro as well as micro level. The results presented in Table 10.5 reveal that the income from livestock both at current and constant prices have registered growth during period under study. The income (NDP) from the livestock in 1980-81 was Rs. 722.68 crores which increased to Rs. 8319.21 crores in 1999-2000 at current prices. The corresponding figures for income from livestock for the base TE 1981-82 prices stood at Rs. 612.39 and Rs. 1715.66 crores for above said period respectively. A study conducted by Sidhu and Sidhu (1986) reported that the per capita annual income for the member of milk co-operative society estimated at Rs. 7975.10 in 1984-85, out of which dairy contributed about Rs. 2133 of the total income as compared to the state level per capita income of Rs. 4602. These findings are further corroborated by the results presented in Table 10.6. The results clearly evince that income from dairying, both for the members of co-operative society and non-members, has increased over time. The income per farm for members of co-operative societies is higher for medium and large categories farmers as compared to the non-members. A comparison amongst the small category farmers exhibits that income per farm from dairying was higher for non-members compared with the members. The reported reason for this difference was that the non-members sold more quantity at the cost of home consumption of milk, as they have to repay the loan taken from milk-vendors during dry season. The results provided in Table 10.6 clearly show that dairying is helping the dairy farmers in supplementing their income along with the utilization of surplus family labour as income is directly related to level of employment.

Table 10.5: Share of livestock in net domestic product (NDP) of the Punjab, 1980-81 to 1999-2000

Year	*NDP at Current prices*	*NDP at Constant prices (Base Triennium ending: 1981-82)*
1980-81	722.68	612.39
1983-84	994.41	796.16
1986-87	1229.24	775.56
1989-90	1992.90	932.57
1992-93	3141.70	1104.29
1993-94	3857.32	1251.97
1994-95	4510.25	1284.24
1995-96	5417.03	1444.54
1996-97	6352.91	1585.06
1997-98	7245.84	1713.78
1998-99	7496.57	1534.30
1999-2000	8319.21	1715.66

Source: Statistical Abstracts of Punjab, 1981-2000.

Table 10.6: Income from dairying of the members of the MPCS *vis-à-vis* non-members in Punjab

Category of the farm	*1989-90**		*1992-93***		*1999-2000***	
	Member	*Non-member*	*Member*	*Non-member*	*Member*	*Non-member*
Small (1-2)	5923	6311	10044	11346	17031	19240
Medium (3-5)	14237	13284	25457	23355	43169	39605
Large (6 and above)	27540	26144	46625	44850	79065	76055

* Chahal, S.S. "An economic analysis of milk marketing in Punjab", Ph.D. Dissertation, PAU, Ludhiana, 1991.

* Estimated on the basis of 1989-90 values computed by Chahal, 1991.

Conclusion

The foregoing discussion clearly shows that milk co-operatives have made a perceptible progress during the study period and helped to promote rural development as the programme is specifically meant for maximum benefit to the poor and the weaker sections of the rural community. The milk cooperative movement has helped to break down barriers between castes, as the members belonging to diverse social and economic status have to stand in same queue to sell the milk to the milk producers' co-operative society. Besides, the milk co-operatives provide a competitive, assured and remunerative market for milk in the producing areas itself. Dairying has also an important role in reducing risk from crop failure, especially under the situation of extreme climatic conditions. As the dairy cooperative under Operation Flood Programme helped in adoption of improved production technologies, especially related to genetic improvement, better feed utilization and animal health cover, it has resulted in improvement of production potential and its better exploitation. Thus, it is quite clear that dairy cooperatives espousing to the rural development by providing self-employment throughout the year to both men and women in the family. An availability of fluid cash from the sale of milk not only helped in improving dairy production through the purchase of balanced feed and other inputs but also helps in improving crop production through the purchase of off-farm inputs like fertilizers, improved seed, etc. Along with this the milk cooperatives are promoting employment for the other skills as it involved a big infrastructure starting from the milk collection to the final disposal of milk and milk products to the consumers. The milk cooperatives not only bring a sense of equality among various sections of the rural society but also promote development of the rural areas. Thus, it can be concluded that milk cooperatives are acting as catalyst for rural development in Punjab.

REFERENCES

Chahal, S.S., (1991), "Case study into factors determining the success or failure of milk producers cooperative societies in Punjab." *Journal of Agricultural Development and Policy*, 3 (1&2).

Chahal, S.S., (1991), "An economic analysis of milk marketing in Punjab", Ph.D. Dissertation, Punjab Agricultural University, Ludhiana.

Chahal, S.S. and Singh, B., (1998), "An economic analysis of activities of MILKFED in production and marketing of milk", *Indian Cooperative Review*, 30(4).

Devasia, Leelamma, (1986), "Cooperatives and rural development", *Kurukshetra*, 34(6).

Sidhu, D.S. and Sidhu, J.S., (1986), "Case Studies on farmers organizations in India", Research Report (Mimeo.), Department of Economics and Sociology, Punjab Agricultural University, Ludhiana.

Sidhu, D.S. and Sidhu, R.S., (1989), "Case studies of successful and unsuccessful cooperative service societies and milk producers' cooperative societies in Punjab", *Indian Journal of Agricultural Economics*, 45(3).

11

IMPLICATIONS OF WTO FOR AGRICULTURE

R.S. BAWA & P.S. RAIKHY

The major objective of the paper is to bring out implications of WTO for Punjab Agriculture. The discussion in the paper has been divided into two sections.

> Section I surveys the different provisions of GATT-94/WTO for agriculture, and
> Section II is devoted to implications for Punjab agriculture and agenda for action at the State level.

SECTION I

Brettonwoods Conference, held in 1944 for new international economic order, recommended setting up of International Monetary Fund (IMF) to deal with exchange rate and balance of payment problems; International Bank for Reconstruction and Development (IBRD) or World Bank (WB) to deal with problems of reconstruction and development, and International Trade Organisation (ITO) to deal with problems of international trade. While the first two organisations were set up in 1945, ITO was not born as U.S.A. opposed its constitution. A temporary arrangement, called General Agreement on Tariffs and Trade (GATT), became effective from January 1, 1948 and afterwards it became a permanent arrangement as its rules accepted by other countries and its membership increased from 23 in 1948 to 125 in 1994.

Before the formation of WTO in 1995, eight rounds of negotiations were held and the eighth round (1986-94), called Uruguay Round, in which 125 countries participated and in which the scope of negotiations was expanded to cover new areas of Agriculture, Textiles, Trade Related Investment Measures (TRIMS), Trade Related Intellectual Property Rights (TRIPS) and services, was the most comprehensive one. This agreement was signed on April 15, 1994, became effective from January 1, 1995 and WTO was born as a part of this agreement to implement it and to develop co-operation with other institutions like IMF and IBRD for better results. The membership of WTO increased to 140 in November 2000 and 28 more countries were engaged in negotiations to become its members.

Agreement on Agriculture (AoA)

The Uruguay Round Agreement on Agriculture has four aspects:

Market Access

The provision regarding market access has three components:

(a) Removal of quantitative restrictions (QRs) or non-tariff barriers (NTBs) on imports,
(b) Tariffication of the NTBs, and
(c) Establishment of tariff rate quotas (TRQs).

Under the commitment regarding removal of QRs, countries with balance of payment problem are required to announce time frame for removal of QRs. Under the provision for conversion of NTBs into tariffs, all quotas, variable levies, minimum import prices, discriminatory licensing, state trading measures, voluntary restraint agreements and other such measures have to be converted into equivalent tariffs. The tariff level for a commodity has to be set equal to difference between domestic wholesale price and c.i.f.* price of imports in terms of domestic currency. However, the developing countries have been given the option to introduce bound tariff levels without the use of tariffication formula. After tariffication of NTBs, the tariffs are to be reduced by 36 per cent in 6 years in case of developed countries, with a minimum reduction of 15 per cent tariff in each line of production. The developing countries are required to reduce the tariff levels by 24 per cent in 10 years with a

* c.i.f. = Cash Insurance Freight

minimum reduction of 10 per cent tariff in each line of production. However, the least developed countries will have non commitment to reduce tariff levels.

For minimum access opportunities, the AoA provides that if imports of primary agricultural products including their prepared products are less than 3 per cent of domestic consumption then minimum access opportunities have to be provided through tariff rate quotas (TRQs). These TRQs have been termed as 'tunnel through the tariff wall' to provide opportunities for trade in agricultural commodities because the markets for such commodities are generally highly protected. The minimum access, which has to be 3 per cent of domestic consumption of agricultural commodities during 1986-88 period in the first year of implementation of AoA, will have to be progressively increased to 5 per cent of domestic consumption in 6 years. However, if the country has serious balance of payment problem then there is no condition of market access.

Domestic Support

Discipline is subsidy regime provided to agriculture is to be brought by fixing the binding and reduction commitments with respect to support, termed as Aggregate Measure of Support (AMS), which is calculated on the basis of each agricultural product receiving price support, non-exempt direct payments and other subsidies which are not exempted from reduction commitment. In AoA, domestic support measures have been divided into three main categories: (a) Product specific (administered prices) and non-product specific (subsidies on inputs) which are subject to reduction commitments, (b) Blue-Box measures (including production limiting programmes based on fixed area, fixed crop yields and fixed number of livestock etc.), direct payments under CAP and deficiency payments under EU programmes, which are exempted from reduction commitment, and (c) Green-Box measures (including decoupled income support, income insurance, crop insurance government expenditure on research programmes of general nature, environmental and particular product related; pest and disease control; training services; extension and advisory services; inspection services; marketing and promotion services; and infrastructural services including electricity, roads, market and port facilities, water supply, dams and drainage schemes, and other environment programmes. It also includes food security programmes which are also exempted from reduction commitments. Two criteria have been laid down for exemption a category from reduction commitment:

(i) the measures should have no or minimal trade distorting effect or effect on production, (ii) the support should be provided through publicly funded government programme not involving transfer from consumers and shall not constitute price support to producers.

The food security programme, public stockholding and assistance provided to private storage for the programme have also been exempted subject to the conditions that (i) such stocks should correspond to predetermined targets solely for food security, (ii) the process of food stock accumulation and disposal should be financially transparent, (iii) food purchasers have to be made at current market prices and sales from food security stock have to be made at no less than prevailing domestic market price, and (iv) if the stocks are acquired and sold at administered price, the difference between the purchase price and external price has to be counted in the AMS. The external price is the average f.o.b. price in case of net food importing country. This means that if administered price for food security programme is higher than external price, then it will be counted in AMS.

Subject to the above conditions for measurement of AMS eligible for reduction commitment, developed countries have been allowed subsidies (AMS) up to 5 per cent of their value of agricultural output; for developing counties the limit has been fixed at 10 per cent. If the subsidies exceed the limits, the developed countries are required to reduce these by 20 per cent in 6 years, while the developing countries are required to reduce these by 13.3 per cent during the same period. The least developed countries have no reduction commitment.

Export Subsidies

AoA lays down that developed countries would reduce export subsidies by 36 per cent in value and 21 per cent in volume as compared with 1986-90 level in 6 years, while the developing counties have been required to reduce these subsidies by 24 per cent in value and 14 per cent in volume in 10 years. The least developed countries do not have any commitment to reduce the export subsidies. These subsidies are to be reduced on commodity-by-commodity basis through a notified schedule. However, the countries which are not giving subsidies in base period have been prevented from introducing these subsidies.

Sanitary and Phytosanitary (SPS) Measures

AoA also seeks to introduce harmonised standards in respect of regulations for protection of human, animal and plant life. The safety standards include measures that

(a) protect human or animal life from risks arising from additives, contaminants, toxins, disease-carrying organisms in food, beverages and foodstuffs,
(b) protect human life from risks arising from diseases carried by animals, plants or products thereof or from spread of pests,
(c) protect animal or plant life from risks arising from the entry, establishment or spread of pests, diseases, disease-carrying or causing organisms, and
(d) prevent or limit other damages from the entry, establishment or spread of pests.

The sanitary provisions relate to human and animal health, while the phytosanitary provisions relate to plant health aspects. The SPS measures may become trade barriers if

(i) domestic SPS standards are lower than those fixed for the imports by another country,
(ii) SPS standards differ across the countries, and
(iii) the processes of one country are not recognised by the other country.

The standards, guidelines and recommendations of Codex Alimentarious Commission (for food safety), International Officer of Epizootics (for animal health) and Secretariat of the International Plant Protection Convention (for plant health) are the basis for harmonisation of SPS standards for the countries. Members can adopt more stringent SPS measures, if there is scientific justification for it. All SPS measures and changes in these are to be notified in transparent manner and the measures are to be applied in no less favourable manner to imports than for similar domestic products.

Besides these four aspects of AoA, there are other areas/provisions of GATT-94, which have major implications for agriculture, agro-food industry and agro-exports.

Technical Barriers to Trade (TBT)

TBT cover the regulations and standards governing the sale of products and aim at correction of market inefficiencies resulting from production, distribution and consumption of these products. These barriers include measures to protect public health, safety, environment and social cohesion. TBT may take the shape of technical specifications like process, product or packaging standards, and/or information remedies and labelling requirements for fresh food products and labelling of textile products.

Agreement on Trade Related Apects of Intellectual Property Rights (TRIPS) and Agriculture

The agreement on TRIPS has implications for agricultural sector also because the provisions will apply to bio-technology and micro-organism with effect from January 1, 2005. In agriculture and food industry, IPRs are of the type of *sui-generis* protection through plant breeders rights (PBRs) for new and distinguishable varieties. This form of protection has been accepted globally through the International Union for the Protection of New Varieties of Plants (UPOV) Convention. However, the privilege provided to the farmers to re-use the seeds for own holding in the UPOV Convention in 1961 was withdrawn in an amendment to UPOV Convention in 1991, wherein now the farmer is required to pay the royalty for re-using the seeds. There is also provision for patents and copyrights for plant varieties, agricultural machinery and technology. The patent protection to the intellectual properties in the agricultural sector has its implications for the costs, productivity and availability of agricultural commodities.

Further, the agreement on textiles and clothing and agreement on anti-dumping also have significant implications for agricultural sector.

Since the formation of WTO on January 1, 1995, three Conferences at Ministerial Level have been held, the first at Singapore during December 9-13, 1996, second at Geneva during May 18-20, 1998 and the third at Seattle during November 29 to December 3, 1999 and more and more issues are emerging. At Seattle Conference, agricultural issues were discussed again but no unanimity could be reached.

SECTION II

Punjab, with 1.57 per cent of geographical area and 2.39 per cent of population of the country, made significant contribution to the food security of the country. Since the inception of procurement policy in the country up to 1998-99, the State contributed about 239 million tonnes of foodgrains to the central pool, which constituted more than 50 per cent share.

Other achievements on the agricultural front during 1970-71 to 1998-99 include:

- Increase in foodgrain production from 73.05 lakh tonnes to 226.91 lakh tonnes.
- Increase in sugarcane production from 5.27 lakh tonnes to 6.08 lakh tonnes.
- Increase in cotton production from 8.18 lakh tonnes to 18.68 lakh tonnes in 1996-97 (then declined to 5.96 lakh tonnes in 1998-99).
- Increase in per capita daily milk availability from 541 grams to 855 grams.
- Increase in egg production and the number reached 2510 million eggs in 1995-96.
- The State produced 25 per cent share (10,000 tonnes) of the total mushroom production of 40,000 tonnes in the country in 1998-99.
- The State produced 25 per cent share (3000 tonnes) of the total honey production of 12 thousand tonnes in the country in 1998-99.
- The area under vegetable increased by 6 times during 1970-71 to 1998-99.
- The fruit production has doubled in the last five years.
- The flower and cut flower production has also picked up in the State.

Other notable features of agricultural development in the State include:

- Highly intensive use of land, with 85 per cent of the geographical area under the crops.
- High irrigation intensity, with 96 per cent of the net area being irrigated.
- Highly intensive use of land with 185 per cent cropping intensity.
- Highest level of mechanisation, (including tractors, tubewells, combines and others), with 4 lakh tractors which constituted 25 per cent of tractors of the country.
- Exports from Punjab, especially of agro-based products increased rapidly.

In spnite of all these developments, the agriculture in the State is at the crossroads and many negative developments have also taken place:

- Production of pulses has gone down from 3.08 lakh tonnes in 1970-71 to 0.47 lakh tonnes in 1998-99.
- Production of oilseeds has gone down from 2.33 lakh tonnes in 1970-71 to 1.67 lakh tonnes in 1998-99.
- Per centage of holdings below 2 hectares increased from 38.6 per cent in 1981 to 44.73 per cent in 1991.
- Per centage of holdings above 4 hectares decreased from 33.4 per cent in 1981 to 29.5 per cent in 1991.
- Agricultural sector employed 62 per cent share of the State Population, contributing 44 per cent of State income, while the remaining 38 per cent non-farm population contributed 56 per cent share.
- Annual growth rate of agriculture (including livestock) has gone down from 5.29 per cent in 7th Plan to 3.00 per cent in 8th Plan and is feared to decline further to 2.38 per cent during 9th Plan.
- Growth rate of overall economy declined from 6.0 per cent in 7th Plan to 5.1 per cent in 8th Plan and is expected to experience 4.96 per cent growth in 9th Plan.
- Total indebtedness of Punjab farmers was estimated at Rs. 5701 crores in 1997-98, which worked out to Rs. 5721 per operated acre.
- There is huge shift towards paddy-wheat rotation, which has reduced organic content of land and further increase in yield is possible at very high marginal cost.
- Underground water is rapidly depleting in the State and water table is falling.
- The State is lagging behind in industrial development as the share of the secondary sector has stagnated around 22 per cent.
- Growth of agro-based industries is not commensurate with the potential of the State and Punjab's share in these industries is much below than that of many foodgrain deficit states.
- Punjab economy has become high cost economy. The per quintal cost of production of wheat in 1996-97 in Punjab was higher than that in Haryana, Rajasthan and Uttar Pradesh. Per quintal cost of production of paddy in Punjab in 1995-96 was higher than that in Orissa and Madhya Pradesh.

The over-dependence of Punjab economy on agriculture has been criticised since early eighties as the gains of green revolution started tapering-off. So long as other states were deficit in foodgrains, the Central Government was keen to procure wheat and rice from Punjab and the share of the State in the Central Pool reached its maximum in case of rice (46.0%) in 1989-90 and wheat (70.3%) in 1992-93. Afterwards, the share of the State in central pool of foodgrains, though experienced fluctuations, but showed declining trend. When agricultural growth in other states like Andhra Pradesh, Karnataka, Bihar, Madhya Pradesh and U.P. picked up bring more area under cultivation and irrigation, the share of the Punjab wheat and rice in the foodgrain production of the country and in the Central Pool started declining. The fear that Punjab foodgrains would not find market started coming out to be true, and in the past 2-3 years, the situation has gone from bad to worse, with farmers waiting in the market for weeks together for the procurement agencies to come and procure their produce. The incidence of these agencies rejecting the foodgrains by terming it substandard also increased and the situation became worst during paddy season in 2000-2001.

While the State's agriculture was reeling under the problem of plenty, GATT-94, with its Agreement on Agriculture appeared on the horizon, involving policy measures for trade liberalisation in agriculture. Though the State openly opposed WTO policies on agriculture, virtually no steps were taken to meet the challenge, which may also offer opportunities.

GATT-94/WTO Agreement on Agriculture has serious implications for Punjab, which is over dependent on agriculture. Under Market Access provisions of the agreement QRs on 772 lines of production, of which about 30 per cent related to agricultural and related activities were lifted by March 31, 2000 and the remaining QRs, which also included larger proportion of agricultural and allied lines of production have been lifted from April 1, 2000. The QRs have been converted into tariffs, with the obligation of reducing these by 24 per cent over a period of 10 years. Thus Punjab agriculture has been thrown open to the world competition. India's acceptance to Tarrif Rate Quota (TRQ) of milk and cream in powder, granules or other solid forms (with the exceeding 6% and 1.5%) at 15 per cent tariff rate shook the dairy sector of Punjab during the first-half of 2000 and there were panic sales of dairy animals. Though the situation was saved due to non-entry of these items, the fear still looms large on the dairy industry and all plans of expansion of dairy enterprise by the entrepreneurs have been abandoned. The provision for imports of 3 per cent of domestic consumption of agricultural commodities (which has to be progressively increased to 5 per cent in 6 years) has also increased the worry of Punjab farmers, who are already not finding market for their foodgrains in the country.

Upto early nineties, Punjab wheat and rice had some competitive advantage, in the international market but due to continuously declining prices in the international market and increase in domestic prices, the competitive advantage is lost. Price of Punjab wheat at Bombay port is considerably higher than f.o.b.* Gulf price of U.S. wheat. The price of Australian wheat at Bombay port in 2000-2001 ranged between Rs. 4,541 to 4,775 per tonne, whereas the procurement price of Punjab wheat was Rs. 5,800 per tonne. By adding transport and other changes, the price of Punjab wheat becomes more than Rs. 8,300 per tonne at Bombay port. Punjab rice is also costlier than Thailand rice and its competitiveness is rapidly declining. Under the circumstances the panic of the farmers and the State Government is but natural. Indian Government has imposed 50 per cent tariff rate on wheat. With the imposition of renegotiated bound tariff rates of 100 per cent in case of wheat and 150 per cent in case of rice, wheat and rice of Punjab will become competitive in the national market but there is no possibility of its becoming competitive in the international market.

Punjab has now planned to export wheat to South Korea, Philippines, Yemen, Vietnam, Dubai and other Gulf countries to Rs. 4,300 per metric tonne delivered at Jamnagar port. Even FCI is making wheat available at ex-godown price of Rs. 4,150 per tonne, which works out to $89 per tonne and after including freight, port handling etc. comes to $100 per tonne f.o.b. USA and Canada have represented before WTO about India highly subsidising wheat exports (Damodaran, 2001).

So far as Domestic Support to Agriculture provisions are concerned, AMS in the Indian Agriculture is negative. Even the non-product specific subsidy is much below the limit specified for AMS for developing countries. Similar has been the case for Punjab also (Table 11.1). However, now when the administered prices of wheat and rice become higher than the external prices, product-specific support may also become positive, though there is no possibility of application of AMS reduction provision for Punjab Agriculture in the near future, but WTO approval to Green-Box and Blue-Box measures largely being taken by developed countries has led to continuous decline of foodgrain prices in the

* f.o.b. = Free on Board

international market and Punjab wheat and rice will not become competitive in the international market. EU and USA paid direct subsidies up to $30,000 per farmer and these subsidies are not covered under reduction commitments. However, if instead of AMS, the concept of PSE, with reduction commitments is included in the WTO provisions, then it is possible that over a medium to long period, Punjab wheat and rice may become internationally competitive.

Table 11.1: Total aggregate measure of support (AMS) to Punjab agriculture on the basis of official exchange rate

(Rs. millions)

Year	*Product Specific AMS*	*Non-Product Specific AMS*	*Total AMS (2+3)*	*Value of Agriculture Production*	*Tatal AMS as % of Agriculture Production (4/5)*100*
(1)	(2)	(3)	(4)	(5)	(6)
1981-82	−10015.6	352.1	−9663.5	28190.3	−34.28
1982-83	−6003.2	631.4	−5371.8	30597.8	−17.56
1983-84	−5955.9	1017.9	−4938.0	32413.5	−15.23
1984-85	−9275.6	2201.7	−7073.9	37728.7	−18.75
1985-86	−26377.0	2904.5	−23472.5	43860.0	−53.52
1986-87	−18174.6	1653.7	−16520.9	44655.9	−37.00
1987-88	−29175.9	2848.8	−26327.1	53646.0	−49.08
1988-89	−14334.6	4381.5	−9953.1	58567.2	−17.00
1989-90	−49224.6	5909.9	−43323.7	68499.0	−63.25
1990-91	−26900.7	4994.0	−21902.7	71365.6	−30.70
1991-92	−27006.0	8085.6	−18920.4	89158.0	−21.22
1992-93	−42959.3	10335.2	−32624.1	95752.6	−34.07

Source: Bhalla, G.S. and Gurmail Singh (1996), *Impact of GATT on Punjab Agriculture*, Institute of Development & Communication, Ajanta Publications, Delhi.

Though input-subsidy policy has fiscal implications, so are those of Green and Blue-Box policies adopted by developed countries, which included deficiency payments and decoupled income payments. However, the inefficiency, high cost, poor targeting, corruption continue to be the major problems of input-subsidy policy. It is argued that appropriate pricing of inputs would lead to saving of budgetary resources, which could be spent on public investment in the agricultural sector and rural infrastructure.

Economic theory also supports income-subsidy policy *vis-à-vis* input-subsidy policy, because through excessive use of inputs, the input-subsidy leads to inefficient allocation of resources. For example, free/subsidised supply of water is considered responsible for excessive exploitation of underground water and fall in water table, which will have long term economic and geographic implications. Small and marginal farmers will be hard hit, because they will not be able to install deep tubewells. There is lot of inefficiency in canal irrigation (due to lack of investment in maintenance of the systems), electricity boards and fertiliser industry etc. due to the input-subsidy policy.

The reduction commitments of export subsidies on agricultural products will have favourable effects on the competitive of Punjab agriculture, because this subsidy is much higher in case of developed countries. For example, out of $7 billion export subsidy provided by EC, 33 per cent was provided to dairy products, 20 per cent to beef, 11 per cent to sugar, 8 per cent to coarse grain, 5 per cent to wheat products and 23 per cent to other agricultural products. It has been estimated that these subsidies worked out to $2169 per tonne in case of butter and butter oil, $1018 per tonne on cheese, $796 per tonne on milk powder, $470 per tonne on sugar and $30.5 per tonne on wheat (Gulati, 2001). Clearly, with such a huge export subsidy, Indian markets will be flooded with agro-products of developed countries and dairy industry of Punjab in particular will close down.

TBT and SPS provisions of AoA also have serious implications for Punjab agriculture because the quality and packing etc. of processed products including fruits, vegetables, honey, milk and milk products, meat products etc. has to be of international standard, otherwise these products can be rejected on technical and sanitary grounds.

So far as implications of TRIPS for Punjab agriculture are concerned, these do not appear to be of serious dimension in the immediate future. Studies have shown that in Punjab 92 per cent seed requirements are met by farmers themselves, while commercial sources constituted only 8 per cent of the required seeds (Sidhu *et al.*, 1998). The seed replacement rate in Punjab has also been very low, it was less than 7 per cent as compared to the norm of 25 per cent (Singh and Asokan, 1997). Moreover, the seed cost constitutes less than 10 per cent of the total variable cost and less than 5 per cent of total cost of production in case of important agricultural crops. Thus the TRIPS and the relevant 'Protection of Plant varieties and Farmers' Rights Bill' when passed in India may not adversely affect the farmers of the State and the rights of the farmers to re-use the seeds and exchange with other farmers have been protected.

Agenda for Future at State Level

Agriculture is the lifeline of Punjab State. But the resource poor and predominantly small and marginal farmers may not be able to compete in the international market without adequate infrastructure, assistance and technology. Certain steps can be taken at the state level to improve the competitiveness of Punjab agriculture, though at the WTO negotiations level only the Central Government will play its role.

First, so far as conforming to WTO provisions are concerned, though Punjab Government justifies direct subsidies to agriculture on economic, social, political and moral grounds, but input-subsidies do involve more distortions and lot of wastage due to poor targeting; therefore, the State Government should make systematic efforts in phased manner to convert these subsidies into deficiency payments or decoupled income support. The beginning may be made withdrawing free electricity to agriculture and giving equivalent amount as deficiency payments. Other input subsidies can also be converted into such payments later on.

Second, assuming that the developed countries will continue with their Blue and Green Box measures, Punjab should also take urgent steps to invest more in agricultural research, extension and advisory services, marketing and promotion services, infrastructural services, environmental and conservation programmes an other payments which are not subject to reduction commitment as per AoA. In view of U.S.A. and Canada's representation before WTO about India's susbsidisation of wheat exports, and administered prices of wheat and rice being much higher than international prices, the procurement prices of wheat and paddy be adjusted accordingly close to the international prices and the difference be accounted for through Green-Box and Blue-Box measures. The resources for such measures may be generated by specific grants from the centre and disinvestment of low utility state agricultural and other related enterprises.

Third, quality consciousness has to be created among the farmers to meet SPS conditions. Agricultural products have to be of high quality with lowest toxic and insecticide contents. Farmers be encouraged to grow Durum wheat variety and basmati rice, processable varieties of potato, tomato, other vegetables and fruits, because quality should be the watch-word in agricultural products. The quality of agricultural products can be ensured from the level of the seeds, cultivation practices and use of herbicides, weedicides and pesticides etc.

Fourth, there is need of diversification of agriculture from wheat and rice to other cereals and pulses, which are processable. Further diversification towards cash crops, vegetables and fruits is required to ease the problem of excess supply of wheat and rice which has led to glut situation. Public Distribution System is being more and more targeted and there is reduced role of Food Corporation of India in procuring the foodgrains. In the budget for 2001-2002, the responsibility of procurement and PDS is being increasingly shifted to the states and state governments will have to create lot of storage facilities, incur huge expenditure on procurement and gear up their procurement agencies. Still the produce will not find market. Therefore, to reduce the burden of procurement of foodgrains, State Government should adopt wheat and rice acreage limiting programmes. In order to encourage the farmers to grow other cereals, pulses, vegetables and fruits etc., subsidy per acre (to the extent of difference in returns from wheat and paddy and alternative crops, which are in short supply) be given by the State Government. Initially such a subsidy may be fixed at 50 per cent of the profitability of the farmer from wheat and rice (approximately Rs. 4,500 per acre per annum) for a period of 5 years for 25 per cent land holding of the farmers. After 5 years it may be reviewed again. The subsidy for diversification may be given out of Agricultural Readjustment Fund to which Central and State Governments should contribute in 75:25 ratio.

Fifth, the State Government should negotiate with other developing countries (as has been done in case of potato with Sri Lanka and wheat with Gulf countries) to explore mutual trade possibilities. The State Government should develop adequate facilities of storage at Kandla port for the purpose. Agricultural Exports and Marketing Facilities Fund may be used for creating such facilities.

Sixth, to strengthen the programme of diversification of agriculture, State should encourage setting up of the agro-processing industries in the State (Raikhy and Nanda, 2000). Following suggestions are given in this context:

- Agro-processing units set up in the rural areas so that rural labour gets employment. The units be set up near the cluster of villages.
- Large/medium units be set up to get the benefit of economies of scale and ensure high quality of product and packing to increase the shelf-life of the products. Alternatively, small units, with sub-contracting arrangements with large/medium units for intermediate processing be set up.
- Farmers must be involved in the processing units, because they

are the suppliers of raw material. Moreover, if farmer's share in consumer's rupee is to be increased such an arrangement becomes necessary, otherwise, there will be monopsonistic exploitation of the farmers by the processing units.

- Farmer's co-operatives appear to be the viable alternative for the purpose. State Government should provide the seed capital and farmers be encouraged to become the shareholders. Liberal credit facilities may also be made available by the commercial banks for the purpose. Later on, Government may sell its shares to the workers of the units.
- Initially such processing units be set up in selected blocks only, depending upon the type of cereals, vegetables and fruits available. After the success of these units, such units be set up in other blocks.
- The role of the State Government is very crucial in planning, co-ordinating and executing the plan for setting up such units. A comprehensive plan be formulated for the State as a whole, through a techno-economic survey. Such plan is essential to minimise the mortality rate of the units.
- Due to the seasonal nature of the agro-processing units, capacity utilisation may be low. Therefore multi-product units, processing different types of products — tomato, potato, fruits, vegetables, milk etc. be set up.
- In case of rice, sugar and cotton units large complexes be set up, processing the products and by-products so as to carry production to the third stage of processing. For example sugar, industrial alcohol, ethanol, alcohol based products, paper and pulp, chemicals and electricity etc.; rice shelling, rice bran oil-solvent extraction, paper and board, specialities from rice etc.
- Alternatively, more schemes of integrated rural industrial townships, as in case of Goindwal, be prepared to generate linkage effects.
- Institute for Agro-Industries be set up in the State to provide information about modern technology, technical knowledge, skill and to act as a link between food-processing units and the markets. Alternatively, collaborative arrangements with big business houses and multinationals may have to be explored.
- The State may settle terms and conditions for inviting multinationals to set up 100 per cent export-oriented units.
- For quality packing, collaborative arrangements may be made

with the Institute for packing or a cell may be set up in the Institute for Agro-Industries in the State.

- For technical manpower in food processing, universities and technical institutes should start relevant courses.
- Raw material for agro-processing units should be purchased in the post-harvest glut season to avoid wastage and fall in prices.
- In case of big business houses/MNCs setting up agro-processing units in the State, contract farming be encouraged in the State.

The State has to play market friendly role under the new economic scenario, by providing export infrastructure, technical expertise, trading houses, storage facilities, good roads, transport facilities, dry port and air transport (for perishable products) facilities so as to create an environment for agro-processing. This will help in sizable value addition and employment generation in the rural areas.

Punjab has tremendous scope for setting up of agro-processing units in dairy products, bakery, animal and poultry feed, liquor, malt and malt products, cotton spinning, weaving, finishing and garments, blankets, shawls and carpets, tanning and preparation of leather and leather products, pulp and paper products, animal and poultry meat and egg powder, canning and preservation of fruits and vegetables, vanaspati and other edible oils, starch and starch products etc. (Shergill & Gurmail Singh, 1994).

Seventh, in view of the fact that developed countries are providing export subsidies to the extent of 100 per cent, Punjab, which is located in one corner of the country, has all the more justification to provide export subsidies, at least till other countries continue with export subsidy. The policy of Indian Railways overcharging the freight to subsidise the passenger traffic goes against remote states like Punjab and Railways must provide special incentives for exports.

Eighth, the possibilities of opening land routes through neighbouring countries to export agricultural products be explored, so that transport costs could be reduced.

Last, the State must formulate its own agricultural policy, so as to delineate the desired cropping pattern, marketing and processing of agro-products and the measures to achieve the objectives of the agricultural policy.

The State Government has taken some measures in the budget for 2001-2002 to create infrastructure for exports and agricultural diversification by setting up Agricultural Readjustment Fund,

Agricultural Marketing and Exports Development Fund and providing Rs. 10 crore for agricultural research. The initial provision for the funds is grossly inadequate and the steps have to be strengthened.

Thus sustained efforts are needed to transform the WTO challengers into opportunities because free and fair trade will be in the interest of all the countries in the long run. Ultimate test of a policy lies in its success to achieve the desired goals and good governance means a lot in this context.

REFERENCES

Aggarwal, Ashish (1994), *GATT and the Developing Countries*, Mohit Publications, New Delhi.

Bawa, R.S. & P.S. Raikhy (ed.) (2000), *Punjab Economy: Emerging Issues*, Guru Nanak Dev University, Amritsar.

Bhalla, G.S. and Gurmail Singh (1996), *Impact of GATT on Punjab Agriculture*, Ajanta Publications, New Delhi.

Bhalla, G.S. and G. Singh (1997), "Recent Development in Agriculture: A State Level Analysis", *Economic and Political Weekly*, March 29.

Chadha, G.K. (ed.) (2001), *WTO and the Indian Economy*, Deep & Deep, New Delhi.

Chadha, Rajesh (2000), "Understanding the WTO Regime," *Economic and Political Weekly*, March, 25.

Chakraborty, Debashis (2001), "WTO and Its Impact on Indian Agriculture and Industry" in G.K. Chadha (ed.) *op.cit*.

Chand, Ramesh (1998), "Removal of Import Restrictions and India's Agriculture: The Challenge and Strategy", *Economic and Political Weekly*, April 11.

Chawla, N.K. and Ravindra Kumar (1997), "International Food Laws and Their Implications for the Indian Dairy Industry", *Indian Dairyman*, Vol. 49, No. 5.

Chowdhary, N.K. & J.C. Aggarwal (1993), *Dunkel Proposals: Implications for India & Third World*, Shipra Publishers, New Delhi.

Damodaran, Harish (2001), "Subsidy Row Behind Wheat Export Move", *Business Line*, March 30.

Dhar, Biswajit and Sachin Chaturvedi (1999), *WTO Agreements and Agricultural Sector: Implications and Options for India*, RIS, New Delhi.

Gill, Khem Singh (1994), *Performance, Prospects and Constraints of Agricultural Development in Punjab*, Oxford & IBH, New Delhi.

Gill, Sucha Singh and Jaswinder Singh Brar (1996), "Global Market and Competitiveness of Indian Agriculture — Some Issues", *Economic and Political Weekly*, Aug. 10.

Government of India (2001), "India Files Proposals on Agriculture", *India & WTO*, Vol. 3 No. 1, Ministry of Commerce and Industry.

Government of Punjab (1999), *Agriculture in Punjab — 1998-99*, Department of Agriculture, Chandigarh.

Gulati, Ashok (2001), "Indian Agriculture and the WTO: Preparing for the New Millennium" in G.K. Chadha (ed.), *op.cit*.

Guleria, Amar S. and Nagesh Singh "WTO and Prospects of Indian Agriculture" in G.K. Chadha (ed.), *op.cit*.

Nanda, Paramjit & P.S. Raikhy (2001), "WTO, Environmental and Labour Standards and India's Textile Exports—Some Implications" in G.K. Chadha (ed.), *op.cit.*

Nanda, Paramjit & P.S. Raikhy (2000), "Exports From Punjab—Performance and Potentials" in R.S. Bawa and P.S. Raikhy (ed.), *op.cit.*

Panchmukhi, V.R. (2001), "World Trade Organisation and India—Challenges and Perspectives" in G.K. Chadha (ed.), *op.cit.*

Raikhy, P.S. & Paramjit Nanda (2000), "Agro-Industries in Punjab—Potential and Suggested Framework" in R.S. Bawa and P.S. Raikhy (ed.), *op.cit.*

Shergill, H.S. and Gurmail Singh (1994), *Scope of Development of Agro-Industries in Rural Punjab*, Institute for Development and Communication, Chandigarh.

Sidhu, M.S. (2001), "Impact of World Trade Organisation on the Indian Seed Industry" in G.K. Chadha (ed.), *op.cit.*

Sidhu, M.S., S.S. Grewal and J.R. Gupta (1998), "Sources of Seed and Rate of Replacement for Wheat Crop in Punjab", *Agricultural Economics Research Review*, Vol. II, No. 2.

Singh, Gurdev and S.R. Asokan (1997), "Seed Industry: Problems and Prospects" in B.M. Desai (ed.) *Agricultural Development Paradigm for the Ninth Plan under New Economic Environment*, Oxford & IBH, New Delhi.

Singh, Joginder (2000), "Implications of World Trade Organization for Punjab Agriculture" in R.S. Bawa & P.S. Raikhy (ed.), *op.cit.*

Singh, Joginder and D.K. Grover (2000), "Environmental Issues and Policy Options in the Agrarian Economy of Indian Punjab" in R.S. Bawa and P.S. Raikhy (ed.), *op.cit.*

Singh, Nishan & P.S. Raikhy (2000), "Economics of Dairy Farming in Punjab" in R.S. Bawa and P.S. Raikhy (ed.) *op.cit.*

Singh, N.P. (2000), "Punjab-Swamped by White Glut", *Outlook*, June 12.

Singh, Sukhpal (2001), "New Barriers to Trade Under W.T.O.: Implications of T.B.T. and S.P.S. Measures for India's Agro-Food Industry and Agro-Exports" in G.K. Chadha (ed.), *op.cit.*

WTO, India-Quantitative Restrictions on Imports of Agricultural, Textile and Industrial Products: Report of the Appellate Body, *WT/DS90/AB/R*, August 23, 1999.

12

CHALLENGES OF AGRICULTURAL RESEARCH IN PUNJAB IN THE WTO REGIME

VIKRAM CHADHA

In the wake of the clamorous hype on the probable repercussions of the WTO obligations for agriculture in the State, the Punjab Government seems to have woken up from its blessed slumber by addressing itself to the issues concerning the making of agricultural production more competitive. In the recently adopted State budget, besides allocating Rs.50 crore to provide export subsidies to farmers and agro processing industry under the green box measures, the State Government has also apportioned Rs.15 crore for agricultural research and Rs.550 crore for an Agricultural Adjustment Fund.

The quintessence of the arguments presented at various fora by the politician, farmers, experts and policy makers alike, is that since the WTO norms will expose the domestic agriculture, based on expensive inputs; inefficient farm practices and pampering subsidies, to unrestricted low priced agricultural imports, it may be difficult for our farm sector to withstand this competitive influx. That is why, of late everyone has been harping on the need to reduce the cultivation costs and also to introduce unorthodox agricultural practices, including new systems of crop rotation, to produce competitive agricultural crops. That is another matter that in spite of the recent nightmarish experience of the wasted deluge of potato crop in the State, much audacious alarming voices for the proper marketing and storage of surplus crops, have yet to be heard.

But nevertheless, the Government's recent budgetary allocation at least does strike a happy note for the farm sector, whereby a thinking has initiated that even the State Government must allocate substantial outlays for carrying out agricultural research aiming at reducing costs, besides researching on the unconventional methods of cultivation, to make this sector viable and internationally competitive. Though agriculture happens to be a state subject, the State Government has so far done precious little as far as agricultural research is concerned, and has largely shifted the responsibility of farm research on the central agencies like ICAR. Perhaps the State Government presumes that its responsibility is only limited to the distribution of seeds, fertilisers and other inputs among agriculturists, which nevertheless is too narrow an outlook from the point of view of developing a sound potential in the farm sector.

The gross neglect of the research scenario in the State, in spite of fabricating a vast grid of research institutions and establishments, is borne out by the fact that the aggregate R&D spending in the State could barely scamper to Rs.48 crore in 1997 from a low of Rs.38 crore in 1994. Exclusive allocation of the plan outlay for the development of Science & Technology (S&T) could be made only as late as in the 8th Plan, when Rs.11.85 crore were allocated for S&T, while only Rs.2.44 crore were actually spent. This plan outlay on S&T and environment has been marginally raised to Rs.53.82 crore during 9th Plan, out of which during the year 2000, only Rs.3.91 crore (0.15 % of the annual plan outlay) were expanded on S&T development, which indeed is a pathetically small effort. How much out of this trivial amount would have been spent on farm research could be anybody's guess. Thus the most vital sector of the Punjab economy—agriculture—continued to remain bereft of the benign benefits of R&D, which indeed is a crucial element in reducing its cost of production to make it competitive. It is in this context, whether driven by the exigencies spewed up by the WTO conditionalities, that even a paltry allocation for farm research in the current State budget is a heartening development.

Now, it is a common place knowledge that R&D happens to be a long drawn and a costly process. A meagre outlay of Rs.15 crore is too miniscule to meet the onerous obligations of the myriad aspects enveloping this vast sector. So the critical issue at this juncture could be, how to narrow down the focus on some of the selected activities of prime importance in the farm sector, which need to be addressed immediately, so as to optimally utilise this meagre sum allocated for this purpose. To my mind, the instant research focus of the research centre set up in PAU Ludhiana for carrying out agricultural research should revolve round some of the following aspects:

Everyone has recently cried hoarse about the outdated traditional cropping pattern being practiced in Punjab agriculture. It has proved to be too uncompetitive besides damaging the ecological balance in the State. The proposed Agricultural Research Centre must concertedly work on evolving new prolific crop rotation cycle that should aim at maximising profitability of the farmers without compromising on the crop productivity and the ecosystem.

Research in biotechnology, an area which is unequivocally known to be raising crop productivity based on genetically engineered robust disease resistant varieties of seeds and plants and manures, should be intensively taken up and applied in Punjab agriculture.

Research in new methods of cultivation, irrigation and growing crops under regulated environments could bring about perceptible increases in productivity and profitability in agriculture.

Research in developing new systems and equipment for preservation and conservation of the surplus food crops, such as silos, bins and warehouses etc. must be stepped up so as to enhance the bargaining strength of the farmers and also for preventing the sinful wastage of food reserves.

Similarly some other such areas of farm operations, involving low cost of development, can be sorted out for a focused research by involving agricultural scientists and experts, which need to be taken up immediately for improving the viability and competitiveness of agriculture in the State, within the constraint of the meagre budgetary allocation for farm research by a resource strapped State.

It is needless to say that along with this concerted research activity, there is an utmost need to monitor its progress. Unlike before, the focus should be on practical applied research on the farm itself, rather than dabbling in its theoretical aspects in the laboratories and research journals. The farmers must be practically demonstrated new developments on the fields for inducing them to adopt these. Let's buckle up to confront the new challenge, may be in a humble way, nonetheless absolutely resolutely.

Of course, as a concomitant measure, the Government should be forthright in assisting the farmers in marketing their produce profitably, both domestically and in foreign markets. The Government should also plan to set up a number of agro-based industries so as to process the surplus agricultural produce without allowing the recurrence of the tragic waste of a bumper crop as it happened in the case of the last potato crop season. The government should itself take up the initiative to set up such industries without abdicating its responsibility to the MNCs.

The current economic scene is hotting up for free market competition. The Punjab farmer is quite progressive and dynamic and would not hesitate to seize upon any fruitful opportunity afforded to him. The only thing he needs is a moral and psychological support from the more astute and enlightened leaders and planners in this hour of flux. He surely has the capacity and courage to turn a dream into a reality and to transform an inhospitable circumstance into a benevolent one.

SECTION–III

RURAL CREDIT INSTITUTIONS

13

ROLE OF INSTITUTIONAL FINANCE AND GOVERNMENT INVESTMENTS IN CAPITAL FORMATION OF PUNJAB AGRICULTURE

M.K. SEKHON & PARMINDER KAUR

Capital formation in agriculture comprises asset creation, directly and indirectly, for augmenting production, land reclamation, preventing soil erosion, irrigation and flood control directly add to the existing stock of capital. Inputs such as equipments, animals, fertilisers, storage, transport and communication, all these are important components of capital formation. Investment on research, science, technology and training are equally important segments of capital formation which improve upon quality and productivity resulting in the shift of the production frontier. Investment in all these various types of activities in agriculture can be financed by individual farmers having surplus funds or by the collective agencies like cooperatives, non-governmental organisations or by the Government.

This paper examines the role of institutional finance for private capital formation and also the trends in public capital formation *versus* government expenditure in agriculture since the planning era. With the large scale adoption of modern production technology, demand for cash inputs went up manifolds. Consequently, the cash requirements of the farming business for the current inputs and for making capital investments increased on the farms bringing the need for agricultural credit in sharp focus. The financial institutions by the Government of India, through the monetary authorities, were directed to pump up credit in the agriculture sector in commensuration with their growing cash requirements. Availability of adequate credit/finance to the agricultural sector is one of the most important factors for achieving the objectives of increased foodgrains production/productivity. Institutionalisation of private capital formation by the involvement of cooperative institutions, scheduled commercial banks and Regional Rural Banks (RRBs) played an important role in accelerating the process of capital formation in agriculture.

Capital Formation in Primary Sector

In the agriculture sector including livestock, gross domestic capital formation showed a declining trend during eighties in the Punjab state. It declined from 20.18 per cent of gross state domestic capital formation, during 1980-81 to 17.59 per cent during 1990-91 at constant prices and maintained almost the same percentage share up to 1995-96 and improved during 1998-99 (Table 13.1). The contribution of other sub-sectors, *viz.* forestry, mining and fishing, is negligible, *i.e.* less than one per cent in the state gross domestic capital formation (SGDCF), whereas in case of manufacturing, it rose from 24 per cent in 1980-81 to about 44 per cent during 1995-96 (near to almost double) and abruptly declined to 27.94 per cent during 1998-99. Rao (1994) and Mishra (1995) and others have also argued that gross fixed capital formation in agriculture by the public sector has been declining in all the states, including the developed ones whose resource position is better. The share of banking sector was also less than two per cent.

Table 13.1: Gross state domestic capital formation by industry of use in Punjab at 1980-81 prices

Categories	*Years*			
	1980-81	1990-91	1995-96	1998-9
Agriculture including livestock	158.42	319.17	417.25	555.11
	(20.18)	(17.59)	(18.31)	(20.40)
Manufacturing	193.79	748.47	1000.97	760.20
	(20.58)	(41.25)	(44.15)	(27.94)
Electricity, gas and water	81.95	207.42	64.36	396.11
supply	(10.44)	(11.43)	(12.82)	(14.56)
Trade hotels and restaurants	104.70	186.27	275.28	262.81
	(13.33)	(10.26)	(12.08)	(9.16)
Public Administration	72.61	114.76	192.78	231.86
	(9.25)	(6.32)	(8.46)	(8.52)
SDCF as percentage to SGDP	15.62	21.66	22.63	21.55

Note : Figures given in brackets indicate percentage.

It should be noted that industry loves infrastructure where it is provided by someone else and does not wish to take over the responsibility of infrastructure building upon itself (Khusro, 1994). In agriculture the intensity of this dependence is many times more due to difference between marginal capacity to invest of an average farmer and an average industrialist when proportion of investment directed towards agriculture was falling, it is important to examine the investment in detail.

The most crucial item of concern for building up the production potential in agriculture is investment made by individual farmers, i.e. in fixed capital investment by the farmers in the form of farm machinery, equipment, farm buildings, irrigation structure, etc. The state consumed 10 per cent of fertilisers, 11 per cent of pesticides, 58 per cent of herbicides and 25 per cent of tractors in the country and annual per capita consumption of electricity in the agriculture sector stands at 252 kWh in the Punjab state compared with 6.8 kWh at the national average (Singh 1999). These figures themselves speak about the level of mechanisation in the Punjab state, needs hardly any vindication. At the state level there are more than 411 thousand tractors, about 250 thousand tillers, more than 3 lakh threshers, about 780 thousand electric motors and 170 thousand diesel engines.

Considering tractors alone as the major investment, the gross margin from wheat and paddy, the most remunerative cropping system in Punjab, form 105,000 hectares would pay for its capital consumption (replacement) in 1981. This requirement increased to about 190,000 hectares in 1991 and further to more than 216,000 hectares in 1996 (Table 13.2). In terms of cultivated area the gross margin from more than 5 per cent of land meet the replacement cost of tractors alone. Since the investment in tractors contribute only about one-third of the total investments by all farmers and more than half by the tractor owning farmers, the gross margins from about 15 to 25 per cent of land to be cultivated intensively and efficiently meet the replacement cost of the capital. The net annual addition to the existing stock of machinery and equipment of modest rates require another Rs.7318 million in terms of capital investment (Singh, 1995). Thus, much more emphasis is required to restore the terms of trade for private capital formation in agriculture, particularly on the capital-costing side.

Role of Credit Institution in Capital Formation

Table 13.3 represents the loans disbursed each year by cooperative credit

Table 13.2: Replacement cost of capital investments for tractors in Punjab, 1981 to 1996

Parameters	Years		
	1981	1991	1996
No. of Tractors	1,44,466	3,07,002	3,98,927
Cultivated area per tractor (ha)	29.14	13.71	10.55
Price of tractor	69,583	1,39,615	2,34,548
Gross returns from Wheat+Paddy (Rs./ha)	9,616	22,673	43,301
Gross margins	4,808	11,337	21,650
Cultivated area of wheat, paddy required to meet the replacement cost of tractors with gross margins	1,04,534	1,89,044	2,16,082
Per cent of NAS*	2.48	4.50	5.04

* National Account Statistics (NAS).
Source : Singh, 1999.

institutions, scheduled commercial banks and Regional Rural Banks (RRBs) from 1970-71 to 1995-96 at current prices. In nominal terms the total agricultural credit advanced (direct) by the institutions, more than doubled from 85.53 crores in 1970-71 to 189.64 crores in 1978-79. In fact this was the period when high yielding varieties of wheat and rice had been widely adopted in the state. The credit availability further went up to Rs.640.40 crores in 1984-85 and almost remained there up to 1988-89. Between 1978-79 and 1984-85, the increase was about 23.8 per cent. During this period, emphasis was on yield increasing inputs and their use had quite considerably gone up. The second significant jump in credit disbursement was noticed in 1989-90, when it increased from Rs.680.24 crores in 1989-90 to Rs.964.58 crores registering an increase of 42 per cent during 1991-92. Then onwards, it generally went up to Rs.1082.95 crores in 1993-94 and Rs.1727.98 crores in 1995-96. During the period of 1989-90 to 1995-96, the yield gains had tapered off and to maintain the existing levels, higher doses of inputs especially fertilisers and weedicides and pesticides were being used as well as the farming became more mechanised. Considering a period after which the green revolution technology has stabilised, the institutional agricultural credit grew during 1984-85 to 1995-96 at a rate of 9.64 per cent per annum.

Looking at the shares of different institutions in this growth, it was observed that cooperative credit structure was the main supplier of agricultural credit in Punjab. Between 1970-71 and 1995-96, cooperative

Table 13.3: Total agricultural credit availability in Punjab, 1970-71 to 1995-98

Year	*Commercial banks*	*Cooperatives*	*Regional Rural Banks*	*Total Agril. Credit (Advanced)*
1970-71	870 (10.18)	7683 (89.92)	–	8553
1977-78	3855 (26.73)	10567 (73.27)	–	14422
1978-79	4503 (23.74)	14461 (76.26)	–	18964
1984-85	16527 (25.81)	47513 (74.19)	–	64040
1985-86	22645 (34.53)	41936 (63.95)	998 (1.52)	65579
1986-87	24559 (38.53)	37437 (58.73)	1751 (2.75)	63747
1987-88	20611 (31.87)	41487 (64.14)	2579 (3.99)	64677
1988-89	23726 (34.88)	41487 (60.99)	2811 (4.13)	68024
1989-90	23123 (23.97)	68646 (71.17)	4889 (4.86)	96458
1991-92	26052 (27.68)	61191 (65.00)	6890 (7.32)	94133
1993-94	28322 (26.15)	70013 (64.65)	9960 (9.19)	108295
1994-95	49149 (31.38)	102851 (65.66)	4639 (2.96)	156639
1995-96	63401 (36.69)	104915 (60.71)	4482 (2.59)	172798

Note : Figures in the parenthes show percentages to total agricultural credit advanced.
Source: Reserve Bank of India, Report of Currency and Finance, Various Issues.

credit grew by 13.6 times from Rs.76.83 crores to Rs.1049.15 crores respectively. The increase was more sharp from 1978-79 to 1984-85 and from 1988-89 to 1989-90. From 1984-85 to 1988-89 the credit even at current prices declined from Rs. 475.13 crores to 414.87 crores. Its share decreased from Rs.74.2 per cent to 61 per cent during the period. Up to 1984-85, the share of institutional credit remained above 70 per cent. It ranged between 60 to 65 per cent in nineties.

In contrast to this the scheduled commercial banks were playing a second fiddle role to the cooperatives in the area of institutional agricultural credit. Its shares remained lower than 40 per cent in all years. However, during the years when the share of cooperatives, in absolute as well as relative terms, decreased that of commercial banks' increased. It seems that commercial banks stepped in when the cooperatives slackened but within a narrow range and *vice versa.* During 1984-87 when cooperative credit declined the commercial banks advanced for agriculture increased from Rs.165.27 crores in 1984-85 to Rs.245.59 crores in 1986-87 and their share went up from 25.8 per cent to 38.5 per cent respectively. Then it came down modestly to 31.9 per cent in 1987-88 and 34.9 per cent in 1988-89 but the fall was drastic in the year 1989-90 at 24 per cent, whereas in absolute terms the credit advanced decreased marginally from Rs.237.26 crores to Rs.231.23 crores. This happened due to the marked increase in volume of agricultural credit advanced by the cooperatives. In the nineties, the credit advances by the scheduled commercial banks have shown some recovery. It has gone upto Rs.491.5 crores in 1994-95, to 634.01 crores in 1995-96 with the share of 31.38 per cent and 36.7 per cent respectively. Over a period of two and half decades, the commercial banks direct advance to agricultural sector has increased from Rs.8.70 crores in 1970-71 to Rs.634 crores in 1995-96 with the share ranging between 10.2 per cent and 38.53 per cent, but if we take the period of 1985-86 to 1993-94, the growth has been slow (Rs.226.45 crores to Rs.634 crores). It appears that the commercial banks after the initial push of credit to agriculture under the government directions when major commercial banks nationalised in the year 1969, developed a cold face and shied away due to low returns and high transaction costs and overdues.

Regional Rural Banks (RRBs) were the late entrants in the field of agricultural (i.e. rural) credit having been created in the year 1982 and their role was confined only to the weaker sections of the rural areas. Then their contribution towards the agricultural credit was limited. The loans made by RRBs stood at Rs.9.98 crores only in 1985-86 which increased continuously to only Rs.44.82 crores in 1995-96. The share of RRBs in the total agricultural credit, which went up gradually from 1.52 per cent in 1985-86 to 9.2 per cent in 1993-94 has decreased to 2.60 per cent in 1995-96.

Outlays and Expenditure of Five Year Plans on Agriculture

The role of capital in the development of an economy is well known hardly needs any emphasis. And this is more so in case of a country where large number of small farmers exist who cannot pour in a significant amount of private investment to keep pace with the development of the new technology/strategy. The vicious circle of low productivity and the income is primarily the cause of lack of capital stocks, low rate of capital formation and inefficient utilisation of existing capital on farms. Table 13.4 shows the outlay and expenditure of the Punjab Government on agriculture and allied activities during the various Five Year Plans. It is evident from the Table that the total expenditure which was Rs.4409.58 lakh during Fourth Plan period has increased to Rs.36791.80 lakh during the Eighth Plan period. As a percentage to total expenditure the share of agriculture and allied activities stood at 10.29 per cent during the Fourth Plan period and it increased to 11.73 per cent during Fifth Plan. After that the absolute share has increased but in percentage terms it has declined continuously and it was found lowest 5.40 per cent during Eighth Plan.

Table 13.4: Outlay and expenditure of five year plans on agriculture

Plans	*Actual Expenditure (In lakhs)*	*Percentage to the total expenditure*
4th Plan (1969-74)	4409.58	10.29
5th Plan (1974-78)	8433.72	11.73
6th Plan (1980-85)	20217.51	10.69
7th Plan (1985-90)	28065.73	7.91
8th Plan (1992-97)	36791.80	5.40
9th Plan (1997-2002)	80173.90	5.60

Although institutional credit has played a significant role ushering in green revolution in Punjab State by helping rapid and widespread adoption of modern seed irrigation-fertilizer technology as well as encouraging private capital formation especially in tractors and tubewells on farms. But on the other hand, Punjab agriculture has become more inputs intensive since late eighties resulting into greater cash requirements. The focus of investment credit needs to be shifted away from tractors and tubewells financing to more productive, high value investment avenues like dairying, poultry, horticulture, vegetable farming, development of land, conservation of water resources, etc. which are required to be promoted in state agriculture under the environment of stagnating productivity, increasing cost of production of the existing paddy-wheat farming system, degradation of soil and water resources and relatively better scope of value addition in these enterprises besides these being helpful in the diversification of agriculture.

Conclusion

The available data on capital formation tells that the private capital formation in agriculture has been increasing in real terms compensating for the slow or sometimes even negative growth in the Public Capital formation in agriculture. The investment in one sector shows the benefits in other sectors. The intensity with which these factors stimulate the economic growth depends upon other factors such as infrastructure, banking, commercial practices, research and development in promoting the trade potential, etc. or in other words social overhead capital. The mutual interdependence of the agriculture sector with other sectors of the economy in the investment linkages scenario makes the agriculture-industry linkages in the production, demand and supply and saving portfolio, operationalise even more so significantly. To sustain improvement in agriculture sector, industrial sector and other sectors of the economy had to improve at relatively much higher growth rates, only then balanced growth model would become sustainable (Sekhon and Singh, 1995).

So the complementarity between public sector and private sector can be explained with the help of inter-sectoral linkages. The increase in the investment of public sector for example in irrigation and other infrastructure that leads to good and argued platform for production that encourage private sector investment which resulted into higher gross domestic product and directly or indirectly increase the revenue of government. So this is a cycle of investment which encourage and discourage inter-sectoral comparison. The need of the time at this stage in the developing state like Punjab is to promote public investment which further creates demand and investment in other sectors and indirectly encourages investment in the private sector.

It can also be concluded that cooperative credit institutions are the major sources of finance to the agricultural sector due to their very strong ground level infrastructure. The commercial banks are still hesitant to provide credit to the agriculture sector after 27 years of their nationalisation due to their preferences for non-agricultural sector lending in urban areas where loans are relatively more secured, size of loan is big and returns are high. The role of RRBs so far has been limited because they are to operate under very adverse conditions, their domain being confined to weaker sections of the rural areas, where rate of loan default is high. The role in future would depend how successfully they counter this menace and build themselves as independent economically viable institutions.

REFERENCES

Bhagwati, I. and T.N. Srinivasan, (1993), *India's Economic Reforms Report*, Ministry of Finance, Govt. of India, July.

Dhawan, B.D. and S.S. Yadav, (1995), "Private Fixed Capital Formation in Agriculture", *Economic and Political Weekly*, Vol. 30 (39), September 30.

Govt. of Punjab, *Statistical Abstracts of Punjab*, various issues, Economic Adviser to Govt. of Punjab.

Gill, K.S., (1993), *A Growing Agricultural Economy: Technological Changes, Constraints and Sustainability*. Oxford and IBH Publishers, New Delhi.

Government of India (1997), *National Accounts Statistics*, Central Statistical Organisation.

Kaur, Milkho, (1990), "Structural Changes in Sectoral Growth Rates in India and Punjab", *Journal of Agricultural Development and Policy*, Vol. 1(2), pp. 58-66.

Kaur, Milkho (1992), *Intersectoral linkages between Agriculture and Industry in Punjab*, unpublished Dissertation, Punjab Agricultural University, Ludhiana.

Khusro, A.M., (1994), "Economic Reforms Saves Employment", V.V. Memorial Lecture, 36th Labour Economics Conference, Indian Society of Labour Economics held at Punjabi University, Patiala, Jan. 5 to 7.

Mishra, S.N. and Ramesh Chand, (1995), "Public and Private Capital Formation in Agriculture: Comments on complementarity hypothesis and others", *Economic and Political Weekly*, Vol. 30(25) June 24.

Mishra, S.N., (1996), "Capital Formation Accumulation in Indian Agriculture Since Independence", *Indian Journal of Agricultural Economics*, Vol. 51 (1-2), Jan.-June.

Rath, Nilakantha, (1989), "Agricultural Growth and Investment in India", *Journal of Indian School of Political Economy*, Vol. 1 (I), Jan.-June, pp. 64-83.

Ram, G.S., (1993), New Economic Policy and Agricultural Investment. Keynote address at seminar on 'Agricultural Policy in the Context of New Economic Policy in India', organised by Agricultural Economics Research Association, IARI, New Delhi, Feb. 24-25.

Rao, C.H. Hanumantha, (1994), *Agricultural Growth, Rural Poverty and Environmental Degradation in India*, Oxford University Press, New Delhi.

Shetty, S.L., (1990), "Investment in Agriculture: Brief Review", *Economic and Political Weekly*, Vol. 25 (7-8), Feb.17-24.

Sekhon, Milkho Kaur and Karam Singh, (1995), "Role of Intersectoral Linkages in a high growth agricultural economy—A simulated scenario", *Agricultural Economic Research Review*, Vol. 8(1), pp. 63-76.

Singh, Karam (1995), "Capital Formation in Punjab Agriculture: Issues and Avenues" (Mimeo), Deptt. of Eco. and Soc., P.A.U., Ludhiana.

Singh, Karam, (1999), "Rural Development: Role and strategies for capitalisation and institutionalisation of the growth process", keynote paper presented at Annual Conference of Agricultural Economics Research Association, Dharwad, Karnataka, Oct.

Dhillon, B.S., M.K. Sekhon and Parminder Kaur (2000), "Capital Formation in Punjab Agriculture: Role of Public and Private Investment", Deptt. of Economics and Sociology, PAU, Ludhiana.

14

COMMISSION AGENTS IN RURAL SETTING
A Socio-Economic Analysis

M.S. GILL & RUPINDER KAUR

The state of Punjab has achieved the present efficiency in agricultural sector through the rational use of available resources alongside the adoption of modern technology. The efforts of the farming community have been strengthened with the development of infrastructure in the form of cooperative credit societies, rural electrification, transportation and marketing. The new agricultural technology heavily profit-motivated and capital intensive requires sufficient supply of credit to meet input demands. Singh (1998) holds that financial and technical support provided by the cooperatives to the farmers have helped tremendously in achieving higher production of various crops and saved the farmers from the exploitative structure of the money lenders. Prasad (1991) holds that the cash requirement for cultivation with new agrarian technologies is eleven times higher than with the traditional methods. With such an increase in the demand for cash, a question arises, can a farmer be able to meet all financial pre-requisites involved in the adoption of new technology? Studies (Kaushal, 1971; Gulati, 1996; Lekshmi *et al.*, 1998) reveal that there exist a big gap between what a farmer owns and what he requires in term of finance. No doubt, cooperative credit societies have been made functional, throughout the state but credit advanced by institutional agencies is inadequate to serve the intended purpose, thereby making certain the cultivators dependency on non-institutional credit agencies (Patel, 1963; Thingalaya, 1978).

Among the non-institutional agencies, commission agents/*arhtiyas* have promoted themselves over the years as the financiers of the farmers of the rural society meeting their credit needs. This is aptly established by the studies conducted by Khan and Tripathi (1972), Desai (1990), Jodka (1995) and others. They have observed that greater proportion of funds and inputs required by farmers for diverse agricultural purposes are provided by *arhtiyas*. *Arhtiyas* have been able to appreciate the multifarious requirements of farmers and have been able to lend in all seasons and for all purposes. In Andhra Pradesh, as against Rs. 20 crores advance by banks and credit societies, Rs. 90 crores of credit is advanced by the *arhtiyas* in the form of inputs (Parthasarthy, 1993). According to a report, commission agents supply 63.85 per cent of the credit to fulfil 61.3 per cent needs of the farmers (Panj Dariya, 1999). In this way, *arhtiyas* are playing a crucial role in the present agricultural development. But does this dominant economic role of the *arhtiyas* lead to the marginalisation of the farming community whereby they get trapped in a vicious circle of indebtedness and come to occupy a subordinate position in the economic structure of the rural society.

Further, the small farmers due to their inability to finance the high cost inputs are forced to cultivate low value and rapid turn-over crops (Walters, 1965). Large farmers on the other hand are rich and as such have large resources to monopolise the new inputs and enjoy the relative advantages of large scale operation and management (Parsad, 1991). This is more true with the globalisation of economy and the property intellectual right. Further, they have access to financial, especially institutional, resources as compared to small farmers. As the large farmers are exploiting financial resources advanced by the credit agencies, their level of indebtedness is high. Mehta and Prasad (1988) have reported that cultivators in most advanced states like Punjab, Gujarat, Tamil Nadu, Haryana and Karnataka have higher average debt. In other words, farming in these states is better supported by the availability of credit. This reflects that the flow of credit from institutional agencies is not evenly distributed. A similar situation prevails with regards to credit availability among various classes of cultivators. Epstein (1978) finds that cooperatives particularly credit societies are serving the wealthy farmers due to which they are able to make use of advanced agricultural technology to raise production on their farms. Under such circumstances, the poor farmers have to depend upon non-institutional sources of credit so as to adopt the new technology. In this context, the present study analyses the role of commission agents in rural society. The specific objectives are:

(a) to analyse the purpose and the amount of credit taken;
(b) to understand the mode and terms of credit repayment;
(c) level of social participation and how this ultimately strengthens the continuity of the flow of credit and mutual social bond.

Setting Study Area

The main cropping pattern followed throughout Punjab with minor exceptions is wheat-rice. With this pattern, there ought to be little variation with regard to credit need and crops grown in different districts. The study has been conducted in one of the agriculturally advanced districts of Punjab that is Ludhiana. Keeping into consideration, the convenience to interact with cultivators, a village in the Ludhiana district has been selected. The average operational holding of the village has been found to be nearly 12 acres. In all, 55 respondents operating, approximately average operational land-holding have been interviewed with the help of a structured pre-tested interview schedule. The study was conducted in 1999.

Main Findings

Agricultural Inputs

Efficiency of the agriculture depends upon the availability of inputs like seed, fertilizers, water, labour etc. Transfer of the possession of such items from one person to another is referred to as delivery system. Indian farmers generally use seeds of very different quality either because the special good quality seed kept for sowing is consumed during off-season or because good seed deteriorates through bad storage. With advancement in seed technology, good quality seed is marketed through retail outlets so that farmers can utilize the best and improved seed to have more production. Data in Table 14.1 show that more than 50 per cent of the respondents use seed produced and stored by them. Nearly one-third of the respondents get seed in cash from Punjab Agricultural University, Ludhiana during Kisan *melas*. The rest get their supply of seed either from the dealers (7.3%) or the commission agents (5.5%) or the cooperative society (1.8%). The supply of seed from above agencies (in their view) is made on credit. In all, the farmers generally use the seed produced on their farm.

Table 14.1: Distribution of respondents by their source of inputs

Inputs	*Source*								
	Self	*Coopera -tive*	*P.A.U.**	*Arhti-yas*	*Dealer*	*Self +PAU**	*LMB***	*Cash*	*Total*
Seed	28 (50.9)	1 (1.8)	17 (30.9)	3 (5.5)	4 (7.3)	2 (3.6)	–	–	55
Fertilizer	–	27 (49.1)	–	18 (32.7)	10 (18.2)	–	–	–	55
Insecti-cides	–	–	–	37 (67.2)	18 (32.8)	–	–	–	55
Water	–	3 (5.5)	–	10 (18.2)	9 (16.4)	–	33 (60.0)	–	55
Labour	17 (30.9)	–	–	–	–	–	–	38 (69.1)	55

Note : Figures in brackets indicate per cent.
* Punjab Agricultural University, Ludhiana.
** Land Mortgage Bank.

As far as fertilizer is concerned, this input in essential especially for the hybrid and improved varieties of crops and is consumed in large quantity by the cultivators. The per hectare consumption of nitrogenous and phosphatic fertilizers in India is 70 kg according to economic survey, 1996-97. The main supplier of fertilizers is the cooperative sector which lends short-term loan for this purpose. This institutional agency provides fertilizers to the consumers at the time of sowing either directly or indirectly through dealers. In the sample, 32.7 and 18.7 per cent of the respondents get their supply of fertilizers from the commission agents and dealers of fertilizers respectively. In most of the Punjab agricultural *mandis* (markets), the commission agents also deal in insecticides, fertilizers, seeds, clothes etc. Thus, fertilizer as an input comes to the farmers predominantly through cooperative societies followed by commission agents and fertilizer dealers.

The new varieties of crops produced under artificial conditions are susceptible to pests and insects and hence require consistent application of insecticides and pesticides to claim the level of productivity of that variety. As new pests/insects attack and certain pest/insect resistant strains develop, the demand for these chemicals increases. Nearly 67 per cent of the respondents purchase these plant protection chemicals from the commission agents whereas the rest buy it from the dealers.

Water is another important input and is indispensable to agricultural production. With changing climate and need of the crop varieties, a regular supply of water is essential to the farm. Most of the Punjab farmers have installed tubewell run either through electricity or diesel. The major source of finance for the installation of pumpset is Land Mortgage Bank which supply credit on medium to long-term basis. Almost 60 per cent of the respondents have taken credit for installation of irrigation facilities from the Land Mortgage Bank. Nearly 6 per cent of the respondents have taken credit from the cooperative society. Commission agents and dealers have financed 18.2 and 16.4 per cent of the respondents for the installation of irrigation facility.

The cultivation process needs hoeing so as to remove weeds from the soil and provide proper circulation of air and water. Ludhiana district has the largest proportion of migrant labourers usually employed during sowing and harvesting time. In the rest of the period, a few labourers along with family labour are employed on the farm. In the sample village, 69.1 per cent of the respondents are dependent upon hired labour whereas the rest employ family labour to carry out farm operations.

In short, various institutional and non-institutional agencies are involved in the deliverance of farm inputs like seed, fertilizers, insecticides, water and labour.

Mode of Payment

The farmers are dependent upon various institutional and non-institutional agencies for the supply of essential agricultural inputs which supply these ingredients either in cash or credit. The data in Table 14.2 reveal that majority of the respondents are getting the supply of inputs on credit. Very few respondents take credit for buying seeds (7.2%). Those who purchase seed from certain dealers or during Kisan *melas* by it in cash, sometime taking money from the commission agent. On the other hand, majority of the respondents take credit to, purchase fertilizers (81.8%) and insecticides/pesticides (94.6%). The fertilizer is purchased either from the commission agent or the dealer specified by the commission agent/cooperative society or the dealer of their choice. The choice of the cultivator is guided by the friendship circle or the agency providing credit. This may account for the sale of poor quality of fertilizers and insecticides/pesticides to the cultivators. With regard to irrigation facilities, the farmers rely on pumpset run either by electricity or diesel after borrowing the money from their respective commission agents. Further, those respondents who have installed pumpsets after taking credit from the Land Mortgage Bank have been advised to get the set from the prescribed dealer. The Bank endorses the credit to the dealer specified by the official, again not ensuring the quality of the product. Interestingly, the initial amount and repayment of installments are usually made after taking cash from the commission agents.

Table 14.2: Mode of payment for inputs

Input	*Mode*				
	Credit	*Cash*	*Credit-cum-Cash*	*Self*	*Total*
Seed	4 (7.2)	23 (41.8)	–	28 (50.9)	55
Fertilizers	45 (81.8)	10 (18.2)	–	–	55
Insecticides	52 (94.6)	3 (5.4)	–	–	55
Water	28 (50.9)	18 (32.7)	9 (16.3)	–	55
Labour	3 (5.4)	35 (63.7)	–	17 (30.9)	55

For this reason, 16.3 per cent of the respondents have reported that they make payment in cash-cum-credit basis. Likewise, payments of the labourers employed during sowing and harvesting time is paid in cash after taking/borrowing money from the commission agent. Thus, majority of the cultivators depend upon credit agencies to bear the expenses of farm inputs. Even those who pay for the inputs in cash invariably take credit from the commission agents. Commission agent on his part extends credit facility on the surety that all sales will be executed through him and in realty, it happens so.

Terms of Credit

With regard to the terms of credit, it has been found that credit agencies advance loan for a harvest season which is to be returned so that future transactions continue. Data in this respect reveal that majority of the respondents repay their debts after six months (Table 14.3). The responses have been categorized as immediate, after one harvest (6 months), after two harvest (one year) and long-term (5 years and above). About 15 per cent of the respondents who have purchased seed on credit repay the same after one harvest season; the rest pay for the seed immediately. On probing, it has been found that more than half of them have taken cash from the commission agent on interest and the rest have taken the amount against the pending sale amount. Same has been the case with those who have purchased chemicals from the shops other than the prescribed ones by the lending agency. Approximately 49 per cent of the respondents repay the credit taken for chemicals (fertilizers, insecticides and pesticides) after six months. Their amount is adjusted against the sale proceeds. Among the respondents who have been taking credit for fertilizers, 32.8 per cent repay it after one year. Similarly, 45.5 per cent of the respondents who have taken insecticides/pesticides on credit repay the amount after one year. In both the cases, adjustments are made from the sale deeds. Interestingly, many of the borrowers keep an account, of the quantity of fertilizers or insecticides/pesticides purchased but not the amount of such items. Very few keep accounts of quantity as well as the price of the purchased items. The farmers have confessed that it is not feasible to keep complete account as sometimes other family members buy these items and are either not reported or recorded. There is always a chance of manipulation at the level of credit advancing agency. This is not the case with cooperative credit society.

The data further discern that 70.9 per cent of the respondents have taken long-term loan from Land Mortgage Bank for the installation of tubewell. At the same time, they hold that to make repayment of installments, money is usually borrowed or adjusted against sale deeds. Same is the case with those who take credit to pay for the labour employed during sowing or harvesting season.

Table 14.3: Terms of credit

Input	*Immediate (purchased on cash)*	*After 6 months*	*After 1 year*	*5 years and above*	*Total*
Seed	23 (85.1)	4 (14.8)	–	–	27 (100.0)
Fertilizer	10 (18.2)	27 (49.1)	18 (32.8)	–	55 (100.0)
Insecticide/ pesticide	3 (5.4)	27 (49.1)	25 (45.5)	–	55 (100.0)
Water	16 (29.1)	–	–	39 (70.9)	55 (100.0)
Labour	–	38 (100.0)	–	–	38 (100.0)

Therefore, the credit advancing agencies are repaid mostly after one harvest and the amount is adjusted against sale proceeds. Many farmers adjust their accounts after two harvest seasons, *i.e.* one year. Nevertheless, the credit advanced is adjusted against sale deed by the commission agent after informing the farmer about the amount deducted by him. The farmer usually accepts but with doubt in mind. They hold that because of the earlier cited reasons, it is not feasible for them to keep tract of accounts of purchases.

Rate of Interest

As commission agents and other credit agencies cater financial needs of the cultivators, it is imperative to analyse the rate of interest charged by these agencies. The data in Table 14.4 reveal that the rate of interest varies between up to 7 per cent to above 21 per cent. Generally the respondents are paying more than 21 per cent of interest on the credit. However, 28.2 and 1.9 per cent of the respondents who have taken credit to pay for water facility and insecticides/pesticides are paying interest rate ranging between 14 to 21 per cent. They hold that they have very good and cordial relations with the commission agent. Interestingly, only 17.9 per cent of the respondents are paying a low interest rate that is up to 7 per cent. These respondents have taken credit for the installation of tubewell from the Land Mortgage Bank. Those who have taken credit from co-operative credit societies are paying interest between 7 to 14 per cent. Some of the respondents might be paying a higher rate of interest because the installments are paid after taking credit from the commission agents.

Table 14.4: Rate of interest

Input	*Rate of Interest*				*Total*
	Upto 7%	*7-14%*	*14-21%*	*Above 21%*	
Seed	–	1 (25.0)	–	3 (75.0)	4 (100.0)
Fertilizer	–	27 (60.0)	–	18 (40.0)	45 (100.0)
Insecticides	–	–	1 (1.9)	51 (98.1)	52 (100.0)
Water	7 (17.9)	14 (35.8)	11 (28.2)	7 (17.9)	39 (100.0)
Labour	–	–	–	38 (100.0)	38 (100.0)

In short, it may be inferred that most of the respondents have taken advances from the commission agents besides institutional agencies like co-operative societies. The amount so taken is usually paid back after each harvest season. Though the rate of interest of the institutional agencies is low but most of the respondents pay high rates of interest for the reason that they have taken credit from the commission agents as well. Even some of the respondents pay their installments after borrowing the same from the commission agent. In the whole process, a farmer has to pay interest on the borrowed amount but the amount of sale proceeds used by the commission agents does not carry any interest. Further, the respondents have been making most of the purchase through the commission agents.

Purpose of Loan

In addition to inputs loan, the cultivators are taking credit for other productive as well as non-productive uses. The data here, pertains to year 1996-97 and 1997-98. Out of the total, 58.2 and 74.6 per cent of the respondents have taken loan for productive and unproductive purposes respectively (Table 14.5). Among the respondents who have taken credit for productive purposes, 87.5 per cent have purchased tractor either through bank or the commission agent. Three respondents have purchased thresher by taking loan from either the bank or the commission agent. Those who have taken credit for purchasing land (3.1%), payment for leased-in land (15.7%), repair of machinery (3.1%) and to pay installments (9.4 %) depend solely on the commission agent for meeting the above needs. No doubt, majority of the respondents have financed their productive needs through institutional credit source that is bank but the role of commission agents cannot be underestimated. For using institutional credit, the land has to be mortgaged by the cultivators whereas this is not so with respect to advances made by the commission agents.

Further, 80.5 per cent of the respondents have taken loan to meet their socio-religious obligations; whereas 14.6 and 29.3 per cent of the respondents have taken credit for house construction and other purposes like education, health, litigation etc. Leaving aside a respondent, the rest have taken credit from the commission agents. Such advances generally are made on the surety that sale proceeds will be carried out through them. Further, advances are extended mostly on the basis of repaying capacity of the loanee and in certain cases on the type of social relationships. In this way, commission agent is the main source of non-productive credit.

Amount of Loan

The data on the amount of loan taken along with the purpose has been shown in Table 14.6. Majority of the respondents have taken credit up to Rs.50,000 (52.7%). This is followed by those who have taken credit of more than Rs.1.50 lakh (21.8%). This credit is advanced for productive and non-productive uses.

Table 14.5: Source and purpose of loan

Purpose	*Agency*				
	Bank	*Arhtiyas*	*Arhityas and self*	*Cooperative*	*Total*
A. Productive					
(i) Tractor	27 (96.4)	1 (3.6)	–	–	28 (87.5)
(ii) Thresher	1 (33.3)	1 (33.3)	1 (33.3)	–	3 (9.4)
(iii) Land	–	1 (100.0)	–	–	1 (3.1)
(iv) Repair of machinery	–	1 (100.0)	–	–	1 (3.1)
(v) To pay installments	–	3 (100.0)	–	–	3 (9.4)
(vi) Payment for leased in land	–	5 (100.0)	–	–	5 (15.7)
B. Non-Productive					
(i) Socio-religious ceremonies	–	32 (97.0)	–	1 (3.0)	33 (80.5)
(ii) Housing	–	6 (100.0)	–	–	6 (14.6)
(iii) Miscellaneous	–	12 (100.0)	–	–	12 (29.3)

Table 14.6: Amount of loan and purpose

Amount (Rs.)	*Purpose*		
	Productive	*Non-Productive*	*Total*
Below 50,000	–	29 (70.7)	29 (52.7)
50,000-1,00,000	17 (53.1)	7 (17.1)	6 (10.9)
1,00,000-1,50,000	5 (15.7)	5 (12.2)	8 (14.6)
Above 1,50,000	10 (31.2)	–	12 (21.8)
Total	32 (58.2)	41 (74.6)	55 (100.0)

Of those taking productive loan, 53.1 per cent of the respondents have credit to their name between Rs.50 thousand to Rs. 1 lakh. Those who have taken loan between Rs. 1 to Rs. 1.5 lakh constitute 15.7 and 31.2 per cent respectively, of the total respondents. This shows that majority of the respondents have taken productive loan up to Rs. 1 lakh.

Contrary to it, the majority of the respondents taking non-productive loan have borrowed upto Rs. 50 thousand (70.7%). This is followed by those taking credit between Rs. 50 thousand to Rs. 1 lakh and Rs. 1 lakh to 1.5 lakh. None of the respondents have taken loan of more than Rs. 1.5 lakh for non-productive purpose. From this, it may be inferred that cultivators are going for advances especially for non-productive purposes according to their repaying capacity. Secondly, productive loan is more than the non-productive one because of the generative capacity of the former as compared to the latter which is a consumption loan.

At this juncture, a question arises, are the farmers able to repay the loan in time? If not, how much amount is outstanding against each use? Data discern that 74.6 per cent of the respondents are under debt ranging between Rs.50 thousand to more than Rs. 1 lakh (Table 14.7).

Table 14.7: Outstanding amount and purpose

Amount (Rs.)	*Purpose*		
	Productive	*Non-Productive*	*Total*
Below 50,000	6 (27.3)	18 (58.1)	10 (24.4)
50,000-1,00,000	8 (36.4)	11 (35.5)	19 (46.3)
More than 1,00,000	8 (36.4)	2 (6.4)	12 (29.3)
Total	22 (53.7)	31 (75.6)	41 (74.6)

Of them, most of the respondents have an outstanding amount between Rs. 50 thousand to Rs. 1 lakh (46.3 %). Nearly 29 per cent are under debt of more than Rs. 1 lakh. Likewise, 24.4 per cent of the respondents have yet to pay less than Rs. 50 thousand.

Data further highlights that outstanding amount for productive purposes is higher as compared to that for non-productive uses. Among the responses, 72.8 per cent have an outstanding of more than Rs. 50,000 against advanced taken for productive purposes. Only 27.3 per cent have yet to pay an amount upto Rs. 50,000 against their advances for productive purposes. Interestingly, the outstanding amount (for productive use) in the case of five farmers is found to be more than Rs. 2 lakh.

Among the respondents (75.6%) having an outstanding loan against non-productive use, 6.4 per cent have yet to pay more than Rs. 1 lakh. Majority of the respondents taking non-productive loan have an outstanding amount of less than Rs. 50,000. It may be inferred that a large section of the farming community is under debt especially the advances taken against non-productive uses and such amount usually does not exceed Rs. 1 lakh.

Interest Rate

The rate at which the money is lent depends upon the type of the lending agency and the purpose of the loan. It is observed that majority of the respondents pay more than 21 per cent of interest on the borrowed amount (Table 14.8). Those who have taken non-productive loan are paying an interest rate of more than 21 per cent. Only one respondent is paying interest between 7 to 14 per cent and the person has diverted co-operative credit to non-productive use.

Table 14.8: Rate of interest

Rate of Interest	*Purpose*	
	Productive	*Non-Productive*
Upto 7%	6 (18.8)	–
7-14%	10 (31.2)	1 (2.5)
14-21%	8 (25.0)	–
Total	32 (100.0)	41 (100.0)

Among the respondents who have taken loan for productive purposes, only 18.8 per cent are paying an interest up to 7 per cent. Nearly 31 per cent are paying interest between 7 to 14 per cent. Those paying higher interest rate of above 21 per cent account for 25 per cent of the respondents. This corroborates our earlier inference that many a cultivators repay their instalments after taking loan from the commission agents who charge exorbitant rate of interest. The high rate of interest charged by non-institutional agencies is because these agencies lend liberally keeping into consideration the output and size of land holding one has. These agencies do not insist on mortgaging the land whereas institutional agencies do besides having cumbersome procedure to lend.

Social Participation

Arhtiyas usually advance loan without keeping anything as security for they know their clients (farmers) and their credit worthiness. At the same time, they make it sure that sale deeds are carried out through them. There is a mutual understanding which forms the basis of their economic interaction. Such relation is not limited to a patron client relationship but mostly extends beyond to take the form of a bond of social solidarity. To give credence to this bond of solidarity, they participate in each other social functions like birth, marriage, death etc. (96.4%) and also exchange gifts on festivals like Diwali, Baisakhi (94.5%).

Table 14.9: Participation and exchange of gifts

Participation	*Yes*	*No*	*Total*
Participate in family function	53 (96.4)	2 (3.6)	55 (100.0)
Exchange of gifts on festivals	52 (94.5)	3 (5.5)	55 (100.0)
Exchange of goods and services on social functions	28 (50.9)	27 (49.1)	55 (100.0)
Exchange favours on demand	5 (10.9)	49 (89.1)	55 (100.0)

This is one of the ways how economic ties are extended to social ones. But is this extension superfluous with the sole motive of achieving one's goal? Data indicate that exchange of favours does not take place on demand (89.1%) and further the exchange of goods/services on social functions is limited to 50.9 per cent of the respondents. This implies that for most of the respondents the social ties are superfluous, artificial and goal-oriented, the values of the modern society. For the rest, the ties are strong and deep. On further probing it is observed that aged respondents (above 45 years) hold the relationship between *arhtiyas* and the cultivators as mutually inclusive and informal. Contrary to it, the young ones that is below 45 years think that it is their mutual dependency and need within which socio-economic ties operate and hence, the relationship should be prescribed within those limits.

Social Relations

The participation on social functions is taking place to keep the economic ties and does not reflect the level of social relations. The respondents have been asked to grade their relationship with their *arhtiyas* as good, average and worst. Approximately 84 per cent of the respondents have good relationship with their *arhtiyas* (Table 14.10). Only one respondent has worst kind of social relation with his *arhtiyas*. In this way, an overwhelmingly proportion of the respondents maintain cordial and good relations with their *arhtiyas*. The main reason propounded by the respondents is that the *arhtiyas* lend them money at that time when no other source of credit is available (63.1 per cent). Another reason which helps to maintain good relations with the *arhtiyas* is transformation of economic ties to a level whereby their families develop close ties with each other (8.7 per cent). Clear adjustments of accounts among the parties also help in the development of good and cordial relations (17.4%). All the above factors have facilitated the growth of close relation among the cultivators and *arhtiyas*. Misunderstanding and improper maintenance of accounts on the part of both the parties leads to the development of worst kind of relations among them. Likewise refusal by the *arhtiyas* to lend money on one or the other pretext may not help good relation to develop. In short, the relations among the parties are cordial and good. This keeps the flow of credit and dependency of farmers *vis-a-vis arhtiyas* intact.

Table 14.10: Social relations between *arhtiyas* and cultivators

Reason	*Good*	*Average*	*Worst*	*Total*
Always help at odd time	29 (63.1)	–	–	29 (52.7)
Family relation	4 (8.7)	–	–	4 (7.3)
Mutual understanding	1 (2.2)	4 (50.0)	–	5 (9.1)
Clear adjustment	8 (17.4)	1 (12.5)	–	9 (16.4)
All the above	4 (8.7)	–	–	4 (7.3)
Payment not clear from other side	–	–	1 (100.0)	1 (1.8)
Sometime refuse to help	–	3 (37.5)	–	3 (5.5)
Total	46 (83.7)	8 (14.5)	1 (1.8)	55 (100.0)

From the above, it may be made out that the relations among cultivators and *arhtiyas* are mutual, inclusive and cordial and depend upon the continuity of mutual financial support. This also explains the complete dependency of the cultivating class upon sources of finances.

Role of Arhtiyas

As the economic dependency of the farming community is established beyond doubt, it becomes imperative to know the ways an *arhtiya* can transform the socio-economic life of a cultivator. Data reveal that *arhtiyas* can and in fact do play an important role in the social and economic transformation of the rural society by extending finance for productive and non-productive uses (Table 14.11). Majority of the respondents hold that by providing agricultural inputs especially fertilizers, insecticides and pesticides the *arhtiyas* can rather they do help the farming community (61.8%). The *arhtiyas* through advances can help the cultivators to purchase cattle (5.5%), farm machinery (1.8%) and to pay for the leased in land (12.7%). As a middle man (7.3%) the *arhtiyas* can watch the interest of the client cultivators in the sale of produce by getting better remunerative price. Further, 9.1 per cent of the respondents opine that through financial assistance for all productive purposes, whether related to farm or to secondary occupation, the *arhtiyas* can help the cultivator to improve their economic conditions and hence lead to rural development.

Table 14.11: Ways a *arhtiya* helps to improve conditions of a cultivator

Ways	*Purpose*	*Number*
Productive loan	(a) to purchase cattle	3 (5.5)
	(b) to pay for leased-in land	7 (12.7)
	(c) to arrange inputs	64 (61.8)
	(d) to purchase machinery	1 (1.8)
	(e) to act as middle man	4 (7.3)
	(f) all the above	5 (9.1)
Non-productive loan		54 (98.1)
No role		1 (1.8)

Further, *arhtiyas* can also assist the cultivator in improving his socio-economic conditions by advancing credit for non-productive uses. In addition to the repair of house, it includes credit for social ceremonies, education of the children and health of the family. Of course, such advances can be and usually are adjusted at the end of the harvest season either in part or in lump sum. Only one respondent holds that none except the man himself can improve his condition by working hard, thinking rationally and judiciously, spending accordingly to the availability of resources and to be contended with what is available. Certainly the supply of the working inputs especially fertilizers, insecticides and pesticides is to be maintained through the *arhtiyas*. In this way, the cordial relations with *arhtiyas* can improve the social and economic condition of the cultivators as the former has the capacity to meet the productive and non-productive needs of the cultivating class.

Generally argument is advanced that the farming community is exploited by the money-lenders and middle men who usurp the returns on the farm. But realizing the needs and purposes served by them, can it be said that other institutional agencies fulfil the gap? Viewed in this context the *arhtiyas* seldom deny credit whereas institutional agencies if extend credit make one to complete a number of formalities including mortgage of the land and getting sureties from influential and rich members of the village. For a *arhtiya* denying credit means loosing a client and having a bad reputation in the business community and the cultivators. As much as 82 per cent of the respondents state that they were never denied credit by the *arhtiyas* (Table 14.12). The basic reason thereof is their good social relations with the *arhtia* (17.7 %). Likewise, 17.8 per cent of the respondents opine that clear adjustment of the accounts among the concerned parties keeps the flow of credit. For others, it is the mutual compulsiveness (11.1 %) of the cultivators and that of the *arhtiyas* that results in the continuity of the flow of the credit for both stand benefited from it.

Table 14.12: Extension of credit with reasons

Refused credit	*Number*		*Reason*		*Number*	
Never	45	(81.8)	(a)	good social relations	32	(71.1)
			(b)	adjustment of account	8	(17.8)
			(c)	mutual co-operation	5	(11.1)
Yes	10	(18.2)	(a)	payment not made (1994-96)	3	(30.0)
			(b)	deal with two *arthiyas* (1996-98)	7	(70.0)
Total	55	(100.0)			55	(100.0)

Some of the respondents have been refused credit in the last few years. Among them, three were denied credit during 1994-96 and seven in 1996-98. The reasons for withdrawal of credit advance facility have been non-payment/clearance of sale/purchase account and dealing with two *arhtiyas*. So as to cope with the problem, two respondents had to sell a small piece of land to clear the debt. This shows that the credit advance has been higher than the repayments and hence leading to indebtedness. Another two respondents on being denied credit in 1996-

98 have arranged the payments for inputs required for farm operation from their relatives whereas three of them have got loan from the banks. This again corroborates the fact that indebtedness among the cultivators is increasing. The rest of the respondents persistently have persuaded the *arhtiya* by making regular visits to him and ultimately restored the system of credit advance. In the process, the farmer has to pay a higher rate of interest for the outstanding amount. Those who have been dealing with two *arhtiyas* ultimately shifted to one with surety that future transactions will be made through him. These tactics of the *arhtiyas* explain the exploitative nature of the economic dependency of the cultivators.

Alternative to Arhtiyas

Under such circumstances can some other institution replace the *arhtiyas*? Nevertheless, cooperative credit societies and banks are extending finances on interest to the farming community, the dependency of cultivators for credit on *arhtiyas* is continuing; rather it is increasing as 61.3 per cent needs of the farmers are fulfilled by the *arhtiyas* against 33.8 per cent by co-operative credit societies and 4.7 per cent by banks (Tiwari, 1997). No doubt, 16.4 and 14.5 per cent of the respondents think that the co-operative credit society and banking institution can replace *arhtiyas* (Table 14.13) but are these institutions ready to advance without guarantee, instantly, on the spot and without administrative hassle. These are the positive aspects of the advance made by the *arhtiyas*. Moreover, the *arhtiyas* maintain personal contact with their creditors which is missing in the institutional agencies.

Table 14.13: Alternative to *arhtiyas*

Alternative	*Number*	
Cooperative Society	9	(16.4)
Banks	8	(14.5)
Relatives and friends	10	(18.2)
From other income sources	12	(21.8)
Sell land	2	(3.6)
No alternative	14	(25.5)
Total	55	(100.0)

Another alternative is getting financial help from relatives and friends (18.2%). Again it is difficult if not impossible as the relatives and friends most probably come from the same occupational background who might expect the same from the respondents. Generating other sources of income by taking subsidiary occupation like poultry, piggery, etc. to meet the credit needs of the farm seems to be an illusionary question as it again demands the inputs of credit. Approximately 4 per cent of the respondents consider selling land and to take up another occupation if such an eventuality arises. The fear of loosing land and source of income besides the symbol of prestige in rural society may be the reason that 25.5 per cent of the respondents find no alternative to *arhtiyas* and the services rendered by them.

Conclusion

The growth of rural sector depends heavily on the availability of inputs like seeds, fertilizers, insecticides, credit and the like. Undoubtedly, the modern agricultural practices demand regular and consistent application of inputs for which the farmers have to invest heavily so as to reap a good harvest. One of the contributing factors is the timely availability of credit at the disposal of the cultivator so that he could buy necessary inputs. The agricultural credit cooperative societies have been strengthened in rural areas to meet above exigencies of the cultivating class. In addition, banking institutions have been spread over the rural areas. The study highlights that cultivators depend upon the above institutions for meeting the expenses of fertilizers, installation of tubewells or pumpsets and agricultural machinery. For insecticides/pesticides and even to purchase seeds and fertilisers, the cultivators are dependent upon the commission agents as well. In this way, various institutional credit agencies are involved in the deliverance of farm inputs. At the same time, the involvement of non-institutional agencies that is the commission agent has been more than that of the institutional ones. It is amply evident from the fact that payment for the inputs irrespective of its nature is made on credit. Even where payments are made in cash, the flow of money is from the commission agents.

The commission agents without doubt charge as high as 24 per cent of interest on the advanced money but the debt is generally cleared after one harvest season. Even the credit taken from the cooperative credit society is returned after one harvest and additional credit is taken again to be returned after the harvest of next crop. Many cultivators take credit from the cooperative society, return a small amount and take credit. In this way, some of the cultivators are burdened with cooperative credit.

Likewise, credit taken from the banks for tubewell/pumpset carries interest between 7 to 14 per cent but the cultivators are unable to return the same in time. Usually, instalments are paid on persuasion of the bank officials but the payments are made after borrowing from the commission agents thus inviting a hefty interest rate besides increasing the debt money. In this way, cultivators indebtedness is increasing and may be paying interest more than the actual cost of the item. This establishes the dependence of the cultivating class upon the commission agents (non-institutional agencies).

Commission agents lend the cultivators for diverse uses including the productive ones. The study shows that the cultivators are dependent upon institutional credit agency (Bank) for agricultural equipments involving large investment but for the small investment, he relies on commission agent. Tractors have been invariably purchased with bank credit. But for the initial amount and the repayments of instalments, taking credit from the commission agent is more or less a common feature among the cultivators. This fact is corroborated from the study that commission agents have provided finances for purchase of land, repair of machinery and to pay instalments, thereby establishing the very necessity of commission agent as a source of credit for carrying out agricultural operations. Mukherjee and Bandhopadhyay (1993) have made similar observations in the light of rich and poor farmers. Not only this, the commission agents meet the non-productive expenses of the cultivators especially connected with social ceremonies, health and education. This finding is supported by the fact that commission agents have provided finance on credit to as many as 60 per cent of the respondents under-study. In this way, the role of commission agent as a financier in the agricultural sector is firmly established.

Rural studies especially published during post-Green Revolution period (Grewal *et al.*, 1986; Desai, 1988; Gill and Dhaliwal, 1991) have referred to blooming fields reflecting thereby the prosperity of rural people. But the reality is altogether different. At present, to say that every cultivator is under-debt will not be a misnomer. The study concludes that the financial burden in terms of debt varies from less than Rs. 50,000 to above Rs. 1,00,000. Those who have taken productive loan especially for tractor are more indebted than those who have availed loan for non-productive uses. This difference owes to the fact that advances (for non-productive use) made by the commission agents are dependent upon the land size, repaying capacity and gross output for sale and personal contacts. At the same time, the commission agent can withhold the sale payments and also make others not to pay for/supply inputs. Due to this compulsive force, the non-productive debt remains within permissible payable limits. For this, the outstanding amount against non-productive use is less than lakh. This is not the case where lending is made by the institutional agencies. Although the fear of mortgage of land, looms large but the legal procedure takes unusually long period and hence, the cultivator can take risk not to repay the loan. Within such circumstances, the indebtedness of cultivator increases. This level of indebtedness accentuates with crop failure and ultimately farmers may go for suicide, mental illness and the like problems.

This dependency of the cultivating class on the commission agents has latently elements of exploitation and subordination. The commission agents supply inputs/credit on the surety that all sale transactions will be carried through them. These agents mostly withhold returns on the farms on one or the other pretext. The cultivator on the other hand is in no position to withhold the sale of his produce due to his indebtedness and subsistence. This creates the condition for perpetuation of the relation of dependency.

Any deviation provides leverage to the *arhtiya* to stop dealing, thereby making the cultivator to suffer economically due to shortage of inputs in the operation of the farm. In this context credit acts as a means to pressurise the cultivator and latently, makes him subordinate to the former. Thus, it can be said that the dependency of the cultivators, or the increased cash requirements of the modern agricultural technology has elements of exploitation and suppression.

To avoid economic hardship, cultivators maintain cordial, good and personal relations with the *arhtiyas*. In addition, the social relations are strengthened through participation and exchange of gifts on social occasions. Since the *arhtiyas* also depends upon the cultivators for their monetary gains and sale of inputs they reciprocate in the same manner. In this way, mutual compulsiveness of the both leads to the growth of economic relations which culminate into social relations among the *arhtiyas* and the cultivators.

The study further concludes that the *arhtiyas* have made such a stronghold among the farming community through satisfying their credit needs and developing personal contacts that no other institution can replace them of their dominant economic role in the rural society. The close and personal social ties reinforce the economic and social dependence. Nevertheless, the study lacks class analysis but the relationship between credit, cultivators and agriculture is amply established. Despite the economic nature of the relationship, it has translated into mutual cooperation, personal, inclusive and informal relationship.

To sum up, with all elements of exploitation and subordination the cultivating class depends heavily upon the services of the commission agents to meet its needs. The survival of the latter depends solely on the existence of the former with its demands for goods and services. In this interdependency syndrome the commission agent is a social reality and functional requisite for the agrarian society.

REFERENCES

Desai, S.S.M. (1990), *Agriculture and Rural Banking in India*, Himalaya Publishing House Bombay.

Desai, V. (1980), *Rural Development*, Vol. VI, Himalaya Publishing House, Bombay.

Epstein, T. (1978), *South India, Yesterday, Today and Tommorrow*, Macmillan, London.

Gill and Dhaliwal (1991), "Economic Implications of Green Revolution" in *Social Economic and Political Implications of Green Revolution* (eds). By Hanssa and Shukla, Classical Publishing Company, New Delhi.

Grewal, Sidhu and Rangi, (1986), "An analysis of Farm Income in Punjab", *Research Bulletin*, Deptt. of Economic and Sociology, Punjab Agricultural University, Ludhiana.

Gulati, A. (1996), "New Economic Policy and Agriculture," *Indian Journal of Economics*, Jan.-June.

Jodka, S.S. (1995), "Changing Structure of informal credit in rural Haryana", *Economic and Political Weekly*, Vol. XXX.

Kaushal, G. (1971), *Economic History of India*, Kalyani Publications, Ludhiana.

Khan, W. and R.N. Tripathi, (1972), *Intensive Agriculture and Modern Inputs*. National Institute of Community Development, Delhi.

Lekshmi, Rukmini *et al.* (1998), "Characteristics of defaulters in Agricultural Credit Use", *Indian Journal of Agricultural Economics*, Vol. 53, No. 4.

Mehta and Prasad, (1998), *Agrarian Relations and Rural Exploitation*, Ashish Publishing House, New Delhi.

Mukherjee & Bandhopadhyay, (1993), "New Horizons for West Bengal Panchayat", *Indian Journal of Agricultural Economics*, Vol. 48.

Parthasarthy, V.P. (1997), "Supply of short-term Credit and estimation of Credit Gaps", *India Cooperative Review*.

Patel, M.L. (1963), "Direction of Cooperative Review", *Indian Cooperative Review*,

Patel, M.L., (1999), Punj Dariya, Vol. 1, No. 22.

Prasad, K.N., (1991), *India's Rural Problems*, Concept Publishing Company, New Delhi.

Singh, Sukhdev (1998). "The Lot of Small, Marginal Farmers remains same", *The Tribune*, May 8.

Tiwari, K.L. (1997), "Planning and Rural Development", *Kurukshetra*, Vol. XLV.

Thingalaya, N.K. (1978), "Report of Rural Credit Structure and Flaws", *Indian Journal of Agricultural Economics*, Vol. 33.

Walter, A. (1965), "Development Planning" cited from *India's Rural Problems* by Prasad. Concept Publishing Campany, New Delhi.

15

TENANCY AND DEMAND FOR AGRICULTURAL CREDIT
Evidence from Border Village in Punjab

GIAN KAUR

The availability and utilisation of credit in time and in adequate quantity is a prerequisite for sustained agricultural growth. Punjab is an agricultural predominant state of the economy. It has experienced big gap in rural credit. It has been existing before green revolution (neglect of the agricultural sector by the financial institutions), periods of green revolution and post-green revolution (period of directed credit by the commercial banks, but enhanced demand for credit for mechanisation of agriculture etc.). The beginning of 1990s witnessed globalisation of agriculture and so changed demand for food products etc. This requires enhanced capital investment in agro-based industries and so increased supply of credit in the State.

The majority of the farmers in rural Punjab depends upon informal sources of credit. The choice of the farmers for this source of finance is because of the absence of adequate supply of institutional credit. In the absence of a perfect and developed credit market, the landless and small farmers remain dependent on the informal sources for most of their credit requirements. Different studies on rural credit (Bardhan, 1984; Basu, 1989; Bell, 1990; Gill, 2001) have observed that such borrowers are debarred from availing institutional credit because of their inability to provide sufficient collateral as security.

Methodology

This study is limited to a single village Ghoga of Amritsar district, a few kilometres from the border line, *i.e.* there is no inhabited village between the border line with Pakistan and this village. The dominant practice of agriculture in the study village is characterised by the institution of tenancy. Tenancy in the state is noted in the form of share-cropping or rent to be paid annually to the landlord. Rent varies from Rs. 6000 to Rs. 12000 per acre annually. The study village bears a special feature where all the farmers have leased-in land from the government for 99 years against a very nominal rent of Rs. 500 per acre per annum. This is the land reclaimed by the Government and leased out mainly to the landless farmers of the village. In most of the cases the owners of the land have emerged by purchasing already leased-in land, again at a very nominal rate of Rs. 7,000 per acre from the government.

The village under study was selected specifically with the objective of examining the credit needs of the farmers cultivating land leased-in from the government and their problems thereof. In all 50 households cultivating land were appreciated for interview, only 45 respondents provided the requisite information. Primary data on land transactions, i.e. leasing-in and leasing-out of land, owned area, family size, number of workers in the family, education level of the heads of the households, sources of income, sources of agricultural credit and use thereof were collected by interviewing the farmers personally with the help of a specifically structured schedule. The data pertain to the agricultural year 1999-2000. Simple tabular analysis has been done for the collected data among different farm size groups. For the purpose of the analysis under study the sample farmers have been categorised into four sub-groups (the maximum size of the owned holding was 8 acres):

(i) Landless: They are pure tenants.
(ii) Marginal Farmers: Farmers with owned land holding upto 2.5 acres.
(iii) Small Farmers: 2.51 acres to 5.00 acres.
(iv) Medium Farmers: 5.01 to 10.00 acres.

The last three categories of the farmers are mixed tenants. The maximum size of the operational holding (owned land + leased-in land– leased-out land) emerges to be 12 acres.

The village under study, though linked with pucca road, has not proper transport facilities. It has no bank office and is facilitated with primary school only. About 20 per cent to 30 per cent of houses of the village are kacha (mud) houses. Wheat and paddy are the main two crops grown, as is the practice of the state. Source of irrigation are tubewells/ pumping sets. The family labour constitutes the major source of agricultural labour.

Results and Discussion

Pure tenants constitute 26.67 per cent of the total sample households and they have 12.21 per cent of the total area leased-in. In terms of area operated by these tenants, they fall in the category of marginal or small farmers. The marginal and small farmers, together constitute 60 per cent of the sample farmers owning 67.66 per cent of the total area (Table 15.1). Pattern of tenancy in the study area is presented in Table 15.2. All the households in the study area have leased-in land. Among the sample households, 12 (26.67%) are pure tenants and others—33-are mixed tenants. However, maximum percentage of area leased-in is by the small farmers, who have 40.59 per cent of the total area leased-in. Area leased-in per household has consecutively increased with increase in the size holding of the farmers. This indicates reverse tenancy, result of mechanisation in agriculture. Heavy capital investment in modern agriculture asks for large size of the farms and so leasing-in land by the larger farmers to get benefits of economies of scale. Leasing-in is usually from the small farmers to the larger farmers (landlords) in case of land transactions among the farmers. But in the study area the operational holdings have been enlarged by leasing-in land from the government and not from the farmers/landlords.

Table 15.1: Distribution of farmers and area according to size group of holding

Size of Group Holding (Acres)	*No. of Households*	*Percentage of households in group*	*Percentage of area owned*	*Percentage of area operated*
Landless	12	26.67	—	12.21
Up to 2.50	11	24.45	7.78	14.06
2.51-5.00	16	35.36	59.88	43.39
5.01-10.00	6	13.33	32.36	25.35
Total	45	100	83.5	100

Source: Field Survey.

Table 15.3 indicates education level of the heads of the sample households. It is observed that majority of landless (58.33%), marginal (63.64%) and small (62.50%) farmers are illiterate. Among the last group (medium farmers) literacy is about 67 per cent, but it is not above the level of matriculation. Low literacy rate is contributed to absence of education facility above the primary level in the sample village and also due to less transport facilities for the school going children to approach the nearby schools providing higher education.

Table 15.2: Pattern of tenancy according to size group of holdings

Size of Group Holding (Acres)	*Number of Households*			
	Mixed tenants	*Pure tenants*	*Percentage of area leased in*	*Area leased-in per household (acres)*
Landless	—	12 (100)	19.56	3.31
Up to 2.50	11	—	19.19	3.71
2.51-5.00	16	—	40.59	5.0
5.01-10.00	6	—	20.66	7.0
Total	33	12 (100)	100	

Source: Field Survey.
Notes : 1. Figures in parentheses are percentages to total amount.
2. '—' implies nil.

Table 15.3: List of farmers according to size-group of holding and education level

Size of Group Holding (Acres)	*Nil*	*Primary*	*Middle*	*Matric*	*Above Matric*
Landless (Pure Tenants)	7 (58.33)	3 (25.00)	2 (16.67)	—	—
Mixed Tenants					
Up to 2.50	7 (63.64)	2 (18.18)	2 (18.18)	—	—
2.51 to 5.00	10 (62.50)	2 (12.50)	2 (12.50)	2 (12.50)	—
5.01-10.00	2 (33.33)	1 (16.67)	1 (16.67)	2 (33.33)	—
Total	26 (57.78)	8 (17.78)	7 (15.56)	4 (8.89)	—

Source: Field Survey
Note: Figures in parentheses are percentages to total amount.

Average family size of sampled households is 4.70 with average earning members per household is 1.66. Ownership of assets/agricultural implements determines the production pattern as implements determine the production pattern as well as credit worthiness of a farmer. Farmers irrigate their land by tubewells/pumping sets. In case of the first three categories—landless, marginal and small farmers—tubewells/pumping sets have been installed by partnership (sharing the cost by two or three farmers). Same is true in case of tractors and oil engines. However, 7 tractors (about 50 per cent of the total tractors) have sole ownership. It is all because of the small holdings and less affordability of such assets by the farmers in the study area.

Table 15.4 gives income level of the sample households. As seen in the table more than 90 per cent of the total income is agricultural income for the landowners. It is about 85 per cent in case of the landless farmers. Income per household has increased consecutively with increase in the size of holding.

Table 15.4: Distribution of farmers according to source of income (per household)

(Amount in Rs.)

Size of Group Holding (Acres)	*Agr. Income*	*Non-Agr. Income*	*Total*
Landless	58683 (84.93)	10375 (15.02)	69058
Up to 2.50	77890 (97.85)	1714 (2.15)	79604
2.51-5.00	169743 (97.91)	36.36 (2.09)	173379
5.01-10.00	230863 (90.23)	25000 (9.77)	255863

Source: Field Survey.
Note: Figures in parentheses are percentages to total amount.

Agricultural Credit

Table 15.5 indicates sources of borrowing of cultivators according to size of holdings. The main sources of credit are the traders. The pure tenants (landless farmers) as well as the mixed tenants (the last three groups of the farmers) have borrowed from this informal source of credit. Only five farmers, that too, in a single size-group (2.5 to 5.00), *viz.* small farmers have borrowed from cooperative societies (formal source). Only one (marginal farmer) of the sample farmers did not borrow from any source of credit, while one sample household (small farmer) borrowed from informal as well as formal sources of finance. Average amount borrowed per household has increased with increase in the size of the holding. However, amount borrowed per acre has decreased with increase in the size of holding. It is because of the small holdings of the cultivators (mainly of the first two groups) and increased demand for consumption loans (as agricultural income is not sufficient to make both ends meet), that makes the amount averaged out higher than the other two groups. These farmers get cash loans from the traders and repay same in cash earned by non-farm activities such as drivers, dairy etc. and also working as agricultural labourers on other farms (Table 15.6).

Table 15.5: Source-wise borrowing according to size of holding

Size of Group Holding (Acres)	Number of Borrowers				
	Traders	Co-operatives	Both	Not Borrowed	Total
Landless	12	—	—	—	12
Up to 2.50	10	—	—	1	11
2.51-5.00	12	5	1	—	16
5.01- 10.00	6	—	—	—	6

Source: Field Survey.

Table 15.6: Source-wise average amount borrowed per household (amount in Rs.)

Size of Group Holding (Acres)	*Formal loan*	*Informal loan*	*Total (Formal & Informal)*	*Per Acre (in Rs.)*
Landless	—	15500 (100)	15500	4679
Up to 2.50	—	18334 (100)	18334	3607
2.51-5.00	7545 (35.47)	13727 (64.53)	21272	2229
5.01-10.00	—	25500 (100)	25500	1855

Source: Field Survey.
Note: Figures in parentheses are percentages to total amount.

Table 15.7 depicts purpose utilisation of credit by the sample farmers. It is observed that 84.67 per cent of the formal loan (in case of small farmers) has been utilised for productive purposes. In case of informal loan (that has been availed by all groups of farmers), use for productive purpose has increased with the size of the farm holding. It was as low as 35.21 per cent in case of landless farmers and as high as 90.71 per cent by the medium farmers (largest class in the study area). As explained earlier it is because the farmers with small farm holdings are not able to fulfil their consumption needs. Major share of their borrowings are utilized for consumption/non-agricultural purposes. Many of these farmers have been observed to have hardly two square meals a day. Among these farmers are such who are not willing to work and so supplement their income from non-farm activities, *i.e.* working as labourers in other fields or in nearby towns. So they are trapped in poverty as well as in debt. As seen in Table 15.7, the landless labourers and the marginal farmers have been found to be defaulters with respective figures of average amount defaulted as Rs. 3835 and Rs. 7331. In the last two categories of the farmers, no one was found to be the defaulter. However, according to the traders/*arhtiyas* (the main source of credit among the sample farmers), the borrowing farmers are always in debt. They repay the old loans and at the same time get fresh loans to be repaid at the next crop (Table 15.7).

Table 15.7: Distribution of farmers according to use of credit for productive purposes

Size of Group Holding (Acres)	*Formal*	*Informal*	*Default (Average, amount in Rs.)*
Landless	—	35.21	(4) 3835
Up to 2.50	—	46.73	(4) 7331
2.51-5.00	84.67	54.22	—
5.01-10.00	—	90.71	—

Source : Field Survey.

Above analysis shows that main source of credit among the sample farmers has been the traders, *i.e.* informal source of credit. Out of 45 sample households only 5 availed formal credit from the cooperative societies, *i.e.* cost of credit in case of informal credit is higher than in case of the formal loans. The rate of interest was found to be 36 per cent per annum in the former case with 12 per cent for the latter one. Still preference of the borrowers is for the informal credit, only due to easy access to this source of finance.

Conclusion

The present study has explored the problems of the tenants in a border village pertaining to access to credit institutions. Most of the sample farmers are dependent upon the informal source of credit, that too, to a single source of local traders/*arhtiyas*. The purpose of the loan has been mainly consumption by the farmers up to 5 acres of land. The remaining few (6) utilised the major share of loans for productive purposes.

The study has highlighted the dominant role of the traders in extending agricultural credit to the farmers. Limitation of the formal institutions to lend to the farmers especially to the landless farmers (pure tenants) has been pointed out. In this context it is suggested that the Government/RBI should evolve some policy measures to extend credit facilities by the formal institutions, especially to such tenants as found in the study area. Over and above, such areas should be provided with proper infrastructural facilities. As in the present case, the village has no banking facilities and also no proper facilities of education beyond the primary level school.

REFERENCES

Bardhan, P.K. (1984), *Land, Labour and Rural Poverty: Essays in Development Economics*, Oxford University Press, Delhi.

Basu, K. (1989), "Rural Credit Markets : The Structure of Interest Rates, Exploitation and Efficiency", in Bardhan, P.K. (ed.), *The Economic Theory of Agrarian Institutions,* Oxford Claredeon Press, New York.

Bell, C. (1990), "Interactions between Institutional and Informal Credit Agencies in Rural India", *The World Bank Economic Review,* Vol. 4, No. 3, September, pp. 297-327.

Gill, Anita (2000), *Rural Credit Markets: Financial Sector Reforms and the Informal Lenders,* Deep and Deep Publications Pvt. Ltd.

16

SOCIO-ECONOMIC ADVERSITIES OF FARMERS
A Case Study of Muktsar District

SUKHDEV SINGH & MANDEEP KAUR

Introduction

Indian economy is predominantly an agricultural economy as majority of the population of the country is dependent on agriculture for their livelihood. The Green Revolution had emerged as a high hope in mid-sixties and consequently, India's production of foodgrains especially that of wheat and rice increased sharply (Bhandari, 1982; Kawi, 1982; Parmar, 1985). With this, the economic conditions of the agricultural community improved a lot.

Punjab, a tiny state of India is known as 'the Granary of India' and its foodgrain share in the central pool is quite high (Sehgal and Arora, 2000). It was the Punjab only where the idea of the Green Revolution was first translated into a reality in India. The success of the Green Revolution in the region removed the chronic food scarcity of the country. Punjab came to be known as the most dynamic and prosperous state, the food basket of India (Jodhka, 2000; Sehgal and Arora, 2000). However, over the past two decades, the story of Punjab seems to have changed a lot and the trends are towards negative sides.

In Punjab, 72 per cent of the farmers have less than 10 acres of land and 45 per cent of the farms are smaller than 5 acres. The small size holdings have increased from 38.6 per cent in 1981 to 44.7 per cent in 1991 (Bobby, 1998) due to continuous subdivision of land holding. The fast multiplying population which is expected to touch 1082 million by 2006 A.D. may further increase the number of small and marginal farmers. The work of various scholars and scientists regarding the problems of small peasants indicate that the farmers particularly the Punjabi farmers are under heavy debt, the amount of which is continuously increasing due to variety of factors thus not only affecting the economic side but also creating lot of socio-psychological problems (Shergill, 1997; Bobby, 1998; Garg, 1999; Jodhka, 2000; Singh, 2000). Apart from these reasons like repeated failure of crops, government policies like failure of regulated markets, saturation of agricultural production, dependence on non-institutional agencies for credit, high cost of production as compared to returns along with mismanagement of funds for socio-religious purposes have led to socio-economic problems for the farmers.

After going through the studies on farmers it comes out that they are facing severe socio-economic adversities particularly in the cotton belt of Punjab due to a variety of reasons. So in this paper a modest attempt has been made to assess the causes of socio-economic adversities of farmers specially in Muktsar district which is one of the cotton growing areas with the following specific objectives :

(i) To study the socio-economic characteristics of respondents.
(ii) To study the contributions of various factors which led to farmers towards severe socio-economic adversities.
(iii) To give suitable suggestions to overcome economic adversities.

Methodology

The present study was conducted in Muktsar district of Punjab. Out of the four blocks of Muktsar district, three blocks, namely Malout, Lambi and Gidderbaha were selected for the present investigation, which almost constitute the whole rural area of this district. Further, five villages from each selected block were chosen randomly and besides these villages some cases of suicide victims were also identified from other four villages and thus the total number of villages comes to nineteen in all. From each selected block 50 respondents were contacted for data collection on the basis of availability of such type of respondents. In all, the total sample consisted of 150 respondents including the family member of those farmers who had committed suicide. Data were collected personally with the help of semi-structured and pre-tested interview schedule.

Results and Discussion

Socio-economic Characteristics of Respondents

The socio-economic characteristics of the respondents, i.e. farmers of the area under study are shown in Table 16.1. It is indicated that more than one-third (35.33%) of the respondents were in the age group of 30-40 years while a little less than one-third (29.33%) were in the age group of 40-50 years. This indicates that majority of the respondents were in between 30-50 years of age which shows that most of the farmers belonged to the Middle-age group. Majority of the respondents (98.00%) hailed from the Sikh religion and belonged to the higher-caste group (98.67%). Most of the respondents (89.33%) were married. As regards the family type the major proportion of respondents (65.33%) belonged to nuclear families while about one-third (34.67%) had been living in the joint families. Nearly half of the respondents, *i.e.* 51.33 per cent had the family size of 5 to 7 members and only a few (6.67%) had very large family, *i.e.* exceeding 11 members. Data indicate that majority of the respondents (38.00%) were illiterate followed by 25.33 per cent of the respondents who had studied uptil Matriculation or 10+2 level. Only a few, *i.e.* 4.00 per cent of the respondents had got some special training like in poultry, bee-keeping, electric works etc. A large proportion of respondents (54.67%) were residing in the pucca houses while one-third of them (29.33%) were having mixed type of houses. A few of the respondents (5.33%) were found to have kutcha houses while remaining had some well-built bungalow type of houses. Sixty-five per cent of the respondents were not engaged in any kind of subsidiary occupation in addition to farming as their main occupation while the remaining 35 per cent of the respondents were engaged in subsidiary occupations like dairy, poultry, bee-keeping, services like teacher in school, bank employees, factory workers etc. with a few respondents having combine harvester as a source of subsidiary income. Majority of the respondents had landholdings less than 10 acres, *i.e.* 28.67 per cent of the respondents had less than 5 acres and 33.33 per cent of them had 5 to 10 acres of land which is indicative that majority of the sampled respondents were in the category of small farmers. Majority of the respondents (90.67%) were having tubewell and canal both as sources of irrigation. It is obvious from the Table that about one-third of the respondents, *i.e.* 32.00 per cent had their total annual income between Rs.50,000 to Rs.1,00,000 while 26.00 per cent of the respondents had annual income up to

Rs.50,000. So, almost 60 per cent of the respondents of the area had their total income below Rs. one lakh per annum.

Table 16.1: Socio-economic characteristics of the respondents

Sl.No.	*Attribute*	*Category*	*Frequency*	*Percentage*
1.	Age (years)	Upto 30	30	20.00
		30-40	53	35.33
		40-50	44	29.33
		50 and above	23	15.34
2.	Religion	Sikh	147	98.00
		Hindu	3	2.00
3.	Caste Category	Higher Caste	148	98.67
		Backward Caste	2	1.33
4.	Marital Status	Married	134	89.33
		Unmarried	16	10.67
5.	Family Type	Joint	52	34.67
		Nuclear	98	65.33
6.	Family Size	Upto 4	35	23.33
		5-7	77	51.33
		8-10	28	18.67
		11 and above	10	6.67
7.	Education Level	Illiterate	57	38.00
		Primary	14	9.33
		Middle	19	12.67
		Matric/10+2	38	25.33
		Graduate and above	16	10.67
		Special training	6	4.00
8.	Housing Type	Kutcha	8	5.33
		Pucca	82	54.67
		Mixed	44	29.33
		Any other	16	10.67
9.	Subsidiary Occupation	Dairy	28	18.67
		Poultry	4	2.67
		Bee-keeping	2	1.33
		Service	11	7.33
		Combine harvester	7	4.67
		None	98	65.33
10.	Land holdings (operational)	Upto 5	43	28.67
		5-10	50	33.33
		10-15	29	19.33
		15-20	16	10.67
		20 and above	12	8.00
11.	Sources of irrigation	Tubewell	5	3.33
		Canal	9	6.00
		Tubewell+Canal	136	90.67
12	Total annual income	Upto 50000	39	26.00
		50000-100000	48	32.00
		100000-150000	29	19.33
		150000-200000	22	14.67
		200000 and above	12	8.00

Factors Contributing Towards Socio-economic Adversities of the Farmers

The thrust of the present paper is to pinpoint the factors leading to socio-economic adversities of farmers and the data in this regard has been given in the forthcoming Tables.

Farm Power and Machinery Owned

The information given in Table 16.2 shows that 65.33 per cent of the respondents had 1 or 2 draught animals and bullock cart. Leaving aside a few, most of the respondents (94.00%) had tractor with trolley. Likewise, most of the respondents had tubewell installed at their farm for irrigation purpose. Only 11.33 per cent of the respondents had thresher and a small percentage of respondents (4.67%) had harvest combine. The statistical test indicates that there were significant differences as regards the ownership of farm power and machinery. The categories with 1 or 2 draught animals, bullock cart, tractor with trolley and tubewell were significantly higher as compared to the other two categories. During field work it was found that people purchase the machinery not only as per their requirement but out of their ego and other social factors.

Table 16.2: Ownership of farm power and machinery

(Multiple response)

Farm power and machinery owned	*Block-I (N=50)*	*Block-II (N=50)*	*Block-III (N=50)*	*G. Total (N=150)*
1-2 draught animals	32 (64.00)	36 (72.00)	30 (60.00)	98 (65.33)
Bullock cart	32 (64.00)	36 (72.00)	30 (60.00)	98 (65.33)
Tractor with trolley	43 (86.00)	50 (100.00)	48 (96.00)	141 (94.00)
Tubewell	46 (92.00)	48 (96.00)	47 (94.00)	141 (94.00)
Thresher	7 (14.00)	5 (10.00)	5 (10.00)	17 (11.33)
Harvest Combine	2 (4.00)	2 (4.00)	3 (6.00)	7 (4.67)
$F_{5,10}$= 255.27**			CD(10d.f.)=3.87	

**Significant at 5 per cent level.
Note: Figures in parentheses indicate percentages.

Ownership of Material Possessions

Table 16.3 shows that ownership of material possessions by the respondents. It was observed during the course of data collection that even the people having less income prefer to have certain material possessions. Scooter (88.67%), television set (84.67%), cooler (85.33%), refrigerator (83.33%) had been found to be possessed by majority of the respondents. The respondents also possessed other material goods like cycle (34.00%), car (29.33%), mixer (31.33%), washing machine (32.00%) showing that almost one-third of the respondents possess modern household-goods. Almost 13 per cent of the respondents owned in addition to the above mentioned, goods like air conditioner, jeep, music system etc. There were significant differences as regards the ownership of material possessions by the respondents. It was found that giving lot of gadgets in dowry was one of the reasons for having a considerable proportion of the above material. So, materialism is increasing considerably among the ruralities.

Table 16.3: Ownership of material possessions

Item	*Block-I (N=50)*	*Block-II (N=50)*	*Block-III (N=50)*	*G. Total (N=150)*
Cycle	21 (42.00)	12 (24.00)	18 (36.00)	51 (34.00)
Scooter/Motorcycle	42 (84.00)	45 (90.00)	46 (92.00)	133 (88.67)
Car	12 (24.00)	13 (26.00)	19 (38.00)	44 (29.33)
Radio	12 (24.00)	8 (16.00)	8 (16.00)	28 (18.67)
Television set	45 (90.00)	46 (92.00)	36 (72.00)	127 (84.67)
Video Cassette Recorder	3 (6.00)	4 (8.00)	2 (4.00)	9 (6.00)
Mixer	19 (38.00)	21 (42.00)	7 (14.00)	47 (31.33)
Cooler	44 (88.00)	40 (80.00)	44 (88.00)	128 (85.33)
Refrigerator	40 (80.00)	44 (88.00)	41 (82.00)	125 (83.33)
Washing Machine	15 (30.00)	14 (28.00)	19 (38.00)	48 (32.00)
Any other	3 (6.00)	7 (14.00)	9 (18.00)	19 (12.67)
$F_{10,20}$ =49.91**			CD(20 d.f.) = 6.78	

** Significant at 5 per cent level.
Note: Figures in parentheses indicate percentages.

Per Farm and Per Acre Return

Table 16.4 indicates that the per farm as well as per acre net returns were much higher in case of rabi crop than the kharif crop in all the blocks. In case of kharif crop the average net returns of all blocks per farm were just Rs.4279 and per acre were Rs.484 as compared to the rabi crop where average net returns per farm were Rs.26211 and per acre were Rs.2968. The overall average net returns for both the crops in a year were Rs.30490 per farm and Rs.3452 per acre. The low returns are attributed largely to the reasons like water logging, salinity, attack of pests, untimely rainfall etc. leading to the overall damage to the kharif crop. Low income per farm may be one of the attributing factors leading to the socio-economic adversities of farmers.

Table 16.4: Per farm and per acre net returns

Season	*Block-I (Rs.)*	*Block-II (Rs.)*	*Block-III (Rs.)*	*Overall average (Rs.)*
Kharif	4972 (546)	4006 (477)	3860 (429)	4279 (484)
Rabi	24920 (2738)	27240 (3227)	26472 (2941)	26211 (2968)
Yearly	29892 (3248)	31246 (3704)	30332 (3370)	30490 (3452)

Note : Figures in parentheses indicate per acre returns.

Annual Family Consumption Expenditure

Table 16.5 gives us the information regarding annual family consumption expenditure on food items, non-food items, socio-religious ceremonies and beverages and drugs. It was observed that majority of the respondents, *i.e.* 67.34 per cent had spent below Rs.20,000 on food items while 31.33 per cent had spent between Rs.20,000 to Rs.40,000. Only two respondents were found to spend more than Rs.40,000 on food items. The first two categories of respondents were quite predominant as compared to the last category. More than half of the respondents, *i.e.* 54.00 per cent had made expenditure between Rs. 20,000 to Rs.40,000 on non-food items followed by 26.67 per cent of the respondents who spent below Rs.20,000. The amount spent on education and medicine was found to be less as compared to that on clothing, housing, fuel etc. There was preponderance of the group spending between Rs.20,000 to Rs.40,000 on non-food items. Most of the respondents, *i.e.* 63.33 per cent spent up to Rs.10,000 on socio-religious ceremonies including expenditure on recreation, participation in marriage, rituals etc. There were significant differences as regards the expenditure on socio-religious ceremonies by the respondents with the preponderance of the category spending up to Rs.10,000. The table spotlights that 40.00 per cent of the respondents spent up to Rs.5,000 on beverages and drugs while 34.00 per cent spent between Rs.5,000 to 10,000 on these items indicating that the rural people spent quite large amount on beverages and drugs like liquor, zarda, tablets etc. leading to their socio-economic adversities.

Table 16.5: Annual family consumption expenditure

Annual Expenditure (in Rs.)	*Block-I*	*Block-II*	*Block-III*	*G. Total*
Food Items				
Upto 20000	31 (62.00)	40 (80.00)	30 (60.00)	101 (67.34)
20000-40000	18 (36.00)	10 (20.00)	19 (38.00)	47 (31.33)
40000 and above	1 (2.00)	-	1 (2.00)	2 (1.33)
Total	50 (100.00)	50 (100.00)	50 (100.00)	150 (100.00)
$F_{2,4}$ = 29.78**			CD (4d.f.) = 11.88	
Non-Food Items				
Upto 20000	13 (26.00)	15 (30.00)	12 (24.00)	40 (26.67)
20000-40000	28 (56.00)	23 (46.00)	30 (60.00)	81 (54.00)
40000 and above	9 (18.00)	12 (24.00)	8 (16.00)	29 (19.33)
Total	50 (100.00)	50 (100.00)	50 (100.00)	150 (100.00)
$F_{2,4}$ = 25.46**			CD (4d.f.) = 7.11	
Socio-Religious Expenditure				
Upto 10000	27 (54.00)	33 (66.00)	35 (70.00)	95 (63.33)
10000-20000	16 (32.00)	13 (26.00)	14 (28.00)	43 (28.67)
20000 and above	7 (14.00)	4 (8.00)	1 (2.00)	12 (8.00)
Total	50 (100.00)	50 (100.00)	50 (100.00)	150 (100.00)
$F_{2,4}$ = 40.91**			CD (4d.f.) = 8.58	
Beverages and Drugs				
No expenditure	7 (14.00)	10 (20.00)	6 (12.00)	23 (15.33)
upto 5000	23 (46.00)	21 (42.00)	16 (32.00)	60 (40.00)
5000-10000	13 (26.00)	14 (28.00)	24 (48.00)	51 (34.00)
10000 and above	7 (14.00)	5 (10.00)	4 (8.00)	16 (10.67)
Total	50 (100.00)	50 (100.00)	50 (100.00)	150 (100.00)
$F_{3,6}$ = 6.80**			CD (6d.f.) = 9.42	

**Significant at 5 per cent level.
Note : Figures in Parentheses indicate percentages.

Amount of Credit Taken

From above we observe that the expenditures of the farmers are more than their earning. To fill the gap, one has to take credit usually from money lender or banks. Data show that a major proportion of the respondents, *i.e.* 28.67 per cent had taken credit between Rs.1,00,000 to 2,00,000 and 25.33 per cent of the respondents had taken credit between Rs.2,00,000 to Rs. 3,00,000 (Table 16.6). A few of the respondents (4.00 %) had taken credit even above Rs.4,00,000. Data further depict that 8.67 per cent of the respondents did not take credit. There were significant differences as regards the amount of credit borrowed by the respondents and the categories whose borrowing was between Rs.1,00,000 to Rs. 2,00,000 and Rs.2,00,000 to Rs. 3,00,000. The amount scenario indicates that borrowing by farmers was quite high which may be a factor leading to their economic adversities.

Table 16.6: Amount of credit taken (1998-2001)

Amount taken (Rs.)	*Block-I*	*Block-II*	*Block-III*	*G. Total*
Not taken	3 (6.00)	7 (14.00)	3 (6.00)	13 (8.67)
Upto 100000	4 (8.00)	8 (16.00)	10 (20.00)	22 (14.67)
100000-200000	16 (32.00)	15 (30.00)	12 (24.00)	43 (28.67)
200000-300000	15 (30.00)	9 (18.00)	14 (28.00)	38 (25.33)
300000-400000	9 (18.00)	9 (18.00)	10 (20.00)	28 (18.66)
400000 and above	3 (6.00)	2 (4.00)	1 (2.00)	6 (4.00)
Total	50 (100.00)	50 (100.00)	50 (100.00)	150 (100.00)
$F_{5,10}$= 11.66**			CD (10d.f.) = 4.61	

**Significant at 5 per cent level.
Note: Figures in parentheses indicate percentages.

Sources of Credit/Loan

It comes out from Table 16.7 that about one-third of respondents (34.31%) took loans from cooperative societies and private money lenders both at the same time followed by those who took loans only from private money lenders (20.43%). The other sources of taking credit were agricultural cooperative societies (18.25%) and commercial banks (7.30%). A few (3.65%) had borrowed from sources other than the mentioned above. There was considerable variability as regards the sources of credit/loan. The data indicate that farmers are not restricted to one source of borrowing; they used to exploit every possible agency/avenue advancing credit to farmers whether it is institutional or non-institutional one. Taking loans from non-institutional sources was quite easy and did not involve tedious paper work. In short, traditional money lender still proved a big source of credit to the farmers.

Since the farmers are drawing credit from various agencies, information was gathered to know the purpose of taking credit. A large proportion of the respondents (84.67%) took loans for the purchase of agricultural input (Table 16.8) followed by 44.52 per cent of the respondents who took loans for the purchase of farm machinery. Nearly equal number of the respondents, *i.e.* 21.16 per cent, 19.70 per cent and 21.89 per cent respectively had taken loans for purposes like purchase of livestock, construction work and repair and for medical purposes.

Table 16.7: Sources of credit/loan

Sources of Credit/Loan	*Block-I (N=47)*	*Block-II (N=43)*	*Block-III (N=47)*	*G. Total (N=137)*
Commercial Banks	4 (8.51)	2 (4.65)	4 (8.51)	10 (7.30)
Agricultural Cooperative societies	7 (14.90)	8 (18.60)	10 (21.28)	25 (18.25)
Private money lenders (*arhtiyas*)	8 (17.02)	11 (25.60)	9 (19.14)	28 (20.43)
Commercial banks and private money lenders	5 (10.63)	4 (9.30)	1 (2.12)	10 (7.30)
Cooperative societies and private money lenders	15 (31.91)	14 (32.55)	18 (38.30)	47 (34.31)
Cooperative societies and relatives	6 (12.77)	4 (9.30)	2 (4.26)	12 (8.76)
Any other	2 (4.26)	—	3 (6.39)	5 (3.65)
$F_{6,12} = 25.52^{**}$			CD(12 d.f.) = 3.27	

**Significant at 5 per cent level.
Note: Figures in parentheses indicate percentages.

Table 16.8: Purposes of taking credit

(Multiple response)

Purpose of taking credit	*Block-I (N=47)*	*Block-II (N=43)*	*Block-III (N=47)*	*G. Total (N=137)*
Purchase of farm machinery	21 (44.68)	18 (41.86)	22 (46.80)	61 (44.52)
Purchase of agricultural inputs	40 (85.10)	35 (81.39)	41 (87.23)	116 (84.67)
Purchase of livestock	9 (19.14)	8 (18.60)	12 (25.33)	29 (21.16)
Construction work and repair	8 (17.02)	10 (23.25)	9 (19.14)	27 (19.70)
Medical purposes	9 (19.14)	11 (25.58)	10 (21.27)	30 (21.89)
To buy durable goods	15 (31.91)	12 (27.90)	16 (34.04)	43 (31.38)
For expenditure on socio-religious ceremonies	13 (27.65)	15 (34.88)	12 (25.53)	40 (29.19)
Any other	5 (10.63)	7 (16.27)	3 (6.38)	15 (10.94)

Note : Figures in parentheses indicate percentages.

Almost 11 per cent of the respondents took loans for purposes such as purchase of shop, to start a business etc. which fall in the 'Any other' category. Thus, majority of the respondents had taken credit for productive purposes. It does not mean that loan for unproductive purposes is not taken by the cultivators. Data discern that one-third of the respondents had borrowed for socio-religious ceremonies and such borrowings invariably add to their adversities.

Outstanding Amount of Credit

As far as the outstanding amount of credit is concerned, it was observed that most of the respondents had outstanding credit between Rs.50,000 to Rs.1,00,000 (27.74%, Table 16.9). Data further show that almost an equal number of respondents constituting 22.63 per cent and 24.81 per cent of the total sample had respectively outstanding amount of credit up to Rs.50,000 and Rs.1,00,000 to Rs.1,50,000. The table further shows that 16.06 per cent of the respondents had outstanding amount of credit between Rs.1,50,000 to Rs.2,00,000 while 8.76 per cent of the respondents had outstanding amount above Rs.2,00,000. This shows that all the respondents who had taken credit had enough outstanding amount leading thereby to economic adversities of farmers.

Table 16.9: Outstanding amount of credit

Outstanding amount (Rs.)	*Block-I (N=47)*	*Block-II (N=43)*	*Block-III (N=47)*	*G. Total (N=137)*
Upto 50000	10 (21.28)	12 (27.91)	9 (19.14)	31 (22.63)
50000-100000	15 (31.91)	9 (20.93)	14 (29.79)	38 (27.74)
100000-150000	11 (23.40)	13 (30.23)	10 (21.28)	34 (24.81)
150000-200000	7 (14.90)	6 (13.95)	9 (19.15)	22 (16.06)
200000 and above	4 (8.51)	3 (6.98)	5 (10.64)	12 (8.76)

$F_{4,8} = 8.41^{**}$ CD(8 d.f.) = 5.46

**Significant at 5 per cent level.

Note: Figures in parentheses indicate percentages.

Reasons for failure of Crops

The respondents told that their crops failed during the past few years due to various reasons.

Table 16.10: Reasons for the failure of crops

(Multiple response)

Reasons for crop failure	*Block-I (N=17)*	*Block-II (N=15)*	*Block-III (N=19)*	*G. Total (N=51)*
Small size of land holding	2 (11.76)	-	-	2 (3.92)
Untimely rainfall	7 (41.17)	9 (60.00)	11 (57.89)	27 (52.94)
Inadequate irrigation facilities	1 (5.88)	-	2 (10.52)	3 (5.88)
Excessive use of chemical fertilizers	3 (17.64)	2 (13.33)	5 (26.31)	10 (19.61)
Attack of pests/plant diseases	10 (58.82)	12 (80.00)	15 (78.94)	37 (72.54)
High cost of inputs	4 (23.52)	2 (13.33)	1 (5.26)	7 (13.73)
Waterlogging	3 (17.64)	4 (26.67)	5 (26.31)	12 (23.52)

$F_{6,12} = 24.60^{**}$ CD(12 d.f.) = 2.72

**Significant at 5 per cent level.

Note: Figures in parentheses indicate percentages.

The most important reason for the failure of their crops had been an attack of pests or plant diseases particularly on the kharif crop of cotton. The percentage of such respondents had been the highest (72.54 %). This was followed by 52.94 per cent of the respondents who held that untimely rainfall was the major reason for the failure of their crops. Interestingly, the overuse of pesticides itself is responsible for the development of pesticide resistant insects/pests. The situation gets aggravated with untimely rainfall. The other reasons for failure of crops were small size of land holding (3.92%), inadequate irrigation facilities (5.86%), excessive use of chemical fertilizers (19.61%), high cost of inputs (13.73%) and waterlogging (23.52%). There was considerable variability in relation to reasons for failure of crops.

Reasons for Expenditure on Socio-Religious Ceremonies

Now the question arises, if the farmers are experiencing failure of crops and their outstanding credit is swelling, how can they continue or afford to spend on socio-religious ceremonies? There must be certain social and psychological factors contributing to making such wasteful expenditures. For majority of the respondents, spending on socio-religious ceremonies either to maintain or enhance their status in the village (62.67%, Table 16.11). Moreover, to show their wealth (20.0%) and to maintain the pride of their ancestors (11.33%), the farmers make heavy expenditures on socio-religious ceremonies. In addition, imitating the well-to-do people, to keep daughter happy after marriage and the like are other reasons for extravagance expenditures on socio-religious functions. There was significant variation as regards the reasons for expenditure on socio-religious ceremonies. The categories spending in order to maintain their status in village and due to social complex *i.e.* cultivators are invariably rich showed their preponderance over other categories.

Table 16.11: Expenditure on socio-religious ceremonies

(Multiple response

Reasons for expenditure	*Block-I (N=50)*	*Block-II (N=50)*	*Block-III (N-50)*	*G. Total (N=150)*
To maintain status in village	31 (62.00)	34 (68.00)	29 (58.00)	94 (62.67)
Show their wealth	10 (20.00)	12 (24.00)	8 (16.00)	30 (20.00)
Due to social complex	27 (54.00)	22 (44.00)	20 (40.00)	69 (46.00)
To maintain pride of ancestors	8 (16.00)	5 (10.00)	4 (8.00)	17 (11.33)
Any other	12 (24.00)	15 (30.00)	18 (36.00)	45 (30.00)

$F_{4,8} = 48.34^{**}$ CD(8d.f.) = 4.81

**Significant at 5 per cent level.

Note : Figures in parentheses indicate percentages.

Conclusion

The results of the study showed that majority of the respondents were in the age group of 30-50 years, hailed from Sikh religion (98.00%) belonged to the high-caste group (98.67%) and were married. They were living in nuclear families and nearly half of the respondents (51.33%) having family size of five to seven members. As regards education level 38.00 per cent were illiterate and most of them had their own pucca houses. Only 35.00 per cent were engaged in any subsidiary occupations and there was preponderance of categories having land less than 10 acres. Majority of the respondents, *i.e.* almost 60.00 per cent had total annual income below one lakh rupees per annum. By and large the respondents possessed certain farm and material possessions irrespective of their economic position. The per farm and per acre returns were much higher in case of *rabi* crop than the *kharif* crop in all the blocks. Most of the respondents spent less on food items as compared to non-food items. Quite a large amount is spent on socio-religious ceremonies and beverages and drugs. The borrowing of credit by majority of the respondents has been quite high for both productive and non-productive purposes, with most important sources being agriculture cooperative societies, private money lenders or both. The study infers that farmers though had enough outstanding amount of credit to repay and experience crop failure still spend sufficiently big amount on socio-religious ceremonies just to maintain social status and prestige without realising its consequences for the future. Pride in self too contributes significantly in this process. It can be thus concluded that the farmers are facing socio-economic adversities due to natural and socio-psychological reasons/factors which have a widespread impact on their economic, social and psychological aspect of life.

Suggestions

On the basis of the results of the study, some suggestions are being made which may be helpful to improve the position of farmers in the state.

1. In most cases farmers spent on durable goods and socio-religious ceremonies in disproportion to their income which quite often leads them towards socio-economic problems. Judicious use of their income may keep them away from the socio-economic adversities. Community level organisations may be helpful to achieve this purpose.

2. There is need for judicious use of fertilisers, pesticides and farm machinery in relation to size of land holding.
3. Besides farming, farmers should adopt subsidiary occupations to supplement their income and practice diverse cropping pattern.
4. Institutional credit structure should be made more active and farmer friendly.
5. In case of natural calamities and successive crop failure government should provide special assistance to the farmers.

REFERENCES

Bhandari, D.K., (1982), Social tensions and political consciousness as a result of Green Revolution, M.Sc. Thesis, Punjab Agricultural University, Ludhiana, India.

Garg, B.S., (1999), "Debts a milestone round farmers neck", *The Hindustan Times*, Jan. 13.

Bobby, J.V., (1998), "Killing fields?", *The Hindustan Times*, Nov. 8.

Jodhka, S.S., (2000), "Green nod to final exit", *The Tribune*, May 21.

Kaur, J., (1982), *Agricultural development and demographic change in rural Punjab*, M.Sc. Thesis, Punjab Agricultural University, Ludhiana.

Parmar, K., (1985), *Effect of increased agricultural production on the living conditions of rural farm families*. M.Sc. Thesis, Punjab Agricultural University, Ludhiana.

Singh, H., (2000), "Why farm sector income low in Punjab", *The Tribune*, Feb. 28.

Shergil, H.S., (1997), *Rural credit and indebtedness in Punjab*. Institute for Development and Communication, Chandigarh.

Sehgal, V.K. and Arora, M., (2000), "Post harvest technologies for rural entrepreneurship through agro-industrial complexes", *Political Economy of India*, Vol. 9, No. 22.

17

FINANCING OF WEAKER SECTIONS
Experience with Regional Rural Banks in Punjab

SAJLA KALRA & KARAM SINGH

The Regional Rural Banks (RRBs) have come a long way since their inception in 1975 and have now become an integral part of the rural financial system. The extensive bank/branch network taking the banking services to the doorsteps of the poor in the far-flung rural areas, mobilisation of rural deposits and meeting the credit needs of the rural clientele are the major strengths of RRBs. The present study was conducted in the Punjab State where no such attempt has been made in the past. Punjab being a progressive agricultural state, the study of RRBs in such a scenario assumes even greater significance to derive out the long-term economic development policies for institutional finance development in the progressive rural areas.

Selection of RRB

There are a total of five RRBs operating in Punjab. The main parameters of these RRBs for the year 1996 are given in Table 17.1. Based on the recovery performance criterion, which is the principal parameter portraying the basic functioning of the financial institution, the Malwa Gramin Bank (MGB), which had the highest recovery performance (94.67%) among the five RRBs in Punjab as well as amongst RRBs of India, was purposively selected for detailed analysis in the study. Malwa Gramin Bank, sponsored by State Bank of Patiala was established on 27-2-1986. It serves the districts of Sangrur, Patiala and Fatehgarh Sahib

Table 17.1: Basic business indicators of RRBs in Punjab, March 1996

Sl. No	*Name of RRB*	*Date of establishment*	*No. of districts covered*	*No. of branches*	*Deposits*		*Outstanding credit*		*Overdue advances*		*% of recovery to demand (As on June, 1995)*
					No. of accounts	*Amount (Rs. lakhs)*	*No. of accounts*	*Amount (Rs. lakhs)*	*No. of accounts*	*Amount (Rs. lakhs)*	
1.	Shivalik Kshetriya Gramin Bank	31-03-83	3	41	105868	56.54	28744	21.33	17051	4.686	63.26
2.	Kapurthala-Ferozpur Kshetriya Gramin Bank	30-03-83	2	43	80761	42.05	28352	25.34	23777	12.22	32.43
3.	Gurdaspur-Amritsar Kshetriya Gramin Bank	30-03-83	2	54	127673	64.36	35967	30.72	8515	10.66	45.12
4.	Malwa Gramin Bank	27-02-86	3	41	45004	34.71	20660	24.35	2040	0.5521	94.67
5.	Faridkot-Bathinda Kshetriya Gramin Bank	22-03-86	3	22	36171	31.27	9763	15.76	5468	2.755	71.28

Source: Financial Statements of RRBs 1995-95, NABARD.

with a network of 41 branches. The head office of the Bank is located at Sangrur which is an industrially backward district of Punjab. The economy of its area of operation is predominantly agrarian.

Profile of RRBs in Punjab has been presented by calculating growth rates of branch expansion, deposits, outstanding advances, CD ratio*, average advances and deposits per branch and average deposits and advances per RRB for the period of five years from 1991-92 to 1995-96 (Table 17.2). The number of RRBs over the corresponding period remained same, *i.e.* 5. The number of branches also remained same, *i.e.* 201. The deposits of RRBs in Punjab increased from Rs. 9831.90 lakhs in 1991-92 to Rs. 22,895.37 lakhs in 1995-96 showing a compound growth rate of 23.59 per cent. Outstanding advances increased from Rs. 6426.53 lakhs to Rs. 11,243.46 lakhs showing compound growth rate of 14.96 per cent. The CD ratio showed decline in Punjab too from 65.4 per cent in 1991-92 to 49.1 per cent in 1995-96. The average deposits and outstanding advances per RRB increased from Rs. 1866.32 lakhs and Rs. 1285.30 lakhs to Rs. 4589.07 lakhs and Rs. 2248.69 lakhs showing growth rate of 23.59 per cent and 14.96 per cent, respectively. Similarly, average deposits and outstanding advances per branch increased from Rs. 48.91 lakhs and Rs. 31.97 lakhs to Rs. 124.38 lakhs and Rs. 60.14 lakhs showing compound growth rate of 23.59 per cent and 14.97 per cent, respectively.

Performance of Malwa Gramin Bank

Malwa Gramin Bank, sponsored by State Bank of Patiala, has its branches located in the district of Sangrur (23), Patiala (13) and Fatehgarh Sahib (5). The issued and paid up capital of Malwa Gramin Bank is Rs. 100 lakhs which is held by Government of India, State Bank of Patiala and Punjab Government in proportion of 50 per cent, 35 per cent and 15 per cent, respectively. The State Bank of Patiala provides managerial and financial assistance to its sponsored Malwa Gramin Bank on the basis of mutually agreed terms.

The MGB besides mobilising rural deposits, lays major emphasis on raising production and productivity through all types of agricultural loans. The loaning policies are targeted on improving the lot of downtrodden and other weaker sections of the society so as to reduce income inequalities and social disparities. Consequent upon various

* CD ratio—Credit-Deposit ratio.

Table 17.2: Profile of RRBs in Punjab, 1992-92 to 1995-96

Year	*No. of RRBs*	*No. of branches*	*Deposits (Rs. lakhs)*	*Outstanding advances (Rs. lakhs)*	*CD ratio*	*Average per RRB*		*Average per Branch*	
						Deposits (Rs. lakhs)	*Outstanding advances (Rs. lakhs)*	*Deposits (Rs. lakhs)*	*Outstanding advances (Rs. lakhs)*
1991-92	5	201	9831.90	6426.53	65.4	1966.38	1285.30	48.91	31.97
1992-93	5	201	12062.47	7364.29	61.1	2412.49	1472.85	60.01	36.63
1993-94	5	201	14487.74	8059.35	55.6	2897.54	1611.87	72.03	40.09
1994-95	5	201	18501.68	9704.74	52.2	3700.33	1940.94	92.05	48.28
1995-96	5	201	22895.37	11243.46	49.1	4579.07	2248.69	113.91	55.94
Compound Growth Rate			23.59* (0.01)	14.96* (0.01)	–7.1NS (0.003)	23.59* (0.01)	14.96* (0.01)	23.59* (0.01)	14.97* (0.01)

Notes: NS indicates non-significant, *indicates significant at 5 per cent level of significance.

Figures in parentheses indicate standard error of estimates.

Source: Reports on Currency and Finance, Reserve Bank of India, Various issues.

relaxations allowed to RRBs by Government of India/Reserve Bank of India, the bank has gone a long way in financing the non-target groups (NTG) ensuring integrated development of the entire area of operation resulting into viability of banks on sustainable basis.

As a result of policy decision taken by Government of India during 1994-95, Malwa Gramin Bank entered into a memorandum of understanding with the sponsor bank (State Bank of Patiala) to swamp the working of the bank which had been incurring losses continuously and accumulated losses as on 31-3-1994 stood at Rs. 44.26 lakhs. Under the continued guidance, assistance and support provided by the sponsor bank, curtailing avoidable expenses, improvement in advances, high yielding investment and proper fund management, MGB has been able to earn profit of Rs. 150.47 lakhs in 1996-97 against 94.89 lakhs during 1995-96 after making adequate provisions.

The profile of MGB has been discussed with the help of physical and financial performance indicators. Physical performance indicators of the bank are presented in Table 17.3.

Branch Expansion

Over a period of nine years the bank had opened a number of branches in various parts of its districts of operation, *viz.*, Sangrur, Patiala and Fatehgarh Sahib. The number of branches of the bank increased from nine in 1988-89 to 39 in number in the next year, *i.e.* 1989-90. Thus major expansion came up only during the year 1989-90. Two more branches were opened during 1990-91 and the total number of branches since then has remained at 41.

Staff Position

In order to manage the increasing business activities of MGB, the strength of staff was increased from 58 in 1988-89 to 127 in 1989-90 and further to 156 in 1990-91. There was some cut back in staff in 1992-93 to 142; it was 135 in 1996-97.

Deposit and Advances Accounts

The number of deposit accounts and advance accounts increased from 3,724 to 48,657 and 1,624 to 20,609, thus accounting for compound growth rate of 29.09 per cent and 28.03 per cent, respectively during the

Table 17.3: Physical performance indicators of the Malwa Gramin Bank, 1988-89 to 1996-97

Indicators	*1988-89*	*1989-90*	*1990-91*	*1991-92*	*1992-93*	*1993-94*	*1994-95*	*1995-96*	*1996-97*	***Compound Growth Rate***
Total bank branches (No.)	9	39	41	41	41	41	41	41	41	**10.91*** **(0.06)**
Staff (No.)	58	127	156	154	142	143	139	136	135	**5.61*** **(0.04)**
No. of deposit accounts	3724	13999	22194	28001	32727	38521	40862	45004	48657	**29.09*** **(0.06)**
Average No. of deposit accounts per branch	414	359	541	683	798	939	997	1098	1187	**16.39*** **(0.02)**
Average No. of deposit accounts per employee	64	110	142	182	230	269	294	331	360	**22.26*** **(0.02)**
No. of advance accounts	1624	6393	12230	16094	18774	19008	19952	20660	20609	**28.03*** **(0.07)**
Average No. of advance accounts per branch	180	164	298	393	458	464	487	504	503	**15.46*** **(0.03)**
Average No. of advance accounts per employee	28	50	78	105	132	133	144	152	153	**21.31** **(0.04)**

Notes: NS indicates non-significant, *indicates significant at 5 per cent level of significance.

Figures in parentheses indicate standard error of estimates.

Source: Compiled from the Annual Reports of MGB, Sangrur.

period 1988-89 to 1996-97. The main reason for the expansion of deposit accounts was an increase in the number of MGB branches and innovative deposit schemes evolved by the bank to mobilise rural savings.

Average number of deposit accounts per branch increased from 414 during 1988-89 to 1187 during 1996-97 which showed a three-fold increase and compound growth rate of 16.39 per cent. Similarly, average advances accounts per branch increased from 180 to 503 showing a compound growth rate of 15.46 per cent. A similar trend was observed with respect to average deposit accounts per employee and average advance accounts per employee. Average number of deposit accounts per employee and average number of advances accounts per employee increased from 64 and 28 to 360 and 153 showing compound growth rates of 22.26 per cent and 21.31 per cent, respectively.

Financial Performance Indicators of MGB

The financial performance indicators of MGB are given in Table 17.4.

Deposits and Advances Outstandings

Deposits of MGB increased from Rs. 206.44 lakhs in 1988-89 to Rs. 4167 lakhs in 1996-97 whereas advances outstanding during the corresponding period increased from Rs. 72.16 lakhs to Rs. 2814.68 lakhs. The compound growth rate of deposits and advances outstandings was 38.37 per cent and 46.91 per cent, respectively. Since there was marked improvement in the technology of farm production and infrastructural facilities such as communication and market facilities, the farmers were tended to increase their marketable surplus through the use of credit by making use of larger amount of investment on their farms to increase production.

Volume of Business

The total business of MGB showed a spectacular increase from Rs. 278.60 lakhs in 1988-89 to Rs. 6981.64 lakhs in 1996-97, *i.e.* at a compound growth rate of 41.23 per cent. This was due to increase in the number of bank branches and the innovative deposit mobilisation schemes undertaken by the bank branches in addition to general growth of the agrarian economy of the area during this period through the adoption of improved technology and complimented by infrastructural facilities like

Table 17.4: Financial performance indicators of the Malwa Gramin Bank, 1988-89 to 1996-97

Indicators	*1988-89*	*1989-90*	*1990-91*	*1991-92*	*1992-93*	*1993-94*	*1994-95*	*1995-96*	*1996-97*	***Compound Growth Rate***
Deposits (Rs. lakhs)	206.44	626.59	1208.23	1530.17	1963.10	2411.40	3090.30	3471.66	4167.00	**38.37* (0.05)**
Advances outstandings (Rs. lakhs)	72.16	324.33	677.56	916.44	1073.62	1229.98	1921.93	2434.18	2814.64	**46.91* (0.06)**
Volume of business (Rs. lakhs)	278.60	950.92	1885.79	2446.61	3036.72	3641.38	5012.23	5905.84	6981.64	**41.23* (0.05)**
Total income (Rs. lakhs)	30.33	39.00	144.77	217.63	296.66	347.17	429.42	573.43	750.13	**48.02* (0.05)**
Total expenditure (Rs. lakhs)	24.96	57.25	142.35	235.76	309.58	352.96	389.79	478.54	599.66	**43.10* (0.05)**
Net Profit/Loss (Rs. lakhs)	5.37	–9.84	2.42	–18.13	–12.92	–5.79	38.63	94.89	150.47	
Overdue amount (Rs. lakhs)	2.06	5.60	10.53	50.01	106.81	116.02	101.24	105.92	136.99	**65.07* (0.01)**
Recovery percentage	94.69	92.55	93.88	92.98	90.87	91.96	93.75	94.67	94.33	**0.07NS (0.01)**
Productivity per branch	30.95	24.38	45.99	59.67	74.06	88.81	122.25	144.04	170.29	**27.34* (0.02)**
Productivity per employee	4.80	7.48	12.08	15.89	21.38	25.46	40.75	43.43	51.71	**34.28* (0.02)**
Credit Deposit Ratio	34.95	51.76	56.08	59.89	54.69	51.00	62.20	70.12	67.55	**6.17%* (0.02)**

Notes: NS indicates non-significant, * indicates significant at 5 per cent level of significance.
Figures in parentheses indicate standard error of estimates.

Source: Compiled from Annual Reports of MGB, Sangrur.

assured irrigation, marketing, transport etc. Productivity per branch increased from Rs. 30.95 lakhs in 1988-89 to Rs. 170.29 lakhs in 1996-97 showing compound growth rate of 27.34 per cent. Similarly, productivity per employee during the period increased from Rs. 4.8 lakhs to Rs. 51.71 lakhs showing compound growth rate of 34.28 per cent.

Credit Deposit Ratio

The credit deposit ratio increased from 34.95 per cent in 1988-89 to 67.55 per cent with compound growth rate of 6.17 per cent. Thus CD ratio clearly indicated that the bank had attached more importance in advancing credit to the rural people.

Overdues and Recovery Percentage

In absolute terms, the overdues amount of MGB increased from Rs. 2.06 lakhs in 1988-89 to Rs. 136.99 lakhs in 1996-97 showing compound growth rate of 65.07 percent. Recovery per centage over the corresponding period has remained above 90 per cent. It was 94.69 in 1988-89 and 93.33 in 1996-97. MGB is the best RRB in India as far as recovery percentage is concerned.

Income, Expenditure and Net Profit

The total income of the bank increased from Rs. 30.33 lakhs in 1988-89 to Rs. 750.13 lakhs in 1996-97 recording compound growth rate of 48.02 per cent. The total expenditure of the bank increased from Rs. 24.96 lakhs to Rs. 599.66 lakhs recording compound growth rate of 43.10 per cent. The net profit also increased from Rs. 5.37 lakhs to Rs. 150.47 lakhs during the corresponding period.

Deposit Break-up

Table 17.5 shows break-up of deposits of MGB for the period 1988-89 to 1996-97 into saving deposits, time deposits, current deposits and other deposits.

The time deposits formed a major part of deposits in all the years under consideration except 1988-89. More than 50 per cent deposits were time deposits, followed by saving deposits and current deposits. The table shows that over the years the share of time deposits in total deposits

Table 17.5: Break-up of deposits of MGB, 1988-89 to 1996-97

Deposits (Rs. lakhs)	*1988-89*	*1989-90*	*1990-91*	*1991-92*	*1992-93*	*1993-94*	*1994-95*	*1995-96*	*1996-97*
Saving deposits	101.80	264.07	505.56	536.70	661.59	782.20	1280.60	1321.88	1600.67
	(49.31)	(42.14)	(41.84)	(35.07)	(33.70)	(32.44)	(41.44)	(38.08)	(38.41)
Current deposits	8.79	37.68	81.68	90.23	94.98	266.84	182.72	277.38	203.34
	(4.25)	(6.01)	(6.77)	(5.90)	(4.84)	(11.07)	(5.91)	(7.99)	(4.88)
Time deposits	95.51	322.68	614.18	901.24	1204.53	1359.45	1622.54	1868.77	2362.34
	(46.26)	(51.50)	(50.83)	(58.90)	(61.36)	(56.37)	(52.51)	(53.83)	(56.69)
Others	0.34	2.16	6.81	2.00	2.00	2.91	4.44	3.63	0.65
	(0.08)	(0.35)	(0.56)	(0.13)	(0.10)	(0.12)	(0.14)	(0.10)	(0.02)
Total	206.44	626.59	1208.23	1530.17	1963.10	2411.40	3090.30	3471.66	4167.00
	(100.00)	(100.00)	(100.00)	(100,00)	(100.00)	(100.00)	(100.00)	(100.00)	(100.00)

Note: Figures in parentheses indicate percentage to total.

Source: Annual Reports of MGB, Sangrur.

Table 17.6: Purpose-wise advance of Malwa Gramin Bank, 1988-89 to 1996-97

Nature of loans advanced (Rs. lakhs)	*1988-89*	*1989-90*	*1990-91*	*1991-92*	*1992-93*	*1993-94*	*1994-95*	*1995-96*	*1996-97*
Agri. Cash Credit (ACC)	34.49	158.30	351.96	540.60	614.62	670.11	827.72	995.15	1172.36
	(47.80)	(48.83)	(53.00)	(58.99)	(57.00)	(54.48)	(43.07)	(40.88)	(42.00)
Agri. Term Loan (ATL)	20.27	69.88	130.58	160.50	202.90	278.96	664.92	921.27	1156.70
	(28.09)	(21.55)	(19.00)	(17.51)	(19.00)	(22.68)	(34.60)	(37.85)	(38.00)
Indirect Agri.	–	–	–	–	–	–	–	73.49	85.11
								(3.02)	(3.00)
Small Scale Industries	2.94	24.04	59.69	69.92	71.79	66.73	72.14	70.70	64.20
	(4.07)	(7.41)	(9.00)	(7.63)	(7.00)	(5.42)	(3.75)	(2.90)	(2.00)
Small Business Finance	6.62	51.89	82.73	82.20	97.21	111.10	188.71	159.54	177.59
	(9.18)	(16.00)	(12.00)	(8.97)	(9.00)	(9.04)	(9.82)	(6.56)	(6.00)
Demand Loan/Overdraft/DD Purchase	7.84	20.14	46.60	63.22	87.70	103.08	168.44	214.05	258.68
	(10.86)	(6.21)	(7.00)	(6.90)	(8.00)	(8.38)	(8.76)	(8.79)	(9.00)
Total	72.16	324.33	677.56	916.44	1073.62	1229.98	1921.93	2434.18	2914.64
	(100.00)	(100.00)	(100.00)	(100.00)	(100.00)	(100.00)	(100.00)	(100.00)	(100.00)

Note: Figures in parentheses indicate percentage to total.

Source: Annual Reports of MGB.

has been increasing up to 1992-93 when it reached a share of 61.36 per cent. It came down to 56.69 per cent in 1996-97. Since time deposits are relatively costlier deposits, their scaling down to some extent is better for the financial health of the RRB.

Purpose-wise Break-up of Advances

Purpose-wise break-up of advances of Malwa Gramin Bank is shown in Table 17.6. The major parts of advances went to agricultural cash credit (ACC) followed by agricultural term loans (ATL), demand loan, small business finance and then small scale industry in that order. Up to 1996-97, ACC and ATL accounted for 42 and 38 per cent of the total advances of MGB, respectively.

Thus RRBs in Punjab have shown a substantial improvement in almost all the business indicators except CD ratio. It may be mentioned that CD ratio is also conditioned by the norms and suggestions of NABARD. In case of Malwa Gramin Bank, there was even more substantial increase both in physical and financial performance indicators.

SECTION–IV

WOMEN EMPOWERMENT

18

POLITICAL EMPOWERMENT OF WOMEN
Lessons from Municipal Corporations of Punjab and Chandigarh

RAJESH GILL

While women's empowerment has been talked about quite extensively both in academic world and outside, its translation into reality has been less frequent. Reasons are many—one, 'empowerment' of women means different things to different people, e.g. feminists/non-feminists; academics/non-academics; men/women; women at different stages of lifecycle; educated/a little educated/highly educated women; rich/poor women; rural/urban women and so on.

Secondly, it is easier to talk about women's empowerment, but much more difficult to translate it into practice because that involves a structural—a more radical transformation, often demanding a spontaneous withdrawal of power from the men as husbands, employers, colleagues, fathers and so on. It is problematic also because empowerment of women involves disempowering other women. For instance, empowerment of a woman as a daughter, daughter-in-law, mother, mother-in-law etc; would imply at the same time, withdrawing a certain amount of power traditionally enjoyed by the mother, mother-in-law, daughter, daughter-in-law, and so on. Its practice therefore is problematic because it creates disturbances in the age-old social relations and power structures.

Out of the educational, economic and political empowerment of women, it is the last, *i.e.* the political, which is most problematic; simply because political arena has continued to be an extremely patriarchal domain, with a negligible visibility of women, especially at the decision making levels. This has been the case not only in a traditional society iike India, but more so in the most developed and liberal democratic societies of the West too. The undercurrents induced by the political empowerment of women in India became evident through the reaction of different political parties towards the reservation of seats for women in the state assemblies and Parliament. Seen from this perspective then, the implementation of 73rd and 74th Constitutional Amendment Acts has been an extremely bold step on the part of the Indian Government. These Amendments mean not only a quantitatively greater visibility of women in local decision making bodies, but more importantly, a qualitative leap for the women (traditionally, debarred from active politics), in the form of a 'voice' which they can utilize for raising issues, high on their agenda. Do they actually use it or not; are they allowed to use it or; are the ones willing to use it being penalized or rewarded; who are the women using it more effectively—are some of the questions which shall find answers only in a due course of time.

Punjab is one of the leading states in the country having undergone tremendous economic and social transformation since independence. On the one hand it has the distinction of having the highest per capita income in the country besides the lowest proportion of population below poverty line, on the other it continues to have considerably low sex ratio besides the lowest rate of female workforce participation in the country. It is heartening to note that the Government of Punjab has responded sympathetically to the problems being faced by the women in the state. The Punjab State Policy for Women (Government of Punjab, 1996) states that the societies and homes with inferior status of women contribute more to malnourishment among children particularly the girl child. Recognizing this, the government has provided greater thrust to programmes for employment of women, rehabilitation, legal and social measures to check atrocities against women and empowerment of women through improvement in their political, economic, educational and health status.

While examining the gender relations in Punjab it is important to note the following factors, which have been instrumental in pushing women, especially the Hindu and the Sikh, within the household:

- Predominantly an agrarian society in which women, though actively participating in agricultural activity along with their men folk, have been mainly entrusted with the domestic chores, bearing of sons and rearing them;
- Invasion of Punjab from time to time by aliens such as Muslims

etc., thereby leaving behind strong implications on women—with the age at marriage coming down and women getting pushed back to the four walls of home;

- This is a status in which a prolonged phase of terrorism of worst kind has left people, especially women—widowed, deserted, pauperized and traumatized. In a pilot study on Victims of Militancy in Punjab conducted by the Institute for Development and Communication, Chandigarh, it is revealed that militancy has left a large number of women victims deserted by husbands, abandoned by families, widowed, with the disintegration of family units and an increasing consumption of alcohol and drugs within the families.

These three factors along with several others have sharpened the demarcation between the public domain and the private domain—with the women's activities getting restricted to the latter. It is this context in which the gender relations in Punjab have to be examined. The impact of 74th Constitutional Amendment becomes very relevant here since this provision is intended to shift the women from private to the public domain. Given the Punjabi socio-cultural milieu, cultural ethos, male chauvinism and historical past, how is this legislative measure going to be received by the public at large? To what an extent is the implementation of this Amendment going to empower women in the state politically and how is it likely to affect gender relations here? These are the questions to which I intend to address myself in this paper.

Constitutionally and legally, equality of opportunity is guaranteed and discrimination on any ascriptive grounds is prohibited in our society. Yet in reality, women's participation in decision-making at all levels—national to the local—is abysmally low. However, this is not the only cause for concern. The other issue is that even when women participate in the decision making bodies as people's representatives, they most of the times remain passive players rather than assuming an effective role in the process. It is time now to probe into such weaknesses and identify ways through which an effective participation of women in the political bodies can be ensured.

Urban government includes municipal corporations, municipalities, town area committees, and notified area committees, cantonment boards and townships. Local government being a subject falling under the jurisdiction of states even though it is since 1993 enshrined in the Constitution of India, the different states have evolved different standards at the operational level. It is important to note that urban governance still remains highly dependent upon the state government for administrative purposes as also for framing of schemes of urban development and their implementation. It is so because it has developed within a system of centralized planning. The strengthening of urban local bodies by democratizing them was initiated very recently with the 74th Constitutional Amendment. After coming to power in 1991, Narsimha Rao Government drafted the 73rd Amendment Bill pertaining to Municipalities which was passed by the Lok Sabha on December 1992. This Amendment became operative since April 1993. It has introduced a new part—namely Part IX-A in the Constitution, which deals with matters relating to urban governance.

Within the urban areas there is a provision of three types of urban bodies—

(a) nagar panchayats;
(b) municipalities; and
(c) corporations.

The nagar panchayats are meant for the transitional areas while the municipalities are made for the smaller urban areas. Municipal corporations are to be constituted for the larger urban areas.

The process of democratization of urban governance has been targeted for, by laying down the provision that all the seats in the municipality are to be filled by direct elections except for those to be filled through nominations. The 74th Amendment ensures a process of decentralization of power from the Centre to the local level and ultimately to the grassroots level. Following are some of the salient features of this amendment:

- Each municipality will be divided into wards. This has been done with a view to reduce the gap between the electorate and the elected. An increased participation of the people in the urban local bodies is also ensured. Provision for the constitution of Wards Committees has been made to reduce centralized system of planning and administration.
- Constitution of various other committees, *i.e.* Standing Committee, Zonal Committee etc. has been made to aim at better administration.
- The most important clause in the 74th Amendment with which

we are directly concerned in this paper relates to the reservation of seats in urban local bodies for women and Scheduled Castes and Scheduled Tribes. It is laid down that the proportion of seats to be reserved for SC/ST to the total number of seats shall be the same as the proportion of the population of SC/ST in the municipal area to the total population of that area. Reservations have been made in case of the seats to be filled by direct elections only.

- *Not less than 1/3rd of the total number of seats reserved for SC/ST shall be reserved exclusively for women belonging to SC/ST.*
- *Seats to the extent of not less than 1/3rd of the total number of seats are reserved for women (including the SC/ST women).*
- *The State Legislatures would have to make provisions by law for reservation of the office of the Chairpersons in Municipalities for SC/STs and women.*
- For an efficient conduct of elections to the urban municipal bodies, each state/union territory has to constitute a State Election Commission headed by a State Election Commissioner.
- The Constitutional Amendment envisages that the Municipalities now would go beyond the mere provision of civic amenities. They are expected to play a crucial role in the preparation of plans for local development and in their implementation.
- In order to review the financial position of Municipalities periodically, the Governor of the state will constitute a State Finance Commission.
- Provision has been made for the constitution of a Planning Committee at the district level for preparing a development plan for the district as a whole.
- The Act provides that in every Metropolitan area, a Metropolitan Planning Committee shall be constituted for preparing a draft development plan for the Metropolitan area as a whole.

Municipal Corporation is the topmost administrative body of urban local government. The Municipal Corporation as an institution is more respectable and enjoys a greater measure of autonomy than other forms of local government. A Municipal Corporation is set out under a special statute, which is passed by the state legislature.

Since the implementation of the 74th Amendment, various state governments in India have amended their Municipal Acts accordingly. Elections to various urban local bodies in the states in conformity with the 74th Amendment have been held atleast once. It therefore is possible at this juncture to assess the discrepancies, if any, between the theoretical vision projected in the 74th Amendment on the one hand, and its practical implementation on the other. While lots of empirical studies have been conducted to examine the implications and effectiveness of 73rd C.A.A., such attempts have been scanty in the case of 74th C.A.A. This paper is based upon one such study conducted in Punjab in 1997, under a research project sponsored by the Institute of Social Sciences, New Delhi. The main focus of the study was on the following questions:

- An assessment of the provisions for women's reservation in the municipal corporations of Punjab;
- How the women elected to the municipal corporations conceptualize their role?
- What have been the motivating factors for them?
- What is the response of male colleagues in the corporations towards women representatives?
- What have been the experiences of women councillors—negative as well as positive?

Research Framework

The study was conducted in the three municipal corporations of punjab—Ludhiana, Amritsar and Jalandhar, where elections took place in 1997. I have supplemented the findings of this study with another study recently conducted on the same issue on the Chandigarh Municipal Corporation. Both the studies are empirical, based on field work, personal interviews being the main source of data collection. While a sample of 25 women councillors was interviewed in Punjab (eight in Ludhiana, nine in Amritsar and eight in Jalandhar), all the 29 councillors (male and female), were personally interviewed in Chandigarh Municipal Corporation. The Chandigarh Municipal Corporation also includes nine nominated members who are experts in diverse fields such as education, administration, planning etc. Commissioners and Secretaries to the Municipal Corporations as well as the Mayors were also interviewed personally. Apart from the primary sources, information relating to municipal elections was also collected from the offices of Chief Election Commission, Punjab, Directorate of Urban Local Bodies, Punjab and offices of the Municipal Corporation at Ludhiana, Jalandhar and Amritsar, besides an analysis of newspaper reportings.

Interviews with the councillors were mainly conducted at their residence since they were not coming to the municipal office very regularly. In many cases, husbands/sons of the councillors used to be present during the interview but special care was taken to elicit the response from women respondents themselves. Of course, the reciprocity with which they provided information varied. Women who had had a political career, were more forthcoming than those who had been thrown into the political arena all of a sudden.

Findings

The time at which the study was conducted is of utmost importance. Elections had just been completed. The incumbents were absolutely new and the municipal bodies thus formed were the first of its kind. Things might be different today, after four long years. Time span is important because for women this was the first and a novel experience. Also, their men (husbands, sons, brothers or uncles) looked at them with a complete lack of trust as effective councillors. In fact in one of the interviews, the son of a councillor remarked "husbands in fact are the trainees who prepare the women for their future roles". Initially, most of the women lacked confidence or a clear conception of the roles they were expected to perform. I am sure the situation must have improved by now as the feedback from rural panchayats has shown. In one such analysis of the case studies of women panchayat members, I have highlighted the existence of both success stories and stories of failure, but certainly, women panches, especially the *Dalits*, had gained tremendous confidence and competence over a period of time. When we interviewed the male officials in the office of the municipal corporation, especially the Commissioners, the response immediately became indifferent and apathetic the moment we asked them about their reactions towards women councillors. It was most difficult to elicit information from these men because of a very stiff mind set, looking at women representatives in the Municipal Corporations, with distrust and disapproval.

Women councillors in Punjab during interviews, except a few, were not very forthcoming, not because of an unwillingness on their part to respond, but primarily because they neither possessed the information on various aspects of 74th C.A.A., nor did they have any opinion on issues confronting them as councillors. The situation was much better in the

Chandigarh Municipal Corporation, where a majority of women were quite responsive in sharing their experiences as councillors. Even those having the support of political parties were articulated enough to bring forth their view points, except the two Scheduled Castes women who were completely illiterate and were most of the time being represented by their husbands. So far as the Commissioners of Municipal Corporations were concerned, the communication generally got blocked the moment the issue of women councillors was brought up for discussion. It appeared as if for them this issue was unimportant, unnecessarily being granted so much of centrality.

Table 18.1: Total Urban population of the three selected municipal corporations of Punjab in 1995

Name of the Corporation	*Total Urban Population*
Ludhiana	10,42,740
Amritsar	7,08,835
Jalandhar	5,27,632

Ludhiana being a metropolitan city according to 1991 Census, has the highest population, followed by Amritsar and Jalandhar. Naturally then, Ludhiana had the highest number of constituencies during the municipal elections of 1997.

Since our analysis centres around reservation for women, it shall be useful to have a look at the number of constituencies reserved for women—SC and General—both (Table 18.2). Every third constituency was identified as a woman constituency in conformity with the Amendment. It is interesting to note that participation of women in the elections in all the three Corporations was quite impressive.

Table 18.2: Number of constituencies/wards reserved for women in the three corporations in Punjab in 1997 elections

Name of the Corporation	*Women (SC)*	*Women (General)*	*Total Wards*
Ludhiana	3	21	70
Amritsar	4	16	60
Jalandhar	5	14	55
Total	12	51	185

On an average, in the constituencies reserved for SC women, the number of contestants was five times the number of seats (Table 18.3). It is significant to compare the data for 1991 and 1997 in this regard. In elections held during 1991 for these three Corporations, there was only one woman candidate who had managed to be elected as a Municipal Councillor. While there was no woman Councillor elected in the Corporations of Ludhiana and Jalandhar, one woman was elected as a Councillor in Amritsar Corporation in the Municipal elections held in 1991. Compared to this, it assumes significance that there are at present 63 women who have been elected as Municipal Councillors in these three Corporations. Entry of women on such a scale has been possible mainly with the enactment of the 74th Constitutional Amendment. The number of women contestants in the wards reserved for SC women was five times that of the total number of seats in Ludhiana and Jalandhar. In Amritsar, however, the average number of women contestants was even more, *i.e.* more than 7. This indicates quite a healthy trend of women's political participation. As we move on to the general category, the average number of women contestants rises further up. While on an average, Jalandhar had the lowest number of women contestants, *i.e.* 4+, more than 5 women were contesting for one seat in Ludhiana, while more than 6 women contested for one seat in Amritsar.

Table 18.3: Number of women contestants in municipal corporation elections in Punjab in 1997

Name of the Corporations	*No. of Women Contestants in SC Constituencies*	*Total Seats*	*No. of Contestants in Women Constituencies*	*Total Seats*
Ludhiana	15	3	111	21
Amritsar	30	4	99	16
Jalandhar	25	5	63	14
Total	70	12	273	51

It is notable that most of the elected women councillors were younger in age (Table 18.4). 56 per cent of the total women interviewed were below 40 years of age. Only 20 per cent of them were aged more than 50 years.

Table 18.4: Distribution of women councillors in Punjab according to age

Age	*Ludhiana*	*Amritsar*	*Jalandhar*	*Total*
Up to 30 years	—	—	3	3
31-40 years	3	6	2	11
41-50 years	3	2	1	6
51+ years	2	1	2	5
Total	8	9	8	25

The most important attribute having direct relevance with political participation of women relates to their educational qualification. The most popular argument, which is, usually put forth against women's reservation is that it is difficult to get many women who are educated and well qualified. For an effective participation, it is further stressed that the women incumbents have to be educated and conscious of their political responsibilities. The argument though very strong does not carry much weight in view of the level of competence our male leaders possess. In an era of gender justice, we must remain conscious that we do not entertain unnecessary expectations from the women, who have only now been allowed to come out into the public life as a matter of right. That not many educated and qualified women initially would come out for elections is borne out by our study. More than half, *i.e.* 52 per cent of the women councillors had educational qualifications only up to matriculation, while 16 per cent were completely illiterate. 36 per cent of the women interviewed were either graduates or post-graduates (Table 18.5). How their educational qualification impact the effectiveness of participation in the municipal council will be discussed a little later.

Table 18.5: Distribution of women councillors in the corporations of Punjab according to educational qualification

Educational Qualification	*Ludhiana*	*Amritsar*	*Jalandhar*	*Total*
Illiterate	1	—	2	3
Upto matric	4	5	4	13
Graduate	1	3	1	5
Post-graduate	2	1	1	4
Total	8	9	8	25

What is important here is not that many of the women councillors do not possess sufficient educational qualification, but more important is the fact that one is not required to possess any specific level of qualifications in order to be eligible to contest the elections. This applies both to the men as well as to the women, with tremendous implementations.

Associated with this is the variablity of occupational status. A vast majority of the women councillors interviewed by us, *i.e.* 21 out of 25, were housewives and thus were not engaged in any gainful employment (Table 18.6). Only two of the women councillors interviewed were professionally qualified. One was dealing with the business in computers, while another was looking after farm/poultry. Occupational status of a person has a tremendous significance since it determines the nature of exposure he/she has in addition to granting him/her with economic independence. A sudden entry of women into the public life may cause certain problems for them in the way of a meaningful participation at the administrative level. Our following discussion will answer some of these doubts. It has to be kept in mind however that such a trend is not totally unanticipated especially at the initial stages of take-off.

Table 18.6: Distribution of women councillors of Punjab according to occupational status

Occupational Status	*Ludhiana*	*Amritsar*	*Jalandhar*	*Total*
Housewife	7	8	6	21
Doctor	—	1	—	1
Advocate	—	—	1	1
Farming/Poultry	1	—	—	1
Business	—	—	1	1
Total	8	9	8	25

The role of political affiliation in an election—at local, regional or national level—cannot be underestimated. The process of democratization is always initiated by politicization. Following the pattern of electoral system at the national level, Municipal elections have also been taking place under an electioneering which is highly politicized, with almost all major national political parties supporting their own candidates. Municipal elections in the states therefore mainly reflect the political currents sweeping the country at large. In fact these elections are likely to evoke greater and more aggressive response than the parliamentary elections since these directly concern the urbanites. In the last municipal elections of Punjab too, different political parties had fielded their own candidates and keen contests were held in most of the constituencies. We have, however, restricted our analysis mainly to women contestants. Almost all major political parties had fielded their women candidates in Ludhiana, Amritsar and Jalandhar (Table 18.7).

Most of the women councillors interviewed by us belonged to the Bharatiya Janata Party and Shiromani Akali Dal. It may be recalled that an alliance of these two political parties had swept the recently held municipal elections in the state of Punjab. There were four women who had contested elections as independents. Since it was for the first time that municipal elections were held with reserved constituencies for women, it would be interesting to trace the political background of these women. Did they already have political standing and if not, then what made them get attached with the particular political parties?

Table 18.7: Distribution of women councillors in corporations of Punjab according to party affiliation

Party Affiliation	*Ludhiana*	*Amritsar*	*Jalandhar*	*Total*
Bharatiya Janata Party	2	5	2	9
Shiromani Akali Dal	3	1	2	6
Indian National Congress	2	1	1	4
Bahujan Samaj Party	—	—	1	1
Independent	1	1	2	4
Others	—	1	—	1
Total	8	9	8	25

Data on the political background of these women provides very interesting insights (Table 18.8). While it was only in 16 per cent of the cases where the women themselves had political linkages with the political party, in most of the cases they were linked with some party through their husbands (72 %). One woman councillor each had a father and a brother who were already having connections with the political parties. There were two cases where the father-in-law of the councillor was associated with a political party. The fact that a majority of women interviewed were linked to a political party through their husbands assumes significance in the context of a patriarchal structure of authority prevailing in our family systems.

Table 18.8: Distribution of women councillors according to their family linkages with political parties

Person with Political Linkages	*Ludhiana*	*Amritsar*	*Jalandhar*	*Total*
Woman Herself	1	1	1	3
Husband	7	7	4	18
Brother	—	1	—	1
Father	—	—	1	1
Father-in-law	—	—	2	2
Total	8	9	8	25

With the constitutional provision for women constituencies in the municipal corporations, the politically active men will naturally look for the women contestants immediately close to them. In these circumstances, they find their wives as the most suitable candidates for elections for obvious reasons. One, it ensures that the political centre does not move out of the family, but remains within it. Two, after winning the election, the political mileage is actually enjoyed by the husband because it is he towards whom the woman would look for decisions and participation. Three, if the wife wins the election, it is as good as he has won because he enjoys a full command over her and can fulfil his own political interests through her status with great ease. Finally, it would help the husband in preserving ties with the political party, not allowing anybody else to hijack the political benefits. Had it not been for these reasons, the husband would never had digested even the thought of throwing the woman of the house into the political field, a public front, forbidden for them. The same thing has happened in the panchayat elections too where women's reservation has forced the politically active husbands to tap the benefit by pushing the wife, in most of the cases into the electoral field. Had the constitutional provision not been there, one could never even think of a such trend. Thanks therefore to the 74th Constitutional Amendment, which has almost forced the men to expose the women closest to them to the political life. It was pointed out by one woman who was the Mayor of a Corporation that had there been no provision for reservation for women, it would just have been impossible for them to have occupied such prestigious positions in the governing bodies. In absence of such a compulsion, men would never have allowed women to enter into the decision-making bodies. However, when women are made to occupy such positions, with a view to empower them as also for decentralization of power, it will definitely have some repercussions which will be taken up for discussion sometime later.

During our interviews, we found that many of these women had still not reconciled with the idea that they were occupying important positions in urban governing bodies and were leading their wards/ constituencies as municipal councillors. A lot of confusion writ large on their faces indicated that they had all of a sudden been pushed into the roles for which they had not been prepared or trained. They would turn towards their husbands for answering any little query. In fact at times it was felt as if their husbands hardly gave them a chance to respond, in their eagerness to react first, believing that they were in a better position to answer questions. It was evident that in spite of their political power, their husbands overpowered these women in every possible way.

Women representatives at the urban local bodies constitute a highly differentiated group. They range from completely uneducated to highly educated; poorest to the most affluent; housewives to the professionally qualified, and so on. Each of these attributes plays a significant role in their perception of the newly acquired role, their commitment towards it, their effectiveness and so on. Also, these had a varied age structure. It is important to note that out of the 25 respondents interviewed in Punjab, 21 were housewives, only 2 were professionals and two were assisting in family business. In Chandigarh, however, the situation is slightly better, half of the women councillors being gainfully employed. While most of the women councillors in Punjab were affiliated to one or another political party, only three had a direct affiliation. Others were associated with a party through their husbands, followed by fathers-in-law, brothers and fathers. This has significant implications as reflected through our interaction with them. These women had confusion writ large on their face, mainly because they had been pushed into the roles they were not prepared for and moreover, they were hardly permitted to function on their own. They would frequently turn to their husbands for every small query. It is important to note here that such an inheritance of political positions by women has invited strong criticism in the recent past. However, it may be absurd since the similar inheritance by males in the family has never been questioned in Indian politics. The change brought about by the Amendments is that now daughters and not only sons; wives and not only husbands; daughters-in-law and not only sons-in-law, are being passed on the political mileage, though out of compulsion.

An important observation emerging out of both the rural as well as urban local bodies so far studied, is that the provisions for the rotation of reserved constituencies often goes against the women incumbents. Women councillors, just like the women panches, initially assume their role hesitatingly, lacking both in confidence and a clear understanding of the new role. By the time they acquire confidence, commitment and an identity of their own, not only is their term over, but their chances of being elected from the same constituency for a second term decline, since it may not be a reserved constituency the next time. The emphasis of political parties being on the constituency, she may never get a second chance as the male aspirants, who had been waiting for the last five years, would grab the chance. This problem can be solved if more and more women contest elections and enter the field on their own and not as passive representatives of their male relatives. A number of cases have come up from the panchayats where women panches, after the completion of their term, have contested from the general constituencies, competing openly with the men. This certainly indicates the successful empowerment of women in a highly patriarchal political field.

Most of our women respondents were found to be only remotely interested in the functioning of the Municipal Corporations in Punjab, and came to the office only for a meeting. These meetings too were mostly attended by the husbands of these women, who, as we were intimated by an official in Chandigarh Municipal Corporation, had to be physically pushed out of the meeting hall. The whole experience of women's empowerment—whether economic, psychological or political, so far has indicated that this exercise involves the total society. Many a times the whole of the issue is taken as if it touches only women. In fact, it touches, or rather 'pinches' men even more. Empowering the women simply means withdrawing power from men. Even the case studies of women's non-governmental organizations which have been success stories show that women in these had carried their men along. Hence it is a gender issue involving both men and women. I found in my study that men, as bureaucrats, officials, subordinate staff, were highly non-cooperative towards women. Women councillors due to the callous attitude of these employees, often had to face a lot of embarrassment, especially when confronted by their constituencies.

For a moment, let us go back to the objectives of the 74th C.A.A., particularly an expectation inherent in it that with the reservation provisions, issues relating to women and child development and those relating to the poor will come up for discussion much more frequently in the municipal corporation meetings and a programmatic shift will take place towards these issues. This expectation has hardly been realized mainly due to the following reasons.

The assumption that women representatives will take up joint issues is ill-founded. Given their diverse composition, clubbed with their political affiliations, issues relating to women and children have often taken a backseat. In Punjab as well as Chandigarh, more often than the women from different political parties, it is the women from the same party, being at daggers drawn. The past experience shows that the candidature of a woman for the post of Mayor has more often been opposed by other women, of the same political party, making it even easier for the men to grab the post ultimately. The fact is that divisions within the women incumbents have done them greater harm, pushing back the women's agenda. Studies from panchayats too reveal that the women panches or Pradhans who have made a wonderful performance, are those who could garner the support of fellow women in the village. Given the age-old patriarchal structures, and monopolized authority of men in politics, women, in order to be effective, will have to have lots of women at their back, irrespective of age, caste, income and so on. As a consequence of political interests ruling the women, just like their male counterparts, issues relating to women and child development often sink to the ground.

A second reason as to why women's issues get a backseat is that even the male colleagues, belonging to the same party, having supported her during elections, never allow the woman councillor to gain prominence, either within the party or the Corporation, thus causing tremendous frustration among women councillors, especially those committed and efficient ones. For instance, the Chandigarh Municipal Corporation, during the last four years, has witnessed maximum infighting within the ruling party, over issues such as election of the Mayor, and nomination to important assignments. Issues, therefore, get sacrificed in favour of wasteful political gimmicks. In line with the experience of panchayats, my analysis too shows that as far as women's issues are concerned, the Scheduled Castes women councillors are more effective as compared to the upper caste. The reason being that low caste women, who also happen to be poor, find it very convenient to approach a woman councillor, belonging to their own group and convey their grievances. The women councillors too have been found to take up these issues in various committee meetings.

With the constitutional provision for women constituencies, the politically active men naturally look upon women contestants, close to them. They find their wives/daughters, as the most suitable candidates for obvious reasons. One, it ensures that the political centre does remain within the family. Two, after winning elections, political mileage is practically enjoyed by the husband. Thirdly, it helps the man in preserving his ties with the political party, not allowing anybody else to hijack the political benefits. Finally, the seat is preserved for the next election, when the constituency is no longer reserved and the man can himself encash upon the last term. Had it not been for these reasons, the husband would never have digested even the thought of pushing the wife into political field a public front, forbidden for her. Thanks to the 74th C.A.A., which has compelled men to expose their women to political decision-making.

Though most of these women initially were confused, hesitant and ineffective, lacking any interest in the role, they have been found to have shed all inhibitions and assume an active participation over time. For instance, the study of Chandigarh Municipal Corporation undertook the appraisal of two male constituencies, two female constituencies (general), and two S.C. women constituencies, in order to gauge the difference in their performance from people's perspective. Assessment of the councillor's role mainly depended upon two factors:

Accessibility of the Councillor

Whether male or female, people had a positive view of the councillor if he/she was easily accessible to them. It may be mentioned here that people in the S.C. women constituencies were more satisfied because these councillors were very accessible to them.

Attributes of People in the Constituency

People constituting the constituency played an important role. For instance, people in the general constituencies were mostly of upper middle classes, with higher expectations from the Corporation. They had more complaints against the councillors. On the contrary, expectations of people in the reserved constituencies (SC women) were low and hence they felt more satisfied.

Performance of women councillors was found to be influenced greatly by their individual traits as well. A woman councillor who was quite articulate, communicative to the people of her constituency, politically strong and assertive in the corporation meetings, was much more appreciated for her role than others who were just killing time. Also, such a woman councillor had excellent chances of getting elected for the second term, even from another constituency, not necessarily reserved. It is important to note that a woman councillor must be politically ambitious, desirous of pursuing a political career, if she wishes to be successful. A woman who assumes her role for five years, waiting for the term to end, with no political aspirations, would not deliver the goods.

On comparing the municipal corporations of Punjab with that of Chandigarh, I find tremendous difference between the women councillors at the two places. Women councillors in Punjab—most of them have remained more or less silent spectators in the process. One of such councillors in Amritsar disclosed during an interview that she had never stepped out of her house alone till she got elected. After that too, she was hardly familiar with the different areas in the city. She did not even know where the office of Municipal Corporation, Amritsar was located. Once, as narrated by her, the Deputy Commissioner, Amritsar was to visit her constituency and she came to know of it only after a few days of his visit. Such experiences are directly related to the socio-cultural melieu of Punjab which is extremely patriarchal in character. The state, in spite of being one of the most developed in terms of per capita income and agricultural productivity, has experienced a further decline in its sex-ratio as per the latest Census reports. We actually need studies relating the cultural ethos of a region with an effective political participation of its women.

Women councillors in Chandigarh, irrespective of their party affiliations or status of the constituency, were much more assertive. Being a smaller city, apart from a capital planned one, Chandigarh Municipal Corporation gets a greater media coverage. A greater number of seminars, workshops and training programmes conducted by various government bodies, N.G.Os and academic institutions in the city makes it possible for the councillors to have a greater exposure. The provision of nominated councillors, though anti-democratic in spirit, has further provided a sobering effect on the Corporation. It is a different thing however that out of the 29 councillors, the 9 nominated members are always looked at as distracters by the ruling political group for blocking the consensus on various issues. As reported by one of the spokespersons of the ruling political group in Chandigarh Municipal Corporation "given such an experience, we will see to it that in the next M.C., the nominated councillors are our own people, providing us support rather than opposition".

Conclusion

Observations drawn from the empirical data highlight the persistence of patriarchal structures backed by a consistent ideology not only among men but even among the women. Substantiating the earlier studies, our analysis too underlines the tendency on the part of men in politics to use this provision for women's reservation in urban local bodies, to their own advantage. Differences between the municipal corporation of Chandigarh and the municipal corporations of Amritsar, Jalandhar and Ludhiana bring out the fact that a greater exposure of both quantitative and qualitative kind, education and training, to the new women representatives can go a long way in making them effective players in the political arena, so far monopolized by men. The analysis leads one to conclude that there needs to be a change in the attitudes of political parties, of society in general, of male counterparts, of media; and above all, of fellow women.

Issues for Future Research

So far we possess very little information on women's role in the Urban Local Bodies. Most of the data we have is of a quantitative nature. To say that so many women have entered the nagar panchayats, municipal councils and corporations and so many have contested elections; and so many are relatives of political men; is, of course, useful as a basic information. But we need studies of a more qualitative kind, to probe as to who among them have been effective and why; and who have been failures and why.

The second lacuna I find is that we so far have had dated studies, covering merely one stage in the cycle of a woman councillor's role. What I mean is that her reaction, experience, performance, self-perception and commitment, on the one hand; and others' perception of her role, on the other, is bound to vary between two points of time, *i.e.* her initiation into the role, in the middle of the tenure and towards the end. My experience has shown that irrespective of whether she was forced by her male relatives or friends, to jump into the role, or she did it voluntarily, her confidence, commitment and aspirations would get strengthened over time. An unintended consequence of all this however is a stronger and politically active woman councillor emerging in the end. But how can her confidence be sustained and how can the social structural barriers blocking her journey are to be minimized, would largely depend upon a systematic analysis of her journey among different stages.

I also find a great deal of difference in the experience as well as performance of women councillors varying in caste status, political strength, economic and educational attributes, personality traits and male support. We need to have a greater knowledge of this differentiation within the women representatives in the urban local bodies. Such an understanding could also help us in removing the hurdles in an effective participation of women in decision making.

Having provided training programmes for women councillors by various government as well as non-governmental organizations in the recent past, we need evaluative studies of these programmes, so as to enhance their effectiveness. Also, the feedback received during these training sessions must be recorded and harnessed adequately for further improvement.

Since most of the municipal bodies, after the implementation of the 74th Constitutional Amendment Act have completed 3/4th of their term, we need to build a data-base on the kind of jobs women councillors in different urban centres have been assigned. For example, out of the different committees formed by the municipal bodies, are women being assigned some peculiar kinds of tasks, e.g. developmental, or cultural, rather than the harder ones such as the financial, administrative and so on.

It would also be quite fruitful to furnish the response of women in general towards women's reservation in urban local bodies. I say this because I feel that there is an urgent need to attract educated, independent and committed women to the role of councillors. With the municipal bodies going the way the state legislative and Parliament have, the same ills of electoral politics and politicization are likely to haunt them too, making municipal bodies an undesirable abode for the competent women. We need more information on the mechanisms through which more women incumbents can counter the male oppression and patriarchy in these bodies.

We also need to look into the role of media in either glorifying or downsizing the performance of women representatives of various kinds. I have found that male councillors and mayors tend to receive greater media coverage than the female counterparts. For example, immediately after the elections to Chandigarh Municipal Corporation, all local news papers carried detailed stories on the Scheduled Castes women who had just been elected as councillors. The negative image these stories created of these women councillors persists even today among the public, in complete absence of an effort to reverse this image even after they have proved to be much more effective than both their male as well female counterparts from the general constituencies.

Finally, whether different political parties push the women candidates consistently ahead like any other male candidate, or they do so only conditionally up to a certain point, needs to be investigated. Studies have shown that even if political parties field their women candidates out of compulsion, they in the process make them politically ambitious, often aspiring for a next term, whether the political bosses like it or not. But the point to be examined is, do the political parties make use of certain tactics in order to shunt out such politically motivated women when they become prominent? How can such women be helped at that moment to continue their political career? Such questions have arisen with the experience of women's reservation to local bodies so far, these must guide further research, enabling us both in a greater enlightenment of the subject and in making the constitutional provision practically more meaningful.

REFERENCES

Gill, Rajesh, (1999), "Seventy Fourth Constitutional Amendment and Political Empowerment of Women in Punjab: A Study in Urban Governance", *Urban India,* Vol. XIX No. 1.

Jolly, Sushma (1982), "Women: Too Soft for Politics", *Femina*, July.

Pandey, Sumana (1990), *Women in Politics*, Rawat Publications, Jaipur.

Punjab State Policy for Women—(1996), Draft Policy presented for discussion by the Govt. of Punjab on 4 March 1996 at Chandigarh.

Singh, K.P., (1994), "Punjab's Population under Changing Socio-economic Conditions", *Political Economy of India,* Vol. 3, No. 3 and 4, Jan.-July.

Towards Equality, Report of the Commission on the Status of Women in India, (1974), Ministry of Education and Social Welfare, Govt. of India, New Delhi, p. 301.

19

WOMEN EMPOWERMENT THROUGH WATERSHED DEVELOPMENT IN PUNJAB

KARAM SINGH, NIRMAL SINGH & RACHHPAL SINGH

The nature and extent of women's contribution in agriculture is of special significance in an underdeveloped area where agriculture is the mainstay of people. Their involvement depends mainly upon the type of farming system, local based family income earning opportunities and above all dominated by the caste, socio-economic and cultural specifications of the resident families and thus varies greatly from region to region (Swaminathan, 1985). Further, they are the real ecologists-cum-conservationists par excellence as far as forests and other natural resources are concerned (Nair, 1991).

The indiscriminate disturbance over a long period in the form of deforestation, logging operations, overgrazing etc. of the forest lands in the Kandi (submountainous) tract of Punjab has led to an imbalance of the ecological system. As an ameliorative measure, the Integrated Watershed Development Project (IWDP) has been in operation since 1990-91 in 17 out of the 42 watersheds in the Kandi area. It aimed at slowing down and reverse the degradation of natural environment and establish the resource base to sustainable pattern of development by using the appropriate menu of treatments of soil and moisture conservation and other technology. Since watershed development is a continuous process and not a discrete rehabilitation operation, the active participation of women engaged in the use of local resources is essential to realise the full potential of watershed based technology for increasing and providing the much needed stability to agricultural production in this underdeveloped hilly area of the Punjab State. In spite of the women's productive efforts and significant contribution towards the sustainable development of the area, their role remains unnoticed and unrewarded. This study is an attempt to highlight the role of women in resource management, impact of various development programmes of the project (such as increased availability of fodder, fuel, water, etc.) on their contribution.

Objectives

The objectives of the study were as under:

(i) to study the socio-economic parameters of women of cultivating and non-cultivating households;
(ii) to analyse the women labour force availability and its role in resource management of livestock, crop production, forest based activities, etc.;
(iii) to ascertain the awareness of women regarding various development activities undertaken in the project area.

Research Framework

The study is based on two-stage surveys : A pilot survey of 800 households (799 effective sample) from 16 villages in three watersheds, all randomly selected, was conducted to assess the general views of the women respondents about the project activities. It was followed by an in-depth survey in six of the 16 villages, i.e. two villages from each watershed, again randomly selected. For this survey, a sample of 50 per cent respondents of the pilot survey was selected randomly without replacement. This gave a random sample of 150 respondent household comprising 90 cultivating and 60 non-cultivating households.

The primary data from the women heads of selected households were collected in detail on socio-economic variables such as family composition, caste, employment status, awareness about the impact of project activities on environment, their perceptions and expectations, development of natural resources in the study area, etc. for the reference year, 1994-95. Some open end questions were also asked from women, enabling them to express their opinion, needs and perceptions without hesitation. Primary data on employment of women in various agricultural, livestock and forestry activities collected in Mid-Term Evaluation Survey of IWDP (June, 1994) was also used.

A Profile of Survey Villages

On an average, human population of 1140 persons resided in a village, in 197 households of whom 71 per cent were landowners, 29 per cent were landless, 37 per cent were Scheduled Castes and about 5 per cent families were having women as head of the household. The proportion of households making *baan*/rope from bhabbar grass (*Eulaliopsis binata*) available in abundance in the local forests was 13 per cent. The average family size was 5.8. In addition to drinking water supplied by water supply department, wells and handpumps were also available for this purpose.

Land statistics of the village showed that the per village geographical area was 873 hectares of which as much as 75.4 per cent was non-arable leaving only 24.6 per cent as arable. Irrigated area was just 7 per cent of the arable land. According to land ownership, about 64 per cent was owned privately whereas 36 per cent were common lands owned by panchayats (10 %) and the government (26%).

The average number of cattle kept by a household was 2.6 for cultivators and 1.4 for non-cultivators. There were 452 adult cattle units per village. The proportion of low yielding milch animals such as local cows and goats was higher with the non-cultivating households than the cultivating households. The fodder scarcity in the area is very serious. Fodders were grown on 6.1 per cent of arable land, mostly during the kharif season. One hectare of grown fodder was available for 13 cattle heads in Punjab State whereas corresponding use for the study area was estimated at 49 cattle heads which indicates that most of the fodder requirements were met from the local forests by bringing fodders or by grazing the animals in these forests.

Nature and Extent of Women's Participation

The nature and extent of women's involvement in agriculture and other activities varies with occupation, caste and status of the family. On an overall basis, 74.7 per cent of the sample households were aware of the project activities (Table 19.1). The awareness was significantly higher among the cultivating (86.6%) than the non-cultivating (55.6%) households. About 73 per cent of the households who were aware of the project had taken benefits under the project. Caste-wise, the percentage of beneficiaries was low for low caste (65.8%) and high for high caste (77.8%). Occupation-wise these differences were quite significant in case of non-cultivating households.

Table 19.1: Awareness about the project and benefits drawn from different components of the project, pilot survey, IWDP (Hills), Hoshiarpur district, 1994-95

Particulars	*Cultivators*			*Non-cultivators*			*Overall*		
	Low Caste	*High Caste*	*Overall*	*Low Caste*	*High Caste*	*Overall*	*Low Caste*	*High Caste*	*Overall*
A. *Awareness*									
(i) Aware	140	287	427	106	64	170	246	351	597
	(90.32)	(84.91)	(86.61)	(55.21)	(56.14)	(55.56)	(70.89)	(77.65)	(74.72)
(ii) Not aware	15	51	66	86	50	136	101	101	202
	(9.68)	(15.09)	(13.39)	(44.79)	(43.86)	(44.44)	(29.11)	(22.35)	(25.28)
(iii) Total	155	338	493	192	114	306	347	452	799
	(100)	(100)	(100)	(100)	(100)	(100)	(100)	(100)	(100)
B. *Beneficiary Households*									
(i) Number	107	226	333	55	47	102	162	273	435
(ii) Per cent of total	69.90	66.86	67.54	28.64	41.22	33.33	46.68	60.39	54.44
(iii) Per cent of aware	76.42	78.74	77.98	51.88	73.43	60.00	65.85	77.77	72.86
C. *Component*									
(i) Agriculture	95	215	310	17	24	41	112	239	351
	(88.78)	(95.13)	(93.09)	(30.91)	(51.06)	(40.20)	(69.13)	(87.54)	(80.69)
(ii) Animal Husbandry	84	209	293	39	41	80	123	250	373
	(78.50)	(92.48)	(87.98)	(70.91)	(87.23)	(78.43)	(75.93)	(91.58)	(85.75)
(iii) Forestry	53	124	177	51	15	66	104	139	243
	(49.53)	(54.87)	(53.15)	(92.73)	(31.91)	(64.71)	(64.20)	(50.92)	(55.86)
(iv) Soil Conservation	79	209	288	10	15	25	89	224	313
	(73.83)	(92.48)	(86.49)	(18.18)	(31.91)	(24.51)	(54.94)	(82.05)	(71.95)
(v) Horticulture	1	5	6	–	1	1	1	6	7
	(0.93)	(2.21)	(1.80)		(2.13)	(0.98)	(0.62)	(2.20)	(1.61)
D. *Employment in forestry work*	11	1	12	26	6	32	37	7	44
	(7.10)*	(0.30)	(2.43)	(13.54)	(5.26)	(10.46)	(10.66)	(1.55)	(5.51)

Note : Figures in the parentheses indicate percentage of benificiary households. *Percentage from total.

Project Components and Beneficiaries

There were a number of components working in the project for the development of the area. About 86 per cent of the households benefited from animal husbandry for artificial insemination (A.I.), subsidized ration, free fodder inputs, etc. followed by agriculture (81%), soil conservation (72%) and forestry (56%). However, more of the benefits of the forestry component are indirect ones and may have not yet been properly perceived by the respondents. In case of high caste cultivators, more than 90 per cent households had taken benefits from agriculture, animal husbandry and soil conservation components. In contrast more than 90 per cent of the low caste non-cultivator households were deriving benefits from the forestry component. About 11 per cent low caste households got employment in forestry works while this was negligible in case of high caste households.

More than 90 per cent households, whether from low caste or high caste, possessed livestock (Table 19.2). The cattle improvement programmes are being executed under the project. Nearly, 50 per cent of the households responded that there was definite positive impact, i.e. improvement in livestock productivity/quality while about 10 per cent gave no response. A higher proportion of cultivator households (59%) perceived the positive impact of the project than the non-cultivator households (31%). Majority of the households (43%) noticed no change in the number of milch cattle in response to improvement in productivity.

Participation of Women

The women play a key role in fetching drinking water for family as well as domestic animals. The livestock owned by more than 50 per cent of households drank water from ponds/*kuhls* (Table 19.3). The non-cultivating households who own smaller number of animals depend more on well/water supply tap/handpump for their animals. Ponds were renovated for harvesting more water, the result was increased supply of water and less distance to cover for fetching water which was reported by about 64 per cent women. Improvement in water supply was reported by 57 per cent households whereas 30 per cent reported no change. More than 70 per cent women reported that quantity of water available had increased and another 14 per cent reported no change. Caste-wise, this benefit was perceived more by the low caste (84%) than the high caste (69%) households. Again, caste-wise analysis revealed that the percentage

Table 19.2: Distribution of households according to livestock possession, observations regarding improvements in livestock productivity/quality and number, pilot survery, IWDP (Hills), Hoshiarpur district, 1994-95

Particulars	Cultivators			Non-cultivators			Overall		
	Low Caste	*High Caste*	*Overall*	*Low Caste*	*High Caste*	*Overall*	*Low Caste*	*High Caste*	*Overall*
A. *Households*									
(i) With livestock	149 (96.13)	328 (97.04)	477 (96.75)	172 (89.58)	103 (90.35)	275 (89.87)	321 (92.51)	431 (95.35)	752 (94.12)
(ii) Without livestock	6 (3.87)	10 (2.96)	16 (3.25)	20 (10.42)	61 (9.65)	31 (10.13)	26 (7.49)	21 (4.65)	47 (5.88)
(iii) Total	155 (100)	338 (100)	493 (100)	192 (100)	114 (100)	306 (100)	347 (100)	452 (100)	790 (100)
B. *Improvement in livestock productivity/quality*									
(i) Yes	79 (53.02)	203 (61.89)	282 (59.12)	52 (30.23)	34 (33.01)	86 (31.27)	131 (40.81)	237 (51.99)	368 (48.94)
(ii) No	62 (41.61)	115 (35.06)	177 (37.11)	78 (45.35)	50 (48.54)	128 (46.55)	140 (43.61)	165 (38.28)	305 (40.56)
(iii) No response	8 (5.37)	10 (3.05)	18 (3.77)	42 (24.42)	19 (18.45)	61 (22.18)	50 (15.58)	29 (6.73)	79 (10.50)
C. *Change in number of milch animals*									
(i) Increased	33 (41.78)	59 (29.06)	92 (32.62)	16 (30.77)	10 (29.41)	26 (30.23)	49 (37.40)	69 (29.11)	118 (32.06)
(ii) Decreased	12 (15.19)	61 (30.05)	73 (25.89)	10 (19.23)	8 (23.53)	18 (20.93)	22 (16.80)	69 (29.11)	91 (24.73)
(iii) No change	34 (43.03)	83 (40.89)	117 (41.49)	26 (50.00)	16 (47.06)	42 (48.84)	60 (45.80)	99 (41.77)	159 (43.21)

Note : Figures in the parentheses indicate percentages.

Table 19.3: Distribution of households according to water source, water supply for livestock, change in quantity of water available and distance covered, pilot survey, IWDP (Hills), Hoshiarpur, 1994-95

Particulars	*Cultivators*			*Non-cultivators*			*Overall*		
	Low Caste	*High Caste*	*Overall*	*Low Caste*	*High Caste*	*Overall*	*Low Caste*	*High Caste*	*Overall*
A. *Source*									
(i) Ponds	64 (42.95)	136 (41.46)	200 (41.93)	35 (20.35)	32 (31.07)	67 (24.36)	99 (30.84)	168 (38.98)	267 (35.50)
(ii) Kuhl	32 (21.48)	76 (23.17)	108 (22.64)	36 (20.93)	13 (12.62)	49 (17.82)	68 (21.18)	89 (20.65)	157 (20.88)
(iii) Water Works	10 (6.71)	32 (9.76)	42 (8.81)	27 (15.70)	19 (18.45)	46 (16.73)	37 (11.53)	51 (11.83)	88 (11.70)
(iv) Well	24 (16.11)	22 (6.71)	46 (9.64)	54 (31.40)	19 (18.45)	73 (26.55)	78 (24.30)	41 (9.51)	119 (15.83)
(v) Hand pump	19 (12.75)	62 (18.90)	81 (16.98)	20 (11.62)	20 (19.41)	40 (14.54)	39 (12.15)	82 (19.03)	121 (16.09)
B. *Water supply*									
(i) Improved	81 (54.36)	230 (70.12)	311 (65.20)	59 (34.30)	61 (59.23)	120 (43.64)	140 (43.61)	291 (67.52)	431 (57.32)
(ii) Deteriorated	44 (29.53)	18 (5.49)	62 (13.00)	26 (15.12)	4 (3.88)	30 (10.90)	70 (21.81)	22 (5.10)	92 (12.23)
(iii) No change	24 (16.11)	80 (24.39)	104 (21.80)	87 (50.58)	38 (36.89)	125 (45.46)	111 (34.58)	118 (27.39)	229 (30.45)
C. *If improved*									
(a) *Quantity available*									
(i) Increased	69 (85.19)	161 (70.00)	230 (73.95)	49 (83.06)	41 (67.22)	90 (75.00)	118 (84.29)	202 (59.42)	320 (74.25)
(ii) Decreased	7 (8.64)	30 (13.04)	37 (11.90)	5 (8.47)	9 (14.75)	14 (11.67)	12 (8.57)	39 (13.40)	51 (11.83)

(*Contd.*)

Table 19.3: (*Contd.*)

Particulars	*Cultivators*			*Non-cultivators*			*Overall*		
	Low Caste	*High Caste*	*Overall*	*Low Caste*	*High Caste*	*Overall*	*Low Caste*	*High Caste*	*Overall*
(iii) No change	5	39	44	5	11	16	10	50	60
	(6.17)	(16.96)	(14.15)	(8.47)	(18.03)	(13.33)	(7.14)	(17.15)	(13.92)
D. *Distance covered*									
(i) Reduced	64	149	213	37	24	61	101	173	274
	(79.01)	(64.78)	(68.49)	(62.71)	(39.34)	(50.93)	(72.14)	(59.45)	(63.57)
(ii) Increased	2	—	2	—	—	—	2	—	2
	(2.47)		(0.64)				(1.43)		(0.47)
(iii) No change	15	81	96	22	37	59	37	115	155
	(18.52)	(35.22)	(30.87)	(37.29)	(60.66)	(49.17)	(26.43)	(40.55)	(35.96)

Note : Figures in the parentheses indicate percentages.

of beneficiaries was significantly higher in case of low caste (72 %) than the high caste (59.4%), the latter already having better access to water even before the project.

It is common practice for women to bring fodder for the animals. Deforestation which leads to lesser fodder availability has direct impact on the women. Thus the responses of the women respondents regarding fodder availability, feeding status of animals and time taken for fodder collection were ascertained (Table 19.4). About 65 per cent of the households brought fodder from common forest lands. Only 17 per cent households reported the improvement in fodder availability; more of cultivator households (21%) than the non-cultivators (10 %) reported this improvement. Significantly, 51 per cent of the households reported decrease in fodder availability, which was being perceived as an implication of control on grazing envisaged under the project. More than 50 per cent of the households revealed that there was no improvement in the feeding status of the cattle. About 58 per cent households reported that they had to spend more time in collecting fodder as a result of the continuously deteriorating productivity of the common lands.

Fuelwood collection is another important activity of the women. In more than 75 per cent of the households, women went for fuelwood collection to meet their domestic fuel needs (Table 19.5). Caste-wise, women in more than 90 per cent of the low caste households collected fuelwood compared to 64 per cent households among the high caste families. The response to change in fuelwood availability differed between the cultivator and non-cultivator or high caste and low caste families. On the overall, 27 per cent reported no change, 81 per cent reported improvement and 40 per cent reported deterioration in the fuelwood availability.

Bhabbar grass, a raw material for paper pulp, is available in plenty in the forest area. It is also used for *baan*/rope making by the local people which provides significant employment and income. About 22 per cent of the sample households were engaged in this profession (Table 19.6). Caste-wise analysis revealed that this profession was adopted mainly by low caste families. Almost in equal proportions, the households reported about the improvement, deterioration and no change in the availability of the grass. The grass was purchased by all the households from the contractors while a few reported its free availability from the common lands. And as is natural, the increase in its price is reported by almost everyone.

Table 19.4: Distribution of households going for fodder collection, observations regarding fodder availability, feeding status of animals and time taken in fodder collection, pilot survey, IWDP (Hills), Hoshiarpur district, 1994-95

Particulars	Cultivators			Non-cultivators			Overall		
	Low Caste	*High Caste*	*Overall*	*Low Caste*	*High Caste*	*Overall*	*Low Caste*	*High Caste*	*Overall*
A. *Fodder from forest/common lands*									
(i) Number	125	171	296	144	47	191	269	218	487
(ii) Per cent of total	83.89	52.13	62.05	83.72	45.63	69.45	83.80	50.58	54.76
B. *Fodder availability*									
(i) Increased	35	28	63	15	4	19	50	32	82
	(28.00)	(16.37)	(21.28)	(10.42)	(8.51)	(9.95)	(18.59)	(14.68)	(16.84)
(ii) Decreased	54	103	157	63	27	90	117	130	247
	(43.20)	(60.24)	(53.04)	(43.75)	(57.45)	(47.12)	(43.49)	(59.63)	(50.72)
(iii) No change	33	40	73	59	15	74	92	55	147
	(26.40)	(23.39)	(24.66)	(40.97)	(31.91)	(38.74)	(34.20)	(25.23)	(30.18)
(iv) No response	3	–	3	7	1	8	10	1	11
	(2.40)		(1.02)	(4.86)	(2.13)	(4.19)	(3.72)	(0.46)	(2.26)
C. *Feeding status*									
(i) Improved	48	59	107	34	8	42	82	67	149
	(38.40)	(34.50)	(36.15)	(23.61)	(17.02)	(21.99)	(30.48)	(30.73)	(30.60)
(ii) Not improved	63	102	165	77	34	111	140	136	276
	(50.40)	(59.65)	(55.74)	(53.47)	(72.34)	(58.11)	(52.05)	(62.39)	(56.67)
(iii) No response	14	10	24	33	5	38	47	15	62
	(11.20)	(5.85)	(9.11)	(22.92)	(10.64)	(19.90)	(17.47)	(6.84)	(12.73)
D. *Time for fodder collection*									
(i) Reduced	16	16	32	5	2	7	21	18	39
	(12.80)	(9.36)	(10.81)	(3.47)	(4.26)	(3.66)	(7.81)	(9.26)	(6.01)
(ii) Increased	67	86	153	105	23	125	172	109	281
	(53.60)	(50.29)	(51.69)	(72.92)	(43.93)	(67.02)	(63.94)	(50.00)	(57.70)
(iii) No change	42	69	111	34	22	56	76	91	167
	(33.60)	(40.35)	(37.50)	(23.61)	(46.51)	(29.32)	(26.26)	(41.74)	(34.29)

Note : Figures in the parentheses indicate percentages.

Table 19.5: Distribution of households going for fuelwood collection and observations regarding improvement in fuelwood availability, pilot survey, IWDP (Hills), Hoshiarpur district, 1994-95

Particulars	*Cultivators*			*Non-cultivators*			*Overall*		
	Low Caste	*High Caste*	*Overall*	*Low Caste*	*High Caste*	*Overall*	*Low Caste*	*High Caste*	*Overall*
A. *Fuelwood collection*									
(i) Yes	139	214	353	181	77	258	320	291	611
	(89.68)	(63.31)	(71.60)	(94.27)	(67.54)	(84.31)	(92.22)	(64.39)	(76.47)
(ii) No	16	124	140	11	37	48	27	161	155
	(10.32)	(36.69)	(28.40)	(5.73)	(32.46)	(15.69)	(7.76)	(35.62)	(23.53)
(iii) Total	155	338	493	192	114	306	347	452	799
	(100)	(100)	(100)	(100)	(100)	(100)	(100)	(100)	(100)
B. *Fuelwood availability*									
(i) Increased	41	98	139	38	15	53	79	113	192
	(29.50)	(45.79)	(39.38)	(20.99)	(19.48)	(20.54)	(24.69)	(38.83)	(31.42)
(ii) Decreased	67	73	140	68	39	107	135	112	217
	(48.20)	(34.11)	(39.66)	(37.57)	(50.65)	(41.47)	(42.19)	(38.49)	(40.43)
(iii) No change	28	41	69	74	22	96	102	63	165
	(20.14)	(19.16)	(19.55)	(40.88)	(28.57)	(37.21)	(31.87)	(21.65)	(27.00)
(iv) No response	3	2	5	1	1	2	4	3	7
	(2.16)	(0.94)	(1.41)	(0.56)	(1.30)	(0.78)	(1.25)	(1.03)	(1.15)

Note : Figures in the parentheses indicate percentages.

Table 19.6: Distribution of women households engaged in *baan* making, observations regarding bhabbar availability, source of collection, purchase and its price, pilot survey, IWDP (Hills), Hoshiarpur district, 1994-95

Particulars	*Cultivators*			*Non-cultivators*			*Overall*		
	Low Caste	*High Caste*	*Overall*	*Low Caste*	*High Caste*	*Overall*	*Low Caste*	*High Caste*	*Overall.*
A. *Engaged in baan making*									
(i) No. of households	67	7	74	95	4	99	162	11	173
(ii) Per cent of total	43.23	2.07	15.01	49.48	3.51	32.35	46.68	2.43	21.65
B. *Bhabbar availability*									
(i) Increased	29	2	31	23	—	23	52	2	54
	(43.28)	(28.57)	(41.89)	(24.22)		(23.23)	(32.10)	(15.18)	(31.21)
(ii) Decreased	20	3	23	32	2	34	52	5	57
	(29.85)	(42.86)	(31.08)	(33.68)	(50.00)	(34.34)	(32.10)	(45.46)	(32.95)
(iii) No change	18	2	20	31	2	33	49	4	53
	(26.87)	(28.57)	(27.03)	(32.63)	(50.00)	(33.33)	(30.25)	(36.36)	(30.64)
(iv) No response	—	—	—	9	—	9	9	—	9
				(9.47)		(9.10)	(5.55)		(5.20)
C. *Source of collection*									
(i) Panchayat/Contractor	67	7	74	95	4	99	162	11	173
	(100)	(100)	(100)	(100)	(100)	(100)	(100)	(100)	(100)
(ii) CPR (free of cost)*	3	—	3	2	—	2	5	—	5
	(4.48)		(4.05)	(2.10)		(2.02)	(3.09)		(2.89)

(Contd.)

Table 19.6: (*Contd.*)

Particulars	*Cultivators*			*Non-cultivators*			*Overall*		
	Low Caste	*High Caste*	*Overall*	*Low Caste*	*High Caste*	*Overall*	*Low Caste*	*High Caste*	*Overall*
D. *If purchased*									
(a) *Its availability*									
(i) Increased	29	3	32	26	1	27	55	4	59
	(43.28)	(42.86)	(43.24)	(27.37)	(25.00)	(27.27)	(33.95)	(36.36)	(34.10)
(ii) Decreased	20	4	24	42	2	44	62	6	68
	(29.85)	(57.14)	(32.43)	(44.21)	(50.00)	(44.44)	(38.27)	(54.55)	(39.31)
(iii) No change	18	Nil	18	27	1	28	45	1	46
	(26.87)		(24.32)	(28.42)	(25.00)	(28.29)	(27.78)	(9.09)	(26.59)
(b) *Price*									
(i) Increased	67	6	73	88	4	92	155	10	165
	(100)	(85.71)	(98.65)	(92.63)	(100)	(92.93)	(95.68)	(90.90)	(95.37)
(ii) Decreased	—	1	1	—	—	—	—	1	1
		(14.29)	(1.35)					(9.10)	(0.58)
(iii) No change	—	—	—	7	—	7	7	—	7
				(7.37)		(7.07)	(4.32)		(4.05)

Note : *Number of households bringing bhabbar from both the sources, *i.e.*, free and purchased.

CPR: Common Property Resource.

Concluding Facts and Figures

1. About 75 per cent of the women were aware of the project benefits; more among cultivating households (87%) than the non-cultivating households (56%).
2. The beneficiary households were also more among the cultivators (68%) than the non-cultivators (33%).
3. Majority of the benefits were perceived to be from animal husbandry (86%) and crop production (81%) components followed by soil conservation (72%) and forestry (56%) components.
4. Improvement in livestock productivity was reported by 59 per cent cultivator and 31 per cent non-cultivator households.
5. Animal pressure is perceived to be still increasing by more households (32%) than those reporting its decline (25%), with 43 per cent reporting no change.
6. The improvement in water supply was reported by 57 per cent households, another 30 per cent reported no change. More of the cultivator (65%) than the non-cultivator (44%) households reported the improvement in water supply. About 75 per cent households considering the improvement also reported increase in the quantity available and 64 per cent reported less distance to be covered.
7. About 65 per cent households depended on forest lands for fodder, more being among non-cultivating households (69 per cent *vs.* 62 per cent) and also more among the low caste households (84 per cent *vs.* 51 per cent).
8. The improvement in feeding status was reported by 31 per cent households only. The saving in time for fodder collection was reported by 8 per cent households but as many as 58 per cent reported the increase in time which may be due to control on grazing envisaged under the project.
9. As many as 76 per cent households collected fuelwood from the forests; higher among non-cultivating households (84 % *vs.* 72 %) and also higher among the low castes (92 % *vs.* 64 %).
10. Improvement in fuelwood availability was reported by 31 per cent, another 27 per cent reported no change but as many as 40 per cent reported decreased availability. The impact of project controls was thus obvious.
11. About 22 per cent households were engaged in *baan* making (a

small scale household cottage industry with bhabbar grass as raw material from the forests), mostly from the low caste (47 per cent *vs.* 2 per cent) and non-cultivator (32 per cent *vs.* 15 per cent) families.

12. Almost equal percentage of families reported improvement, deterioration and no change in the availability of bhabbar grass.
13. As many as 86 per cent women were engaged in tending of cattle, 48 per cent in crop production (68 per cent among cultivating households) and 8 per cent in casual labour (17 per cent among non-cultivators).
14. In respect of forest related activities, 70 per cent women were engaged in fuelwood collection, 58 per cent in fodder collection, 34 per cent in *baan* making and 21 per cent in bhabbar grass harvesting.

The Policy Dialogue

The women play a significant role through participation in income augmenting activities of both the farm and non-farm families, which has a direct bearing on issues related to watershed development. The participation is particularly significant in such activities as livestock rearing, fodder and fuelwood collection for own domestic consumption and cutting of bhabbar grass for wage employment and for collection as raw material for further value addition through self-employment in *baan* making. Their awareness on matters of energy conservation (smokeless *chulhas*) would have direct bearing on reducing the pressure on forests for fuelwood and thereby yield better response to watershed management practices carried out in these areas. Likewise, the involvement of women in carrying out livestock development programme would facilitate in sustaining the improvement in livestock productivity. The women of the area should be equally involved to appreciate the role of other watershed development activities planned for the overall development of the area. These measures would also complement the rehabilitation of degraded environment in these areas.

REFERENCES

Nair, G.R. (1991), "Women as Guardians of Forest Wealth", *Social Welfare*, Oct. 4-5.

Sharma, Anju, *et al.* (1995), Mountain Resource Management – Strategies for Involving Women. International Seminar on National Resources Management and Their Linkages with Farming Systems, June 8-9, Deptt. of Social Sciences, Dr. Y.S. Parmar, Univ. of Horti. and Forestry, Nauni, Solan (H.P.).

Singh, Karam *et al.* (1995), "Concurrent Evaluation of Watershed Development Project : A Case Study of Punjab", *Man and Development*, Dec.

Singh, Karam *et al.* (1994), Concurrent Evaluation Report, IWDP (Hills), Punjab, A Mimeograph, Deptt. of Economics and Sociology, P.A.U., Ludhiana.

Swaminathan, M.S. (1985), *Imparting a Rural Women User's Perspective to Agricultural Research and Development*, IRRI, Philippines.

Thakur Vidya, (1995), Rural Women and Natural Resources, Contributed Paper Vol. II, International Seminar on National Resources, June 8-9, Deptt. of Social Science, Dr. Y.S. Parmar Univ. of Horti. and Forestry, Nauni, Solan (H.P.).

Govt. of Punjab, (1990), Feasibility Reports of Dasuya-Langerpur, Nara-Dada Manjhi and Arniala Watersheds, Joint Development Commissioner, IWDP (Hills), Punjab, Chandigarh.

20

RURAL DEVELOPMENT AND WOMEN
Visibly Changing Lifestyle and Invisible Hands

KUMOOL ABBI

This paper is part of an ongoing study of the productive and social roles of Punjabi rural women in the present socio-economic development scenario. The work is however in a preliminary stage and the paper presents the findings of only part of the work carried out in a village of Malwa region. In undertaking this study our broad aim is to document the present pattern of women's domestic and non-domestic work and interlinked social roles and relate them to the patterns of agriculture and other forms of economic activity in the village. The paper in particular focuses on understanding the interlinkages between techno-economic change centring on patterns of production and earning a living and social transformation relevant to women's lives, socio-economic positions, maintenance and change of lifestyles and social identities. While doing so the paper highlights the complexity of life lived by the women, their overly busy day-to-day schedule and daily race against time which remains invisible to many blinkered economists, census enumerators and others who continue to categorise these women as mainly non-workers. Although a good deal of relevant quantitative data was collected, the emphasis of this presentation is on qualitative explication of the lived experience of the various categories of women and the direction of changes in their pattern of living. The data has been collected in periodic visits over a period of two years as part of a continuing fieldwork, and there has been a deliberate stress on obtaining detailed interviews to bring out the complexity of the situation as well as the diversity of women's voices by allowing them to speak for themselves where possible.

Findings of Previous Studies

The focus of most studies concerned with women's work participation has been that the capital intensive technology, associated with higher agricultural productivity and resulting prosperity has led to the withdrawal of women from the agricultural process in the green revolution areas of Punjab and Haryana. This has not only affected more prosperous large landholders and others but also not so well off landless labourers, artisans and small and marginal farmers, though the nature of women's respective response, as we shall discuss presently varies considerably. The studies of Sandhu (1976), Singh (1980), Sethi (1982), Das Gupta (1987), Shiva (1988), Agarwal (1989), Bhalla (1989), Chowdhry (1994), Abbi and Singh (1997), Kaur (1999) and Rastogi (2000) highlight withdrawal from agricultural production activities and marginalisation of women in terms of superfluousness, discriminatory wage differentials, undervaluation of specific tasks associated with women, lower proportion of female workers in specified populations (FLP rates), higher incidence of dowry, domestic violence, greater intra-household discrimination, low female survival rates, etc.

These studies draw attention to certain characteristic features of the female labour force in Punjab, some referring to cultural norms relating to women, others to the empirical observation of actual behaviour. These include: (1) the *purdah* ideology as well as values of honour or *izzat* leading to a number of taboos in traversing the distance between the home and the outside world, (2) the practice of village exogamy, (3) the percentage of female workers being twice as high in urban areas than in rural areas, (4) other female workers being the highest in Punjab as compared to other states of India, (5) unfavourable attitude towards sending females to work, specially unmarried girls both in urban and rural areas, and a higher representation of widows, separated and divorced women in the workforce.

Selected Village

Punjab has several thousand inhabited villages representing a large variety in size, caste composition, crop productivity, electrification, irrigation, drinking water facilities and social amenities such as post offices, schools, dispensaries, linked roads, paved streets and other indices of development. Even Patiala district wherein the study was carried out has about 1500 villages showing similar variety. Although no village, or a combination of a few villages could be fully representative of this variety, yet each village, while being a unique intersection of similar socio-cultural and developmental forces, is also, in its own way, a representative of a broader milieu. However apart from its academic suitability, our identification of the village selected was also guided by considerations of convenience of access, manageability and resource constraints.

Accordingly, we selected the village Shahpur (name changed) which is small in size, multicaste in composition and has a fair number of cultivators, agricultural labourers and non-agricultural occupations represented in it. Shahpur is located 9 km. from Patiala city, and, in terms of access, a 5 km. long link road connects it to the highway linking Patiala with the cities of Chandigarh and Ambala. According to 1991 census, Shahpur has a total population of 547–299 males and 248 females — distributed into 73 households. Apart from the dominant Jat Sikhs, ten additional castes are represented in it. As the industrial focal point of Bahadurgarh, having a branch of Escorts tractors, Milkfood, Bakeman's bread making unit and a number of other manufacturing units, is only 4 km. away, the villagers also have, in addition to agriculture, access to various non-agricultural employment activities.

The Census figures of 1991 put the total main workers at 168, the total male and female non-workers at 131 and 240 respectively giving an impression of an almost total withdrawal of women from the work force. The socially constructed nature of this withdrawal and its significance will, we hope, become clear as the analysis proceeds.

Sample Selection

Of all households, every alternate house was selected for study and canvassed by means of a schedule listing the main points to be explored. This yielded a sample of 36 households constituting about 49.5 per cent of the total. To ensure ease of communication and avoid stereotyped response, open ended informal conversation in Punjabi language was considered preferable to more structured questionnaire administration. The informants were allowed to talk freely with only minimal prompting, to either get the flagging conversation flowing, or to seek a necessary clarification, the emphasis being on understanding the women's own views of their lived experience.

Land being the most important resource and the main source of economic and social disparity in the village, for the purpose of analysis, the households were initially classified in terms of operational landholdings into extra-large, large, medium, semi-medium, small, marginal and landless categories. However because of very considerable overlapping in values and behaviour due to common caste, educational levels, non-agricultural income, urban consumerist influence, etc. it was considered desirable to group together the adjacent categories of landholdings, yielding three categories: (A) Upper farmers (extra-large landowners 25 + acres, large landowners — 12.5-24.99 acres); (B) middle farmers (medium landholders 7.50 to 12.49 acres, semi-medium landholders — 5.0 to 7.49 acres); (C) Lower farmers (Small landholders — 2.49 to 5.0 acres and marginal landholders — 1.0 to 2.49 acres). As the landless were a purely negative category consisting of a very heterogeneous grouping of people differing very considerably in income, occupations, caste affiliations, skills as well as values and behaviour, it was considered desirable to further differentiate between D(i) — Upper landless (skilled workers, professionals, businessmen, etc.), D(ii) — Lower landless (agricultural workers, sweepers, casual unskilled labourers etc.). This procedure yielded 7,7 and 6 households respectively of upper, middle and lower farmers, in addition to 8 households each of upper landless and lower landless, making a total of 5 categories.

We are well aware that classifying households according to land and other assets owned and even income may not unambiguously define the position and entitlements of women within them, for in Punjabi patriarchal society men's relation to property greatly differ from those of women. Even women's use of their own property and income (occasionally not excluding personal jewellery) is hedged in by gendered kinship and cultural constraints. Further women may differ considerably in their rights, responsibilities, privileges and disabilities. A widowed or divorced sister dependent on the brother, despite her supposed rights of inheritance and maintenance from ancestral property may be reduced to a family drudge even in relatively prosperous households.

There are further problems of categorisation which, to my mind, have not been adequately addressed, if at all, in the available studies. Upper farmers, and to a varying degree those at other levels, have started diversifying into transport, commercial dairying and other business and professional work. Their sons, daughters, daughters-in-law, having become educated, have taken to government service, law, medicine, teaching and other professional and clerical jobs yielding considerable additional income. Although they may live in the countryside and commute to nearby urban centres for work, their lifestyles and domestic division work may resemble closely those of their urban counterparts. Any landholding based classification tends to violate this diversity and leads to an overly simplified and distorted presentation. Yet their life is so closely and intricately bound up with their farm based households that a classification based on their respective individual occupation/ profession would perhaps be no less distorting. However in the absence of any more variation and gender sensitive ordering procedure, we felt that a classification of households based on difference in operational landholding, supplemented where necessary by subsidiary information on other occupational sources of income, will adequately bring out significant structural features and other nuances of the lived conditions of women in terms of their common and variant responses to their respective productive roles.

Cultural and Social Constraints Affecting Women

Before we discuss the present day productive and social roles of women categorywise in terms of our classificatory scheme, we would like to draw attention to certain traditional, cultural and social structural features of women's relation to land and agricultural work which continue to affect women's productive and social roles at all category levels, though with some modest more recent changes in certain respects.

Punjabi society is both patrilineal and patrilocal and except among the minority Muslim population village and patri-clan exogamy and strictly adhered to, social reaction to breaches if any being very strong. People prefer to marry off their daughters at a considerable distance away, so that the frequency of interaction between the two set of affines and the daughters and their natal home is suitably restricted. Traditionally, women's rights to inheritance of their ancestral property were severely circumscribed: they had a right to maintenance in case of lack of marriage, marital breakdown or other such exigencies, but they could not pass on any property rights to their children or in-laws, even the present laws providing for equal inheritance subtly discriminate against them to the greater advantage of their brothers. Furthermore, in the village setting they are under social and moral pressure to relinquish their inheritance rights to land in favour of their brothers or close agnatic cousins, with the latter undertaking to carry out performing brotherly ritual gift exchanges and certain welfare functions for them and their children.

The situation is fraught with a lot of covert tension, because quite a few women resent giving up their rights and, in certain cases, even voice their resentment. There have also been a few court cases filed mostly at the instigation of some covetous husbands or in-laws. However, most people, women included, consider such action too, shameful to take. So women's rights to land and other ancestral property remain mostly unexercised.

Even when they do inherit some land, they face a serious problem of managing it as absentee landlords. For this again they have to depend on some male relative. As Gurdev Kaur, one of our informants reacting sharply to this predicament says, 'something rightfully belongs to you when you can call the shots. Who bothers if you get a patch of land from your parents? What about the means of cultivating it?' Another woman, Gurinder Kaur, who had similarly inherited four acres voiced a related practical difficulty. 'How can one keep shuttling between one's *peke* (father's village) and *sauhre* (husband's village) to manage it? My husband had to lease it out.'

Thus deprived of land and capital and hedged in by social and cultural taboos restricting their agricultural activities, social contact with unrelated men and moving freely outside the home, the role of women of all categories in agricultural production has always remained ancillary to that of men, though the kind of chores actually falling to the lot of women and the extent of drudgery involved have varied with the availability of male family hands and hired labour and other material and social circumstances of the families concerned.

Upper Farmer Households

All the 7 upper farmer households in the sample belong to persons of dominant Jat Sikh caste, except one belonging to an upwardly mobile Sikh carpenter. Their operational holdings vary from 13 acres to 85 acres. The largest landholders also owns a petrol pump and a dairy farm consisting of a substantial herd of buffaloes. His wife is a doctor. While the other households don't have so ample resources, in two of them, wives are school teachers, and all have, in addition to farming, substantial dairying interests. All have school or college going children and own atleast one car and a tractor. These factors as we shall discuss presently, condition in certain important respects the productive and social role of the women of upper landholder category.

Most of these women have not visited their family fields for years and treat these like any other source of income. Their interaction with agriculture is limited to the cleaning and storing of the grain meant for domestic consumption. They have no involvement in the productive process of grain crops. Even their traditional role of feeding the men in the fields is hardly ever performed.

Since in the village structure most of the outside work is performed by men, the task of transmission of knowledge about the high yielding varieties of crops too, has become entrusted to men, and being so transmitted it has become a man-to-man affair. As the supervisory personnel were also men, the interaction with the market became further male-centred in relation to buying and selling of produce, purchase of fertilizers, pesticides, weedicides, interaction with government personnel, banks, etc., for loans, buying of tractors, threshers, combines, payments of electricity bills and so on. This gap of information and knowledge between men and women has reinforced the already well entrenched patriarchal structures and created an exclusion for the women. As Gurinder Kaur responds, 'yes, attachment is there; but what does one do by going to the field? I can't imagine myself on the tractor. Only last year when my husband and son had gone out of station did I feel duty bound to see how things were going. Well my nephew was supervising a pesticide operation. I hardly knew the ABC of pesticides and came back patting him on the back.'

However, among this category of women there is a tendency to be nostalgic and reminiscent about the past, particularly in relation to the daughters-in-law (and in some cases the grand daughters-in-law), with regard to help in harvesting, taking food to the men on the fields, cleaning up and sifting the harvest, churning butter milk and taking out butter, etc. The daughters-in-law are seen to have it 'so easy with all the time in the world to apply powder, *bindi* and lipstick' and indulge in *Sair sapata* (sight-seeing), enjoying the fruits of labour of the previous generation'. As Jagir Kaur says regretfully, 'Earlier one was so conversant with what was going on in the fields. I would often be asked to advise about seeds, sowing and harvesting. I would discuss with my friends' and neighbours' wives and help finalise these things. But now all this talk of pesticides and procurement boggles me.'

Another tendency of these women relates to a growing acceptability of work in the tertiary sector which provides an avenue to move outside the house. This is exemplified by Devinder Kaur who is a doctor in the local medical college and Pritam Kaur who is a government school teacher. Devinder Kaur provides an interesting example of intrahousehold exploitation of dependent kinswomen, as she has managed to pass on all the household responsibilities to her widowed sister-in-law, Jagrup Kaur.

Pritam Kaur though herself doing the cooking, takes the help of a *Jeor* woman for cleaning the utensils and has also employed a local Mazhabi girl as a maid. Both represent the emerging trend among Jat Sikh women to move out for professional work and in the process inculcate the ideas, values and lifestyles of middle or upper-middle class urban women. However, at the same time there is a self-deprecating tendency among such women to undermine the economic significance of one's own earnings, which are modestly presented as only a small part of the wider consumption pattern of the household. The work itself is apologetically presented as just an activity to 'pas time'.

Though Devinder Kaur has handed over all the chores to her sister-in-law, she keeps the controls in her hands. At the same time she has joined a kitty club in the city and is proud of her husband's Maharani Club membership. Her salary is used to buy clothes, gold things for herself, etc. After long conversations in a number of visits over a couple of weeks she confesses using her salary secretly to help out her younger sister financially. The younger sister is similarly married into a landowning family at Malout but unlike her own 'sardarji' the sister's husband is addicted to alcohol and opium and often beats her up. 'He has sold off most of his land. That good for nothing, amli is only living for his intoxicants', she scorned. She finds it easy to divert her resources as her 'sardarji' provides well for the children, the household and other needs.

Despite her marginal involvement in housework, just to make a sweet dish and *prashad* on special days, she too feels, like Pritam Kaur and others, that with an improvement in standards of living work in the household has greatly increased, for expectations have become *shehari* (urban). Food three times a day unlike the previous two meals served in the morning and evening, different varieties of dishes, cutlery, cleaning up, maintaining hygienic standards, and dusting. Even household gadgets like mixies, washing machines, electric motors, butter churners, need to be handled by oneself which increases the burden.

The women of this category feel the increasing dependence they have on cash incomes, unlike previous times when a lot of things were exchanged in kind, now 'one needs money for everything'. Unlike Devinder and some others with their own earnings, most of them get a fixed amount of money every month. 'But if you want to buy something' as Gurpreet puts it 'one has to wheedle the money out of the husband through extra attentions'. Although most of the consumption behaviour is family comfort and status maintenance centred, as distinct from personal craze for fashion. It is the latter aspect of their consumption expenditure and its irrational extravagance which gets critical attention from their husbands and others, who, for some reason, feel not altogether happy with the emerging trends in lifestyles, especially women's taking to the new trends in make-up. It is women's consumerist orientation which gets singled out for blame for the purchase of expensive consumer durables though the whole household may enjoy the comforts and reflected glory of possession and display of modern status symbols. As one such male critic commenting disparagingly on his wife's consumption role said, 'All she does is sit and eat and has become a *gaindi* (female rhino). I have already bought a Maruti, a colour T.V., mixie grinder, washing machine,... now she is after an air conditioner. The land does not give me so much that one can keep giving in to her demands all the time...' Such images of unproductive and irrational consumer oriented role of women highlight the attribute of women as financial liability and an additional burden on the husband's family requiring compensation in the form of a larger dowry.

All the women interviewed accept the increasing demand for dowry as well as expenditure on weddings as a social reality and a traditional value. The inclusion of consumer durables is essential in a status appropriate dowry, particularly the latest model of car, followed by cash or fixed deposits, gold, items of utility, etc. The occasion of the wedding also becomes grand as it involves, hiring marriage palaces in the city, as well as caterers for feeding the groom's party and a large number of invited guests. The rituals too have increased in number and become more elaborate and expensive.

Similarly the items and clothes included in the dowry are not traditional works of embroidery like phulkaris, baghs, woven durries and khes, waistbands, quilts, etc. which have lost their value and interest and are at best symbolically represented, but those specially ordered from Barkha Ram of Patiala and one or two prestigious boutiques from the recently opened A.C. market. Even for the purchase of utility items orders may be placed in famous shops of Bombay, Delhi, Saharanpur, Ludhiana or Chandigarh. The good offices of a relative abroad may be sought for buying a suitable make up kit for the bride. Here again the educational qualifications of daughters are highlighted to attract a good match, though it is realised that education carries with it an element of protection in case of marital breakdown and girls need for financial self-reliance.

Because of status considerations and the greatly increased work involved, women of this category do not participate in the milking and taking care of buffaloes and other milch animals. The milk production having been commercialised has now entered the male domain. The legends of love and romance associated with milking and caring of buffaloes are hardly relevant in the present context. The tendency among most of these families on the contrary is for a separation of cattle from living space and keeping the animals away on the family farm to be looked after by the hired labour. Connected with changes in values and lifestyle is also the remodelling of houses to include more bedrooms and toilets.

Drawing attention to the growing burden on women of emerging lifestyle; Pushpinder asserts, 'The gas, electric motor, mixers, washing machines may have reduced the manual tasks but bringing them in has increased manifold our burden of tasks'. These include serving food on the dining table, preparing the meals; even the ritual of tea has undergone a transformation. Now serving tea requires porcelain cups, and items like sweets, biscuits, cakes, namkeen brought from the city. Similarly even entertaining guests and meals served to them have become elaborate. At the same time the pressure to maintain living standards becomes immense, which includes proper upkeep of the interior decoration of the house, installing marble flooring, new upholstery and suitably matching curtains purchased from the city. The family has to be well turned out in terms of well-stiched clothes, either readymade or made to measure by the reputable city tailor, which do not give a *paindu* look. The proper upkeep and bringing up of children implies socialising them to be familiar and at ease with city ways', particularly eating manners and playing with toys; and preparing them to gain entry into the desired public schools and at the same time insulating them from the village atmosphere. Thus the major burden of these women is to make sure from the domestic end that the status of the husband and his family is maintained or enhanced in relation to others of similar position.

Middle Farmer Households

Of the seven middle farmer sample households, one is upwardly mobile *Jeor* and the remaining are Jat Sikhs. The operational holdings range from 5 acres to 12. The *Jeor* with his twelve acres being the largest in the category. Two of them with 8 to 10 buffaloes combine a balanced interest in farming and dairying while others place greater emphasis on farming though in addition keep 2-4 buffaloes for selling milk. All have a scooter each for transport and a colour or black and white T.V. Most of them send their children to English medium schools and some of the children have reached college level.

Women of the middle farmer category have a tendency to imitate the upper farmers who represent the coveted urban middle class lifestyles, though the limitations of their resource forces them to either settle for cheaper versions and less variety. The difference mainly remains of being able to afford or not to a second hand car or a new scooter, a colour or black and white T.V. and a video or a two-in-one. Readymade clothes of cheaper material and similar look may also be bought. In matters of food these households demand from women three cooked meals a day or two. The availability of resources also govern the withdrawal of women from agricultural work, looking after milch cattle, preparing the feed, cutting and carrying of fodder themselves or through hired labour. In fact there is a somewhat arbitrary point where women for their own reasons or as a sop to the masculine pride of their husband as breadwinners declare themselves as homemakers and withdraw from farm related activities and other outside work.

Moreover, there is a tendency among some of the middle farmer women of older generation to hold on to old work related activities and values. Satinder Kaur (59) continues to cook on her *chulah* and along with her daughter looks after the buffaloes and milks them. Similar is the case of Ram Parmeshwari's household. Ram Parmeshwari (72) is a widow and maintains an iron control on the house, where she is referred to as 'lady police'. Food is still cooked on the *chulah* (the family uses gas in an emergency) and water drawn from the hand pump and the task of looking after the buffaloes is divided among the daughters-in-law. Ram Parmeshwari goes alone to the city for her marketing. 'I carry all things in a big bundle put it on my head take it to the bus stop, and bring it back.' She looks after all the outdoor work of the family and feels comfortable in the men's *baithak* having given up domestic work for years. However the same standards do not apply to the *bahus* who can't leave the house unescorted as it is a question of *ghar di izzat* (family honour).

A somewhat exceptional case is that of Daljit Singh's wife who keeps a keen interest in what is happening on the farm. 'Here I sit blowing the *chulah* but my heart pains when I think of the *mandy*. My husband is a bloody pawn in the hands of the *arhtia*. However she feels there is little she can do about it, 'Just imagine standing alone in the bazar surrounded by lecherous men, people would only say 'this women's husband is a good for nothing fellow'. Moreover she fears a violent reaction from her husband to any attempt at interference from her 'I can first see his *juti* on me.'

Lower Farmer Households

The six lower farmer sample households are quite heterogeneous caste-wise and consist of two households of Jat Sikhs and one each of Khatri, Rajput, Jeor and Julaha castes. The land owned by them ranges from less than an acre to 3.5 acres. All of them except the Khatri own two to four buffaloes and sell milk. The Khatri does contract work and leases out his land. Four of the households have scooters, one a bicycle and one has no means of transport. As their holdings don't yield enough income to maintain a family, they either lease out their land and take up some other work or combine agriculture with some other work to supplement their income.

Women's participation in agriculture and other types of work is thus dependent on whether or not the household leases out its land and adequacy or otherwise of income earned. Those who can afford it entrust the task of looking after the milk cattle to the hired labour and buy the fodder in bulk if they do not grow it themselves. The others with less resources have to forage for the fodder.

The women of the cultivating households generally do help their men in the fields. Sukhvinder Singh and his wife for example together cut the wheat harvest. 'If you have an able bodied wife, why not get together and do the work, after all labour, does not come cheap' reasoned Sukhvinder. And his wife chipped in 'Nobody is diminished doing one's own family work'. She regularly visits the fields to look after the odd jobs needing to be done whenever he goes to the city. Rajender Singh, who has only retained about a half acre of his land after selling off the rest for investing in dairying is also similarly helped by his wife at sowing and harvesting time. Such farm labour is however treated as an extension of their household work and the women concerned would themselves disclaim that they do any farm work. Such disclaimers are part of women's complicity in minimising their own contribution to agricultural work in conformity with the prevailing male centred norms of respectability.

Most women of this category however feel the need to find supplementary sources of income. Preet, for example, sews clothes and knit sweaters for people in the village. She does this informally and whatever is earned she spends on the children, their school uniforms and sometimes for the kitchen.

Her husband is determined to continue with agriculture and rents in a couple of acres to make it economically viable. But Preet feels 'it is not really worth the while when you come down to making both ends meet.' Similarly Mohinder Kaur who together with her husband has taken to dairying as the main source of livelihood, has four buffaloes and two calves to look after. She combines rather well the rigours of housework with dairying to perform effectively, the task of looking after the buffaloes, milking, washing and feeding them.

She also makes cowdung cakes and looks after a few hens kept for selling. Her son delivers the milk to the buyers. The sale proceeds of milk are generally collected by her but after deducting a fixed sum she hands them over to her husband who has to meet a number of outside expenditures. The general ration for the house is brought by her husband but the stuff from the cooperative ration shop is bought by her. She has also started a rotating credit society and with that money bought a television. The women of those households that have leased out their land and withdrawn from agriculture find themselves at a serious disadvantage in finding a supplementary source of income to meet some of their own as well as their children's needs. Very few of them are skilled, educated or trained enough to find respectable non-agricultural jobs. They also have status constraints in accepting manual employment. The self-employment promotion schemes of the government relating to piggeries, poultries, fisheries or other tiny enterprises are, as one of them put it, 'All are only on paper. You will surely not get anything without approach.' Thus they have a certain compulsion to confine themselves to household work.

Upper Landless Households

The eight upper landless households are quite heterogeneous in caste, income and the levels of living they can afford. Castewise there are two Jat Sikhs, two Khatri and one each of Brahman, Ramgarhia, Ramdasia and Harijan households. The higher income households are represented by the two Khatris and one of the Jat Sikh households having business, professional and white collar sources of income and corresponding lifestyles. They all have a scooter, fridge, T.V. and in one case even a Swaraj Mazda truck. All the others are skilled workers in tertiary employment or working on their own. Generally these households have more than one source of income. All households have at least a T.V. and a scooter or bicycle for transport.

The heads of the two Khatri households have both a police background. One, is a retired Assistant Sub-Inspector who has taken up business after retirement. With the help of government loans, he has managed from a small beginning to develop a successful transport business. He also owns a ration shop. His wife and two daughters-in-law between themselves, cook the food on the family gas stove, clean the house and furniture, look after the only buffalo owned by the family, milk and process the milk for household needs. The fodder is brought by a servant. The women don't do any outside work. The other household head on the other hand is a serving Sub-Inspector and his wife Pushpa a school teacher. She bicycles to work everyday and also earns extra money by taking tuitions of the village children. She represents the growing number of educated village women at virtually all levels taking to various tertiary occupations. She herself looks after cooking, cleaning the house, washing clothes and other household chores. Living in the village and commuting to her urban school, she fells an extra burden of work, for, as she puts it, 'one has to be both, an urban and rural woman.' Such considerations are alien to the women of the other Khatri household. Pushpa, however, always tries to reach home in time to serve her husband a hot cooked meal.

Similar is the working and living pattern in the corresponding Jat Sikh household where the husband works as a clerk and the wife as a cashier in the State Bank of India at Chandigarh. The wife cooks food and gets all the other housework done before taking a bus to Chandigarh. The husband purchases rations and gets the children ready for school. The house has no milch animal and no agriculture based activity, the husband having had sold his patch of land to make his house *pucca.* The family has a motorised hand pump, a scooter, a gas stove and a cooker, all pointing to a partially modernised non-farm lifestyle. However, as a token of her acceptance of the husband's role as breadwinner and head of the family she dutifully hands over her monthly salary to him and he in turn returns a part of it to her for her own and household expenses. Like this Jat household, in the Ramdasia household also, where the husband Inderjit is a skilled worker and earning well; there is no involvement of the wife in either agricultural labour or livestock related work. Inderjit has earned enough to purchase a T.V., a refrigerator, a gas stove and is planning to buy a scooter. Intervening in a discussion about his wife's work, he said with pride 'I don't send my wife to work. She stays at home and cooks for us'.

In the remaining households of the category there are two to five women. One Brahmin man has his widowed mother staying with him while all the other households have a couple and their one to four sons living jointly. The fathers are all skilled workers but the sons occupations range from combine and autorickshaw driving to semi-skilled regular labour to casual labour. One has a cow and all the others have two to three buffaloes which are looked after by the women of the households, with men bringing the fodder, feed and attending to the sale of milk. While the grandmothers confine themselves to general supervision, looking after grandchildren and occasionally milk. The rest of the household work including tending the milk animals is done by the daughter-in-law. No woman of this category does any farm or other outside work.

Lower Landless Households

Although like the upper landless, the eight lower landless, households also represent six different castes, with the exception of one Jat Sikh household, all others represent lower castes, mostly Scheduled Castes. Further they represent the lower end of the living styles of the village, though at times they may manage to possess certain consumer durables like those possessed by more well off groups such as a T.V., radio or a second hand scooter. Most households and even many individuals within them combine two or more manual jobs, mostly low paid, such as agricultural labour—casual or steady, sheep herding, construction labour, autorickshaw driving, gardening, domestic help, daily wagers in a factory.

An example of such a combining of jobs, perhaps a little to the extreme is that of a Ramdasia household of Hari Singh. Twice a year, at harvest times, he works on the farm of the local landholder and in addition goes around to other farms to look for work. Moreover to supplement his income he has taken a loan to set up a small flour mill. Besides these he undertakes cotton threading and filling quilts. Moreover he fully acknowledges that his wife Beero 'is an equal partner, even more,' in these tasks. The entire family, including his two sons, works together in the fields. They have also kept a buffalo to meet the family's need for milk. Beero, in addition to housework takes active part in harvesting, gleaning the wheat ears, collecting firewood, making dung cakes, picking cotton, milking the family buffalo and bringing and cutting fodder to feed it. Yet, she feels that there is not enough labour available for women like her. 'Even men have to go around other villages looking for work. Where can we go?' She complained. The household is obviously quite well off, but the values, livingstyles and work patterns are closer to the lower landless than those of the upper. Her complaint regarding non-availability of agricultural work, however, does point to certain opportunity constraints applicable specifically to women which may partly account for their withdrawal from such work except in the peak seasons of wheat harvesting, rice planting, etc., when every available hand can be accommodated. As to the opportunity constraints Abbi and Singh's (1997) study on Post-Green Revolution Punjab draws particular attention to the competition from cheaply available migrant labour as a significant factor making for withdrawal of the local landless labour from agricultural labour to construction work, factory labour and other non-farm activities in neighbouring towns.

The other Ramdasia household in this category, though providing a similar illustration of combining different kinds of farm labour with other kinds of jobs, also highlights certain gender specific social constraints and related internal inhibition affecting women's taking up of outside work. Ramnath the head of the household is regularly employed as a gardener in the nearby Escorts factory. But his income is not enough to meet the needs of his two wives and their seven children. He takes leave twice a year and along with his whole family takes part in harvesting on contract basis. In addition his wives like the above Beero, do various farm jobs from time to time. His second wife, Janko, actually an older widowed sister-in-law, in addition works as domestic help at the nearby University, for, as she admits with some reluctance, she has to make some little arrangement for her own children. She gives the earnings partly to her husband, partly to her co-wife and partly she keeps secretly with her. During the harvest season she takes leave from domestic work and actually participates in harvesting. Although she does not quite like the idea of going for work everyday but the fringe benefits, money, old clothes, something to eat are attractive enough to reconcile her to it. Moreover she feels that she has an advantage 'being a widow and over the hill, people can understand my efforts to fend for myself'. Her co-wife, however, feels embarrassed to move out into the world beyond the village, for 'it is full of dirty men who keep eyeing you'. Further, she feels it below her dignity to wash 'anyone's dishes'. So she consoles herself with the thought, 'Anyhow it is the husband's duty to feed me.' She, however, willingly cuts the fodder, feeds and milks the family buffalo.

Prakash, wife of Lakhwinder, Chamar of this category, however finds some other compelling circumstances to take up domestic employment outside the village. Lakhwinder is addicted to country liquor and whatever he earns as casual labour is spent on it. Prakash, with her four children, had to seek the help of an acquaintance in the village to get a domestic job. Though Lakhwinder protested against her going outside the village to do this kind of work, she has kept on doing it anyway. As she puts, 'who does not like some extra money'. She conceals from Lakhwinder the actual number of houses she works in and the amount earned. However, she takes care to give him some money for his liquor, 'otherwise he get violent'. She keeps one buffalo and she and her daughter together go out to collect fodder and firewood. During the harvest season she too takes leave from work to engage in harvesting to meet the family needs for grains. In the other Chamar household, Maya, wife of Darshan Singh, a permanent farm labourer has no problem either in doing domestic service or working outside the village. During the morning she works as a domestic help in the village itself and in the afternoon she goes to the dispensary at Bahadurgarh to work as a dai (midwife) for which she gets a regular salary, with the saving from which she has managed to buy two fans and an electric iron.

The remaining three households in this category belong one each to a Shepherd, Balmiki and a Nongar. While their level of living and the relationship to agricultural work of their women is similar, the men and women of the three also have their own specific types of work and associated patterns.

Jagir Singh Gadri (Shepherd) maintains a commercial relationship with an upper farmer by selling wool sheared from the sheep twice a year. His wife Santo and children look after the goats, milk them and deliver milk at their customers houses. Santo goes out to the farmers' fields collecting fodder and wood for the *chulah*. Moreover during the harvest season the whole family takes up on contract one or more fields to harvest, managing thus to store grain for a year. After harvesting she does casual jobs to glean the corn, weed the fields, pick cotton, transplant rice, etc. 'I want to earn money to make a pucca house but they don't want women for anything' she said regretfully.

Jagdish (Nongar) takes orchards on rent from the farmers on an agreed instalment basis in accordance with the traditional practice. For the duration of the contract the Nongar's reside in the orchard. Nongar women though actively participating in domestic and other productive work play an active role in supervising the orchard leaving the men folk free to find some other supplementary work. Jagdish's wife Parmeshari, who keeps two buffaloes and sells milk, herself goes to the farmer's fields to collect fodder.

Similarly Ram Krishan Balmiki works as a casual labourer, while his wife maintains the traditional role of collecting the dung from an upper farmer's house and cleaning the bathrooms. The dung she carries home to make cakes which are sold as *chulah* fuel. She also works in two or three other houses of the village on cash payment. Collecting fodder for the family buffalo is also her responsibility. At the time of the harvest, the family jointly participate in harvesting, on contract basis and the women in addition go for scavenging, weeding, gleaning, etc.

The Caste Factor

Finally a word about the caste factor would seem to be in order here. As already stated, our classification of the landholders is based on the size of the operational holdings and that of the landless, on skilled work, professional or business status not caste, although the latter may be relevant as an indirect factor affecting the availability of land, skills, inherited property and other resources. The fact that all the upper and middle farmers, except two, are Jats does show both the indirect linkage and absence of absolute linkage. The considerable heterogeneity of caste composition among the lower land holders, however, show an appreciable delinking of caste and operational land holding at that level. Further, despite a considerable caste heterogeneity at the upper and lower landless levels, the first have a predominant representation of upper and middle level castes and the latter of the lower castes. Yet values, behaviour and lifestyles under discussion appear to be more related to the respective category membership and within category differences in skills and resources, than to caste affiliation.

Conclusion

This paper has highlighted the significance of the growing complexity of the productive and social roles of women, the changes in the paid work undertaken outside as well as in the work related to non-wage duties of looking after the household, children and guests, maintaining social contacts and generally upholding the social status of the family by projecting a status appropriate pattern of living. The increasing withdrawal of women from agricultural labour and other paid work is seen as complexly linked to it both as a consequence and promoting and sustaining factor.

Among the lower landless, however, agricultural labour, particularly seasonal undertaking of harvesting on contract basis, continues to be important for both men and women including even some of those in regular factory or household employment. Further, there is a clearly discernible and even verbally expressed preference in some cases for withdrawing from such labour as the family resource position improves with the acquisition by oneself, one's wife, or one or more child of regular better paying skilled or tertiary employment. This withdrawal may be just a symbolic marker of improved family status in some cases, yet in others it may constitute a significant step towards upward social mobility and greater modernisation of the household. The validity of this view becomes particularly evident when we look at the upper landless, some of whom represent such upward modernising movement from the lower to the upper landless status. Most others of this category, with the possible exception of a very conservative minority, show similar, if not greater, upward strivings and modernising orientations. Almost total withdrawal of their women from agriculture related activities and growing involvement in tertiary occupations atleast to this change in orientation. Further, the greater interest of the upper landless in children's education and their choice of such consumer durable as scooters, T.V.s, radios and other modern gadgets signify the same value preferences.

At each of the upper, middle and lower farmer category levels, the study takes note of the significant variations in the specificities of this modernising upward mobility process and its manifestations in emerging values, behaviour and lifestyles. While doing so, it points out how the technological modernisation of farming and associated prosperity, withdrawal of women from agricultural work at .ll levels of the village society, their increased involvement in catering to household consumption and status appropriate lifestyle maintenance needs as well as taking to professional and other tertiary occupations, both signify and help to promote Punjab's characteristic modernisation process. By positively viewing women's withdrawal from agricultural work in this broader development context, the paper attempts to correct its prevailing reified conceptualisation and negative understanding in scholarly studies.

REFERENCES

Abbi, B.L. and Kesar Singh (1997), *Post-Green Revolution Rural Punjab – A Profile of Economic and Socio-Cultural Change (1965-95)*, CRRID, Chandigarh.

Agarwal, Bina (1989), "Rural Women, Poverty and Natural Resources; Sustenance, Sustainability and Struggle for Change", *Economic and Political Weekly*, Vol. XXIV, No. 43, P WS-46-'WS-65'.

Bhalla, Sheila (1989), "Technological Change and Women Workers: Evidence from the Expansionary Phase in Haryana Agriculture",. *Economic and Political Weekly*, 28 Oct. Vol. XXIV, No. 43, P WS67-WS87.

Brass, Tom (1990), "Class Struggle and the Deproletarianisation of Agricultural Labour in Haryana (India)", *Journal of Peasant Studies*, Vol. 18, No. 1, pp. 36-37.

Chand, R., Sidhu, D.S. and Kaul, J.L. (1985), "Impact of Agricultural Modernisation and Labour Use Pattern in Punjab with Special Reference to Women Labour", *Indian Journal of Agricultural Economics*, Vol. XL, No. 3, pp. 352-59.

Chowdhry, Prem (1994), *The Veiled Women-Shifting Gender Equations in Rural Haryana 1880-1990*, OUP, Delhi.

Dak, T.M. and Sharma, M.L. (1988), "Social Framework of Female Labour Participation in Rural Sector" in T.M. Dak (ed). *Women and Work in Indian Society*. Manohar Publications, New Delhi.

Das Gupta, Monica (1987), "Selective Discrimination Against Female Children in Rural Punjab, India", *Population and Development Review*, March, Vol. 13, No. 1, pp. 77-100.

Dixon, Ruth B. (1978), *Rural Women at Work: Strategies for Development in South Asia*, John Hopkins University Press, Baltimore.

Jain, Devaki and Nirmala Banerjee (eds) (1985), *Tyranny of the Household, Investigative Essays on Women's Work*, Shakti Books, Delhi.

Jeffery, Roger, Jeffery, Patricia, Lyn, Andrew (1989), "Taking Dung Work Seriously: Women's Work and Rural Development in Northern India", *Economic and Political Weekly*, 29 April Vol. XXIV, No. 17, pp. WS32-WS37.

Kak, Shanti (1994), *Subsistence Economies and Women's Work: A Case Study of India*. NMML: Delhi No. XLVII.

Kaur, Rupinder (1998), "Female Work Participation: Caste, Class and Gender Analysis in Rural Indian Punjab", *International Journal of Punjab Studies*, Vol. 5, No. 1.

Lourdes, Beneria (ed.) (1998), *Women and Development*. New York: Praeger Publishers, New York.

Mann, R.S. and Mann, K. (1988) "Status Versus Work and Role of Jat Women" in T.M. Dak (ed) *Women and Work in Indian Society*, Manohar, Delhi.

Nayyar, Rohini. (1989), "Rural Labour Markets and Employment of Women in Punjab and Haryana" in AV Rose (ed) *Limited Options: Women Workers in Rural India*, New Delhi: ILO, ARTEP, pp. 234-55.

Rastogi, Preet, (2000), "Identifying Gender Backward Districts Using Selected Indicators", *Economic and Political Weekly*, Nov. 25-Dec. 1.

Sandhu, H.K. (1976), "Technological Development versus Economic

Contribution of Women in Rural Punjab", *Social Change*, Vol. 6, Nos. 3 & 4.

Sharma, Urusula. (1980), *Women Work and Property in Northwest India*, Tavistack, London.

Sen, Gita. (1982), "Women Workers and Green Revolution' in Lourdes Beneria", (ed.) *Women and Development*, Praeger Publishers, New York.

Sethi, Raj Mohini. (1982), *Female Labour in Agriculture*, Punjab University, Chandigarh,.

Shiva, Vandana. (1988), *Staying Alive: Kali for Women*, New Delhi.

Singh, K.P. (1986), "Female Labour Force, Population Growth and Development: The Case of Punjab" in S.L. Sharma (eds) *Development–Socio-cultural Dimensions*, Rawat Publishers, Jaipur, pp. 85-103.

21

WOMEN EMPOWERMENT THROUGH LABOUR PARTICIPATION IN INDUSTRIAL SECTOR

HARNEK SINGH & M.K. DHILLON

In the family economy, the role of women has been and still is auxiliary to that of the men of household. Accordingly, it is difficult to draw a line between those working substantially and those whose work is considered minor. Generally, the women in the lower strata of society shoulder much drudgery which is often ignored as unproductive not because it does not add to production but due to that they are not directly earning any income out of it. Actually, the female labour participation is conditioned by several factors. It has been considered that there are four major conditions for the supply of female labour such as child care and other domestic duties, nutrition, local customs and other socio-economic factors and the family subsistence needs. The extent of mobility allowed to women, availability of suitable jobs, desire on the part of women to avail of job opportunities, educational attainment, income level and the husband's occupational status are also the factors which influence the female employment.

Empirical evidence shows that in the urban areas, there is only 13.07 per cent employed women labour force. The overall labour participation rates in the rural area are, however, determined by the extent to which women and children participate in the labour force. As the employment opportunities increase, more number of women come in labour force especially in the industries of electronic, textile, communication etc. This study was conducted to know the effect of working, social environment and feelings of the industrial women workers. Textiles industry in Ludhiana (Punjab State) has been selected purposively as a large number of women work in this field. An equal number of women from rural (R) as well as urban (U) area were taken into consideration. Data were analysed with the help of suitable statistical techniques.

A number of parameters were taken into account to know the effect of employment of industrial women workers. Out of all, social background, reasons of doing this work, effect of this job on self, family and other members of society, consultation, involvement of women in the decision of household matters and grievances while working were considered as most important variables. These are given as under:

Social Background

A number of characteristics such as age, education, religion, marital status, family size and family income per month were taken into consideration to know the social background of the rural as well as urban industrial women labour.

It was observed from Table 21.1 that a majority of the women were young (up to 30 years) in age in the total sample. Out of it, a large number of them were from the rural areas. Though, women of higher age (above 31 years) also work in the factory but only 15 per cent were from rural areas. The number of women above 31 years of age were more from urban area due to the reason that it was easy for them to come for work because of living in the same city. The factory owners encourage young girls for employment because of the fact that after marriage they will go to new place. In this way, there will be no problem of labour unrest.

The level of education of these women was low. Only about 29 per cent had education up to matric level whereas 16.67 per cent were illiterate in the total sample. The level of education was high in case of rural than that of urban women. As in the city, the opportunities were available for work, so they sent their girls for work from the very beginning. In the rural area, there were no opportunities for work at native place, so, some of them afforded to give education to their daughters upto matric level. Moreover, this industrial work is not restricted to any education level nor to any religion. In the total sample, 58.33 per cent were from Sikh and 40.83 per cent from Hindu religion. The majority of the respondents of rural area were Sikh and Hindu from urban area. All of them had different marital status, *viz.* unmarried, married, widow and divorced. In the total sample, half of them were unmarried. In case of respondents of rural area, a majority of them were unmarried and married in case of urban area. There was no divorced respondents from rural area as compared to 8.33 per cent from the urban.

Table 21.1: Social background of the respondents

Characteristics	*Rural*	*Urban*	*Total*
Age			
Upto 20 years	32(53.33)	14(23.33)	46(38.33)
21-30 years	19(31.67)	24(40.00)	43(35.83)
31 years and above	9(15.00)	22(36.67)	31(25.83)
Education			
Illiterate	4(6.67)	16(26.67)	20(16.67)
Primary	13(23.33)	21(35.00)	35(29.17)
Middle	21(35.00)	10(16.67)	31(25.83)
Matric	21(35.00)	13(21.67)	34(28.33)
Religion			
Hindu	15(25.00)	34(56.67)	49(40.83)
Sikh	45(75.00)	25(41.67)	70(58.33)
Muslim	–	1(1.67)	1(0.83)
Marital Status			
Unmarried	39(65.00)	21(35.00)	60(50.00)
Married	17(28.33)	29(48.33)	46(38.33)
Widow	4(6.67)	5(8.33)	9(7.50)
Divorcee	–	5(8.33)	5(4.17)
Family Size			
Upto 4 members	16(26.67)	20(33.33)	36(30.00)
5 members and above	44(73.33)	40(66.67)	84(70.00)
Family Income Per Month			
Upto Rs.1000	7(11.67)	3(5.00)	10(8.33)
Rs.1000-1500	19(31.67)	20(33.33)	39(32.80)
Rs.1500-2000	21(35.00)	22(46.67)	43(35.83)
Rs.2000 and above	13(21.67)	15(25.00)	28(23.33)

In case of composition of family, a majority of the respondents were from large family (above 5 members) in the total sample. The pattern was almost the same in both types of localities (rural and urban) of the respondents. The income level of all the respondents was low and almost all of them were at the subsistence level. There were only 23.33 per cent of the respondents in the total sample who had family income above Rs.2000 per month. A large number of them fell in the income category of Rs.1000 to Rs.2000 per month per family. All this indicates that women workers were young in age, less educated and from poor families. They were not able to have more savings out of this meagre income.

Reasons of Taking up this Work

The main reason of doing industrial labour was economic necessity. The other reasons associated with it were large family size, no other source of income, to pastime, undesirable habits of husbands, etc. Almost same pattern prevailed with the respondents of both type of localities (Table 21.2). Only a few women workers said that source of income was limited to them. About 22 per cent of urban workers said that they had to work because there was no one and no other work available to them. On the other hand, 30.00 per cent rural respondents considered that due to large family size, it was the necessity to work and mobilise more resources for easy living. Even, some of them considered that due to bad habits of their husbands and other members of the family, they had to do work. On the whole, it was economic necessity which forced them to do this job.

Table 21.2: Reasons of taking up this work by women workers

Reasons	*Rural*	*Urban*	*Total*
Economic necessity	56(93.33)	56(93.33)	112(93.33)
No other source of income	7(11.67)	13(21.67)	20(16.67)
To pass time	4(6.67)	11(18.33)	15(12.50)
Large family size	18(30.00)	6(10.00)	24(20.00)
Habit of husband	6(10.00)	4(6.67)	10(8.33)

Multiple responses
$\chi^2 = 12.32$, d.f. = 4, significant

Effects

The employment of women brought many changes in the family, society and on standard of living. It is evident from Table 21.3 that in the total sample, a majority of the working women got respect and considered independent in the family. Their self-dependence gave them moral courage and integrity. This was more so with the rural women workers. With this employment, they were able to fulfil most of the needs of the family.

In case of urban respondents, large number of them said that they participated in making decisions about different matters in the family. This was not so before employment. In addition to this, they were able to take care of health of self and also of the family members. It all shows that all the workers irrespective of their place of residence, got upward mobility in their social status.

Table 21.3: Effect of employment of women workers

Effect on	*Rural*	*Urban*	*Total*	*Chi-square value*
Family				
Got respect from family	58(96.67)	46(76.67)	104(86.67)	
Participated in decision making	8(13.33)	37(61.67)	45(37.50)	23.15 S
Better health of family members	18(30.00)	36(60.00)	54(45.00)	
Became independent	41(68.33)	25(41.67)	66(55.00)	
Able to fulfil family needs	33(55.00)	11(18.33)	44(36.67)	
Society				
Got respect from friends & neighbours	47(78.33)	38(63.33)	85(70.83)	
Encouraged others	22(36.67)	42(70.00)	64(53.33)	9.66 S
Neighbours don't liked job	14(23.33)	29(48.33)	43(35.83)	
Friends felt jealous	5(8.33)	10(16.67)	15(25.00)	
Improvement in food standard	58(96.67)	49(81.67)	107(89.17)	19.18 S
Able to get good clothes	40(66.67)	30(50.00)	70(58.33)	
Able to purchase luxury items	4(6.67)	27(45.00)	31(25.83)	

Multiple responses
S = Significant at 5 per cent level.

The effect of employment of these workers was also in the right direction among their friends, neighbour and other members of society. The same Table indicates that a large number of them got encouragement and respect from the neighbours and other persons. One-fourth of the workers in the total sample said that their neighbours and friends had not liked their working. Some of them were jealous but others said that girls/housewives should go outside for work. This type of thinking is still going on in the backward sections of our society. This was more so in the case of urban workers. The rural workers were from very poor families. So, a large number of village people liked their working in the factory. According to the views of the rural workers, the village people appreciated their parents/husbands for allowing to do work in the city.

They said that now, they (worker's family) will be able to marry her with a right person. In case of urban workers, friends encouraged them but neighbourers had not liked their working. On the whole, these workers were liked by most of the persons of our society.

These workers also got improvement in their own household. In the total sample, about 90 per cent of the workers were able to purchase all the eatables which were not possible before this employment. Some of them purchased all the needed items in the household. About 25 per cent of them were able to purchase the items which they considered as luxury goods such as electric fan, cycle, sewing machine, watch etc. In addition to this, 58.33 per cent of them were able to purchase clothes for all the times and for all members of the family. These improvements were witnessed more by rural than that of urban workers. But the so called luxury items were taken more by urban than rural workers.

So, these workers felt differently after getting the employment. The major change which was considered by most of them was respect from family members as well as other members of the locality. Almost all of them were able to express themselves in a better way.

Consultation

These women industrial workers were consulted in making decision in and outside the family (Table 21.4). A large number of them were consulted in money matters, such as, how much should be spent and saved in the family. Similarly, they were taken into consideration for household purchase of costly and grocery items.

Table 21.4: Consultation in family matters

Matters	*Rural*	*Urban*	*Total*
Money matters	39(65.00)	59(98.33)	98(81.67)
Household purchase	38(63.33)	56(93.33)	94(78.33)
Ceremonies	31(51.67)	34(56.67)	65(54.17)
Marriage function	16(26.67)	24(40.00)	40(33.33)
Dowry	13(21.67)	14(23.33)	27(22.50)
Children education	19(31.67)	16(26.67)	35(29.17)

Multiple responses
$\chi^2 = 3.47$, d.f. = 5, Non-significant

But in case of dowry, only about one-fourth of them were consulted from the total sample. The urban respondents were consulted more than that of rural. Almost all the urban women were consulted in the money and household matters. Actually, rural women were not very particular whether they are consulted or not. They considered it the male's prerogative. So, their participation in marriage function, *i.e.* how much to be spent and how much to be given to relatives, where to put the children for schooling, upto which class they should be taught, etc. was not very encouraging. In case of urban respondents, they got involved in deciding the expenditure on marriage, purchase of different items, celebration of religious and other ceremonies, etc.

The unmarried girls were not much consulted in making decisions in the family. Especially in the low and just middle class families, it was the head of household who always decides all the matters. There was a little scope for the consultation of women folk.

Grievances

These textile workers were satisfied by getting some work in the factory. But, with the passage of time, they felt that something more is required at the work place. Almost all of them said that wages were less. They were not able to purchase all the items of household with these meagre wages (Table 21.5). They were paid for the work done but even then these workers considered that working time is more. After coming from work in the evening, they were not able to take care of the children, washing clothes, visiting relatives etc. This was more felt by urban workers. Rurals had not considered these matters as most important.

Table 21.5: Grievances of the workers

Grievances	*Rural*	*Urban*	*Total*
Low wages	54(90.00)	55(91.67)	109(90.83)
More working hours	8(13.33)	41(68.33)	49(40.83)
Non-availability of medical facility	15(25.00)	22(36.67)	37(30.83)
No refreshment is given	14(23.33)	22(36.67)	46(38.33)
No free uniform	19(31.67)	30(50.00)	49(40.83)
Lack of entertainment	3(5.00)	4(6.67)	7(5.83)
Lack of rest days	2(3.33)	5(8.33)	7(5.83)

Multiple responses
$\chi^2 = 25.79$, d.f. = 6, Significant

Though the medical facility is being provided by E.S.I. Hospital but workers considered it difficult. They had to get leave to get medical facilities and to spend money on medicines. The uniform, which they are to wear while at work was also not freely available to them. Even at work, there was no refreshment and entertainment in the factory. Moreover, they had no rest day. They can had it themselves, but will not be paid. So, they desired that factory owners should keep at least two days as rest days in a month. These grievances were more pronounced by urban workers. Though, the rural workers also felt these, but were satisfied by getting work in the factory. Otherwise, it was difficult for them to meet with both ends meet.

Conclusion

The study infers that textile women workers no doubt belong to all the age group but a majority of them are young with low level of education. They have little saving from their work and what so ever they are able to save, is utilised to purchase household. This indicates that textile women workers come from poor social and economic section of the society. Most of them are doing work in factories to augments their meagre economic resources and to meet the economic necessities of the life.

Further, the employment of the women has helped in their empowerment. The most important effect of their work has been that these women now get respect from the family members and others in the society. They are able to build confidence and courage to become more independent than looking towards others for guidance. Their employment has sufficiently exposed them to register their presence in the family and outside. These women are often consulted in deciding matters pertaining to household, children, and relatives.

No doubt, the owners of the factories provide a number of facilities to the workers; still the urban workers have more grievances than their counterpart rural workers. The main grievance is related to the provision of work. These women can contribute more towards their social development provided the owners employ or give regular work. This will take care of their grievances, as well.

In short, it can be concluded that employment empowers women and enhances their social capability to improve upon low social and economic status among the significant others. Education, which most of the studies on women empowerment, holds good for their emancipation, has to be supplemented by employment to generate confidence among them to play a significant role in decision making within and outside the family.

REFERENCES

Brown, I. David, (1977), "Women in labour force", *Journal of Home Science*, 69 (5), pp. 21-22.

Desai, T.P., (1993), "Stress and mental workload: A Study in an industrial organisation", *Indian Journal of Industrial Relations*, 29 (3), p. 258

Mishra, T.K., (1989), "Indian Women—unorganised agents of rural change", *Kurukshetra*, 44(5), pp. 27-28.

Singh, K.P. (1980), "Economic development and female labour force participation: The case of Punjab", *Social Action*, 30 (2), pp. 128-57.

Usha, S., (1983), "Labour market discrimination against women", *Indian Journal of Industrial Relations*, 18 (4).

22

WOMEN AND SOCIETY
Empowering Through Work

M.S. GILL

The dominant models of development adopted in the Capitalist and Marxist systems are based on the doctrine of material progress, the theory of growth and manipulative view of science and techno-managerial approach to human welfare. In the process the women especially in the rural areas and those of low socio-economic position lost control over their labour and knowledge besides access to resources. Men on the other hand, have gained control over resources and technology. This process has sharpened gender inequalities. Despite planning, constitutional commitment, laws and legislations, the women feel deprived of the gains of development as the question of women's development has been always a "marginal one". The devaluation of women's work and her marginalisation have resulted in a devaluation of the women herself (Venkateswaram, 1995). The devaluation and reduced status has led to practices such as gender discrimination in food and wages, dowry and violence against women. The origin of such inequalities in the view of Beneria (1979), Mies (1980) and others stem from division of labour and unequal position of men and women in family and society. Many social scientists believe culture as the main determinant of such inequalities. Oakley (1974) provides evidence that gender roles are culturally determined in which women are relegated to lower position as compared to men. This culture in the form of values, ethics, norms and roles is learnt and socially transmitted. Such situation coupled with the present mode of development has not only sharpened the inequalities but at the same time has aggrandized the pursuit of profit and power in all sphere of life thereby determining the status on wealth, power and skills to manipulate means to achieve these ends.

The desirability to increase the production with new production forces has ensured supremacy of exchange value against use value which has resulted in the domination of man at home as well as work place besides limiting woman's capacity to participate effectively in production process. Blau and Jusenius (1976) see women's secondary position in the labour market as a consequence of overcrowding of women in low productivity occupations, difference in educational background and imperfection in labour market. The present struggle to control people through arms, police and weapons, too, has been responsible for the infiltration of such values in family which are associated with patriarchy. As a result, women continue to suffer from subjugation.

Further earlier women movements whose membership was drawn from the urban middle class have needs different from the large majority of the poor Indian women. The "women question" was addressed to equality which linked feminism and anti-casteism saying that religious texts were used to subordinate both women and the lower castes and attempts to re-appropriate traditionally accepted women space and to interpret myths, practices, and folklores to discover traditional sources of women's strength rather than their sufferings were made (Kumar, 1989). Later on, their emphasis centred on class basis of women oppression, roads to women's liberation and the role they themselves could play in this. The efforts were thrusted on how to organize and represent themselves to generate a consciousness of women's oppression at home (dowry deaths) and outside (rape, child sacrifice, forcible widow immolation etc.). Such protests and representations culminated into enactment of new rules and regulations pertaining to wages, work hours, holidays, women's rights and so on. In spite of this, her position in society is invariably linked to her assets and her control over her earning and other assets which she or her family may have (Kalbagh, 1991). In this context, women's status is linked to her education and place in the economic structure of the society. This is the reason for the present study to be particularly confined to the educated working women only.

The basic thrust of the paper is to understand the status as perceived by the working women, the factors that enhance their status and to find out link between employment and status.

The Study

The study is focused on the working women in Guru Nanak Dev University, Amritsar. A list of the working women was drawn from the teachers and non-teachers voter lists. Out of this, the respondents were selected randomly from the total number of female employees working in different capacity; of course, class IV employees were intentionally excluded because of their low educational and economic level. In all, 59 respondents were interviewed with the help of a structured schedule. The analysis is limited to women employee without distinction of teaching/non-teaching category.

Results

Status refers to one's position in the society. It entails duties and privileges for the beholder of a status. Status is valued higher or lower depending upon the duties, responsibilities, and privileges along with a number of ascriptive and achievemental factors. But when it comes to sexes, men are ranked higher than women traditionally because of their activities and confinement of the latter to home. Her responsibility of home and care of the youngones (and also the aged) may somehow prevent her from transcending group relations in production process that ultimately may lead to unequal status of men and women. Out of this has originated the response that 74.6 per cent of the women respondents consider their status not equal to that of the men (Table 22.1).

Table 22.1: Status of male and female

Status	*Number*	*Percentage*	*Reasons*		
A. Equal	15	(25.4)	(i) People say so	4	(26.7)
			(ii) Legislation	9	(60.0)
			(iii) Equal opportunities	2	(13.3)
B. Unequal	44	(74.6)	(i) Society accepts unequal status	19	(43.2)
			(ii) Ideology of male superiority	12	(27.3)
			(iii) Restriction on women	8	(18.2)
			(iv) Lack of occupational mobility	5	(11.4)
Total	59	(100.0)			

The society still holds unequal status for sexes and the same is handed down to the coming generation through socialization (43.2%). In addition, the ideology of superiority of the male over the female because of the former's role and status culturally defined with authority vested in male has pushed the latter to secondary position (27.3%). Likewise restrictions imposed on women concerning her ways of behaviour and acting in home and outside (18.2%) and denial of mobility even in the occupation by terming her role more inclined towards home than work place (11.4%) are the other reasons for her low status. Contrarily, majority of those stating equality of status holds that legislations enacted from time to time, which give rights to women predominantly, have put their status at par with that of the men (60.0%). Similarly, availability of equal opportunities of education, health, and others has enhanced their status (13.3%). Some of the respondents consider that as people say so, they have no option except to believe in equality of sexes (26.7%). Hence, majority of the respondents still find difference in the status of man and woman and society transcends the same through socialization. Even the equality of status is considered more because of the legislations enshrined in the Constitution than opportunities and perception of equality of sexes in the cognitive world of the people. As far as rights of the women are concerned, 72.9 per cent of the respondents are of the opinion that legislation enacted in the Constitution of India have given equal right to vote, education, health, property, employment and so on (Table 22.2).

Table 22.2: Rights of male and female

Status	*Number*	*Percentage*	*Reasons*		
A. Equal	43	(72.9)	Constitutional provisions	43	(100.0)
B. Unequal	16	(27.1)	(i) Social environment	12	(75.0)
			(ii) Discrimination	4	(25.0)
Total	59	(100.0)			

Despite this, the social environment in which one lives (75.0%) and discrimination one suffers at various places/occasions (25.0%) are infringing upon their rights and squarely blame such attitude responsible for inequality of sexes. No doubt, the number of such respondents is low but refers to significant factors contributing to unequal rights.

The above view is supported by 79.7 per cent of the respondents who consider that women are a discriminated lot (Table 22.3). The discrimination arises out of the attitude of the society that still holds women as subordinate (44.7%). A large proportion of the respondents consider their exploitation at work place (34.0%) and blockage to their promotion in profession (21.3%) amount to discrimination and this leads to their unequal status in one way or the other. On the other hand, some of the women find that performance at work place better than the men and their participation in all activities including political leave no place for discrimination.

Table 22.3: Discrimination against women in society

Discrimination	*Number*	*Percentage*		*Reasons*		
A. Yes	47	(79.7)	(i)	Blockage in promotion	10	(21.3)
			(ii)	Exploitation at work place	16	(34.0)
			(iii)	Attitude of people	21	(44.7)
B. No	12	(20.3)	(i)	Perform better than men	5	(41.7)
			(ii)	Equal participation	7	(58.3)
Total	59	(100.0)				

The above analysis shows that the rights of the women are, of course, equal to that of men as prescribed in the Constitution of India but in reality, the status of women is not equal to that of men and they are discriminated at their place of work and at home. Their service gives them opportunities of self-expression and a better lifestyle but sense of neglect prevails in their sphere of activities manifestly or latently because of cultural preferences and expectations which govern their role behaviour. In this regard, data indicate that due to lack of geographic movement and occupational mobility, the promotion of women is hindered (80.0%) and they are exploited at their work place (20.0%) by assigning those tasks that are not accepted by their counterpart or are labelled as woman/household jobs (Table 22.4).

Table 22.4: Reasons for unequal status and discrimination

Reasons for Unequal Status	*Discrimination*							
	Blockage to promotion		*Exploitation at work place*		*Attitude of people*		*Total*	
Society	–		6	(37.5)	10	(62.5)	16	(41.0)
Ideology of male superiority	4	(33.3)	3	(25.0)	5	(41.7)	12	(30.8)
Restriction on movement	–		4	(66.7)	2	(33.3)	6	(15.4)
Lack of occupational mobility	4	(80.0)	1	(20.0)	–		5	(12.8)
Total	8	(20.5)	14	(35.9)	17	(43.6)	39	(100.0)

$\chi^2 = 19.65$; d.f. = 6 at 0.005 = 18.5

Further, restriction over their movement to transcend group relations or mediating among a large section of people inhibit their pro-active participation at workplace and this provides ground for exploitation at workplace (66.7%). The attitude of the people towards women frequenting in male company sufficiently clear ground for the restrictions in their interaction and movements as stigmatized words or phrases often form the part of the male's discussion; these are 'she enjoys the company of male', 'she shows her figure' and the like. To avoid such labelling in male dominated workplace, women restrict their movements and this speaks of unequal status (33.3%) and discrimination. Similarly, the attitude of people in society is more governed by the collective consciousness than individual rational thinking about women and out of this originates the notion of inequality and discrimination. The association between the status and discrimination has been found to be high (χ^2=19.65) which means unequal status gives way to means of discrimination and *vice versa*.

Under such circumstances, certain factors in the view of the respondents contribute towards their empowerment through which one can assert one's status and overcome discrimination to a large extent. Among such factors, education is found to be the most determining one (69.5%, Table 22.5) which helps in improving the status of women. Education supports women to cope with superstitions, social system that exploit them in the name of family ties, religion, social mores and so on besides helping them to learn to demand a politically and socially more equitable position. Gill (1996), Narayan (1998), Khaira (1999), too, have made similar remarks. Education furthers their chances of entering into the economic or occupational structure whose professing helps women to gain status on society (18.6%). Constitutional provisions and ownership of property are the other factors contributing to status enhancement of the women in the society.

Table 22.5: Factors responsible for equal status

Factors	*Number*	*Percentage*
Education	41	(69.5)
Constitutional provision	4	(6.8)
Service	11	(18.6)
Ownership of property	3	(5.1)
Total	59	(100.0)

While talking of equality, women are to be integrated into the main stream of social life and that means active participation in the development process. Interestingly, Indian society considers family and society in general to be more important than the self (individual) which in the west is considered as a road to women empowerment. The participation of the woman in activities other than home has exchange value and their working outside the home carry prestige and power. For this, 89.8 per cent of the women opine that women should work outside the home. Only 10.2 per cent of the respondents do not favour this because it increases rather double their burden of work and responsibilities besides leaving room for exploitation (Table 22.6).

Table 22.6: Opinion regarding working of women outside home

Should Work	*Number*	*Percentage*	*Reason*			
A. Yes	53	(89.8)	(i)	Economic	25	(47.2)
			(ii)	Status of family	12	(22.6)
			(iii)	Freedom to spend	10	(18.9)
			(iv)	Self-confidence	6	(11.3)
B. No	6	(10.2)	(i)	Duel responsibility	4	(66.7)
			(ii)	Exploitation	2	(33.3)
Total	59	(100.0)				

Joining the occupational structure not only augment the resources of the family (47.2%) but also raises the economic status of that family in the society (22.6%). Further, 18.9 per cent of the respondents find that their job has enhanced their freedom to make independent economic decisions. For 11.3 per cent of the respondents, the participation in the work force has given them self-confidence to make rational decisions regarding family, self, and society. At least, it has enabled them to grab a solid space in the family of one's in-laws. In short, their employment has enhanced their status in the society. But one wonders why majority of the working women carries the notion of unequal status and discrimination. For this, I think one has to look into the psychology of the issue of reservation policy which has besides opening avenues of status enhancement has created a sense of status neglect in the cognitive world of a section of society called downtrodden. Anyhow to analyse and understand this issue, the working of the women has been computed against the status and discrimination factors.

Data in Table 22.7 reveal that though the women' work augment economic resources of the family, the attitude of the society at large has not changed (68.4%) and this account for their statement that women are not equal to men. The working women have been able to raise the economic status of the family but the attitude of the society and the ideology of male superiority still prescribe unequal status to women (45.4% respectively). Moreover, the working women have got freedom to make economic decisions and spend as desired but restriction on their movement curtails their power to make independent expenditure (44.4%). It is equally associated with the ideology of male superiority (33.3%) and general view prevailing in the society (11.1%). As stated, the engagement of women in the occupational structure raises one's self-confidence but restriction imposed by way of prescribing norms of behaviour and action (75.0%) coupled with their lack of mobility (25.0%) amount to unequal status of sexes. For this, the association between women's status and her working is found to be significant (χ^2=28.65). Thus, woman may join the occupational structure to augment resources of the family or family may give her right in the decision making by allowing her to spend; the attitude towards woman coupled with ideology of male superiority transgressed through socialization attribute to unequal status for woman in society and paving way for her exploitation and discrimination.

Table 22.7: Reasons for working and status of women

Reason for working out of home	*Reasons for unequal status*				
	Society	*Ideology of male superiority*	*Restrictions*	*Lack of mobility*	*Total*
Economic	13 (68.4)	4 (21.1)	1 (5.3)	1 (5.3)	19 (43.2)
Family status	5 (45.4)	5 (45.4)	–	1 (9.1)	11 (25.0)
Freedom to spend	1 (11.1)	3 (33.3)	4 (44.4)	1 (11.1)	9 (20.4)
Self-confidence	–	–	3 (75.0)	2 (25.0)	5 (11.4)
Total	19 (43.2)	12 (27.3)	8 (18.2)	5 (11.4)	44 (100.0)

χ^2 = 28.65, d.f. = 9 at 0.001 = 27.9

Table 22.8: Reasons of working and discrimination

Reasons for working out of home	*Reasons for discrimination*			
	Blockage to promotion	*Exploitation*	*Attitude of society*	*Total*
Economic	4 (16.7)	7 (29.2)	13(54.2)	24 (42.1)
Family status	3 (27.3)	3 (27.3)	5 (45.4)	11 (19.3)
Freedom to spend	1 (16.7)	3 (50.0)	2 (33.3)	6 (12.8)
Self-confidence	2 (33.3)	3 (50.0)	1 (16.7)	6 (12.8)
Total	10 (21.3)	16 (34.0)	21 (44.7)	47 (100.0)

χ^2 = 3.95; d.f. = 6 at 0.001 = 10.6

Attempt has also been made to find out an association between reasons for working out of home and discrimination as perceived by the working women. Data in Table 22.8 discern that the women who are working to improve their resources find attitude of the society as a major factor contributing to their discrimination (54.2%) followed by their exploitation at work place (29.2%). Similar observations are made by women who think their job has enhanced the social and economic status of the family. Those who have improved upon their confidence find their exploitation (50.0%) and hindrance in their promotion (33.3%) contributing to their discrimination. For this the women have not been able to participate and contribute fully at their work.

Conclusion

The above analysis reveals that majority of the working women find their status unequal to that of men because of the inbuilt attitude of the society where male is considered superior to his counterpart. Out of this originates the behavioural pattern that restricts her mobility; geographic as well as occupational. The lack of mobility is further constrained by her biological and social functions, which are valued higher by the society and are enforced through religious and social ideas. Such ideas are transmitted as a cultural value through socialization and define one's way of behaving, acting, and thinking in the society. In this way, the traditional logical interpretation of one's role sufficiently contributes to the unequal status of sexes.

The Constitution of India gives equal rights to women such as right to vote, to health, to property, and the like and to safeguard their interest has further enacted laws and legislation. With all such means and measures, social environment has not been conducive in which a woman is free to exercise her rights. This is the reason for majority of the women to refer to their discrimination in society expressed especially in attitude of people, exploitation at work place, and blockage to promotion. All these pursuits block the avenues of extending group relations and positions of power and prestige for the women. Out of this originates dissatisfaction, felling of neglect, unequal status and discrimination. Gill (1996) has inferred this while talking of equality as a perception and as a belief. For this the discrimination of women is found to be associated with unequal status.

Education is one of the most important factors that can empower women and help them to cope with exploitative social system as per the study. Likewise, the economic and occupational structure opens avenues of implicit interaction with worldly activities associated with power and prestige. The legal structure gives power and rights but exercise of power and rights is possible through education and employment. The study infers that women through their employment augment their family's economic resources paving a way to improve socio-economic status of the family. Their power to earn and improve economic status contains a sense of right *i.e.* liberty to spend and play a role in economic decisions. It also contains elements of independence as it enhances self-confidence. Certainly the participation in worldly activities through education and employment is inimical to their proverbial powerless situation; instrumental to their low status.

Contrarily, the relation between the reasons for working outside the home and the reasons for unequal status and discrimination explains that subordination and powerlessness of women are uncritically ascribed to biological differences and gender-based inequality perpetuated in the society. No doubt the women have achieved positions of power and prestige, they are generally assigned tasks that their counterparts deny or are equated to feminine activities. Women's entry into the occupational structure, of course, helps to prove their competency and equality in services but does not empower them. The route to women's empowerment is undoubtedly through their joining the occupational structure. Feminist, too, insists that a woman must be able to go out and work and earn as an expression of her right to equality (Gagote, 1986) but the present study concludes that such opportunities help in self-actualization and not enough to achieve equality in status with man. Their empowerment still is recognized in 'housebound' and 'feminine' tasks and services.

Further, joining the occupation structure is a mean to women's empowerment but does it take care of the institution of family and marriage or lead to gender struggle where each one is trying to gain at the cost of the other? So long the ideology of male superiority continues to be advocated and culturally transferred through socialization with control of resources in the hands of man, may be at home or at work place; the struggle between the sexes for status, equality, or empowerment of women ought to assume a diabolic situation in which the interests of the one will confront with that of the other. This necessarily requires a consciously derived attitude in which the changing realities of sharing the resources should be incorporated into the institutionalized roles and group relations. Otherwise, web of group relations will continue to be flaunted by processes of conflict and disorganization culminating into struggle for equality.

In addition, with the entry of women into the production process, child-care and education is being transferred from the family to the specially carved out institutions like creche, kinder garten, television and the like (more true for the urban areas), the child is being devoid of (if not devoid of atleast finding a replacement) values of love, affection, sympathy, care for others and so on; values essential for the maintenance of social relations with warmth and generosity. This type of socialization is responsible for the growth of uni-dimensional man for whom community is secondary to individual interest and has ample space for struggle among sexes; thereby adding another base of struggle in a society already driven with conflicts and struggles based on caste, class, religion, and the like. Under such circumstances not only the family but also the society at large will be under threat. Hence, the question of women's empowerment should be visualized in the light of familial and community solidarity.

REFERENCES

Beneria, Lourdes (1979), "Reproduction, Production and Sexual division of labor", *Cambridge Journal of Economics*, vol. 3, no. 3.

Beneria, Lourdes (1982), *Women and Development*, Praeger Publishers, U.S.A.

Blau and Juesenius (1976), "Economists Approach to Sex Segregation in the Labor Market" in Laxall and Reagen (ed.) *Women in Work Place*, University of Chicago Press, Chicago.

Gagote, Sudha (1986), "Feminism and Sociology" in Krishna Raj (ed.) *Women Studies in India*, Popular Prakashan, Bombay.

Gill, M.S. (1996), "Women and Equality" in Upadhayay (ed.) *Women in 21st century*, Harnam Publications, New Delhi.

Kalbagh, Chetna (1991), *Women and Development*, Discovery Publishing House, Bombay.

Khaira, Simranjit (1999), "Women's Empowerment Through Economic Independence" (unpublished) M.A. Thesis, Department of Sociology, Guru Nanak Dev University, Amritsar.

Kumar, Radha (1989), "The Women's Movement", *Seminar,*355.

Mies, Maria (1980), *Indian Women and Patriarchy*, Concept Publishing Company, New Delhi.

Narayan, Usha (1998), "Conditions of Women over the last fifty years", *Mainstream*, Vol. xxxvi.

Oakley, Ann (1974), *House-wife*, Allen Lane, London.

Venkateswaram, S. (1995), *Environment, Development and Gender Gap,* Sage Publication, New Delhi.

SECTION–V

DEVELOPMENT AND ENVIRONMENT

23

DEVELOPMENT, ENVIRONMENT AND SOCIETY

M.S. GILL

Human activities are increasingly depleting the available natural resources and degrading the environment as well. The problem has assumed such a great nuisance that efforts are afoot to revitalize the degraded environment through the active intervention of international bodies such as United Nation Environment Agency, United Nation Development Programme and the like. Environment has also been taken up as an human right issue and many Nations have incorporated this as a Fundamental Right as in India. This paper is an attempt to understand the effect of development on natural resources and the population. It equally endeavour to look into the environment awareness perspective and the role of technology in its sustainability.

Development in the capitalist and Marxist system is based on the theory of growth, material progress and a manipulative view of techno-managerial approach to human welfare. The basic ingredients of development are materialism and technology; measured by Gross National Product of a country. Gradually the experience of development with growth has led to the incorporation of social indicators such as education, health, sanitation and so on. The third world countries added components like 'self-help', 'basic needs', 'minimum need programme' to bridge the widening inequalities among the people and the nations (Sharma, 1986). But development on the whole was and is still identified with physical and economic growth in terms of production, industrial and agricultural growth rates, export of commodities, commissioning of power plants and irrigation projects etc. There is a growing realization that besides dividing the globe into disparate world, the development path has severely impaired the protective system by increasing emission of greenhouse gases, toxic pollutants etc. and the supportive system through erosion of bio-diversity, deforestation, soil, water and air pollution. At the same time the principle of 'growthmanship' has overstrained the natural resource base without relating it to people and nature. This realization came in early seventies when the world experienced its first shock of oil price hike. This has more effect on developing economies like India which was building their industries on commercial energies such as petroleum, electricity, and nuclear power (Kaushik, 1996).

Again, the capitalist development ushered by industrialization is considered as the prime causative factor that has altered the man-nature relationship. The generation of surplus and non-local uses, the crux of industrialization, has eroded the traditional values pertaining to nature which have developed out of close symbiotic interaction of man with nature. These values used to justify nature as supreme that provides protective cover and sustenance to man who is subordinate and dependent. The process of industrialization has altered the whole system and nature now has come to be at the mercy of the former. This has threatened the very survival of the vast section of people, numerous natural species and even the planetary life. According to World Watch, State of the World 2000, the use of earth resources has threatened global environment by raising temperature due to continued use of uncleaned technologies and increasing population pressure on groundwater, cropland, oceans and forests. These are speedily leading to ecological collapse. Bonan holds that human use of land especially clearing of forests for agriculture is an important cause of regional climatic changes (cited from *Down to Earth*, 2001). The intensive and extensive use of natural resources with materialistic approach to life and nature — central to the present model of development — has adverse effect on the poor, the tribal, the forest dwellers, and the women who heavily depend upon them as primary source of their livelihood. It has equally deprived these communities of their age-old habitat and vital subsistence resources. Also, the long run sustainability of the resources is endangered (Kothari, 1996). In real sense, development has to relate itself to the people and communities affected by dams and hydroelectric projects, roads and railways and such other projects. But the situation is otherwise to a great extent. For instance, thermal power plants emanate approximately 500 metric tons of ash everyday and it is usually dumped in ponds, marshy lands and agricultural fields thereby affecting the people surviving on these resources. The super thermal plant at Roopnagar is proving slow poison because of pollution generated from it and other negative consequences; the seepage of slurry from the dykes is creating a water logging problem to a large area (*The Tribune*, 2000). According to UNDP, a large proportion of 20 to 30 million migrants moving to urban areas each year has a big proportion of environmental refugees whose land is so eroded or exhausted that it can no longer sustain them. The pattern of development in India has degraded more than 75 per cent of agricultural land because of soil erosion, water logging and salination and six billion of top soil is lost every year as a result of deforestation, overgrazing etc. (cited from Sheth, 1997). Similarly, the use of chemical fertilizers, toxic as they are, kill the earthworms and other bacteria that convert material on earth to natural nitrogenous and phosphatic manure and thus, prevent earth from regaining fertility in a natural way (Nath, 1996). So as to keep production, consistent application of agro-chemicals becomes the necessity of the cultivators. This shows that eco-material available to man is being used in the name of development without proper care for its sustenance.

Equally the provision of infrastructural inputs may be useful from the viewpoint of a section of the society who want to extract or exercise control over the resources. But it may not be able to enhance the ability or power of the people for equitable share in the resources. Development in the broader sense means enhancing the power and ability of the people to direct their lives in the context of their environment, history and aspiration for the future (Sheth, 1997). It involves enlarged range and quality of choices of lifestyles, of occupations encompassing better health, education, and freedom from oppression and poverty. It has to be eco-friendly and all sectors and strata of society should have access to the use of natural resources in an equitable and sustainable way. The stringent rules of the government quite often do not allow the people to meet their aspirations of sustaining their resources. For example, the people of the drought hit areas especially of Rajasthan, Gujarat, Andhra Pradesh have adopted a novel method of rain harvesting through check dams to meet their water needs. In the case of Orissa, check dam at Goudpali village in Nadtideul of Sambalpur built by the people was not allowed completion by the government (*Down to Earth*, 2001). On the other hand, the Rajasthan government believes that it has a right over every raindrop and makes a move to demolish water harvesting structure set up by local people (*Down to Earth*, 2001). Looking at these one wonders why the notion of equitable and sustainable way of access to natural resources is incorporated in the concept of development.

Secondly, all higher forms of production lead to the division of the population into different classes with different often, antagonistic interests. The interest of the ruling class becomes the driving factor of production; since production no longer restricted to providing the barest means of subsistence for the oppressed people (Engels, 1972) rather to meet the production and consumption demands of the dominant class and subsistence of the dominated sufficient to ensure surpluses. They pay little attention to natural or social effect of the surpluses. Their concern is with profit and generation of surplus; even their concern for the commodity and its purchasers is guided by their limited interest. For instance, in Cuba forests were burnt down on the slopes of the mountains to obtain sufficient fertilizers for one generation very high profitable coffee trees. The tropical rainfall afterward washed away the unprotected upper stream of the soil leaving behind bare rock thus affecting the subsistence of the people dependent upon these. Further, a large irrigation project in Madhya Pradesh which was originally expected to increase crop production by atleast ten fold has led to extensive water logging thereby reducing corn and wheat fields. Farmers there now refer to their once fertile fields as 'wet deserts' (Sandra, 1985). Likewise in Rayagada district of Orissa — home of Paroja Kondha tribe — the private mining companies have got mining right to extract bauxite which would eventually dry up around 700 streams and chew up forests, the lifeline of the district's 85 per cent tribal population (*Down to Earth*, 2001). The United States responsible for 24 per cent of the global green house gases emission refuses to take domestic measures till developing countries also do the same. Such examples explain the neglect of the interest of the poor disadvantageous groups or states.

Also the main cause of environmental destruction in the world is the demand for natural resources generated for the consumption of the rich: whether they are rich nations or rich individuals or groups within the nation. The Prime Minister of Malaysia has stated at the Earth Summit 1992 that the high per capita consumption in developed countries place a far heavier burden on the environment than that in the developing countries. In this regard, per capita the US residents consume 33 times more aluminum, 183 times more natural gas, and 385 times more pulp-wood than the Indians. Likewise the rich are spending much higher on electrical equipment, motor vehicles, and scooters (Sheth, 1997). Even among the developed nations there is a difference in the environmental pollution caused by their populace. The Australian Institute analysis reports that average Australian green house gases (GHG) emissions are

30 per cent higher than those of the US citizens. An Australian is responsible for 27.6 tons of GHG emitted against one ton by an Indian (*Down to Earth*, 2001). This discerns that materialistic culture and consumeristic lifestyle developed by economically advanced countries and being imitated by the developing ones have precipitated the degradation of land and forests and overuse of water, energy, and other resources.

Moreover, the factories and farms to have more production are overusing at least 40 per cent more of water thereby putting a pressure on the available water. The extensive irrigation projects to tap water resource for meeting the consumption need of the factories and farms have created problem of floods, recharge of ground acquifers in addition to changing the courses of rivers and streams. With the adoption of wheat-rice rotation under green revolution areas has encouraged canal irrigation and excessive use of ground water for irrigation. Punjab which produce 60 per cent of wheat and 40 per cent of rice of the central pool finds water table falling at a rate of 25 to 30 cm a year. The State of World Report, 1998 published by Worldwatch Institute, says the gap between water use and sustainable yield of the acquirer is so high that the acquifer under Punjab could be depleted by the year 2025 (Mahapatra, 1999). In addition, the use of canal irrigation without proper arrangement of drainage is resulting in soils become alkaline or saline (Nadkarni, 1987). Cultivators of Abohar, Fazilka, Ferozpur and adjoining areas acutely feel these problems. At the same time the problem of water logging in these canal irrigated areas is an example of misuse of precious water resource.

With emergence of irrigation projects, changing course of rivers, submission of forests, and falling water table, the problems of the poor, the tribal, the women and the children have increased who face increasing difficulty in gleaning fuel wood, finding fodder, and fetching water. In the process, state too supports the dominant ones to earn revenue and profits. With respect to the newly carved out states of Jharkhand, Uttaranchal and Chattisgarh in India, Aggarwal (2001) holds that Government of India loves to talk about poverty but usually serve the interests of contractors and companies which exploit and destroy rich natural resource base of the poor, *i.e.* forests and bio-diversity in particular. Even the changed crop rotation pattern to achieve high productivity in cereal crops in Punjab to feed increasing masses has excluded oil seeds, pulses, vegetables and the like, thereby the poor masses are deprived of their cheap vegetable protein (Bhullar, 1990).

Equally in the name of national interest, the poor people are asked to support the big projects such as Sardar Sarover, Congentrix, Tehri Dam and others which in reality serve the purpose of the few well-off resourced agriculturists, industrialists and the like; depriving at the same time others of the traditional access to land, forests and water. Nevertheless, in the long run all are going to face the problem of ecological imbalance created in the name of development. So, development as well as ecological destruction disproportionately affects the poor and the rich and in this regard, environmental degradation and social justice are two sides of the same coin.

Not that the poor and tribal are robed of their resources with all logic of ameliorating their conditions, these people lack environmental and ecological awareness as do the rich. Among such people, there is awareness that their subsistence system has greater community control and helps in positive interaction with nature, but lack of knowledge about ecological consequences. The question that arises: is there disjuncture between perception regarding availability of natural resources and comprehension of ecological damage? The struggle of traditional artisan fisher people against mechanized fishing vessels, local people's movement against hydro-electric dam in Kerala and other parts of the country, Chipko movement against felling of trees and so on were initially directed towards their very survival as their livelihood was threatened. The ecological dimension which was not immediately perceived was added later on as the mechanized fishing will destroy fish breeding grounds, will destroy rich bio-diversity of the catchment areas on which their subsistence depends, will threaten the fragile ecosystem and so on. The ecological consciousness is also observed among the owners of electroplating units operating in Ludhiana city of Punjab. The owners are adopting housekeeping method to control pollution. In their view, it controls 80 per cent of water pollution and helps reuse of collected nickel and different acids (*The Tribune*, 2001). This consciousness arises out of becoming aware of their polluted ground water and dangerous effect of the chemicals on the health of the people and the workers. Examples like this indicate that ecological awareness is limited to immediate environment of the community and governed by the relation with natural resources within it. Further, the poor have little ability to desist from using the subsistence natural produce —fuel, fodder, fibre etc. —rather wisely or with restrain.

Under such circumstances, the natural resources get neglected both in the hands of the rich and the poor. In the process, the degradation may reach an irreversible stage where the crisis of the economy and the society at large may emerge. According to Shiva (1991, 342), "the neglect of the role of natural resources in ecological processes and its people's sustenance economy, the division and destruction of these resources for community production and capital accumulation, are the main reasons for the ecological crisis and the crisis of survival in the Third World." This prediction can be true for the world if the process of degradation continues.

Further, the sustainability of society requires decision on technologies taking into account environmental constraints. Technical solution to specific problems can be actualized through research but the global and long term solutions to environmental problems require concomitant support from all quarters of society including developed and developing countries. So far, there are no clear scientific criteria that mutually commensurate development and environment. Kyoto proclamation on greenhouse gases emission is one such example. In spite of this, progress towards sustainability demands measures and comparisons of the ecological price of the commodity production in addition to social and ethical ramifications. National and even international bodies usually refrain from explicit normative statements and the social and ecological price involved because of lack of political judgement or their being at variance with other considerations. Partial enforcement of Kyoto proclamation at international level and controversy over Narmada Valley project, use of banned agro-chemicals like endosulfan, phorates and many others are such issues that require technological inputs with environmental consideration. At the same time it is felt that do environmental friendly technologies have all the answer to this malice. For instance if a country shifts from coal energy to wind power, the demand for energy for air-conditioners, dishwashers, geysers and freezers continue to grow unabated. It means that farms will be replaced by windmills thereby making the poor peasants to die without work and food.

In these conditions, how to direct the process of development? The development supported by science and technology has strengthened the survival of man on the earth besides improving his quality of life. So blaming science and technology for all ills do not hold well. In reality, the growing environmental awareness is itself the outcome of increased scientific knowledge. Even the success of people's struggle for the maintenance and management of their eco-system owes it to the active intervention of the scientists abreast with the consequences of ecological degradation and mismanagement. Rejecting science and technology for all malice on the earth may pose a serious problem in the context of the struggle for ecological and implicit social reality to overthrow the existing social formation. The answer lies in strengthening the scientific knowledge to evolve socially rational and appropriate technologies. Such technologies instead of stripping the traditional knowledge base, developed under natural process of man-nature interaction, should fall in with it and let local communities manage their eco-material on this blended knowledge. The success stories of harvesting rain water to meet drought in Andhara Pradesh with the fusion of traditional and modern scientific knowledge (*Down to Earth*, 2000) should be the encouraging point for the modern civil society.

Conclusion

The problem of development has ecological consequences is understandable but their role in generating inequalities and widening the gap between 'have' and 'have-nots' is not given adequate attention. The analysis reveals that the dominant and affluent sections of the society/ nations indiscriminately use the natural eco-material with/without realization that it will overtake and engulf them as well. It is important to quote Marx who once said that the oppressor oppresses himself in the process of oppressing others (cited from Jhunjhunwala, 2000). To avoid such 'no return' situation, the affluent societies or section of the society should redefine their interests and limits within a broader environmental perspective. In other words, to have sustainable development structural adjustments in the organization of the society is required which demands altering the relationship of dominance and subordination. It requires economic transformation without jeopardizing the interests of different groups within the society that of the poor, the tribal, and the women. It requires realization on the part of the rich that another underprivileged and underdeveloped section exists whose survival depends upon the ideology of 'sharing the resources' and 'not me but you' rather than appropriating the resources and limiting to self-interest. It requires decisions on sustainable agriculture that takes into account both food and non-food crops with genetic diversities and negative repercussion that their inputs produce on society at large. This realization will provide a base for judicious handling of eco-materials on which culture and civilization has developed.

The reckless advancement in the field of science and technology without relating it to traditional knowledge may not be conducive for establishing symbiotic man-nature relationship. The study provides that new scientific development takes along with it the traditional knowledge for strengthening the eco-base of the society. Gill and Singh (2000) too, conclude that the symbiotic man-nature relationship can be established and strengthened through the use of common man's knowledge and skills whose roots lie in strong familial and community ties. Such attempt will repose the faith of the underprivileged and underdeveloped communities that scientific advances are not against their interests rather strengthen their subsistence system.

REFERENCES

Aggarwal, Anil (2001), "Ecological Poverty", *Down to Earth*, Vol. 9, No. 16, Jan.16.

Bhullar, N.S. (1990), "Development Strategy for the Nineties", *The Economic Times*, May 10.

Engels, F. (1972), *Dialectics of Nature*, Progress Publishers, Moscow.

Gill, M.S. & Singh A.M. (2000), "Sustainable Society: Social and Cultural Issues", Proceedings of the Fourth International Conference on Eco-Balance held at Japan from Oct. 31 to Nov. 2.

Jhunjhunwala, B. (2000), "Environmental Half Truth", *The Tribune*, March 30.

Kaushik, K.K. (1996), "Agricultural Policy in the light of New Economic Policy", in *Agriculture, Rural Development and Panchayati Raj* (ed.) V.S. Mahajan, Deep and Deep Publications, New Delhi.

Kothari, Smitu, (1996), "Whose Nation, the displaced victims of development", *Economic and Political Weekly*, Jan. 15.

Kumar, A. (2000), "Receding Water Level", *The Dainik Jagran*, Dec. 26.

Kumar, Maroj (2001), "Electroplating Units Pollute Ludhiana", *The Tribune*, Jan. 29.

Mahapatra, R. (1999), "Punjab Facing Ground Water Crisis", *The Tribune*, Oct. 28.

Nadkarni, M.V. (1987), "Agricultural Development and Ecology: An Economist View", *Indian Journal of Agricultural Economics*, Vol. 42, No. 3.

Nath, K.P. (1996), "Environmental Issues in Indian Agricultural Development", in *Agriculture, Rural Development and Panchayati Raj* (ed.) Mahajan, Deep and Deep Publications, New Delhi.

Panda, R.and B. Das (2001), "Action Reaction", *Down to Earth*, Vol. 10, Vo. 8, Sept. 30.

Prasad, E. and B. Das (2000), "Tryst with Rain", *Down to Earth*, Vol. 9, No. 1, Oct. 31.

Sharma, S.L. (1986), *Development; Socio-Cultural Issues*, Rawat Publishers, Jaipur.

Sheth, Pravin (1997), *Environmentalism*, Rawat Publishers, Jaipur.

Shiva, V. (1991), *Ecology and Politics of Survival*, Sage Publications, New Delhi.

Shiva, V. (2001). "Who owns the river?", *Down to Earth*, Vol. 10, No. 4, July 31.

Singh, P.P. (2000), "Thermal Plants Pollution hits 30 villages", *The Tribune*, Sept. 29,

Society for Environmental Communication (2000), "The South", *Down to Earth*, Vol. 9, No. 13, Nov. 30.

Society for Environmental Communication (2001), "Worst Polluters", *Down to Earth*, Vol. 10, No. 10, Oct. 15.

24

PESTICIDES, ENVIRONMENT AND SOCIETY
Issues and Options

BALWINDER SINGH & G.S. DHALIWAL

The present world population of 6 billion is likely to cross 8 billion mark by 2025 and about 90 per cent of this increase would occur in developing countries. Therefore, the provision of adequate food and environmental security would remain the key issues confronting mankind in the third millennium. There are limits to the expansion of land area under cultivation, hence, most of the gains in agricultural production would come from increased productivity (Dhaliwal *et al.*, 1999).

India has achieved a major breakthrough in agricultural production. The production of food grains has increased from 72.3 million tons in 1965-66 to 206 million tonnes in 1999-2000. The state of Punjab, often called the granery of India has played an important role in achieving self-sufficiency in food grains. The state contributes about 21 per cent to India's wheat and 9 per cent to paddy and 21 per cent to cotton production. In fact, the state is confronted with a problem of plenty at the turn of the century (Jai Singh, 2000).

Pesticides have made a great impact on human health, production and preservation of food, fibre and other cash crops by controlling disease vectors and by keeping in check many species of unwanted insects and plants. Although, various methods are used to control pests in different pest management systems, pesticides continue to be the major component of most of the pest control programmes and will probably remain so during the near future.

Pesticide Consumption

There has been tremendous increase in consumption of fertilisers and pesticides. The per hectare consumption of fertilisers in India increased from 1.9 kg in 1960-61 to 90.0 kg in 1998-99. However, in Punjab per hectare use of fertilisers has increased from 1.06 kg in 1960-61 to 177.41 kg in 1998-99, which is the highest among all the states in the country. The total amount of pesticides used in India increased from 154 metric tonnes in 1953-54 to 84,000 metric tonnes in 1993-94. Thereafter, the consumption of pesticides has declined due to the ban/restriction on the use of DDT/HCH and availability of low dosages pesticides. During 1999-2000, the total consumption of pesticides in India was 54135 metric tonnes, i.e. 288g/ha (Agnihotri, 2000). At present, the intensity of pesticide use is the highest in Punjab (923 g/ha) as compared to other agriculturally advanced states like Haryana (843), Tamil Nadu (410), Andhra Pradesh (548), Gujarat (447) and Karnataka (216) (Table 24.1). Cotton accounts for the highest consumption of pesticides at the state as well as at the national level (Agnihotri, 2000). However, the consumption of pesticide continues to rise in Punjab (Table 24.2). There has been a marginal decline in insecticide consumption which has been more than off-set by the increase in the use of herbicides.

The insecticides have played a major role in increasing cotton productivity, mainly due to the various constraints in the adoption of cultural practices, non-availability of resistant varieties with good potential and lack of efficient biocontrol agents. The exploitation of insecticides further increased with the release of high yielding varieties, which were more susceptible to insect pests. As a result, the cotton crop is grown under the insecticide umbrella. The cost of insecticides as a percentage of cost of cotton cultivation has increased from 2.1 per cent in 1974-75 to nearby 13 per cent in 1994-95 in the state (Table 24.3).

Environmental Impact of Pesticides

The excessive and indiscriminate use of pesticides has led to new pest problems and development of resistance in insect pests and weeds to pesticides. Moreover, pesticides have entered into the food chain and contaminated all components of the environment. Some of these issues have been highlighted in the present paper.

Table 24.1: Trends in pesticide consumption in selected states in India

Sl.No.	*State*	*Metric tonnes technical grade*							*g/ha*
		1993-94	*1994-95*	*1995-96*	*1996-97*	*1997-98*	*1998-99*	*1999-2000*	
1.	Andhra Pradesh	14500	13000	12775	12100	9000	9000	7000	548
2.	Arunachal Pradesh	41	42	40	10	19	18	19	75
3.	Assam	650	630	525	350	290	280	260	68
4.	Gujarat	5300	5100	5250	5179	5291	5036	5000	447
5.	Haryana	5200	5250	5300	5050	5045	5035	5030	843
6.	Karnataka	4450	4400	4000	3600	3000	3000	2600	216
7.	Kerala	720	700	1167	1469	940	1228	1168	383
8.	Madhya Pradesh	3779	2757	2947	1878	1517	1410	1299	53
9.	Maharashtra	6770	6900	4898	6146	5625	3898	3942	184
10.	Orissa	1400	1700	1401	1293	994	961	1006	103
11.	Punjab	6300	6450	7600	7300	7300	7300	7100	923
12.	Rajasthan	3600	3900	3500	3500	3325	3350	300	162
13.	Tamil Nadu	10500	9500	4000	3232	2929	2950	2882	410
14.	Uttar Pradesh	11000	11000	11500	8000	7800	7600	7400	288
15.	West Bengal	6084	5823	5338	5200	5025	4521	4626	531

Table 24.2: Consumption of pesticides (M.T. technical grade) in Punjab during 1998-99 and 1999-2000

Pesticide Group	*1998-99*			*1999-2000*		
	Kharif	Rabi	Total	Kharif	Rabi	Total
Insecticides	2629	639	3268	2605	532	3137
Fungicides	256	234	490	257	253	510
Herbicides	1525	1427	2952	1810	1515	3325
Total	4410	2300	6710	4672	2300	6972

Table 24.3: Cost of cultivation and value of insecticides used on cotton crop in Punjab

Year	*Cost of cultivation (Rs./ha)*	*Cost of insecticides*	
		Value (Rs./ha)	*As percentage of cost of cultivation*
1974-75	1394.80	30.42	2.1
1979-80	1531.82	70.17	4.6
1984-85	2642.93	314.67	11.9
1989-90	4199.37	651.91	15.5
1994-95	17311.03	2243.19	13.0

Pesticide Resistance

Large-scale use of pesticides to control pests has resulted in the development of resistance (Table 24.4). The American bollworm, *Helicoverpa armigera* (Hubner) has attained the status of key pest. It has developed resistance to all the major groups of conventional insecticides. A 12-fold resistance to cypermethrin has been reported in the populations collected from Ludhiana. Low level of resistance to chlorpyrihos has also been observed in some populations. The reduction in field efficacy of dimethoate, oxydemeton methyl and phosphamidon has also been observed. High frequencies of insecticide resistance to cypermethrin, fenvalerate, quinalphos and endosulfan have been reported from Mansa. The cotton whitefly, *Bemisia tabaci* (Gennadius) has developed resistance or even cross-resistance to insecticides like dimethoate, oxydemeton methyl and phosphamidon. Among the vegetable pests, *Plutella xylostella* has developed multiple resistance to nearly all the commonly used insecticides. High levels of resistance to synthetic pyrethroids have been reported at three locations in Punjab, namely Amritsar, Jalandhar and Mansa. Resistance to cypermethrin was 2880-fold at Amritsar, 2150-fold at Jalandhar and 2133-fold at Mansa whereas to fenvalerate it was 1770, 2100 and 2700-fold at Amritsar, Jalandhar and Mansa, respectively. Resistance to several organophosphate and organopchlorine insecticides has been reported in the mustard aphid, *Lipaphis erysimi* (Kaltonbach). More than 100-fold resistance was recorded in case of endosulfan and phosphamidon; lower levels of resistance to malathion, parathion and dimethoate were also reported in aphid population from different areas of the state. Another aphid species, *Myzus persicae* (Sulzer) has also been reported developed resistance to several insecticides including endosulfan, malathion and dimethoate (Dhaliwal and Singh, 2001).

Table 24.4: Insecticide resistance and insecticide-induced resurgence of insect pests

Insect pests	*Insecticide*	*Resistance factor*
A. Insecticide resistance		
Bemisia tabaci	Oxydemeton methyl	High
	Dimethoate	High
	Phosphamidon	High
	Cypermethrin	High
	Chlorpyriphos	High
	Monocrotophos	Moderate
	Quinalphos	Moderate
	Deltamethrin	Moderate
Helicoverpa armigera	Cypermethrin	High
	Chlorpyriphos	Low
Plutella xylostella	All groups of insecticides	High
B. Insecticide-induced resurgence		
Bemisia tabaci	Cypermethrin	High
	Fenvalerate	
	Deltamethrin	
	Acephate	
	Monocrotophos	
Amrasca biguttula	Chlorpyriphos	High
	Quinalphos	

Insecticide-Induced Resurgence

The indiscriminate use of synthetic pyrethroids like deltamethrin, cypermethrin and fenvalerate has led to resurgence of whitefly and aphid (Table 24.4). The excessive use of quinalphos and chlorpyriphos also resulted in resurgence of cotton jassid during flowering phase. The overall increase in jassid population in north zone is due to the extensive use of both these insecticides for management of the *H. armigera*. The use of phytotonic insecticides like acephate and monocrotophos after mid-September also resulted in whitefly resurgence (Dhawan *et al.*, 2000).

Pesticide Poisoning

Almost all the pesticides are inherently poisonous. It has been estimated that more than one million poisoning cases occur in the world annually with about 15,000 deaths. India accounts for one-third of the total pesticide poisoning cases in the world. Cases of blindness, cancer, diseases of liver and nervous system from pesticide poisoning have been identified in cotton growing areas of Maharashtra and Andhra Pradesh.

A comparative analysis of 1995 data for Punjab shows that poisoning appears to be the most convenient means of suicide. In Punjab, among all the cases of suicide 58 per cent have been reported to be committed by consuming pesticides. This is revealing as it shows the impact of green revolution on the mode of suicide in the state. Aluminium phosphide is most effective fumigant for protecting food grains during storage. A survey conducted by All India Institute of Medical Sciences, New Delhi in 1988 shows that there are widespread cases of aluminium phosphide poisoning in North India. The use of pesticides is rapidly becoming a serious health hazard in Punjab villages. There are cases where accidental deaths of some farm labourers were reported (Dhaliwal and Arora, 2001).

Environmental Contamination

During the last 4-5 decades, organic pesticides have become increasingly important in controlling pests of crops, animals and man. These chemicals have greatly increased agricultural yields and saved millions of lives from insect-borne diseases. Unfortunately, their unscrupulous use has resulted in the pollution of the environment. The main reasons for environmental pollution and serious ecological problems with pesticides are:

- Pesticides are biological poisons.
- Large quantities are applied to the ecosystem.
- Poor application technology is used which results in large amounts of pesticides being widely spread in non-target areas.
- Little pesticide (<1%) ever hits the target pests.

Pesticides persist in the environment for periods longer than required or intended.

A brief account of pesticide residues in various components of the environment, with special reference to Punjab scenario, is given here.

Soil

A large proportion of pesticides, when applied reach the soil, which acts as a reservoir for these chemicals. Studies conducted at PAU in 1976-77 on pesticide residues in soil revealed the presence of mainly DDT followed by HCH, lindane, methyl parathion, phorate etc. The highest mean level of 0.08 mg/kg of DDT residues was found in cotton growing areas, which was more than four times the mean level of 0.017 mg/kg for the Punjab soils. This may be ascribed to the then recommended use of DDT on cotton for pest control (Kalra and Chawla, 1983). But after the imposition of ban on DDT and HCH in agriculture, the residues of these insecticides started declining and the latest survey done to study the residues of insecticides in soil reveals the absence of these insecticides at the detection limit of 0.01 mg/kg (ppm).

Food Commodities

Pesticide residues in food are often a matter of major concern to the public. Nevertheless, it is very difficult to produce crops that contain no insecticide residues without serious losses due to pests. Domestic animals are also continuously exposed when they eat insecticide contaminated feed. This results in the contamination of milk and meat. Studies, conducted at PAU reveal that residues of various insecticides in different food and feed commodities.

Milk and Milk Products

Bovine milk and its products, because of their special significance in human diet, have been extensively monitored for DDT and HCH residues. During 1976-80, detectable amounts of DDT residues were found in all the 215 samples of milk collected from different locations of Punjab (Table 24.5). Out of these, 174 samples (81%) exceeded the prescribed maximum residue limit (MRL) of 1.25 mg/kg Apart from DDT, HCH residues were also found to be predominant contaminant of bovine milk in Punjab. Though at that time, no limit was prescribed for HCH in milk, its residues in a number of samples seemed quite excessive (Kalra and Chawla, 1983). During 1984-89, the analysis of 142 samples of milk also revealed 100 per cent contamination with 70 and 48 per cent milk samples exceeding the MRL limits for DDT and HCH residues, respectively.

However, the analysis of 263 samples during 1988-93 revealed that only 50 per cent samples exceeded the MRL of DDT while HCH residues exceeded in 55 per cent samples (ICMR, 1993). After the ban on the use of DDT and HCH, the residues of these insecticides have started showing decline as is evident from 24 samples analysed during 1999-2000, that only two samples showed the presence of DDT residues at the detection limit of 0.01 $mgkg^{-1}$ while in case of HCH only lindane (χ-isomer of HCH) residues were found to be present in 23 samples and that too above the prescribed MRL of 0.01 $mgkg^{-1}$. However, these levels were calculated to be below the theoretical daily intake (TDI) of 480 μg/day for a 60 kg person.

Table 24.5: Pesticide contamination of bovine milk in Punjab

Year	*No. of samples analysed*	*No. of samples contaminated*	*Nature of residues*	*Range of residues(ppm)*	*No. of samples above MRL*
1976	215	215	DDT	0.02-0.044	174
		215	HCH	0.006-0.91	75
1985-86	142	142	DDT	0.01-2.99	99
		142	HCH	Tr.0.301	69
1989-93	263	257	DDT	ND-0.37	133
		236	HCH	ND-0.65	145
1999-2000	24	2	DDT	Tr.0.01	Nil
		23	HCH (only lindane)	0.09-1.046	23

The problem of contamination of dairy products with pesticide residues in India was studied by Kalra *et al.* (1979) by analysing popular brands of butter and found most of the samples to be contaminated with DDT residues above the MRL of 1.25 mg/kg. However, later studies conducted in 1984-89 revealed that only 57 and 47 per cent samples of butter exceeded the MRL of DDT and HCH, respectively (Table 24.6).

Table 24.6: Residues of DDT and HCH in butter in Punjab

Year	*No. of samples analysed*	*No. of samples contaminated*	*Insecticides detected*	*Range (ppm)*
1983	120	120	DDT	0.32-12.35
			HCH	0.22-6.39
1989	95	95	DDT	0.11-9.80
			HCH	0.05-7.63

Cereals and Pulses

The studies conducted at PAU showed the presence of DDT and HCH residues in almost all the 140 samples of wheat flour collected from different cities in Punjab. Eighty-six out of 140 samples contained DDT residues above the MRL of 0.1 mg/kg. However, during 1989, only one out of 30 samples collected was found to be contaminated with DDT residues above the MRL. The analysis of 99 samples of rice grain reveals that only 9 per cent samples exceeded the MRL (Table 24.7). Thus, with time there has been a considerable decline in the contamination of cereals as its use in agriculture has been banned and for malaria control it has been restricted.

Table 24.7: Pesticide contamination of different food and feed commodities in Punjab

Commodity	*Year*	*No. of samples analysed*	*No. of samples contaminated*	*Nature of residues*	*Range of residues (ppm)*	*No. of samples above MRL*
Cereals	1984-85	30	30	DDT	Tr-0.58	1
		30	30	HCH	Tr-1.60	Nil
Rice grain	1990-98	99	19	DDT	Tr-0.27	Nil
			99	HCH	Tr-0.32	9
Vegetables	1990-98	96	24	DDT	Tr-0.29	Nil
			49	HCH	Tr-0.10	Nil
			64	Commonly used OP's	0.01-0.46	7
Animal feed	1984-89	15	15	DDT	0.05-0.33	MRL not prescribed
			15	HCH	0.02-0.26	-do-
Animal feed and fodder	1990-91	105	85	DDT	0.002-6.703	-do-
			105	HCH	0.004-2.281	-do-

Vegetables

The residues of DDT and HCH were found to be invariably present in vegetables when these insecticides were widely used in agriculture and public health. However, recent analysis of 96 samples of vegetables collected directly from farms revealed that contamination scenario with these insecticides has considerably been changed as none of the samples was found to contain residues of these insecticides above the MRL. However, 7 samples were found to contain residues of some commonly used organo phosphorous insecticides like monocrotophos, quinalphos, triazophos, etc. above their prescribed MRL's (Table 24.7).

Human Milk

Mother's milk is the primary food for an infant. All the 130 samples of mother's milk collected from the Punjab during 1979-80 were found to be contaminated with the residues of DDT and HCH at levels far more than those reported from most other countries in the world (Kalra and Chawla, 1983). The contamination scenario was almost the same during 1988-89 when the analysis of 122 samples also revealed the residues of these insecticides at almost the same levels (Joia and Battu, 2000). However, the samples analysed during 1999-2000 project show quite a safer picture with significant low levels of residues of these insecticides (Table 24.8).

Table 24.8: Mean DDT and HCH residues (ppm) in human milk in Punjab and other countries

Country	*No. of samples analysed*	*DDT*	*HCH*
India (Punjab) 1979-80	129	0.52 (0.03-2.35)	0.18 (0.01-0.82)
India (Punjab) 1988-89	121	0.55 (0.03-0.30)	0.26 (0.02-4.25)
India (Punjab) 1999-2000	22	0.07 (0.024-0.25)	0.13 (0.06-0.38)
Canada 1975	–	0.024	0.001
Japan 1971-75	–	0.05-0.07	0.05-0.07
Sweden 1971-75	–	0.07-0.08	0.08-0.10
Switzerland 1973	–	0.07	0.001
USA 1971-74	–	0.09-0.20	0.02

Animal Feed

The contamination of animal products such as milk, eggs and meat with DDT and HCH results mainly from the intake of feed contaminated with these insecticides. The analysis of various feed and fodder samples revealed the presence of both DDT and HCH residues. The highest levels of DDT and HCH in wheat straw were found to be 1.48 and 6.6 mg/kg respectively. Since these insecticides were not recommended for direct use on crops, their residues may, therefore, result from their usage in malaria control programme (Kalra & Chawla, 1983). However, the recent studies show the presence of these insecticides at comparatively low levels. Still, the occurrence of these insecticides in various types of feed and fodder needs thorough investigations so as to identify the sources of contamination.

Dietary Intake

Commodity surveys are sometimes considered inadequate in providing realistic estimates of dietary intake of pesticide residues. The need for measuring the actual intake of pesticides through totaldiet studies has been felt. The results of the total diet studies by Singh (1982) showed that the mean levels of dietary intake of DDT and HCH residues were 238 and 224 μg/person/day from the vegetarian and non-vegetarian diets, respectively. The corresponding levels of HCH residues were 124 and 133 μg/person/day. However, the studies conducted in 1999 revealed the much lower intake of residues of these insecticides. The intake of DDT residues through vegetarian and non-vegetarian diets was calculated to be 6.2 and 3.0 μg/person/day, respectively, while for HCH, the corresponding values were found to be 5.90 and 6.20 μg/person/day (Table 24.9). These values have been found to be much lower than the acceptable daily intake (ADI) of 300 μg/person/day for a man weighing 60 kg. This declining dietary intake of these persistent pesticides can be attributed to be restrictions imposed on the use of these chemicals in India.

The problem of the pesticides contamination of food faced by a country would depend upon the consumption, nature and pattern of usage of pesticides and the effectiveness of the regulatory or other methods being followed for their control. The problem pesticides should yield place to safer and more effective pesticides. The decisions on the use of pesticides must be made by considering certainty and uncertainty of benefits and risks, as well as allowable alternatives.

Table 24.9: Average dietary intake of DDT and HCH residues in various countries (μg/person/day)

Country	*DDT*	*HCH*
Australia	20.0	–
Canada	10.8	2.5
Italy	35.4	16.7
USA	6.5	1.1
India-1982		
Vegetarian	238.1	124.4
Non-vegetarian	224.1	133.2
India-1999		
Vegetarian	6.2	59.0
Non-vegetarian	3.0	62.0

Pesticides and Social Problems

The unrecommended and overuse of pesticides has led to many problems which directly or indirectly affect man and his environment. These pesticides have innate capacity to cause injury to all living organisms as well as to the quality of our environment. There is a constant fear that society is being slowly poisoned by the intake of food contaminated with pesticides. The presence of residues of these pesticides in food commodities and other components of the environment has proved toxic to humans, domestic animals, birds, fishes and non-target fauna of agro-ecosystems. In addition to these side effects, the insect pest problems in many crops have aggravated following continuous application of pesticides. This, in turn, has further increased the consumption of pesticides resulting in the phenomenon of pesticide treadmill.

Economics of Pesticide Use

Taking the example of cotton in Punjab, the cost of insecticides as percentage of the total cost of cultivation of the crop increased from 2.1 per cent in 1974-75 to 13.0 per cent in 1994-95. While the cost of cultivation has increased more than twelve times between 1974-75 and 1994-95, the cost of insecticides use has multiplied over 73-fold during this period. In spite of phenomenal increase in the cost of plant protection chemicals, the losses due to insect pests have been increasing steadily. All these environmental problems caused by the pesticides need to be taken into account for making critical appraisal of their role in agriculture.

Although real full estimates of damage caused by pesticides are not available, it has been reported that every rupee worth of pesticide used has caused an estimated 5-10 rupees worth of damage to environment and public health alone.

Pesticides and Human Health

The unregulated use of pesticides is very detrimental to the human health. The Natural Resource Defence Council (NRDC) of USA reported that one of every 3400 children between 1 and 5 years of age could one day get cancer because of the pesticides they ate as young children (NRDC, 1989). If pesticides could cause so much damage to child health in the country which imposes the most stringent regulations on their use, the extent of damage in developing countries like India where the pesticides use is more or less unregulated, can be well imagined.

In fact, cases of blindness, cancer, diseases of liver and nervous system from pesticide poisoning have been identified in cotton growing areas of Maharashtra and Andhra Pradesh. Even occupational workers regularly involved in spraying operations revealed high incidence of psychological symptoms like anxiety, sleep disturbance, depression and severe headache. Cases of pesticide poisoning are also not uncommon from cotton growing areas of Punjab, Haryana, Andhra Pradesh and Maharashtra.

Awareness Among Farmers

Pesticides are poisonous chemicals and the farmers lack the knowledge of their proper use. The selection of right pesticide and its application at the recommended dosage are vital for timely control of pests (Singh *et al.*, 1997). The surveys conducted in cotton growing areas of Punjab have revealed that the farmers usually purchased pesticides from the commission agents on loan. Failure to repay the loan and suffer heavy losses due to pest outbreaks, many farmers have been reported to commit suicide by consuming one or the other pesticide. The agents advise the farmers to purchase unrecommended pesticides to promote their sales, use them at lower dosages or at a longer interval to reduce the cost of application. It was found that only 11 per cent of the sprays on cotton were correctly directed against the bollworms with right insecticides. In 28 per cent of the cases, farmers used insecticides which were not effective against bollworms, and 61 per cent of the sprays were carried out with recommended insecticides but at low concentrations (Atwal, 1986).

A subsequent study (Sidhu *et al.*, 1994) also revealed that 81.25 per cent of the farmers purchased pesticides on credit, mostly from the commission agents of the grain markets. Most of the farmers (80.41%) used various types of insecticidal mixtures for bollworm control against the PAU recommendations. Some of the synthetic pyrethroids like fenvalerate which were available at cheaper rate were used in higher than the recommended dosages whereas lower dosages were used in case of non-pyrethroid insecticides which were costly. Only 3.13 per cent of the farmers followed the PAU recommended schedule of sprays. The recommended spray interval was followed by only 29.90 per cent of the cotton growers.

According to their findings of yet another study (Mangat *et al.*, 1998), 60.67 per cent of the farmers applied the recommended number of sprays for the control of cotton pests as per the calendar based spray schedule (Table 24.10). About one-third of the farmers applied excessive sprays and the remaining 6.0 per cent less than the recommended number of sprays. As regards the dosages of insecticides used, only about one-third of the farmers applied the recommended dosages. Synthetic pyrethroids were mostly applied at higher dosages and organophosphate and carbamate insecticides at lower than the recommended dosages. In general, cheaper insecticides like fenvalerate and cypermethrin were used at higher than the recommended dosages while costlier insecticides like chlorpyriphos, carbaryl and deltamethrin were used at sub-optimum dosages.

Table 24.10: Adoption pattern of pesticides use for management of insect pests of cotton

Parameter	*Adoption pattern (%)*		
	Recommended	*Lower*	*Higher*
Number of sprays	60.7	6.01	33.3
Insecticide dosage			
Synthetic pyrethroids	32.1	13.5	54.5
Carbamates	33.3	66.7	0
Organophosphates	33.1	62.8	0
Organochlorines	70.0	28.0	2.0

Thus, there is an urgent need to educate the farmers regarding the efficient and judicious use of pesticides so that they can get maximum returns from the benefits of these chemicals and social as well as health risks associated with the use of pesticides can be minimised.

Future of Pesticides

Pesticides will continue to play an important role in integrated pest management programmes. But their use must be made compatible with other components of pest management. Therefore, development of selective pesticides favouring arthropod natural enemies is presently receiving more attention from the chemical industry due to environmental impacts of pesticide misuse. Additional research efforts are needed to obtain safer pesticides for the future. There is an urgent need to determine environmentally based economic threshold values for all the important insect pests in different agroclimatic conditions. The efficacy of existing pesticides can be enhanced by developing more efficient formulations. Systemic insecticides applied as granules, seed dressings, root zone application, stem injection and leaf-axil application avoid damage to natural enemies moving on the plant surface. Ecological selectivity can be accomplished through judicious use of pesticides based on critical selection, timing, dosage, placement and formulation of pesticides.

Sublethal concentrations of a number of insecticides along with respective nuclear polyhedrosis viruses have been found highly effective for the control of a number of important pests (Battu *et al.*, 1993). Fenvalerate, endosulfan and chlorpyriphos at one-third of the recommended dosages when combined with entomopathogenic fungi *Beauveria bassiana* (Balsamo), Vuillemin were found to be quite effective against *Spilosoma oblique* Walker (Patel and Kanaujia, 1998).

Many botanical pesticides have been extensively evaluated against major insect pests of agricultural crops and the results have been quite encouraging. In view of their multifacet action, botanicals are quite useful and can help to reduce the load of synthetic pesticides in agriculture. For example, alternate application of neem-based products and synthetic insecticides have reduced the pesticide load upto 40 per cent in rice and cotton ecosystems under Punjab conditions (Dhaliwal *et al.*, 1996; Mann *et al.*, 2001).

Pesticide misuse can also be attributed to an error in transfer of technology. Sometime ignorant or over-enthusiastic farmers extract carbofuran from granular formulations by soaking in water and apply as foliar application. There is also urgent need to improve quality of pesticide formulations being marketed. Attempts should be made to enforce pesticide regulations by establishing required enforcement machinery adequately. A strong network should be created for forecasting/ forewarning of pests and monitoring of pesticide usage. Safety and education must be encouraged in the rational use of pesticides. Research thrust on biological control, and resistant varieties should be given consideration possibly using biotechnological approaches.

Conclusions

Pesticides are essential tools of modern agriculture and form an integral part of overall strategy because production has hardly any meaning without protection. Pesticides are also a help to the environment when they are used carefully and wisely. The use of pesticides is energy-efficient, because it safeguards high productivity per unit area. Pesticide use in developing countries is indispensable in the struggle against hunger and disease. Emphasis should, therefore, be given to their judicious and safe use. In view of the adverse effects resulting from pollution of the environment by these chemicals, there is a great need to monitor pesticide usage.

Innovative strategies for crop protection, the development of new active ingredients and on-going programmes to develop resistant varieties will help to maintain and, where necessary increase the effectiveness of the available crop protection measures. It is very important to ensure better protection for workers engaged in pesticide handling and application. More efficient use of present pesticides, use of alternate methods of pest control and use of ecofriendly pesticides in well organised pest management programmes will greatly increase our capacity to produce more food and feed for the expanding population. Society expects manufacturers to develop safe and environmentally friendly active ingredients and it also expects farmers to use these products properly and in a responsible manner so as to get wholesome food of high quality.

REFERENCES

Agnihotri, N.P. (2000), "Pesticide consumption in Agriculture in India – an update", *Pesticide Res. J.* 12(1), pp. 150-155.

Atwal, A.S. (1986), "Future of pesticides in plant protection", *Proc. Indian Natn. Sci. Acad.* B52(1), pp. 77-90.

Battu, G.S., Ramakrishnan, N. and Dhaliwal, G.S. (1993), "Biotechnology: Perspectives in insect pest management", In G.S. Dhaliwal and R. Arora (eds.) *Trends in Agricultural Pest Management*. Commonwealth Publishers, New Delhi, pp. 417-468.

Dhaliwal, G.S. and Arora, R. (2001), *Integrated Pest Management: Concepts and*

Approaches. Kalyani Publishers, New Delhi.

Dhaliwal, G.S. and Singh, B. (2000), *Pesticides and Environment*. Commonwealth Publishers, New Delhi.

Dhaliwal, G.S., Arora, R., Dhawan, A.K. and Singh, B. (2000), "Intensive agriculture and pest problems: A case study of Punjab", *Indian J. Ecol.* 27(2), pp. 109-130.

Dhaliwal, G.S. Arora, R. and Dhawan, A.K. (1999), "Sustainable agriculture: Issues and strategies", In G.S. Dhaliwal, R. Arora and A.K. Dhawan (eds.) *Emerging Trends in Sustainable Agriculture*. Commonwealth Publishers, New Delhi, pp. 1-14.

Dhaliwal, G.S., Singh J. and Dilawari, V.K. (1996), "Potential of neem in insect pest management of rice", In R.P. Singh, M.S. Chari, A.K. Raheja and W. Kraus (eds.) *Neem and Environment*. Vol. 1. Oxford & IBH Publishing Co. Pvt. Ltd., New Delhi, pp. 425-431.

Dhawan, A.K., Dhaliwal, G.S. and Chelliah, S. (2000), "Insecticide-induced resurgence of insect pests in crop plants", In G.S. Dhaliwal and B. Singh (eds.). *Pesticides and Environment*. Commonwealth Publishers, New Delhi, pp. 86-127.

ICMR, (1993), *Surveillance of Food Contaminants in India*. Indian Council of Medical Research, New Delhi, pp. 171.

Jaisingh, H. (2000), "Greying of Green Revolution: Faulty Policies: Rusted tools", *The Tribune*, October 26.

Joia, B.S. and Battu, R.S. (2000), "Occurrence of DDT and HCH residues in breast milk in Punjab (India)", *Indian J. Envir. Toxicol.* 10(10), 16-18.

Kalra, R.L. and Chawla, R.P. (1983), *Studies on Pesticide Residues and Monitoring of Pesticidal Pollution*. Final Technical Report, PL-480 Project, Punjab Agricultural University, Ludhiana.

Kalra, R.L., Chawla, R.P. 'Sharma, M.L. and Tiwana, M.S. (1979), "Pesticide residues in milk and milk products in India." *Symp. Control of Pests of Diseases of Agricultural Crops/Commodities and Animals*, Feb. 23-24, Punjab Agricultural University, Ludhiana.

Mangat, I.S., Gill, K.S. and Arora, R. (1998), "Adoption status of IPM in American cotton in Punjab", *Indian J. Ecology* 25(1), pp. 50-54.

Mann, G.S., Dhaliwal, G.S., and Dhawan, A.K. (2001), "Effect of alternate application of neem products and conventional insecticides on population build-up of *Bemisia tabaci* (Gennadius) and its impact on bollworm damage in upland cotton", *Ann. Pl. Prot. Sci.* 9(1), pp. 22-25.

NRDC, (1989), *Intolerable Risk: Pesticides in our Children's Food*. Natural Resources Defence Council, Washington, DC, USA,

Patel, P.S. and Kanaujia, K.R. (1998), "Mass multiplication pathogenicity and feasibility of mycoinsecticides in integrated pest management", In G.S. Dhaliwal, N.S. Randhawa, R. Arora and A.K. Dhawan (eds.). *Ecological Agriculture and Sustainable Development*, Vol.2. Indian Ecological Society and Centre for Research in Rural and Industrial Development, Chandigarh, pp. 222-231.

Sidhu, A.S., Singh, J., Arora, R., Brar, D.S., Dhaliwal, C.S., Bal, R.S. and Singh, J. (1994), "Adoption pattern of plant protection measures *vis-à-vis* effectiveness of recommended insecticides against *Helicoverpa armigera* (Hubner) during 1990—a year of cotton crop failure in Punjab", *J. Insect Sci.* 7, 1994: 10-13.

Singh, J., Dhaliwal, G.S. and Randhawa, N.S. (1997), *Changing Scenario of Punjab Agriculture: An Ecological Perspective*. Indian Ecological Society and Centre for Research in Rural and Industrial Development, Chandigarh, 63 pp.

Singh, P.P. (1982), Insecticide residues in food in the Punjab—A typical dietary survey, Ph.D. Thesis, Punjab Agricultural University, Ludhiana.

25

STATUS OF STAKEHOLDERS IN WILDLIFE-PROTECTED AREAS
A Case Study of Harike Bird Sanctuary

ANISH DUA & CHANDER PARKASH

Introduction

India by virtue of its extensive geographical stretch and varied ecological conditions supports rich biodiversity. People living in the vicinity of these ecological hot spots and declared "Protected Areas" play an important role in the sustainable development and management of natural resources. For centuries together these people have lived in harmony with their surroundings. May it be wild stocks or plants or the important animal life, they acted as the custodians of our natural heritage. But unfortunately the last century saw the fastest rate of depletion of our resources and, many a time, communities living in these protected areas were held responsible for this damage.

Are these natives really the culprits, or are they the obstruction to the Machiavellian tendencies of the policy makers to cover up the failures of various governmental schemes in these remote but very important ecological systems? May it be the Maldharies of the Gir National Park in Gujarat or the fishermen of Chilka Lake, efforts were to uproot them and for decades together put them in the grind of land and resource compensation (Kaul, 1995). The end result in all such cases is that communities are transformed from landowners to being labourers. Various schemes in the name of development never reach these people and they continue to live in the never-ending hope that some day justice would be done and their problems would be redressed (Ghuman, 1989; Ladhar *et al.*, 1994).

This paper is an endeavour to highlight the status of stakeholders in a wildlife-protected area, Harike Lake—a Ramsar Site, situated in the state of Punjab.

Topography

Harike Lake is situated at the confluence of rivers Sutlej and Beas, two main tributaries of the Indus river system and forms a part of large wetland ecosystem called Mand area in the state of Punjab. This permanent wetland came into being after the construction of a barrage on the river in the year 1952. The major objective of engineering this structure was to supply water for irrigation and drinking purposes to Southern Punjab and the Rajasthan State through canals (Mavi, 1993). Earlier, the area was a part of large floodplain of the two rivers and was inhabited by the agrarian community. With the construction of the barrage many low-lying areas were flooded and people had to move out to neighbouring areas. They were given compensation but some of them still claim to have their lands right in the middle of the wetland. They still till that land and are in constant conflict with the civil authorities.

Harike and its Importance

As of now the wetland has an expanse of 148 sq. km and has the water storage capacity of 67900 acre-feet. It attracts thousands of migratory birds from Eastern Europe, Pakistan, Siberia, Tibet and other erstwhile USSR countries (Vishwakarma, 2000). Harike has its recognition internationally for being an important wetland because it attracts thousands of water birds every year. For this reason it has been identified as one of the six Ramsar Sites of the country. Every year tourists throng this small town to watch birds and school children come to participate in nature camps. The wetland has been drawing the attention of researchers from Universities and Natural History Societies for it is an ecological heaven for biologists/ecologists. Till two years back the wetland was annually auctioned for fishing and at times the Punjab State was earning up to Rs.1 crore a year as contract money (Ray, 2000).

But all these years people living in the area were completely ignored, they were never told about the rich resource in their backyards, or how to exploit these resources in a better manner and be a part of the overall sustainable development programme.

Community Profile

There are 12 villages in the vicinity of Harike Wetland and the primary occupation of people living here is agriculture. The farmers have moderate to high land-holdings and the major concern for them is the land that they wish to possess deep in the core area of the wildlife-protected stretch. The government labels such activities as encroachments and the conflict is a never-ending phenomenon in the area. The families of these farmers are of fairly good size (i.e. 8-10 persons per family); they indulge in an intensive level of farming with modern agriculture tools like tractors. Female-male ratio is poor and the literacy level is not very good. Despite all this the people are aware, influential and their viewpoints are always of the kind where they wish to exploit the natural resource bank completely but do not want to participate in the constructive pursuit to maintain and develop this fragile ecosystem.

The other two communities in the study area are of very poor strata and have reed cutting and fishing as their main occupation. The detail account of these communities as stakeholders is discussed in this paper.

Reed Cutters

No. of Families:	130
Family size:	6-7 persons
Female: Male:	8:10
Education:	Illiterate or at the most primary level
Castes:	Rao and Majhabi Sikhs
Financial Status:	Poor

The members of this community are staying in three villages, *viz.*, Manu Machi, Old Makhu and Shakina Wali Basti in the districts of Kapurthala and Ferozpur. They harvest the plants of the spp. *Phragmites karka, Sachhrum spontaneum, S. bengalensis, Typha latifolia, T. elephantina*, and *T. angustata*. These plants are utilised to make *rassi, moodahs*, thatching of the huts, and as fuel and fodder. The whole operation of reed cutting is done for only four months in a year when the plants are extracted, dried and processed for different uses. The final produce is sold at a very low price and the middlemen who transport and sell this product in the other areas harness the real benefit. The reed cutters are in constant conflict with the wildlife department as they are checked for making an entry into the wetland. For a major part of the year these people work as labourers in the fields of the bigger farmers.

Fishermen Community

No. of families:	25
Family size:	5-6 persons
Education:	Totally illiterate

Originally migrated from eastern Uttar Pradesh, West Bengal and Bihar, these fishermen are living in two temporary settlements, one close to Harike village and the other in the Sultanpur Lodi area. Earlier they were working for the local fish contractors but the banning of fishing in the wetland area has decreased the average income of these families who are now doing fishing in the canals etc. Fishing is mainly done using gill nets and the catch is sold to the contractor in the mornings at the landing centres. All these families live below the poverty line, they have no access to civic services and frequently fall prey to waterborne diseases. In the conflict between the Wildlife Department and fishery contractors it is these fishermen who bear the brunt when many of them are caught for trespassing in the protected but unmarked boundaries of the wetland.

Conclusion

The wetland has international repute, is known for its rich diversity in bird, fish and plant life, and serves as a tourist site for a small limited number of people. The state of Punjab is planning to establish ecotourism at an industrial level in the wetland and the preliminary work for the same has been initiated by various agencies. But it is feared that the marginal farmers, reed cutters and fishermen would be ignored in this mega venture and would be pushed to the boundary. It is suggested that these communities are included in the mainstream and are asked to guide tourists; indulge into indigenous skills and craft and thus initiate an ideal development process where people are part of the improvement scheme.

REFERENCES

Ghuman, J.S. (1989), "Report and recommendations of the working group for development of the Mand area in river Beas and Sutlej in Punjab". A report by Town and Country Planning and Urban Department, Government of Punjab, Chandigarh.

Kaul, S. (1995), "The conservation of Indian freshwater resources", *Journal of Lakes and Reservoirs: Research and Management*. Vol. 1. 49-54.

Ladhar, S.S., Chauhan, M. and Jerath, N. (1994), "Harike Lake": A report by WWF-India, New Delhi.

Mavi, H.S. and Tiwana, D.S. (1993), *Punjab Geography*, National Book Trust, New Delhi.

Mitsch, W.J. and Gosselink, J. (1990), *Wetlands*, Van Nostrand Reinhold, New York.

Parkash, C. (1999), "An overview of biodiversity at Harike Wetland, Punjab" A M.Sc. dissertation. Guru Nanak Dev University, Amritsar.

Ray, J. (2000), "Sustainable fisheries development of Harike Wetland" A M.Sc. dissertation, Barkatullah University, Bhopal.

Vishwakarma, M. (2000), "Biodiversity Conservation of Harike Wetland". A M.Sc. dissertation, Barkatullah University, Bhopal.

26

DIMENSIONS OF DRUG-ADDICTS
A Comparative Analysis

B.K. AGGARWAL, SHALINI SHARMA & NISHA DUA

Drug use is not only the problem of Indian society in the modern times but it has been a feature of all the societies in the world since times immemorial. Undoubtedly, it is spreading like wild fire amongst youth in the developed, developing and underdeveloped countries. According to the World Health Organisation, drug addiction is 'a state of periodic or chronic intoxication, detrimental to the individual and to the society, produced by the repeated consumption of drug (natural or synthetic).' Tracing the genesis of drug abuse in society, it is one of the root causes of many social problems, being experienced in different regions. Today drug addiction has reached an alarming level. It has in fact started becoming a part of daily life of youth and has gripped them all over the world. Realising the severity of the problem, the present study was conducted in Ludhiana district of Punjab with the following specific objectives:

1. To correlate degree of drug use with socio-economic variables of drug-addicts.
2. To study the extent of drug use in the study area.

Research Design

The study was conducted in Ludhiana district of Punjab. Ludhiana has de-addiction centres and drug addicts are treated in different hospitals under psychiatry departments. A list of drug addicts was prepared from the four hospitals, *i.e.* Dayanand Medical College and Hospital, Christian

Medical College and Hospital, Guru Teg Bahadur Hospital and Deol Hospital. The addicts were divided into two categories on the basis of their place of residence, *i.e.* rural and urban. Fifty respondents from each category were randomly selected. Data was collected with the help of an interview schedule.

The drug addicts were divided into three categories on the basis of their frequency of drug use:

1. *First Degree Drug Addicts:* They were the moderate kind of drug addicts and their consumption level was (a) one-fourth to one bottle (alcohol); (b) 10-20 gm powder drugs; (c) 2-5 cigarettes; (d) 2-5 tablets/capsules/injections.
2. *Second Degree Drug Addicts:* They were the regular kind of drug addicts and their consumption level was (a) one and half to two and half bottles (alcohol); (b) 21-40 gm powder drugs; (c) 6-12 cigarettes; (d) 6-12 tablets/capsules/injections.
3. *Third Degree Drug Addicts:* They were the excessive kind of drug addicts and their consumption level was (a) more than two and half bottles (alcohol); (b) more than 40 gm powder drugs; (c) more than 12 cigarettes; (d) more than 12 tablets/capsules/ injections.

Results and Discussion

The appraisal of socio-economic dimensions of drug addicts is very important for determining the basis of their turning to drug addiction. The variables included in the study were age, caste, education, marital status, occupation and family type.

Socio-Economic Variables

1. *Age:* Age of an individual is a significant factor for determining the attitudinal and behavioural changes towards various social aspects. The relationship between age group and type of drug addict is presented in Table 26.1. It is evident from the Table that majority of the third degree drug addicts were in the age group of up to 20 years in rural (52.2%) as well as in urban area (50%). Inter-area comparison showed that percentage of third degree (46%) drug addicts was higher in rural area as compared to urban area (40%) whereas percentage of first degree (34%) drug addicts was higher in urban area as compared to rural area (20%).

When a person is young he is more volatile, emotional, make new friends, experiment new things without a thought of the consequences. Chi-square test did not reveal a significant relation between type of drug addict and age. Although it has not attained the level of significance. It is yet suggestive that further collaboration can be attained in subsequent studies ($\chi^2 = 20.12$, d.f. = 6).

2. *Caste:* The respondents were categorised on the basis of caste. It is evident from Table 26.2 that among high castes the percentage of third degree drug addicts were more in urban area (45.0%) than in rural area (34.8%). Among low castes the percentage of third degree drug addicts was little bit high in rural area (34.8%) as compared to urban area (30.0 per cent). The percentage of first degree and second degree drug addicts was almost the same among the high and medium castes in both the study areas whereas among low castes second degree drug addicts were more in urban area (38.5%) than in rural area (29.4%). Chi-square test found that relationship between type of drug addict and caste was significant at 5 per cent level ($\chi^2 = 11.00$, d.f. = 4).

3. *Education:* Table 26.3 highlighted the relationship between type of drug addicts and educational level of respondents. It is apparent from the Table that 78 per cent drug addicts have matric and above educational level in both the areas. The Table also highlighted that majority of third degree drug-addicts were having educational level of matric and above in both rural (60.9%) and urban (90%) areas. From the above it can be concluded that in rural area a person who is illiterate or less educated (matric and below) are more prone to drug-addiction than an educated person. But in urban area, more educated persons are more prone to drug-addiction. Chi-square test showed the significant association between type of drug addicts and educational level ($\chi^2 = 4.91$, d.f. = 4).

4. *Marital Status:* Marital status of drug addict was ascertained to determine whether it was a factor impinging on addiction. It is evident from Table 26.4 that 85 per cent third degree drug addicts were unmarried in urban area, as compared to 43 per cent in rural area. On the whole in rural area married persons were more prone to addiction (58%) than unmarried (42%) but in urban area percentage of unmarried addicts was more (72%) than married addicts (28%). χ^2 test reveals a significant relationship between type of drug addict and marital status ($\chi^2 = 0.22$, d.f. = 2).

5. *Occupation:* Occupation is accepted as the most effective indicator to measure the status of an individual. The occupation influences their own lives as well as of their family members. Table 26.5 shows that 40 per

Table 26.1: Relationship between type of drug-addict and age

Age (in years)	Rural				Urban				Grand Total
	First degree	Second degree	Third degree	Total	First degree	Second degree	Third degree	Total	
Upto 20	2(20.00)	4(23.53)	12(52.17)	18(36.00)	5(29.41)	3(23.08)	10(50.00)	18(36.00)	36(36.00)
20-30	3(30.00)	4(23.53)	7(30.43)	14(28.00)	4(23.53)	5(38.46)	6(30.00)	15(30.00)	29(29.00)
30-40	2(20.00)	7(41.18)	2(8.70)	11(22.00)	3(17.65)	4(30.77)	2(10.00)	9(18.00)	20(20.00)
Above 40	3(30.00)	2(11.76)	2(8.70)	7(14.00)	5(29.41)	1(7.69)	2(10.00)	8(16.00)	15(15.00)
Total	10(20.00)	17(34.00)	23(46.00)	50(100.00)	17(34.00)	13(26.00)	20(40.00)	50(100.00)	100(100.00)

Note : Figures in parentheses indicate percentages.

Table 26.2: Relationship between type of drug-addict and caste categories

Caste	Rural				Urban				Grand Total
	First degree	Second degree	Third degree	Total	First degree	Second degree	Third degree	Total	
High	4(40.00)	7(41.18)	8(34.78)	19(38.00)	7(41.18)	5(38.46)	9(45.00)	21(42.00)	40(40.00)
Medium	2(20.00)	5(29.41)	7(30.44)	14(28.00)	4(23.53)	3(23.08)	5(25.00)	12(24.00)	26(26.00)
Low	4(40.00)	5(29.41)	8(34.78)	17(34.00)	6(35.29)	5(38.46)	6(30.00)	17(34.00)	34(34.00)
Total	10(20.00)	17(34.00)	23(46.00)	50(100.00)	17(34.00)	13(26.00)	20(40.00)	50(100.00)	100(100.00)

Notes : Figures in parentheses indicate percentages.

High – Brahmins, Jat, Khatri, Arora, Medium – Saini, Nai, Tarkhan, Suniar, Low – Adharmi, Mazahabi, Balmiki, Ramdasia.

Table 24.3: Relationship between type of drug-addict and education level

	Rural				Urban				Grand Total
	First degree	*Second degree*	*Third degree*	*Total*	*First degree*	*Second degree*	*Third degree*	*Total*	
Illiterate	3(30.00)	5(29.41)	9(39.13)	17(34.00)	2(11.76)	1(7.69)	2(10.00)	5(10.00)	22(22.00)
Matric	7(70.00)	11(64.71)	12(52.18)	30(60.00)	8(47.06)	6(46.15)	14(70.00)	28(56.00)	58(58.00)
Graduate and above	-	1(5.88)	2(8.69)	3(6.00)	7(41.18)	6(46.16)	4(20.00)	17(34.00)	20(20.00)
Total	10(20.00)	17(34.00)	23(46.00)	50(100.00)	17(34.00)	13(26.00)	20(40.00)	50(100.00)	100(100.00)

Note : Figures in Parentheses indicate percentages.

Table 26.4: Relationship between type of drug-addict and marital status

Marital Status	Rural				Urban				*Grand Total*
	First degree	*Second degree*	*Third degree*	*Total*	*First degree*	*Second degree*	*Third degree*	*Total*	
Unmarried	2(20.00)	9(52.94)	10(43.48)	21(42.00)	11(64.71)	8(61.54)	17(85.00)	36(72.00)	57(57.00)
Married	8(80.00)	8(47.06)	13(56.52)	29(58.00)	6(35.29)	5(38.46)	3(15.00)	14(28.00)	43(43.00)
Total	10(20.00)	17(34.00)	23(46.00)	50(100.00)	17(34.00)	13(26.00)	20(40.00)	50(100.00)	100(100.00)

Note : Figures in parentheses indicate percentages.

cent drug addicts were self-employed in both the areas. The study further highlighted that majority (80%) of the third degree drug addicts were engaged in self-employed and government service in urban area whereas in rural area 74 per cent third degree drug addicts were agriculturists and self-employed. Chi-square test did not reveal a significant relation between occupation and type of drug-addict ($\chi^2 = 23.8$, d.f. = 6).

6. *Family type:* Family is the most basic institution of socialisation which determine the total personality and character of a person. It is apparent from Table 26.6 that a large percentage of drug-addicts come from nuclear families, *i.e.* 57 per cent; 38 and 76 per cent respectively from rural and urban areas. Inter-area comparison showed that in urban area 70 per cent third degree addicts come from nuclear families, whereas in rural area 43.5 per cent third degree drug addicts were from nuclear families. On the basis of above data it can be stated that nuclear family is one cause of drug addiction. The relationship between the type of drug addict and family type was found statistically significant ($\chi^2 = 0.67$, d.f. = 2).

7. *Income:* Economic status also influences the attitude of the individual. The study revealed that majority of drug addicts (51%) come from high income group, *i.e.* above Rs.60,000/annum in both the areas. Table 26.7 further highlighted that majority of the third degree drug addicts were from high income group in both rural (52%) and urban (60%) areas. Few of the third degree drug addicts were from middle income group both in rural (9%) and urban (10%) areas. Second degree drug-addicts were more in rural (34%) areas than in urban (26%) area. While first degree drug-addicts were higher in urban (34 per cent) area as compared to rural (20 per cent) area. The relationship was found statistically significant ($\chi = 4.16$, d.f. = 4).

Frequency of Drug Use

In order to examine the extent of drug use in rural as well as urban areas, different type of drug had been analysed as follows:

Alcohol: It is a kind of depressant drug. It depresses the central nervous system. It is an organic compound with a formulate of carbon, oxygen and hydrogen. The alcohol consumed by human being is known as ethyl alcohol. It is evident from Table 26.8 that majority of rural addicts took desi (78%) alcohol while urban addicts took foreign (60%) alcohol.

Table 26.5: Relationship between type of drug-addict and occupation

Occupation	*Rural*				*Urban*				*Grand Tota*
	First degree	*Second degree*	*Third degree*	*Total*	*First degree*	*Second degree*	*Third degree*	*Total*	
Government servant	1(10.00)	2(11.76)	2(8.69)	5(10.00)	6(35.29)	5(38.46)	7(35.00)	18(36.00)	23(23.00)
Self-employed (Business/technical and professional)	3(30.00)	5(35.29)	8(34.78)	17(34.00)	8(47.05)	6(46.15)	9(45.00)	23(46.00)	40(40.00)
Agriculture	5(50.00)	7(41.19)	9(39.14)	21(42.00)	2(11.76)	1(7.69)	2(10.00)	5(10.00)	26(26.00)
Any other (students and labourers)	1(10.00)	2(11.76)	4(17.39)	7(14.00)	1(5.89)	1(7.69)	2(10.00)	4(8.00)	11(11.00)
Total	10(20.00)	17(34.00)	23(46.00)	50(100.00)	17(34.00)	13(26.00)	20(40.00)	50(100.00)	100(100.00)

Note : Figures in parentheses indicate perecntages.

Table 26.6: Relationship between type of drug-addict and family type

Family type	*Rural*				*Urban*				*Grand Total*
	First degree	*Second degree*	*Third degree*	*Total*	*First degree*	*Second degree*	*Third degree*	*Total*	
Joint	9(90.00)	9(52.94)	13(56.52)	31(62.00)	3(17.65)	3(23.08)	6(30.00)	12(24.00)	43(43.00)
Nuclear	1(10.00)	8(47.06)	10(43.48)	19(38.00)	14(82.35)	10(76.92)	14(70.00)	38(76.00)	57(57.00)
Total	10(20.00)	17(34.00)	23(46.00)	50(100.00)	17(34.00)	13(26.00)	20(40.00)	50(100.00)	100(100.00)

Note : Figures in parentheses indicate percentages.

Table 26.7: Relationship between type of drug-addict and their income

Income per annum (in Rs.)	*Rural*				*Urban*				*Grand Total*
	First degree	*Second degree*	*Third degree*	*Total*	*First degree*	*Second degree*	*Third degree*	*Total*	
Upto 30,000	5(50.00)	4(23.53)	9(39.13)	18(36.00)	6(35.29)	7(53.85)	6(30.00)	19(38.00)	37(37.00)
30,000-60,000	1(10.00)	4(23.53)	2(8.69)	7(14.00)	2(11.76)	1(7.69)	2(10.00)	5(10.00)	12(12.00)
Above 60,000	4(40.00)	9(52.94)	12(52.18)	25(50.00)	9(52.94)	5(38.46)	12(60.00)	26(52.00)	51(51.00)
Total	10(20.00)	17(34.00)	23(46.00)	50(100.00)	17(34.00)	13(26.00)	20(40.00)	50(100.00)	100(100.00

Note: Figures in parentheses indicate percentages.

Table 26.8: Distribution of respondents according to their type of drugs

Type of Drugs	*Rural No. of Respondents*	*Urban No. of Respondents*
Alcohol		
Desi	39(78.00)	10(20.00)
Indian	15(30.00)	20(40.00)
Foreign	6(12.00)	30(60.00)
Narcotics		
Opium	35(70.00)	25(50.00)
Bhooki	30(60.00)	23(46.00)
Dode	33(66.00)	25(50.00)
Codeine	32(64.00)	35(70.00)
Corex	25(50.00)	30(60.00)
Phensydril	20(40.00)	25(50.00)
Morphine	15(30.00)	19(38.00)
Norphine	10(20.00)	7(14.00)
Avil	27(54.00)	35(70.00)
Heroine	3(6.00)	5(10.00)
Hypnotic Sedatives		
Dizapam	10(20.00)	13(26.00)
Proxyvon	7(14.00)	10(20.00)
Tranquilizers	20(40.00)	25(50.00)
Barbiturates	15(30.00)	15(30.00)
Cannabies		
Bhang	25(50.00)	21(42.00)
Charas	20(40.00)	19(38.00)
Ganja	18(36.00)	18(36.00)
Hashish	5(10.00)	5(10.00)
Marijuana	10(20.000	9(18.00)
Miscellaneous		
Cigarattes	42(84.00)	45(90.00)
Cough syrup	35(70.00)	39(78.00)
Sleeping pills	40(80.00)	9(18.00)
Iodex	5(10.00)	4(8.00)
Shoe polish	2(4.00)	–

Note: Figures in parentheses indicate percentages.

Narcotics: These are drugs which dull consciousness and used to induce sleep at night or alleviate anxiety or pain by day. These are opium, bhooki, dode, codeine, corex, morphine, phensydril, norphine, avil and heroine. The Table reveals that from this category of drugs rural respondents were more addicts to opium (70%); dode (66%) and codeine (64%) while majority of the urban addicts used codeine (70%), avil (70%) and corex (60%). Heroin was used by only few rural (6%) and urban (10%) addicts.

Hypnotic-sedatives: These drugs are classified together because each drug has the ability to depress the central nervous system into a condition resembling sleep. The difference between a hypnotic action and a sedative action is one of the degree of depression. Drugs comes under the hypnotic sedatives are diazepam, proxyvon, tranquilizers and barbiturates.

It is apparent from the Table that tranquilizers and barbiturates were used more from this category of drugs. 40 per cent and 50 per cent of the rural and urban addicts respectively used tranquilizers and 30 per cent each used barbiturates.

Cannabis: This is psychoactive substance causing the mood modification and behaviour changes in the user. Under this family most common drugs used are bhang, charas, ganja, hashish and marijuana. No significant difference in the intake of these drugs was found in rural and urban areas. But it can be inferred from the Table that bhang and charas were consumed widely by addicts.

Miscellaneous: Under the miscellaneous drugs, commonly used drugs are cigarettes, cough syrups, sleeping pills, iodex and shoe polish. Table shows that from this miscellaneous category most of the respondents took cigarettes, sleeping pills and cough syrups. Few addicts were also found taking iodex and shoe polish.

Conclusions

The growth of drug addiction and its accelerating momentum is an undeniable worldwide phenomenon. Drug addiction is a complex process and it is an outcome of critical combination of various factors. The socio-economic variables of the drug addicts were studied for determining the reasons for their turning to drug addiction. It was found that majority of drug addicts (65%) belong to the age group of upto 30 in rural as well as urban areas. So, menace of drug abuse afflicts lower or productive age group because taking drugs starts in adolescence age. Majority of the respondents belonged to high caste (40%) and low caste (34%) and less among medium caste. It appears that 59 per cent of drug addicts were illiterate and having a low level of education, whereas only 20 per cent of the drug addicts had a high level of education. It has also been found that proportion of unmarried addicts (57%) was higher as compared to married addicts (43%). The study reveals that significant number of addicts were self-employed (40%). Respondents from nuclear family (57%) were indulged more in drug addiction than respondents from joint family (43%).

The study further reveals the frequency and extent of drug use. It was found that majority of respondents took desi alcohol in rural and foreign alcohol in urban area. In natural origin narcotics, cough syrups and opium were most prevalent. In the category of synthetic drugs morphine, avil were found more while in cannabis category bhang and charas were widely used. Iodex and shoe polish were also used by a few rural and urban addicts.

Preventive Measures

Drug abuse is a serious socio-economic and medical problem which damages the health and well being of productive persons. It is detrimental to the family, society and the nation. Thus, following preventive measures should be given priority:

1. The Government should strictly implement the laws to control supply and demand of illicit drugs.
2. A stringent punishment against smugglers, peddlers, pushers should be provided.
3. Sex, alcohol and drug (SAD) education should be introduced from atleast Vth class onwards to create awareness regarding harmful effects of drugs.
4. The Government should provide more recreational and co-curricular facilities like sports, music, dramatics, etc. for exploring and channelising the energies of youth in positive direction.
5. Communication channels and counselling and guidance services should be extensively used to create awareness.
6. Provision of more employment opportunities.
7. Detoxification, de-addiction, social and vocational rehabilitation and after care centres should be increased.

REFERENCES

Broota, K.D. and Singh, S. (1986), "Adjustment problems and socio-personal variables in drug abuse", *Indian Journal of Clinical Psychology*, 13 (1), 59.

Chitnis, S. (1974), *Drug on the College Campus*, Tata Institute of Social Science, Bombay.

Deb, P.C. (1977), *Social dimensions of Drug-abuse in India*, Punjab Agricultural University, Ludhiana.

Dube, K.C. (1975), "Drug abuse in Northern India: Observations concerning Delhi-Agri. Region", *Bulletin on Narcotics*, 18 (1), 49-53.

Hundleby, J.D. and Mercer, G.W. (1987), "Family and friends as social environment and their relation to adolscent's use of alcohol, tobacco, and marijuana", *Journal of Marriage and Family*, 49 (1), 151-164.

Mohan, D., Darshan, S. and Neki, J.S. (1977), *A study of drug abuse in rural areas of Punjab.* A preliminary report submitted to the Ministry of Social Welfare, Govt. of India.

Singh, A. and Singh, S. (1980), "Drug-abuse amongst students in Punjab", *Indian Psychological Review*, 19(4), 1-7.

INDEX